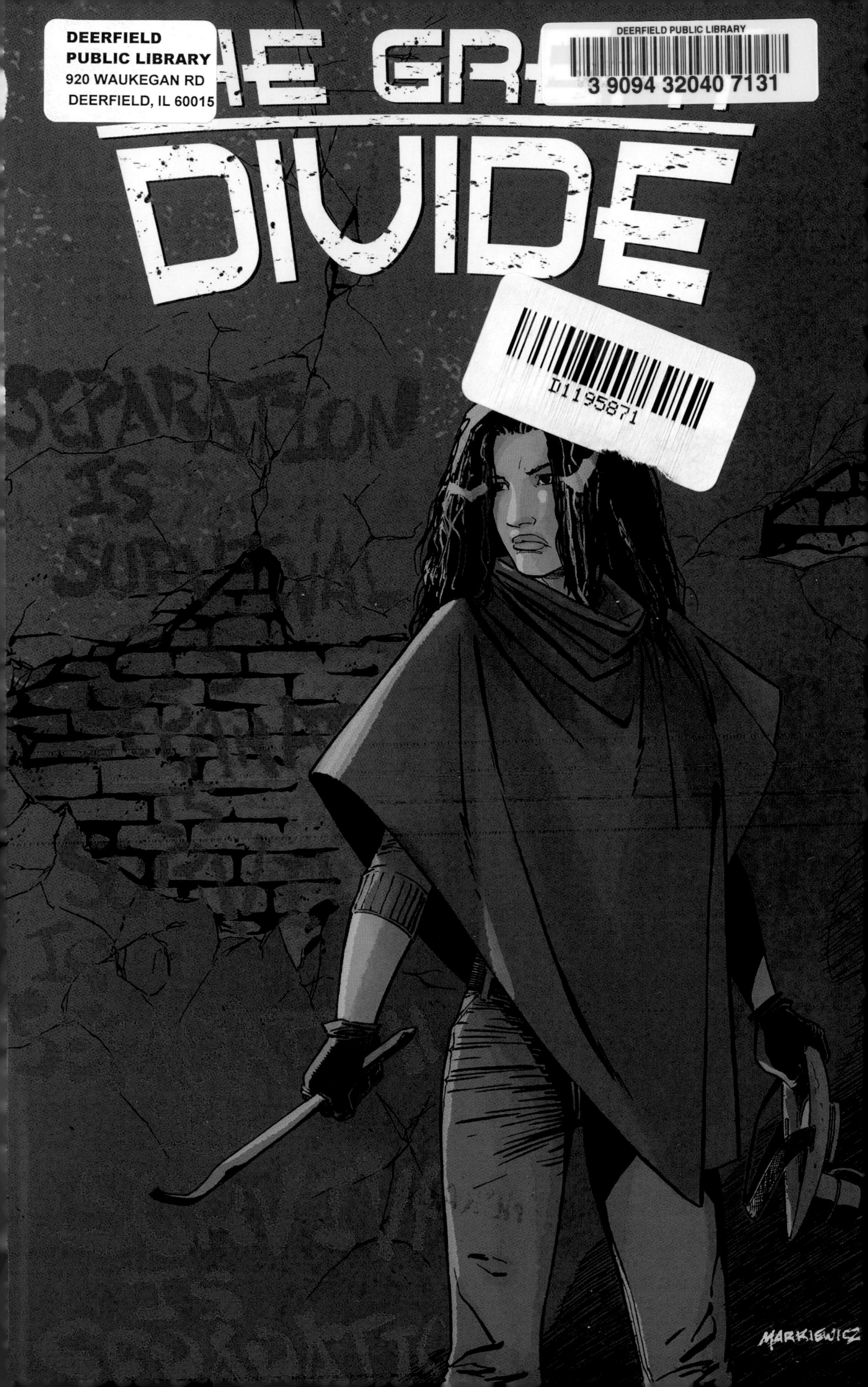
DIVIDE
SEPARATION
IS
MARKIEWICZ

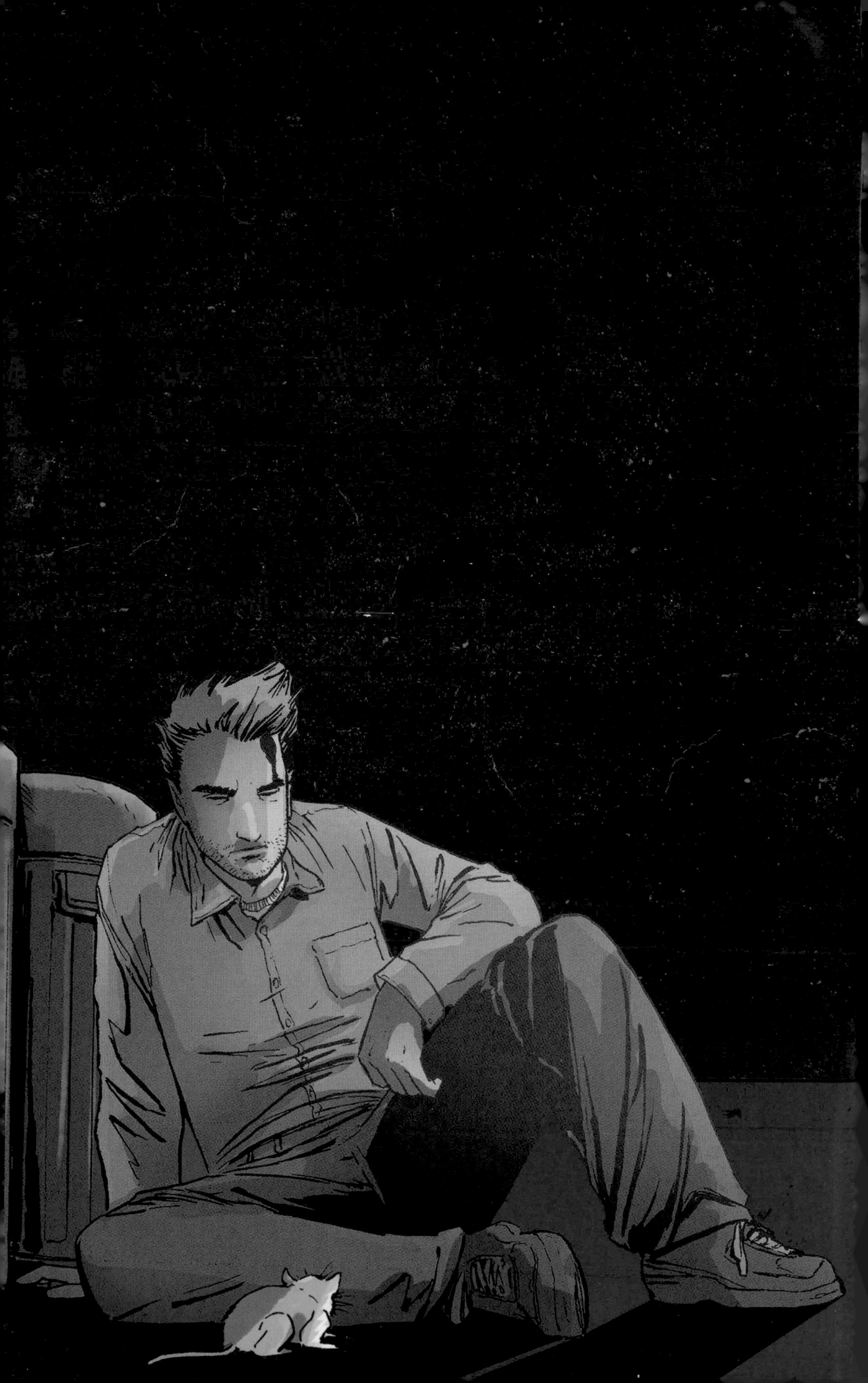

THE GREAT DIVIDE

STORY
BEN FISHER

ART + LETTERING
ADAM MARKIEWICZ

COLORS
ADAM GUZOWSKI

LOGO DESIGN
PATRICK BROSSEAU

STORY EDITOR
JONATHAN STARK

COLOMBIAN TRANSLATIONS
MARIA VELEZ

COLLECTION DESIGNER
GEOFF HARKINS

SPECIAL THANKS TO STEPHEN HALL, JASMINE HITES, AND BLAINE SUNDWALL
FOR THEIR CONSULTING EXPERTISE.

Online at www.DYNAMITE.com
On Facebook /Dynamitecomics
On Twitter @dynamitecomics

ISBN-13: 978-1-5241-0334-7
First Printing   10 9 8 7 6 5 4 3 2 1

DYNAMITE®

Nick Barrucci, CEO / Publisher
Juan Collado, President / COO

Joe Rybandt, Executive Editor
Matt Idelson, Senior Editor
Anthony Marques, Associate Editor
Matt Humphreys, Assistant Editor
Kevin Ketner, Assistant Editor

Jason Ullmeyer, Art Director
Geoff Harkins, Senior Graphic Designer
Cathleen Heard, Graphic Designer
Alexis Persson, Production Artist
Chris Caniano, Digital Associate
Rachel Kilbury, Digital Assistant

Brandon Dante Primavera, V.P. of IT and Operations
Rich Young, Director of Business Development

Alan Payne, V.P. of Sales and Marketing
Keith Davidsen, Marketing Director
Pat O'Connell, Sales Manager

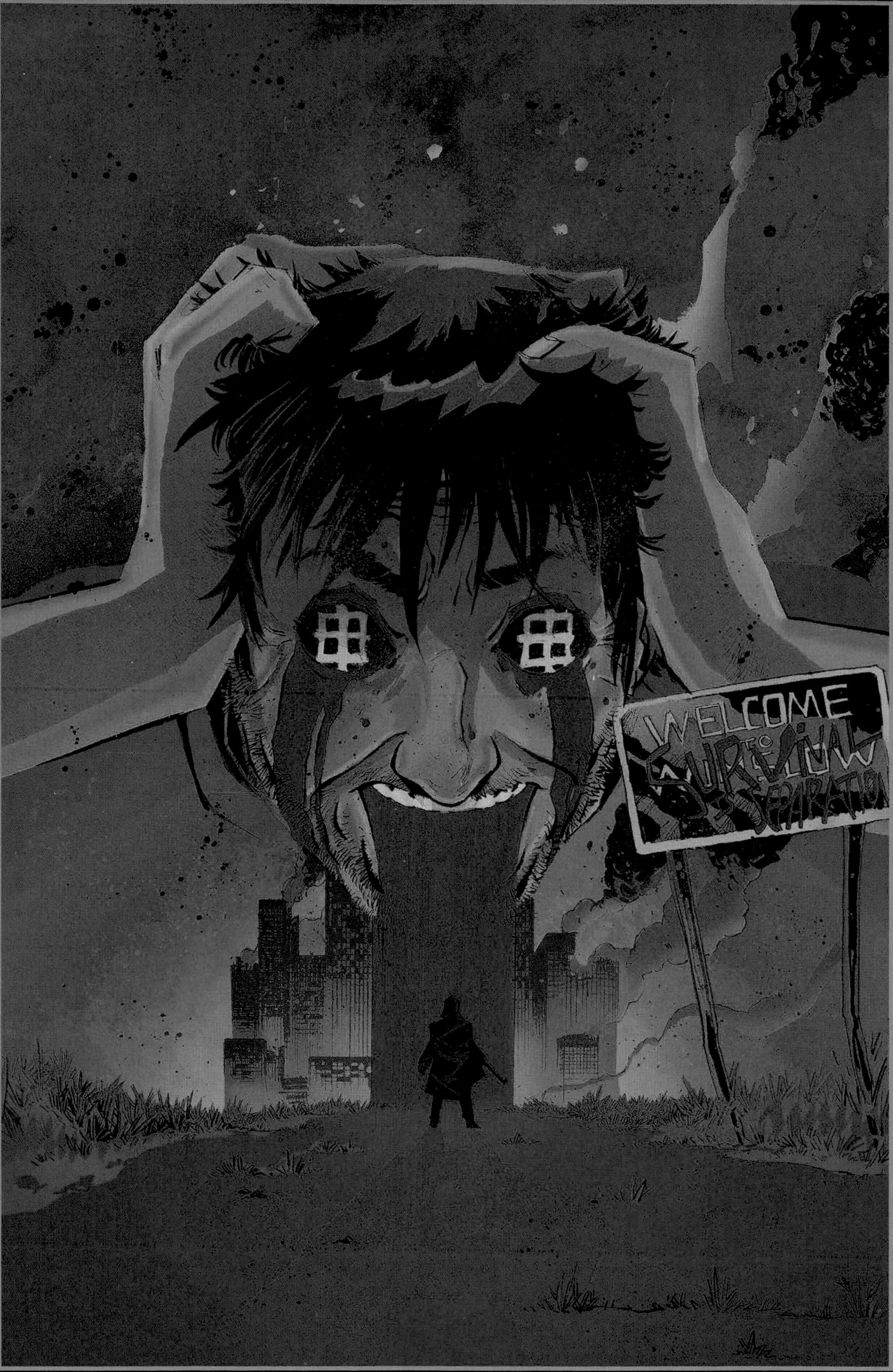
WELCOME

ISSUE ONE
COVER ART BY MIKE HENDERSON
COLORS BY ADAM GUZOWSKI

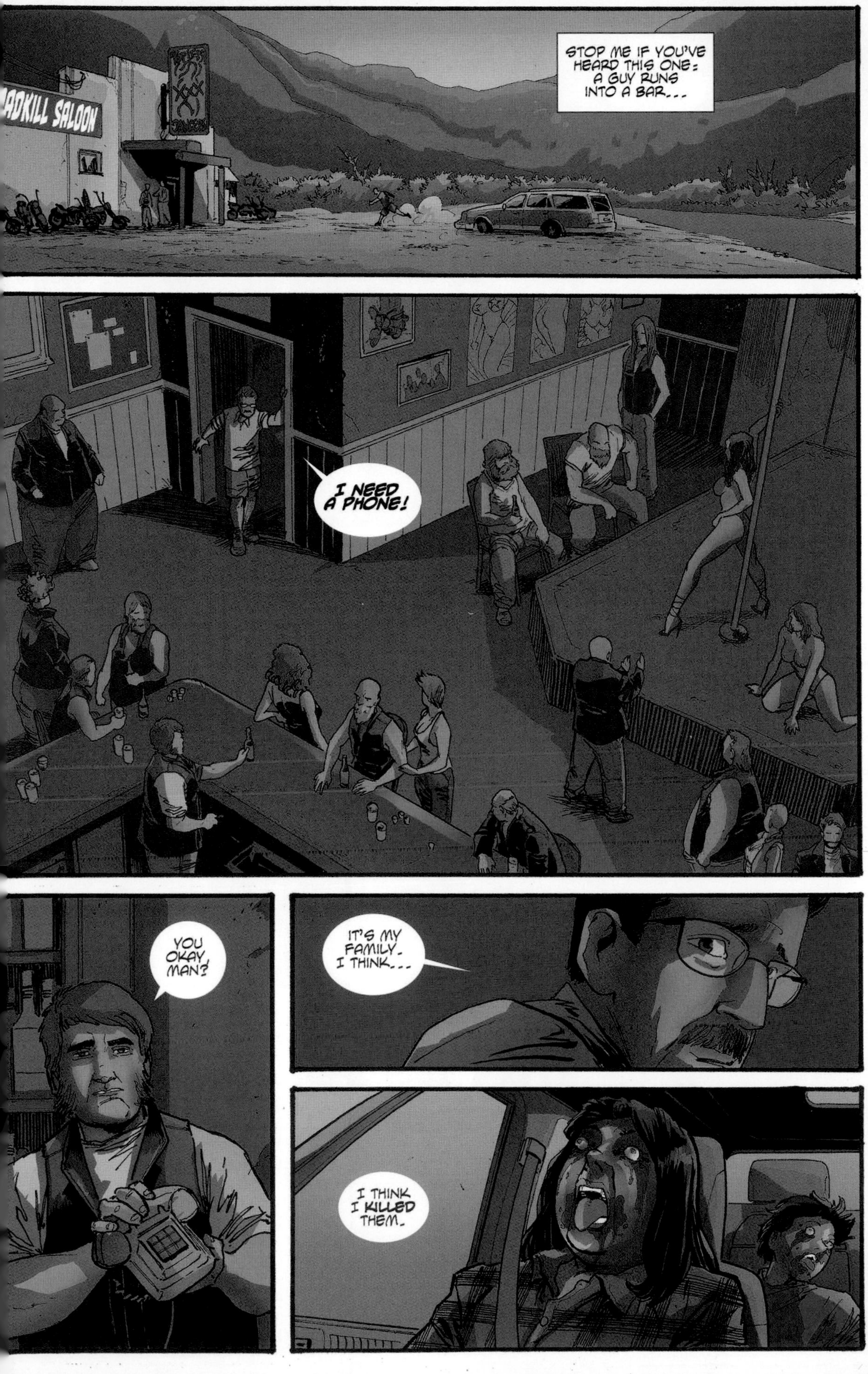

ADKILL SALOON
STOP ME IF YOU'VE HEARD THIS ONE: A GUY RUNS INTO A BAR...
I NEED A PHONE!
YOU OKAY, MAN?
IT'S MY FAMILY. I THINK...
I THINK I KILLED THEM.

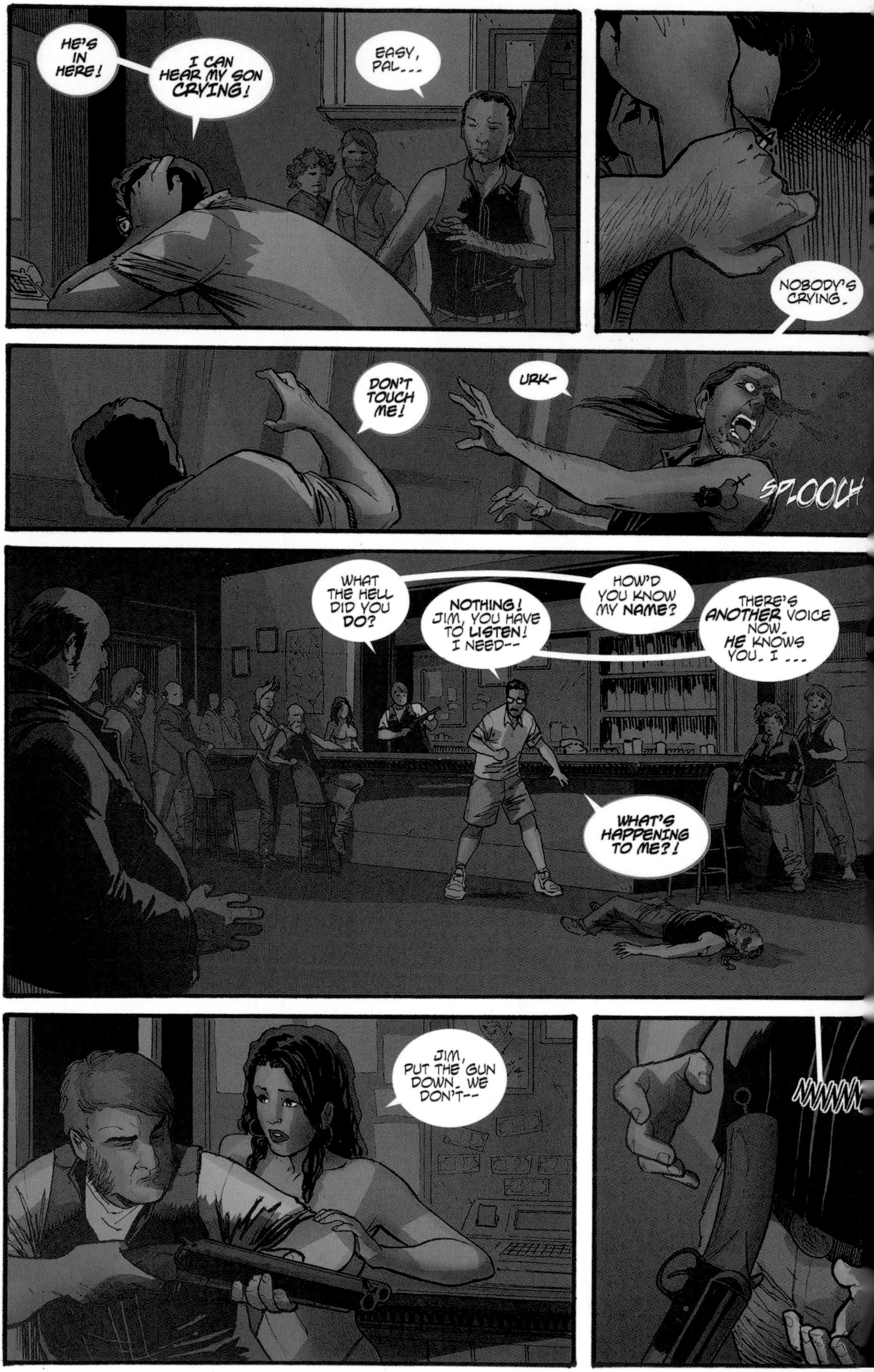
HE'S IN HERE!
I CAN HEAR MY SON CRYING!
EASY, PAL...
NOBODY'S CRYING.
DON'T TOUCH ME!
URK-
SPLOOCH
WHAT THE HELL DID YOU DO?
NOTHING! JIM, YOU HAVE TO LISTEN! I NEED--
HOW'D YOU KNOW MY NAME?
THERE'S ANOTHER VOICE NOW. HE KNOWS YOU. I...
WHAT'S HAPPENING TO ME?!
JIM, PUT THE GUN DOWN. WE DON'T--
NNNNNN

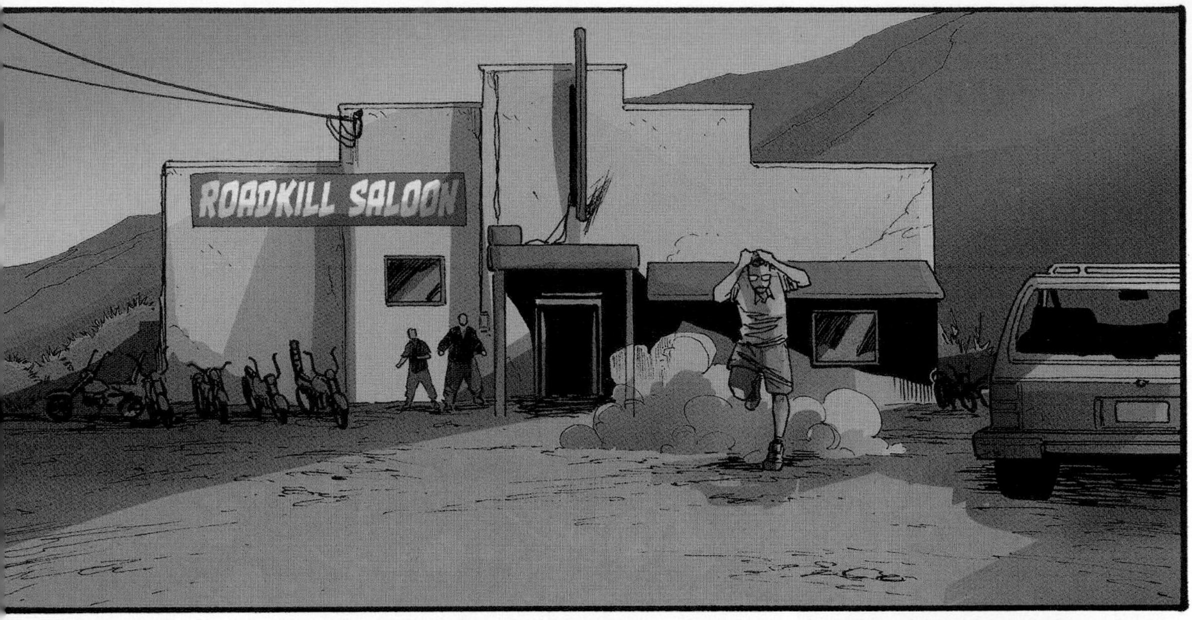
ROADKILL SALOON

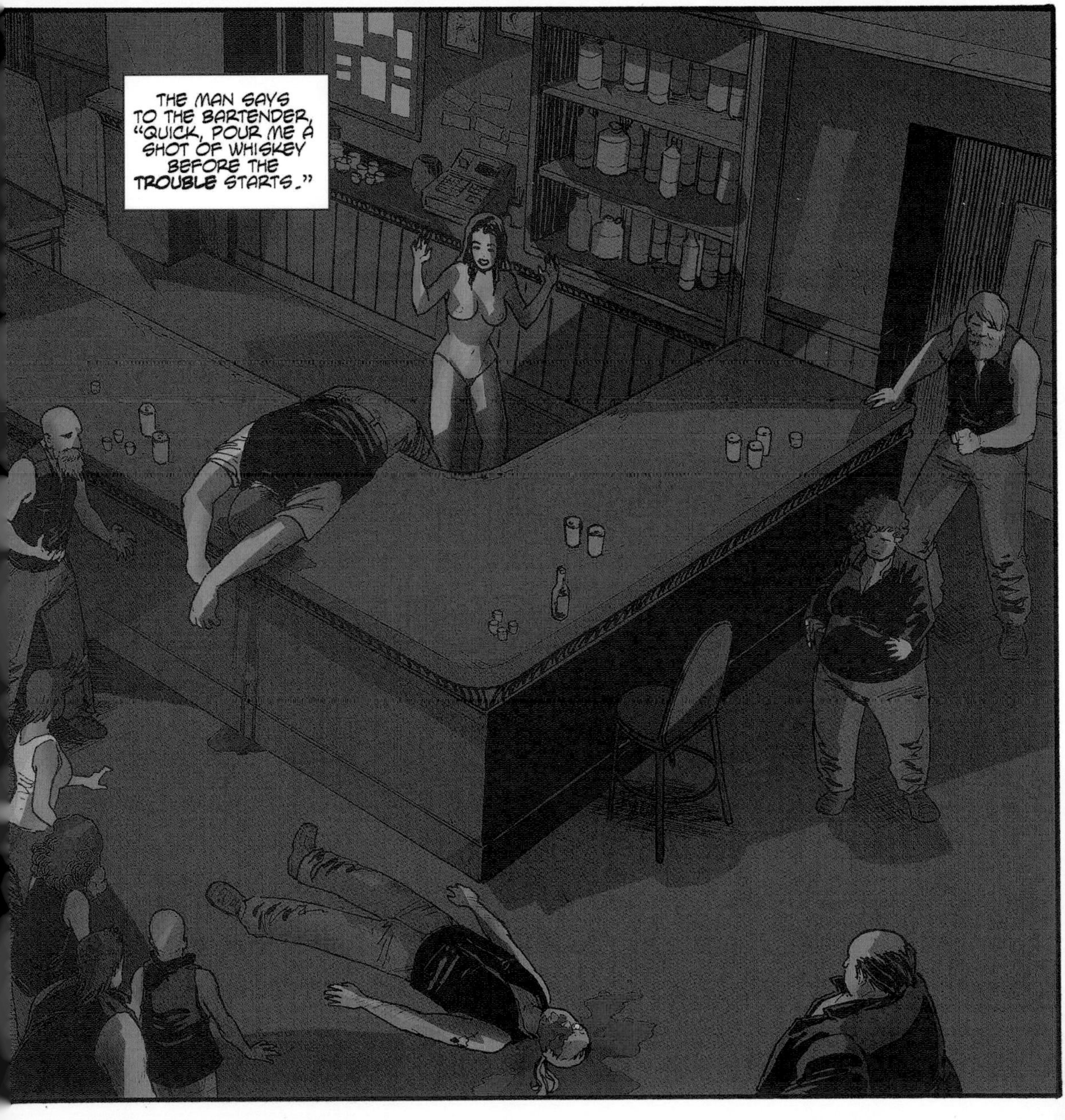
THE MAN SAYS TO THE BARTENDER, "QUICK, POUR ME A SHOT OF WHISKEY BEFORE THE TROUBLE STARTS."

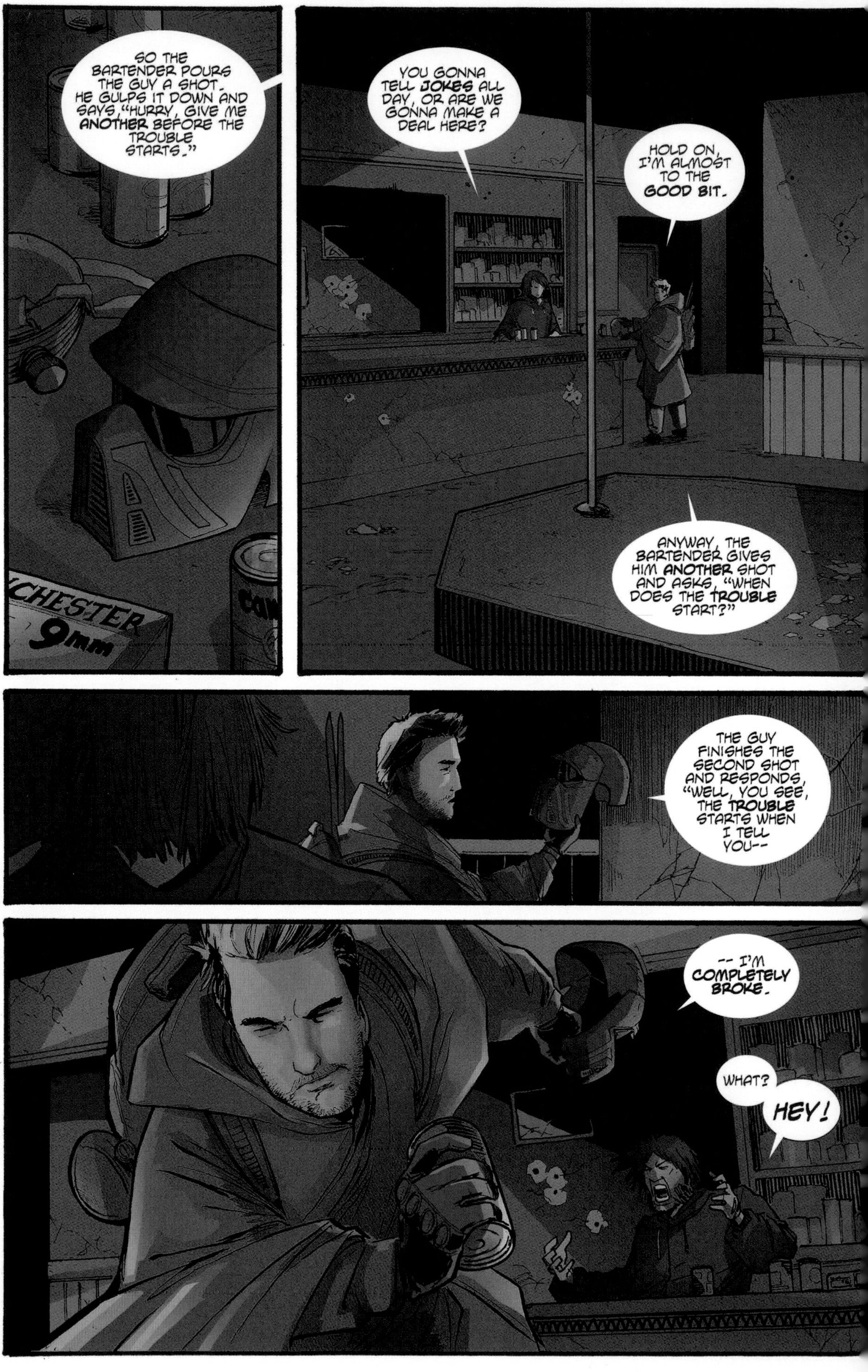
SO THE BARTENDER POURS THE GUY A SHOT. HE GULPS IT DOWN AND SAYS, "HURRY, GIVE ME ANOTHER BEFORE THE TROUBLE STARTS."
YOU GONNA TELL JOKES ALL DAY, OR ARE WE GONNA MAKE A DEAL HERE?
HOLD ON, I'M ALMOST TO THE GOOD BIT.
ANYWAY, THE BARTENDER GIVES HIM ANOTHER SHOT AND ASKS, "WHEN DOES THE TROUBLE START?"
WINCHESTER 9mm
THE GUY FINISHES THE SECOND SHOT AND RESPONDS, "WELL, YOU SEE, THE TROUBLE STARTS WHEN I TELL YOU--
-- I'M COMPLETELY BROKE.
WHAT?
HEY!

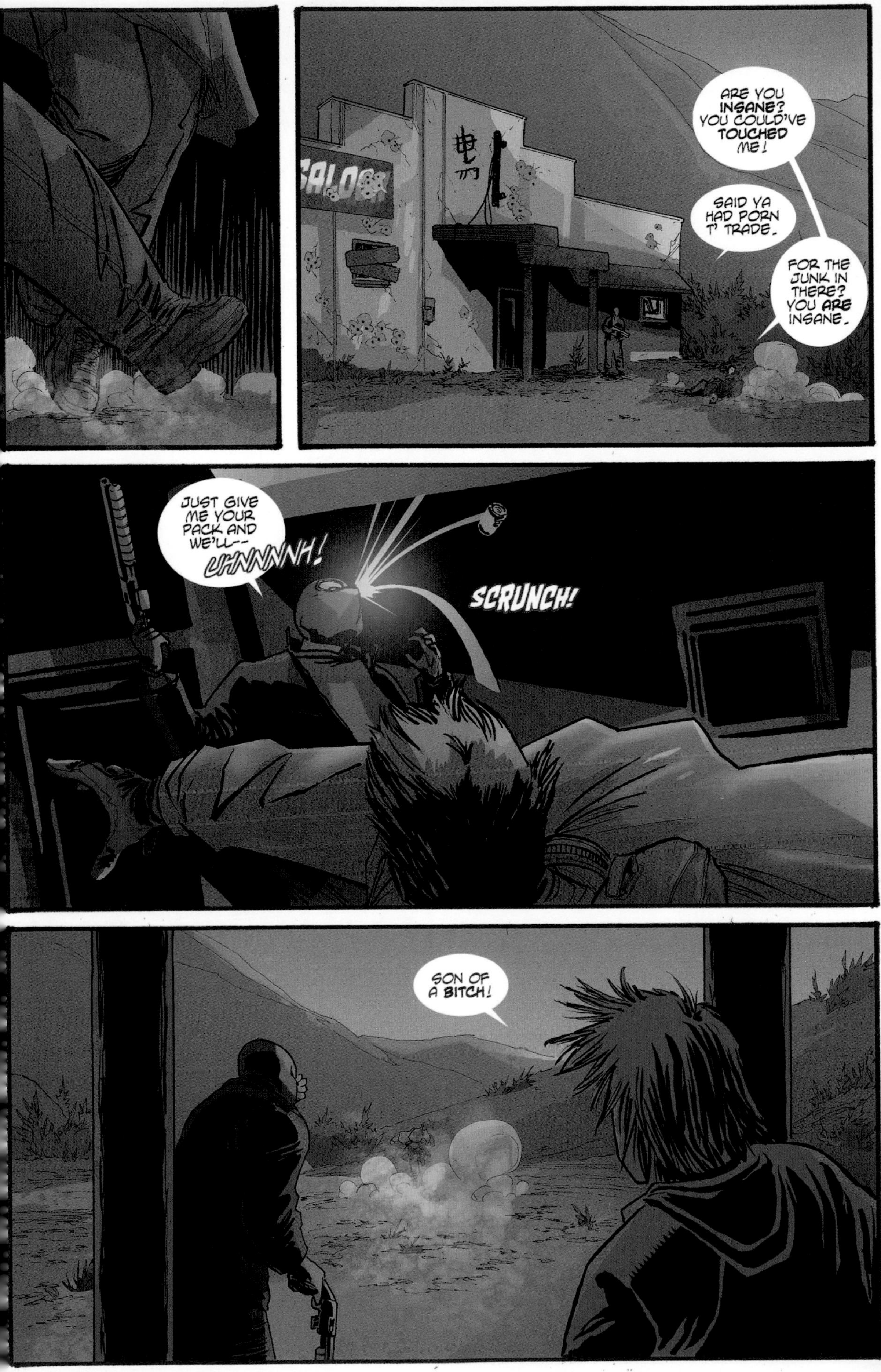
ARE YOU INSANE? YOU COULD'VE TOUCHED ME!
SAID YA HAD PORN T' TRADE.
FOR THE JUNK IN THERE? YOU ARE INSANE.
JUST GIVE ME YOUR PACK AND WE'LL-- UHNNNNH!
SCRUNCH!
SON OF A BITCH!

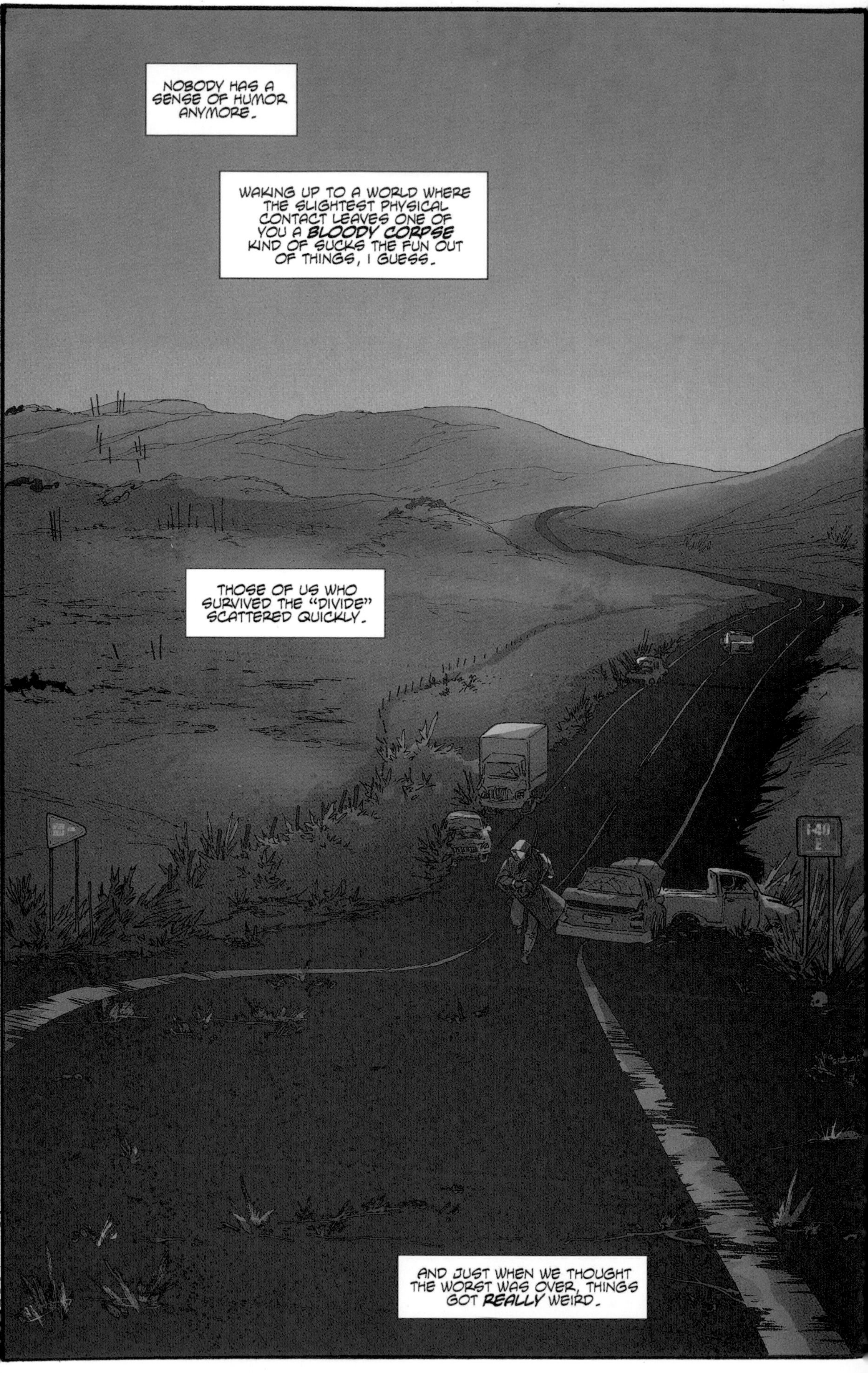
NOBODY HAS A SENSE OF HUMOR ANYMORE.
WAKING UP TO A WORLD WHERE THE SLIGHTEST PHYSICAL CONTACT LEAVES ONE OF YOU A BLOODY CORPSE KIND OF SUCKS THE FUN OUT OF THINGS, I GUESS.
THOSE OF US WHO SURVIVED THE "DIVIDE" SCATTERED QUICKLY.
I-40 E
AND JUST WHEN WE THOUGHT THE WORST WAS OVER, THINGS GOT REALLY WEIRD.

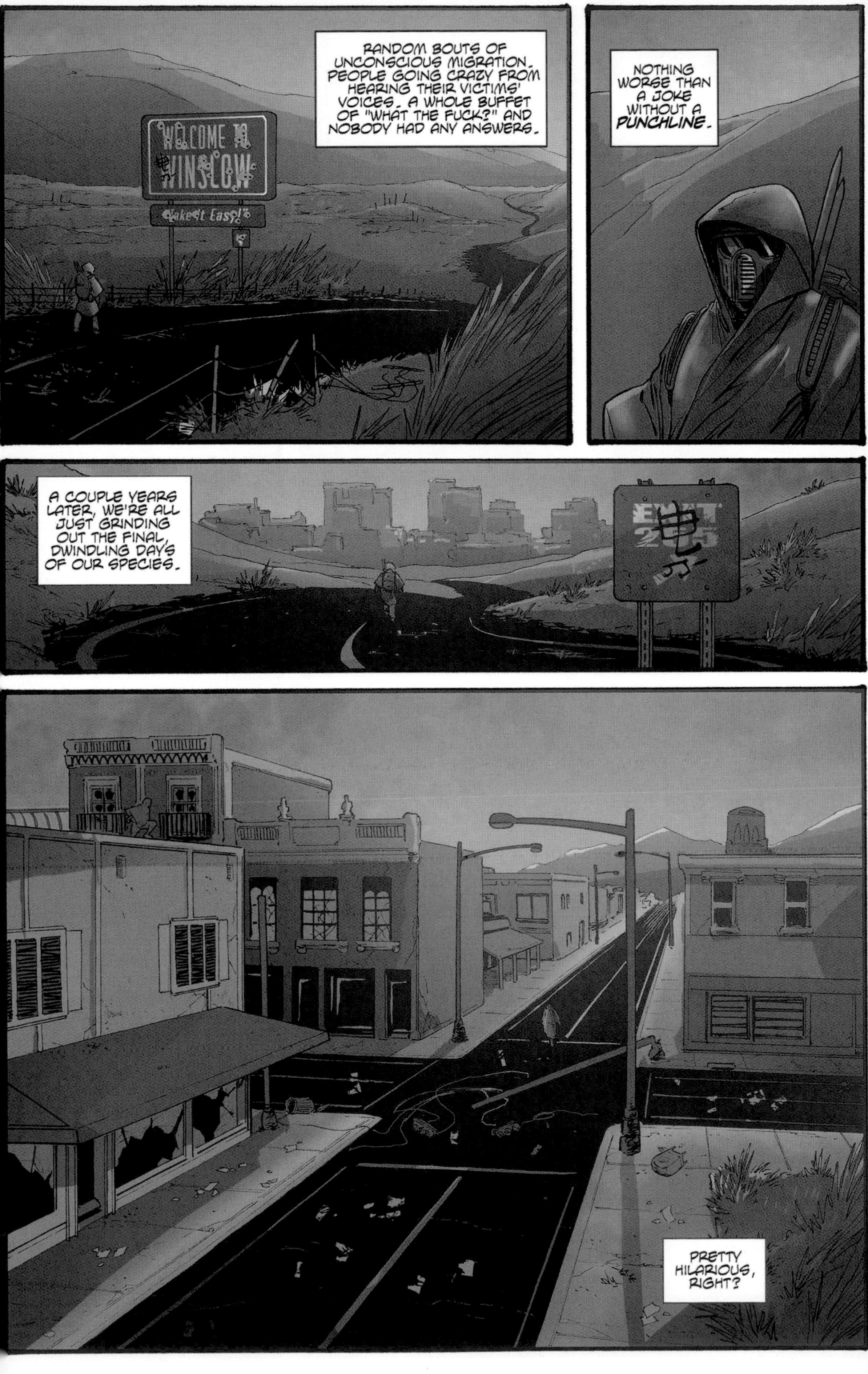
RANDOM BOUTS OF UNCONSCIOUS MIGRATION. PEOPLE GOING CRAZY FROM HEARING THEIR VICTIMS' VOICES. A WHOLE BUFFET OF "WHAT THE FUCK?" AND NOBODY HAD ANY ANSWERS.
WELCOME TO
WINSLOW
NOTHING WORSE THAN A JOKE WITHOUT A *PUNCHLINE*.
A COUPLE YEARS LATER, WE'RE ALL JUST GRINDING OUT THE FINAL, DWINDLING DAYS OF OUR SPECIES.
PRETTY HILARIOUS, RIGHT?

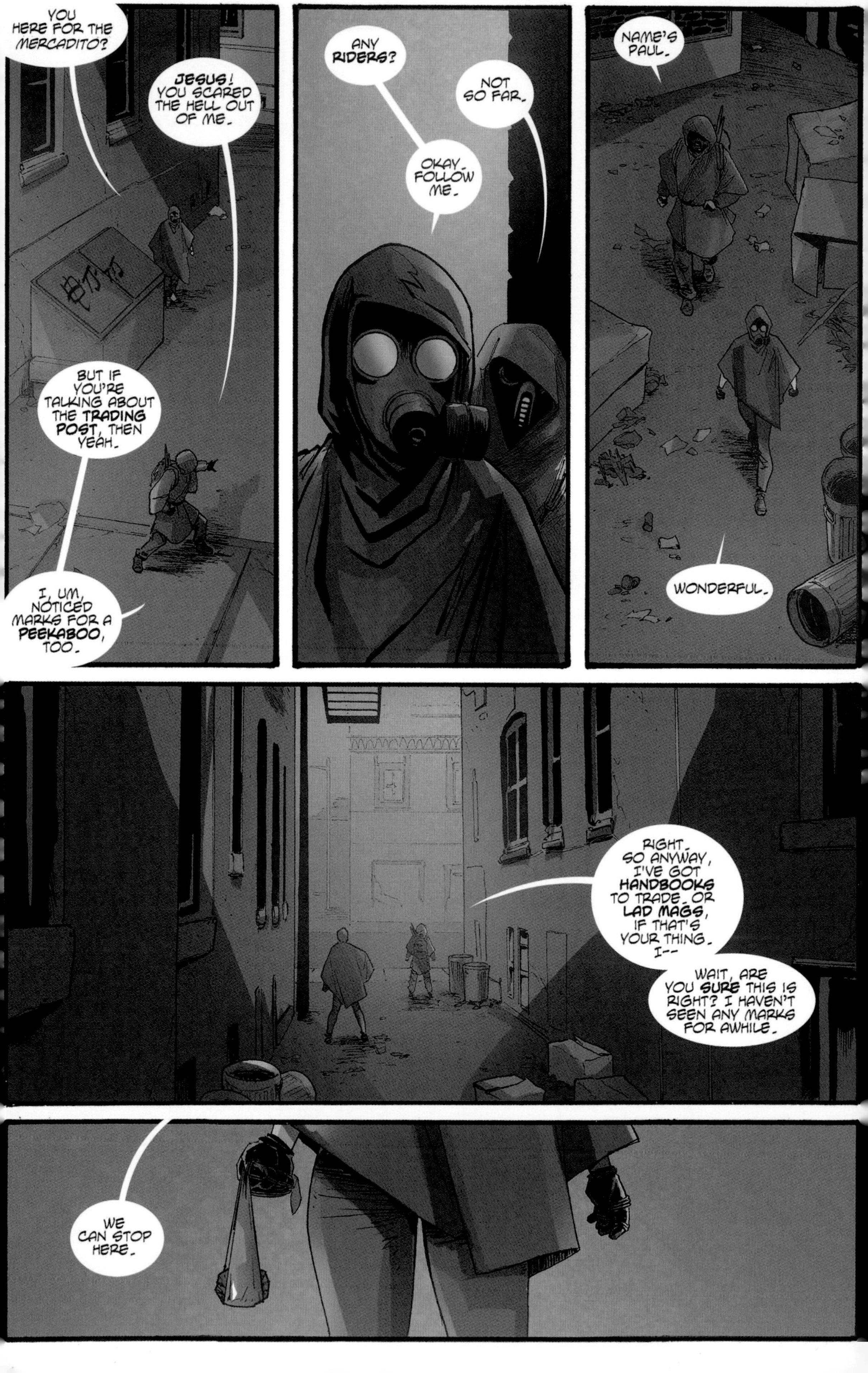
YOU HERE FOR THE MERCADITO?
JESUS! YOU SCARED THE HELL OUT OF ME.
BUT IF YOU'RE TALKING ABOUT THE TRADING POST, THEN YEAH.
I, UM, NOTICED MARKS FOR A PEEKABOO, TOO.
ANY RIDERS?
NOT SO FAR.
OKAY. FOLLOW ME.
NAME'S PAUL.
WONDERFUL.
RIGHT. SO ANYWAY, I'VE GOT HANDBOOKS TO TRADE. OR LAD MAGS, IF THAT'S YOUR THING. I--
WAIT, ARE YOU SURE THIS IS RIGHT? I HAVEN'T SEEN ANY MARKS FOR AWHILE.
WE CAN STOP HERE.

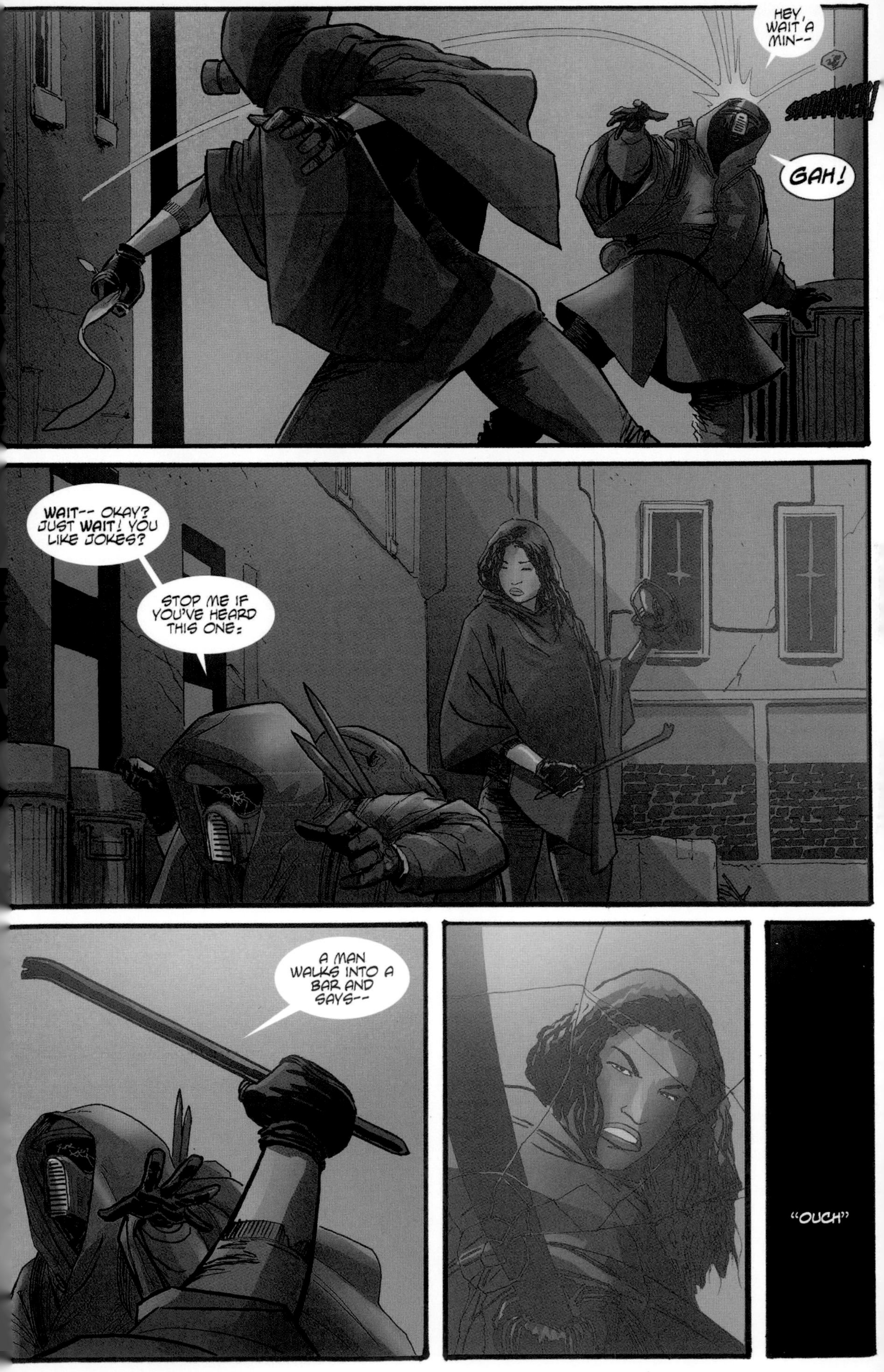
HEY, WAIT A MIN--
GAH!
WAIT-- OKAY? JUST WAIT! YOU LIKE JOKES?
STOP ME IF YOU'VE HEARD THIS ONE:
A MAN WALKS INTO A BAR AND SAYS--
"OUCH"

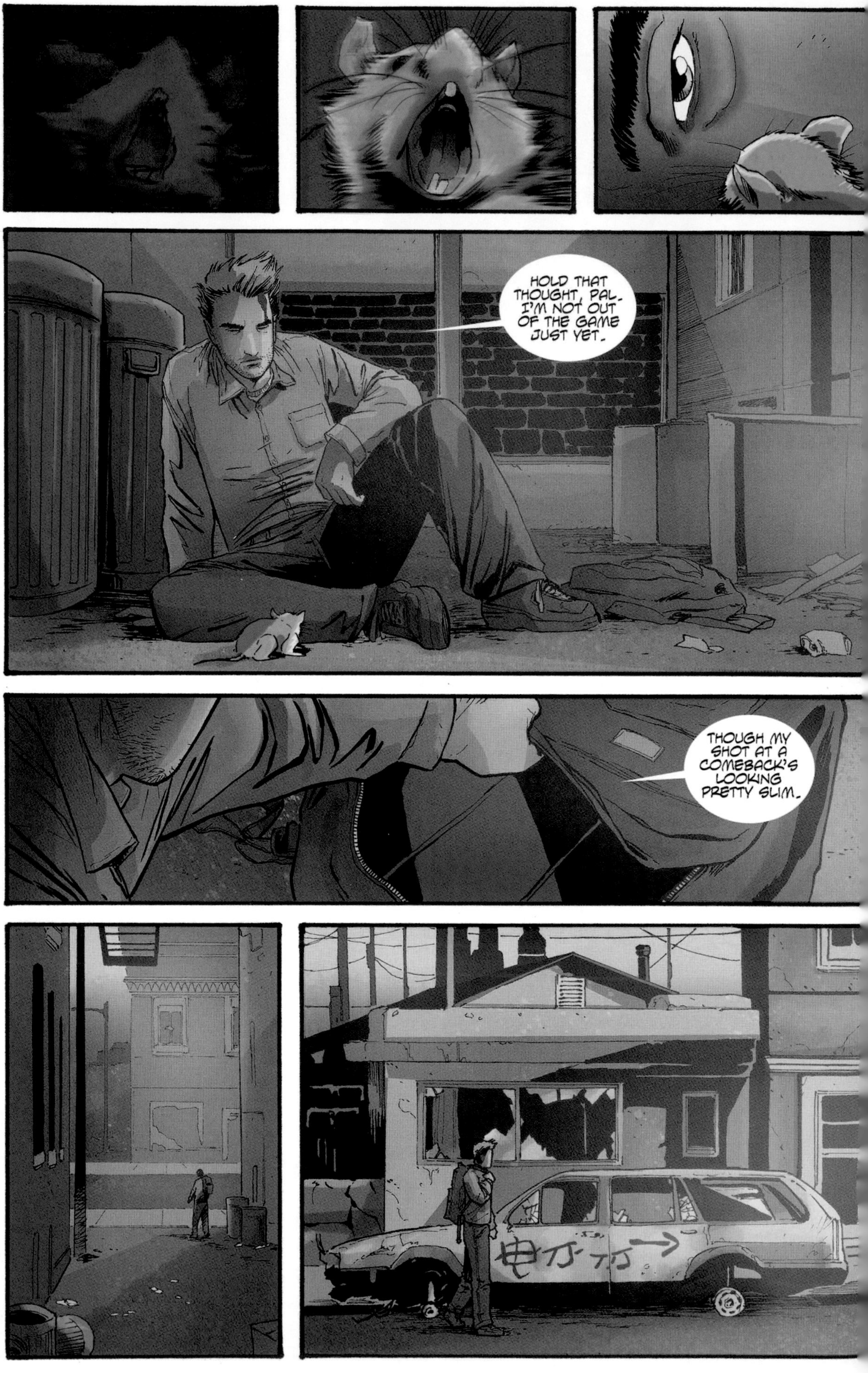
HOLD THAT THOUGHT, PAL. I'M NOT OUT OF THE GAME JUST YET.
THOUGH MY SHOT AT A COMEBACK'S LOOKING PRETTY SLIM.

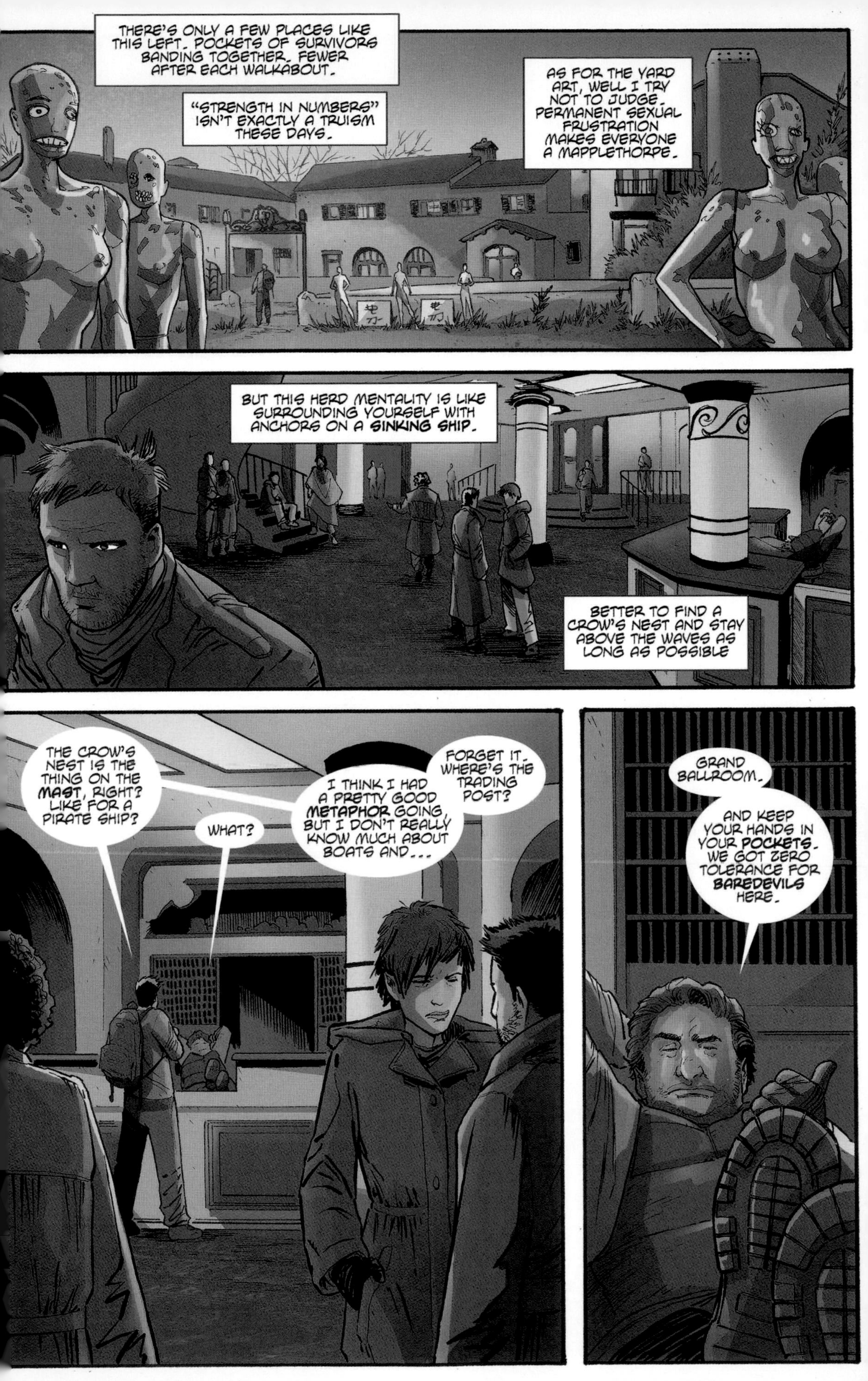

THERE'S ONLY A FEW PLACES LIKE THIS LEFT. POCKETS OF SURVIVORS BANDING TOGETHER. FEWER AFTER EACH WALKABOUT.
"STRENGTH IN NUMBERS" ISN'T EXACTLY A TRUISM THESE DAYS.
AS FOR THE YARD ART, WELL I TRY NOT TO JUDGE. PERMANENT SEXUAL FRUSTRATION MAKES EVERYONE A MAPPLETHORPE.
BUT THIS HERD MENTALITY IS LIKE SURROUNDING YOURSELF WITH ANCHORS ON A **SINKING SHIP**.
BETTER TO FIND A CROW'S NEST AND STAY ABOVE THE WAVES AS LONG AS POSSIBLE
THE CROW'S NEST IS THE THING ON THE **MAST**, RIGHT? LIKE FOR A PIRATE SHIP?
WHAT?
I THINK I HAD A PRETTY GOOD **METAPHOR** GOING, BUT I DON'T REALLY KNOW MUCH ABOUT BOATS AND...
FORGET IT. WHERE'S THE TRADING POST?
GRAND BALLROOM.
AND KEEP YOUR HANDS IN YOUR **POCKETS**. WE GOT ZERO TOLERANCE FOR **BAREDEVILS** HERE.

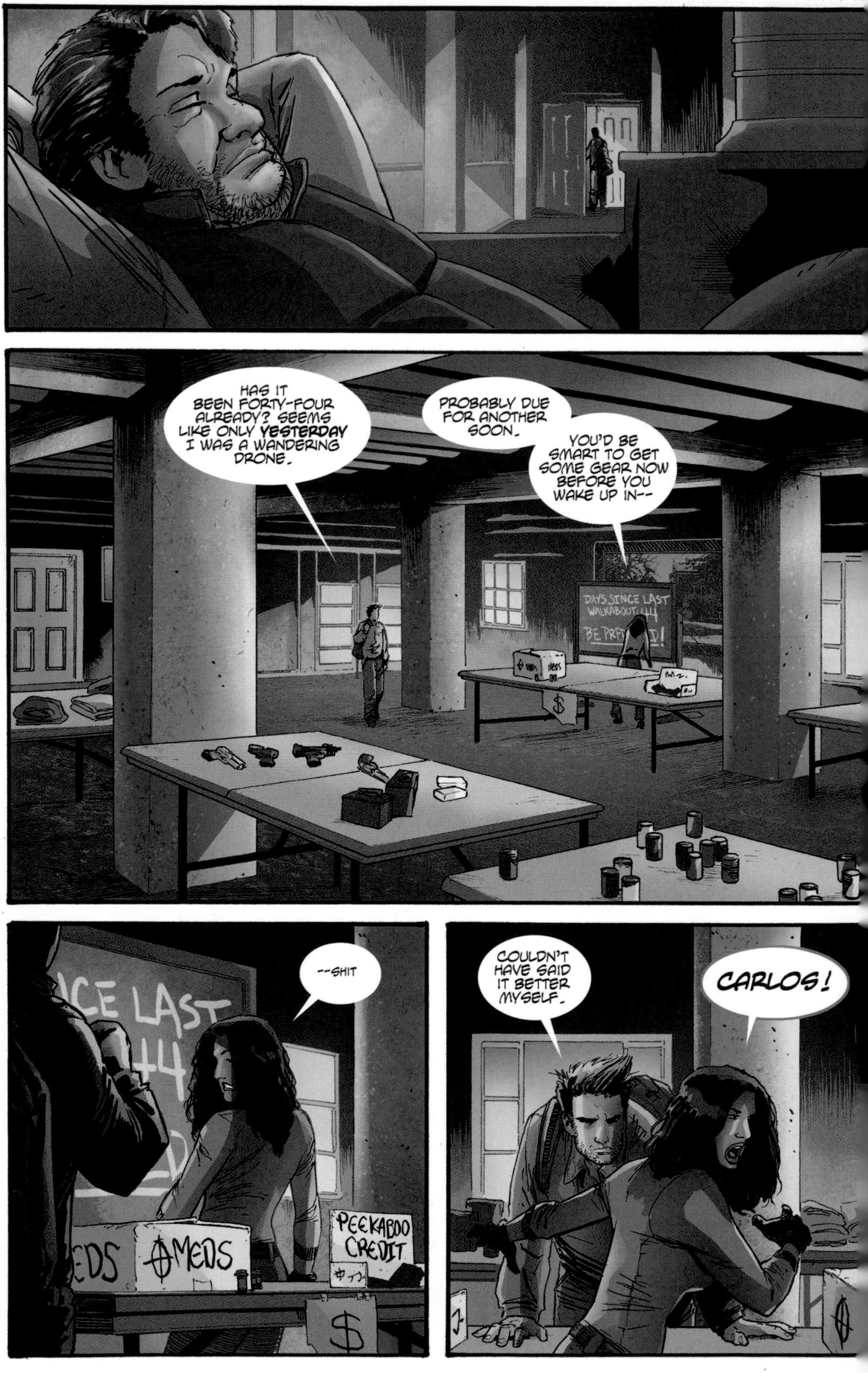
HAS IT BEEN FORTY-FOUR ALREADY? SEEMS LIKE ONLY **YESTERDAY** I WAS A WANDERING DRONE.
PROBABLY DUE FOR ANOTHER SOON.
YOU'D BE SMART TO GET SOME GEAR NOW BEFORE YOU WAKE UP IN--
DAYS SINCE LAST WALKABOUT: 44
--SHIT
MEDS
PEEKABOO CREDIT
COULDN'T HAVE SAID IT BETTER MYSELF.
CARLOS!

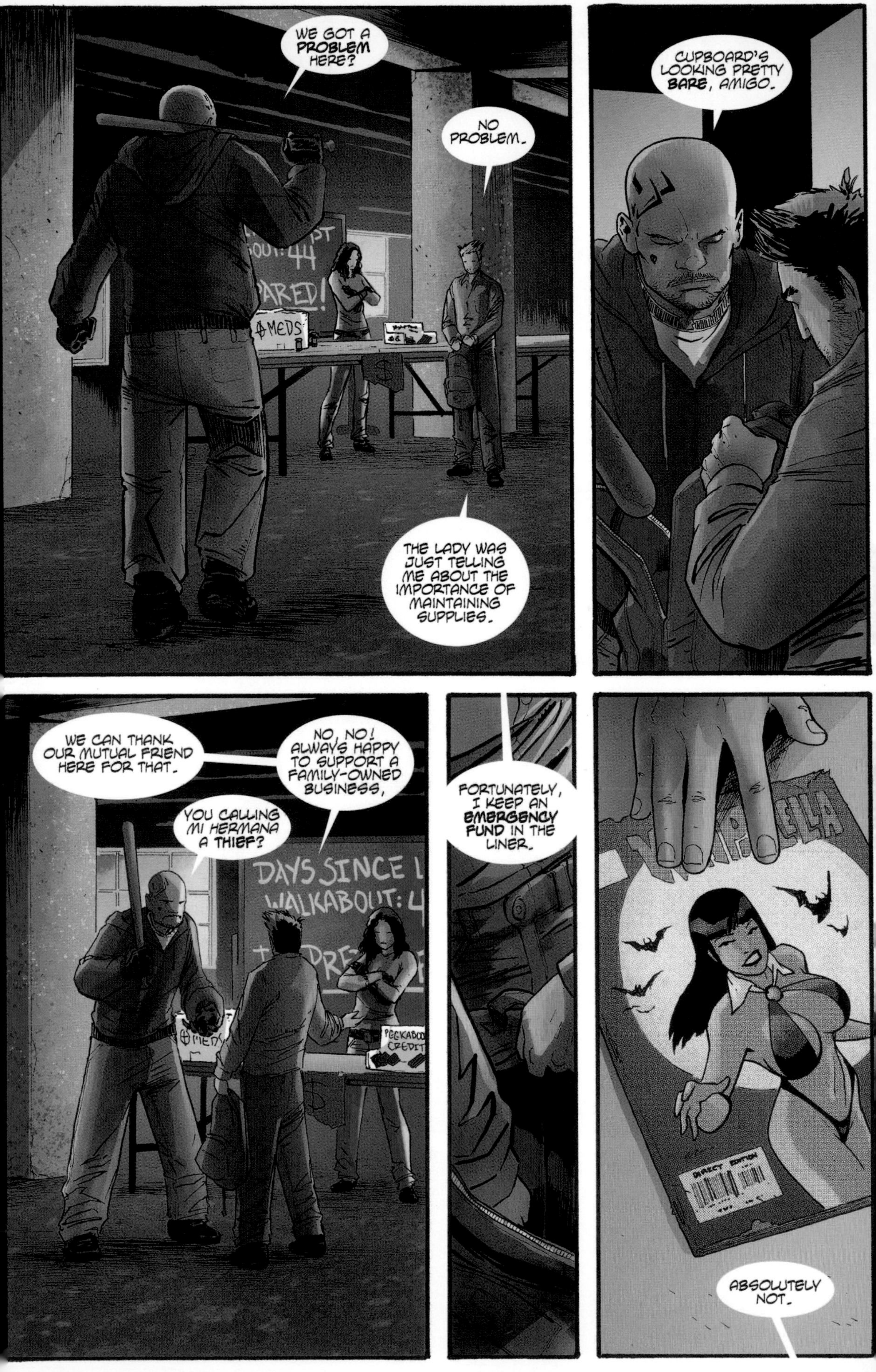

WE GOT A PROBLEM HERE?
NO PROBLEM.
THE LADY WAS JUST TELLING ME ABOUT THE IMPORTANCE OF MAINTAINING SUPPLIES.
MEDS
CUPBOARD'S LOOKING PRETTY BARE, AMIGO.
WE CAN THANK OUR MUTUAL FRIEND HERE FOR THAT.
YOU CALLING MI HERMANA A THIEF?
NO, NO! ALWAYS HAPPY TO SUPPORT A FAMILY-OWNED BUSINESS,
DAYS SINCE L
WALKABOUT: 4
PEEKABOO CREDIT
FORTUNATELY, I KEEP AN EMERGENCY FUND IN THE LINER.
ABSOLUTELY NOT.

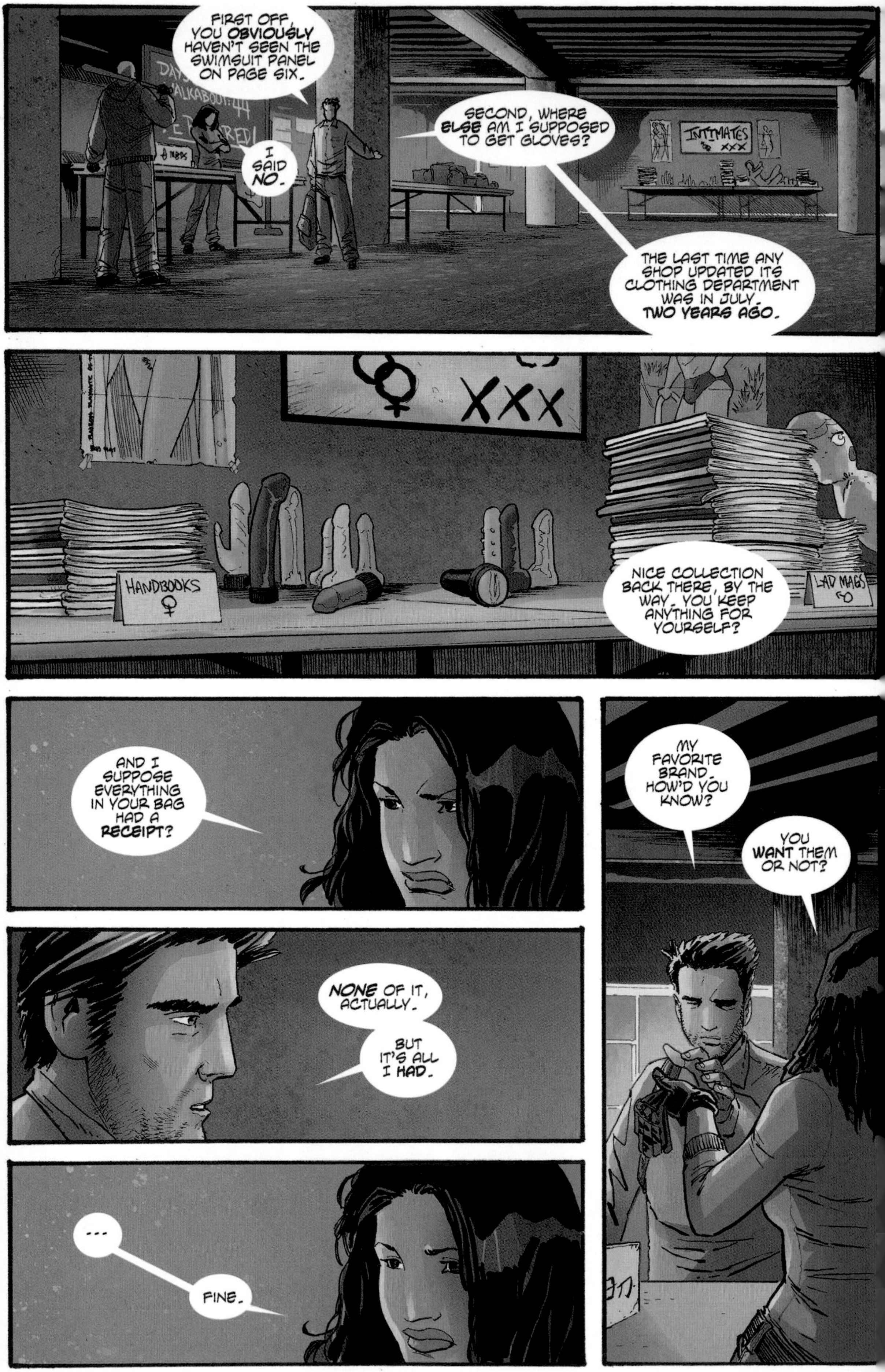

FIRST OFF, YOU OBVIOUSLY HAVEN'T SEEN THE SWIMSUIT PANEL ON PAGE SIX.
I SAID NO.
SECOND, WHERE ELSE AM I SUPPOSED TO GET GLOVES?
THE LAST TIME ANY SHOP UPDATED ITS CLOTHING DEPARTMENT WAS IN JULY. TWO YEARS AGO.
INTIMATES XXX
XXX
HANDBOOKS ♀
LAD MAGS
NICE COLLECTION BACK THERE, BY THE WAY. YOU KEEP ANYTHING FOR YOURSELF?
AND I SUPPOSE EVERYTHING IN YOUR BAG HAD A RECEIPT?
NONE OF IT, ACTUALLY.
BUT IT'S ALL I HAD.
...
FINE.
MY FAVORITE BRAND. HOW'D YOU KNOW?
YOU WANT THEM OR NOT?

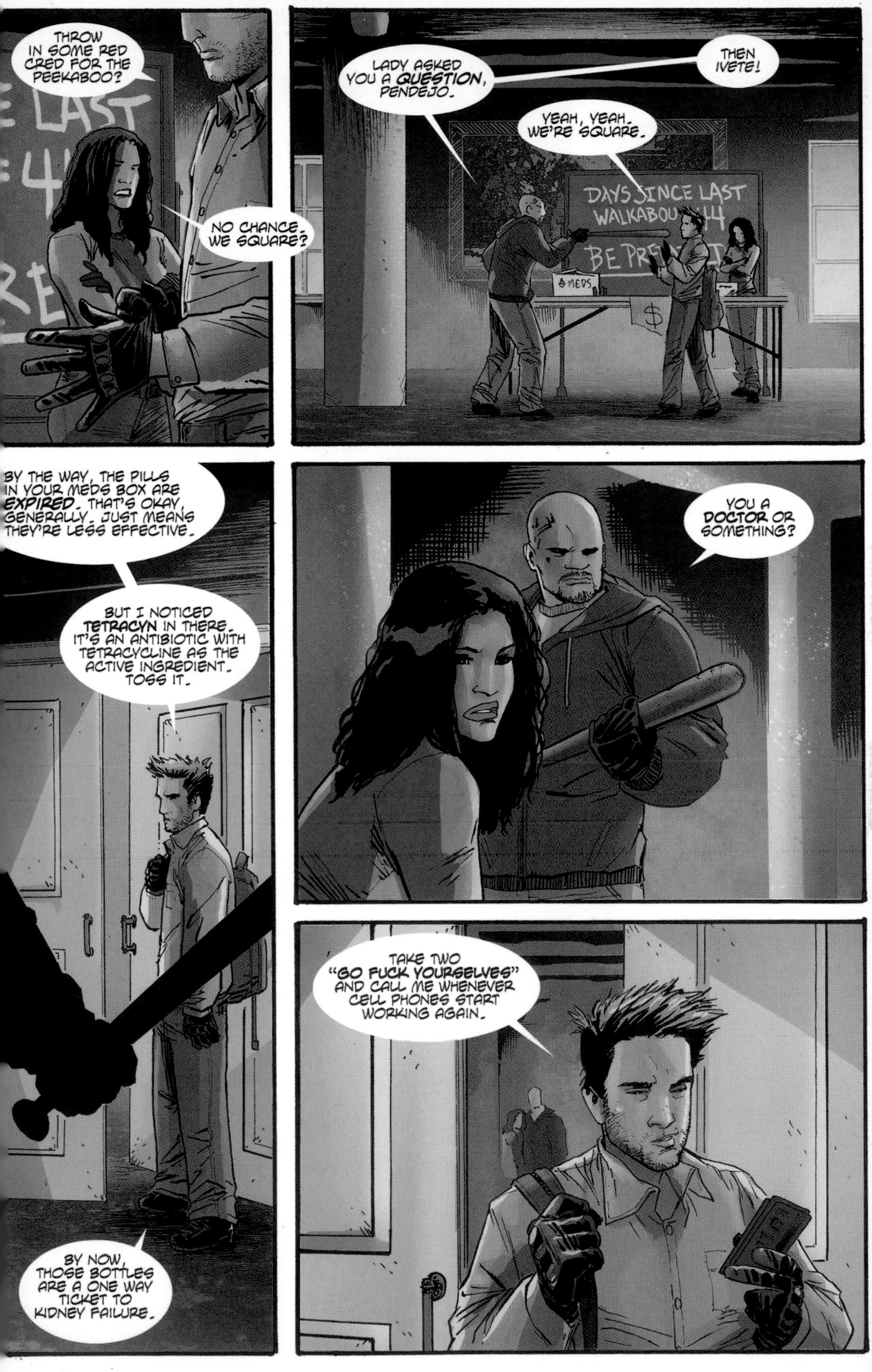

THROW IN SOME RED CRED FOR THE PEEKABOO?
NO CHANCE. WE SQUARE?
LADY ASKED YOU A **QUESTION**, PENDEJO.
THEN IVETE!
YEAH, YEAH. WE'RE SQUARE.
DAYS SINCE LAST WALKABOUT 44
BE PRE
MEDS
BY THE WAY, THE PILLS IN YOUR MEDS BOX ARE **EXPIRED**. THAT'S OKAY, GENERALLY. JUST MEANS THEY'RE LESS EFFECTIVE.
BUT I NOTICED **TETRACYN** IN THERE. IT'S AN ANTIBIOTIC WITH TETRACYCLINE AS THE ACTIVE INGREDIENT. TOSS IT.
BY NOW, THOSE BOTTLES ARE A ONE WAY TICKET TO KIDNEY FAILURE.
YOU A **DOCTOR** OR SOMETHING?
TAKE TWO **"GO FUCK YOURSELVES"** AND CALL ME WHENEVER CELL PHONES START WORKING AGAIN.

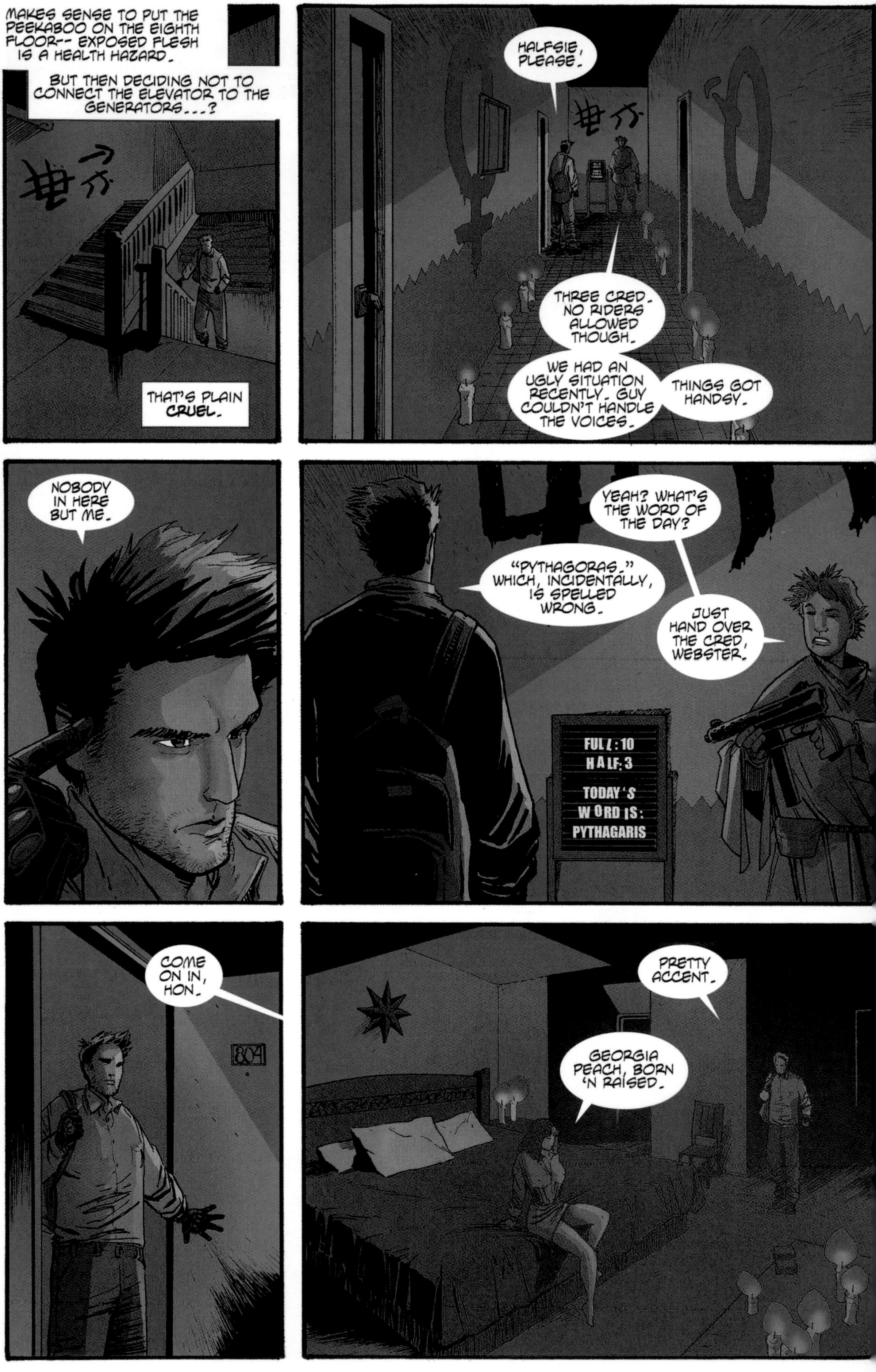
MAKES SENSE TO PUT THE PEEKABOO ON THE EIGHTH FLOOR-- EXPOSED FLESH IS A HEALTH HAZARD.
BUT THEN DECIDING NOT TO CONNECT THE ELEVATOR TO THE GENERATORS...?
THAT'S PLAIN CRUEL.
HALFSIE, PLEASE.
THREE CRED. NO RIDERS ALLOWED THOUGH.
WE HAD AN UGLY SITUATION RECENTLY. GUY COULDN'T HANDLE THE VOICES.
THINGS GOT HANDSY.
NOBODY IN HERE BUT ME.
YEAH? WHAT'S THE WORD OF THE DAY?
"PYTHAGORAS." WHICH, INCIDENTALLY, IS SPELLED WRONG.
JUST HAND OVER THE CRED, WEBSTER.
FULL: 10
HALF: 3
TODAY'S WORD IS:
PYTHAGARIS
COME ON IN, HON.
804
PRETTY ACCENT.
GEORGIA PEACH, BORN 'N RAISED.

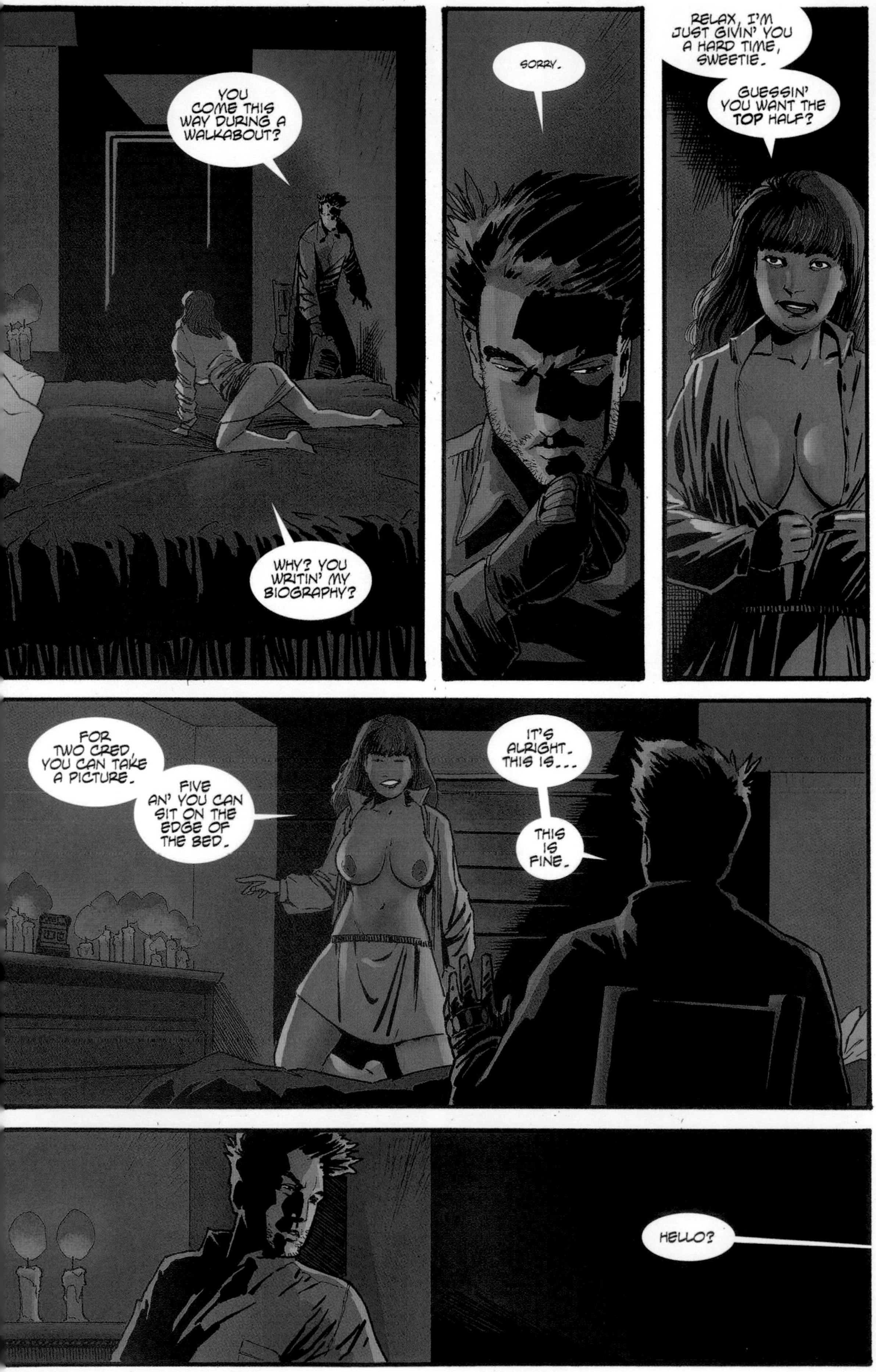
YOU COME THIS WAY DURING A WALKABOUT?
WHY? YOU WRITIN' MY BIOGRAPHY?
SORRY.
RELAX, I'M JUST GIVIN' YOU A HARD TIME, SWEETIE.
GUESSIN' YOU WANT THE TOP HALF?
FOR TWO CRED, YOU CAN TAKE A PICTURE.
FIVE AN' YOU CAN SIT ON THE EDGE OF THE BED.
IT'S ALRIGHT. THIS IS...
THIS IS FINE.
HELLO?

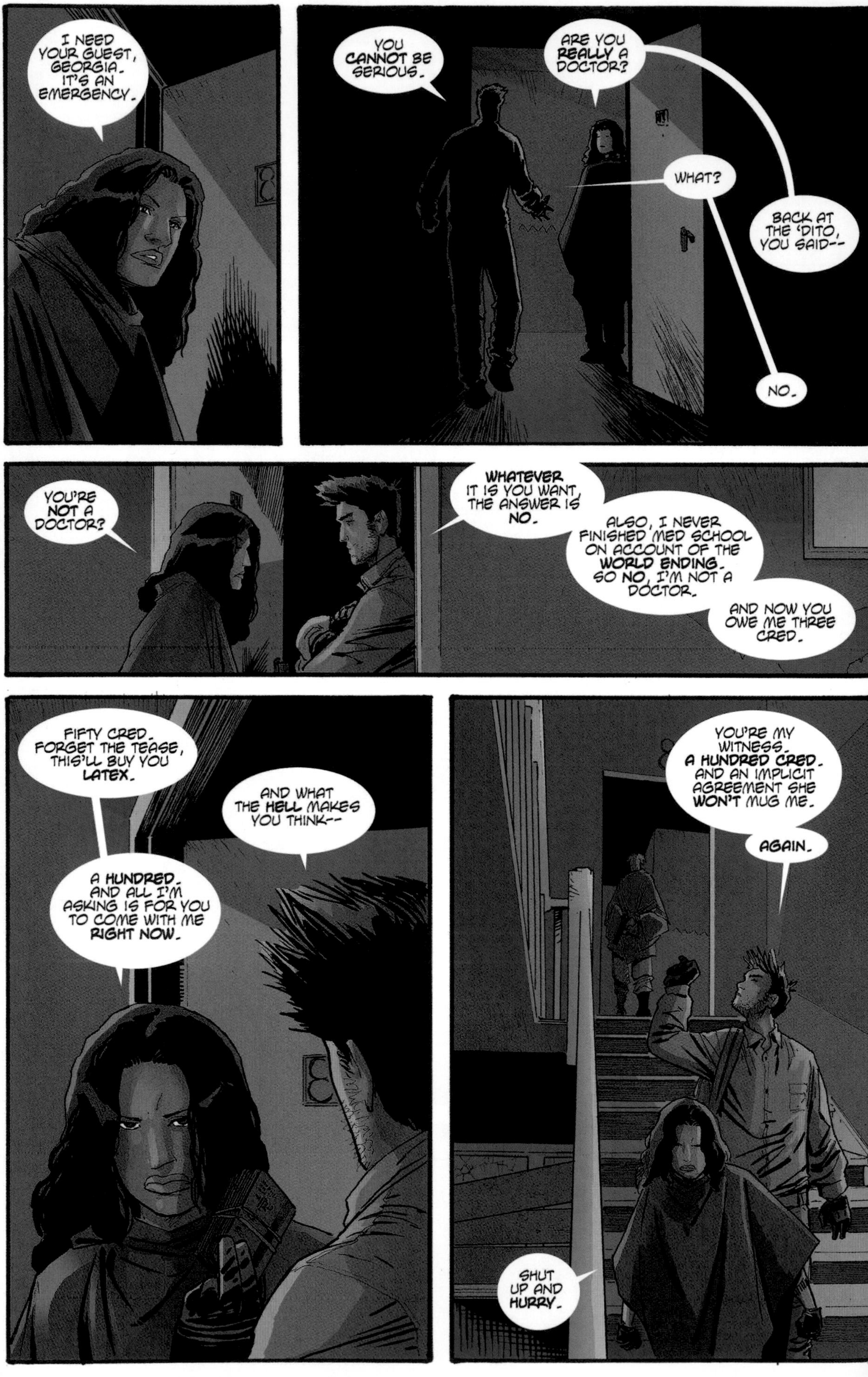
I NEED YOUR GUEST, GEORGIA. IT'S AN EMERGENCY.
YOU CANNOT BE SERIOUS.
ARE YOU REALLY A DOCTOR?
WHAT?
BACK AT THE 'DITO, YOU SAID--
NO.
YOU'RE NOT A DOCTOR?
WHATEVER IT IS YOU WANT, THE ANSWER IS NO.
ALSO, I NEVER FINISHED MED SCHOOL ON ACCOUNT OF THE WORLD ENDING. SO NO, I'M NOT A DOCTOR.
AND NOW YOU OWE ME THREE CRED.
FIFTY CRED. FORGET THE TEASE, THIS'LL BUY YOU LATEX.
AND WHAT THE HELL MAKES YOU THINK--
A HUNDRED. AND ALL I'M ASKING IS FOR YOU TO COME WITH ME RIGHT NOW.
YOU'RE MY WITNESS. A HUNDRED CRED. AND AN IMPLICIT AGREEMENT SHE WON'T MUG ME.
AGAIN.
SHUT UP AND HURRY.

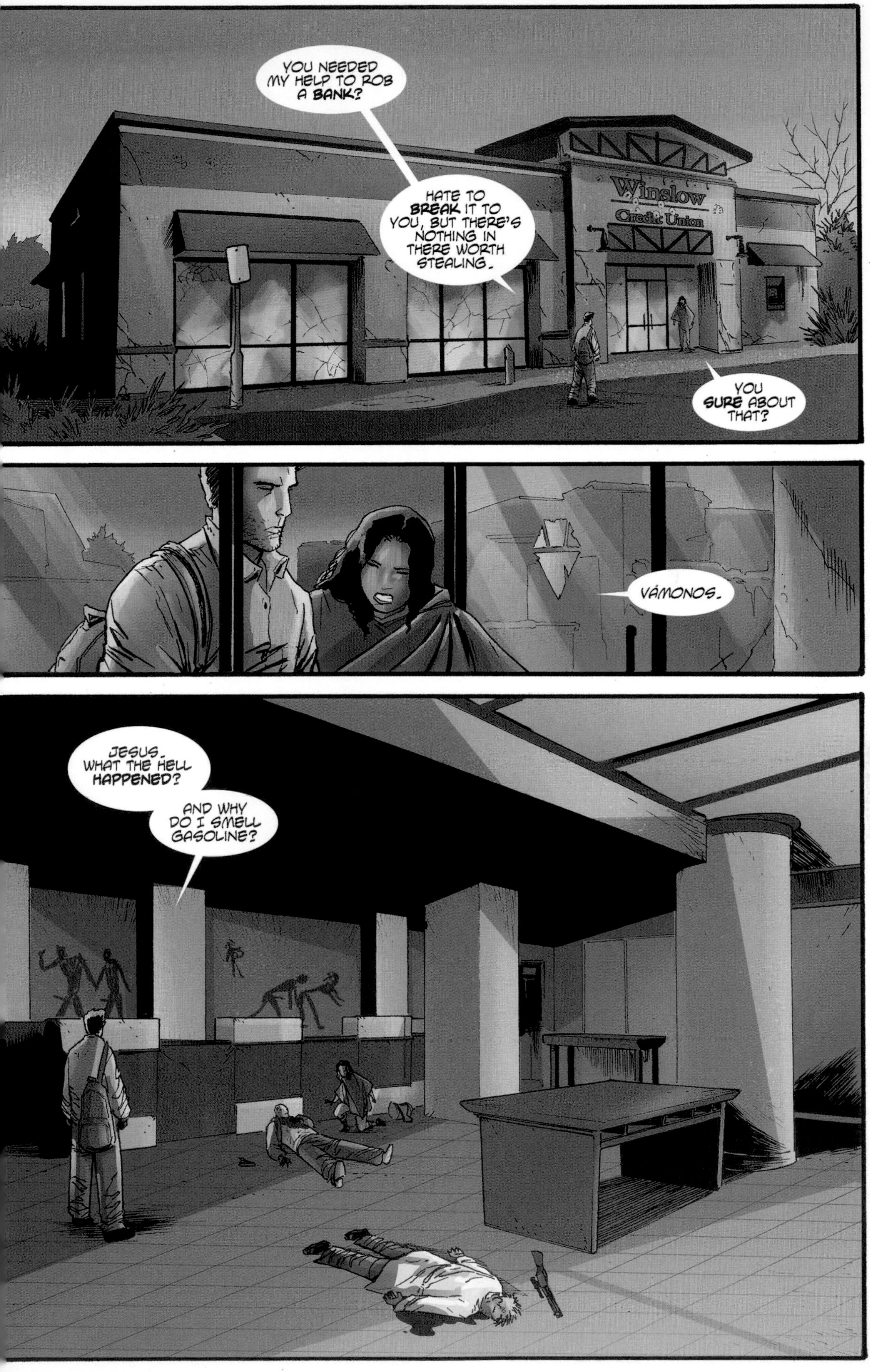
YOU NEEDED MY HELP TO ROB A BANK?
Winslow Credit Union
HATE TO BREAK IT TO YOU, BUT THERE'S NOTHING IN THERE WORTH STEALING.
YOU SURE ABOUT THAT?
VÁMONOS.
JESUS. WHAT THE HELL HAPPENED?
AND WHY DO I SMELL GASOLINE?

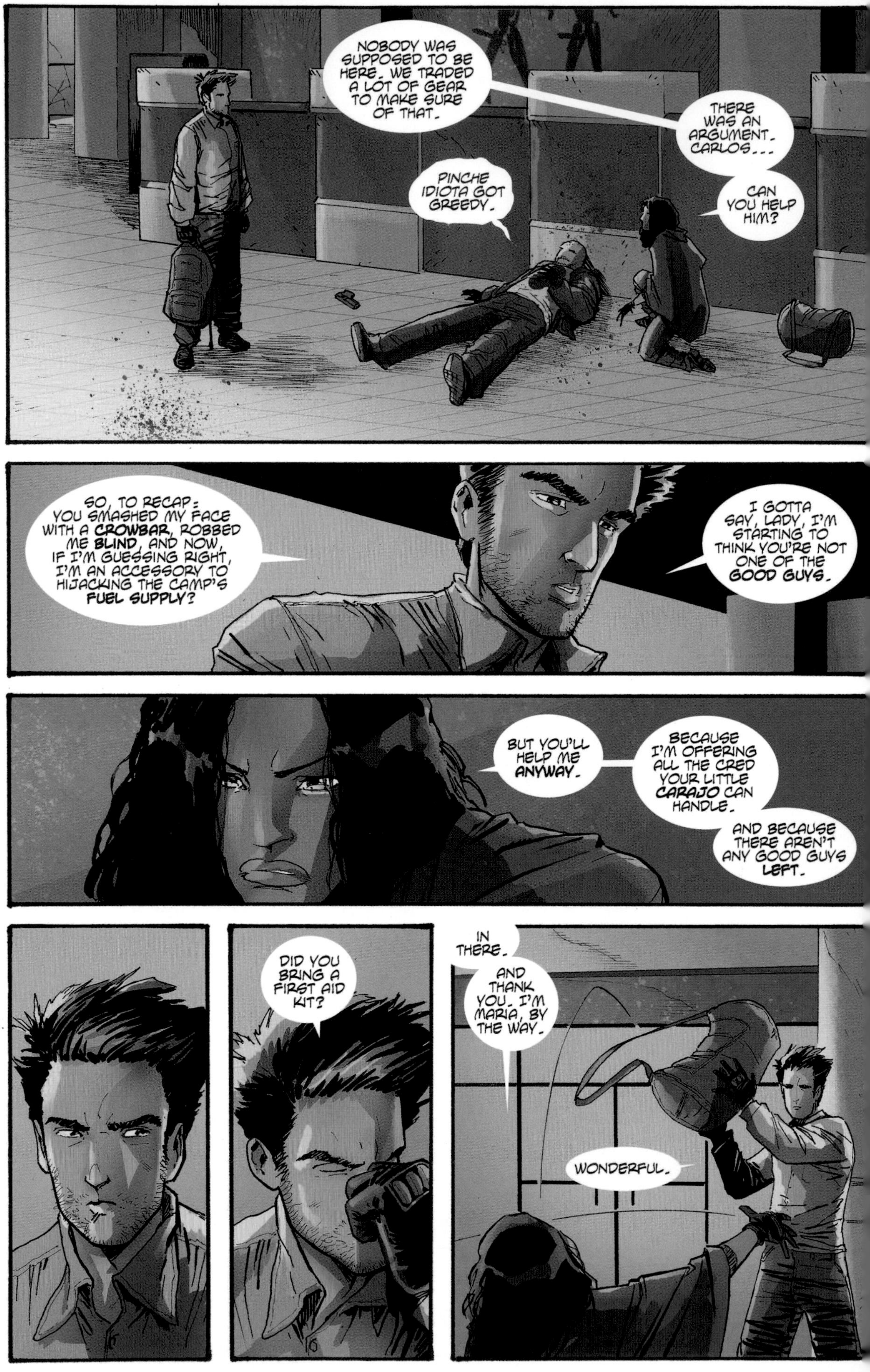
NOBODY WAS SUPPOSED TO BE HERE. WE TRADED A LOT OF GEAR TO MAKE SURE OF THAT.
THERE WAS AN ARGUMENT. CARLOS...
PINCHE IDIOTA GOT GREEDY.
CAN YOU HELP HIM?
SO, TO RECAP: YOU SMASHED MY FACE WITH A CROWBAR, ROBBED ME BLIND, AND NOW, IF I'M GUESSING RIGHT, I'M AN ACCESSORY TO HIJACKING THE CAMP'S FUEL SUPPLY?
I GOTTA SAY, LADY, I'M STARTING TO THINK YOU'RE NOT ONE OF THE GOOD GUYS.
BUT YOU'LL HELP ME ANYWAY.
BECAUSE I'M OFFERING ALL THE CRED YOUR LITTLE CARAJO CAN HANDLE.
AND BECAUSE THERE AREN'T ANY GOOD GUYS LEFT.
DID YOU BRING A FIRST AID KIT?
IN THERE.
AND THANK YOU. I'M MARIA, BY THE WAY.
WONDERFUL.

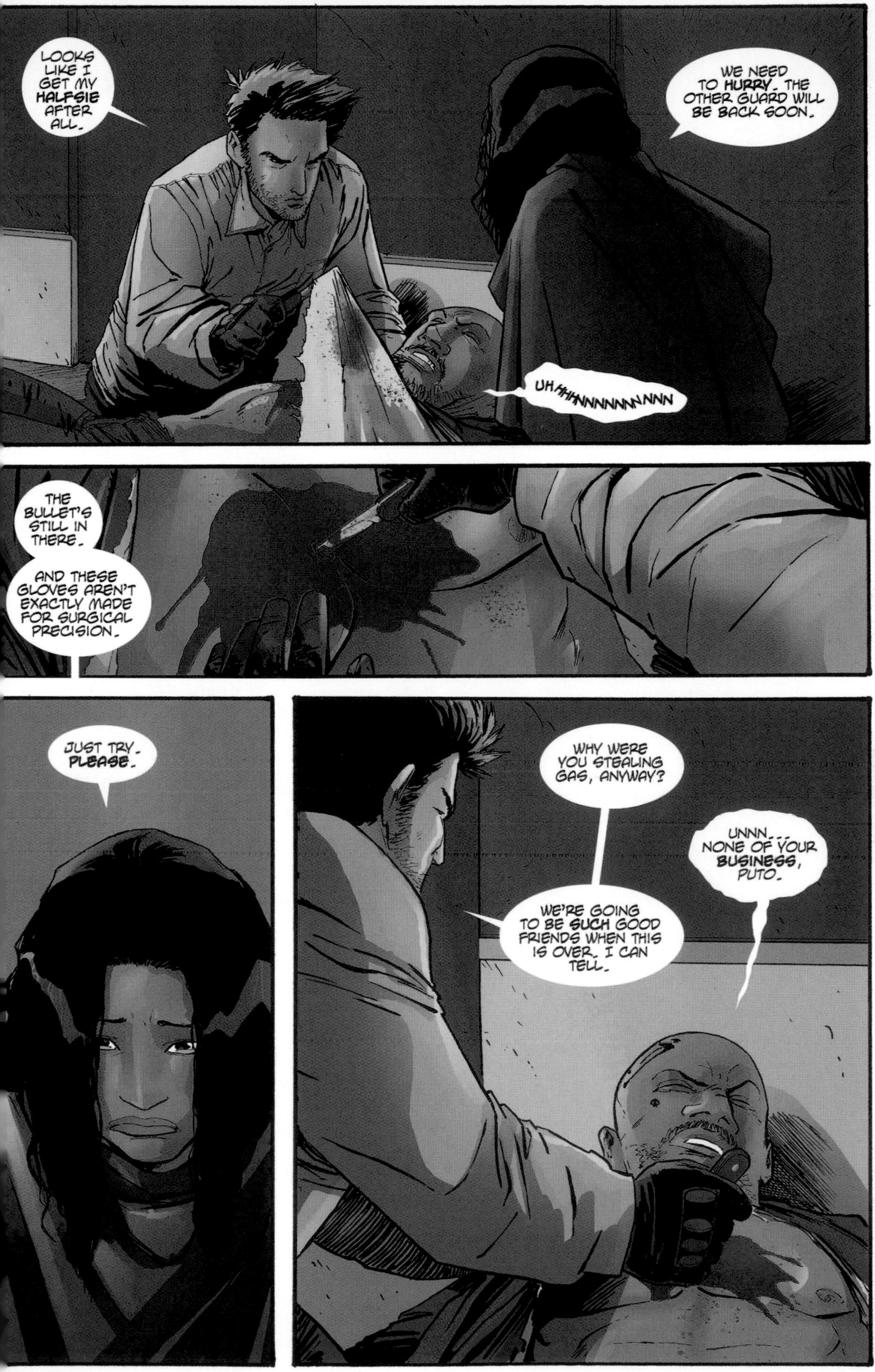
LOOKS LIKE I GET MY HALFSIE AFTER ALL.
WE NEED TO HURRY. THE OTHER GUARD WILL BE BACK SOON.
UHHHHNNNNNNNNN
THE BULLET'S STILL IN THERE.
AND THESE GLOVES AREN'T EXACTLY MADE FOR SURGICAL PRECISION.
JUST TRY. PLEASE.
WHY WERE YOU STEALING GAS, ANYWAY?
UNNN... NONE OF YOUR BUSINESS, PUTO.
WE'RE GOING TO BE SUCH GOOD FRIENDS WHEN THIS IS OVER. I CAN TELL.

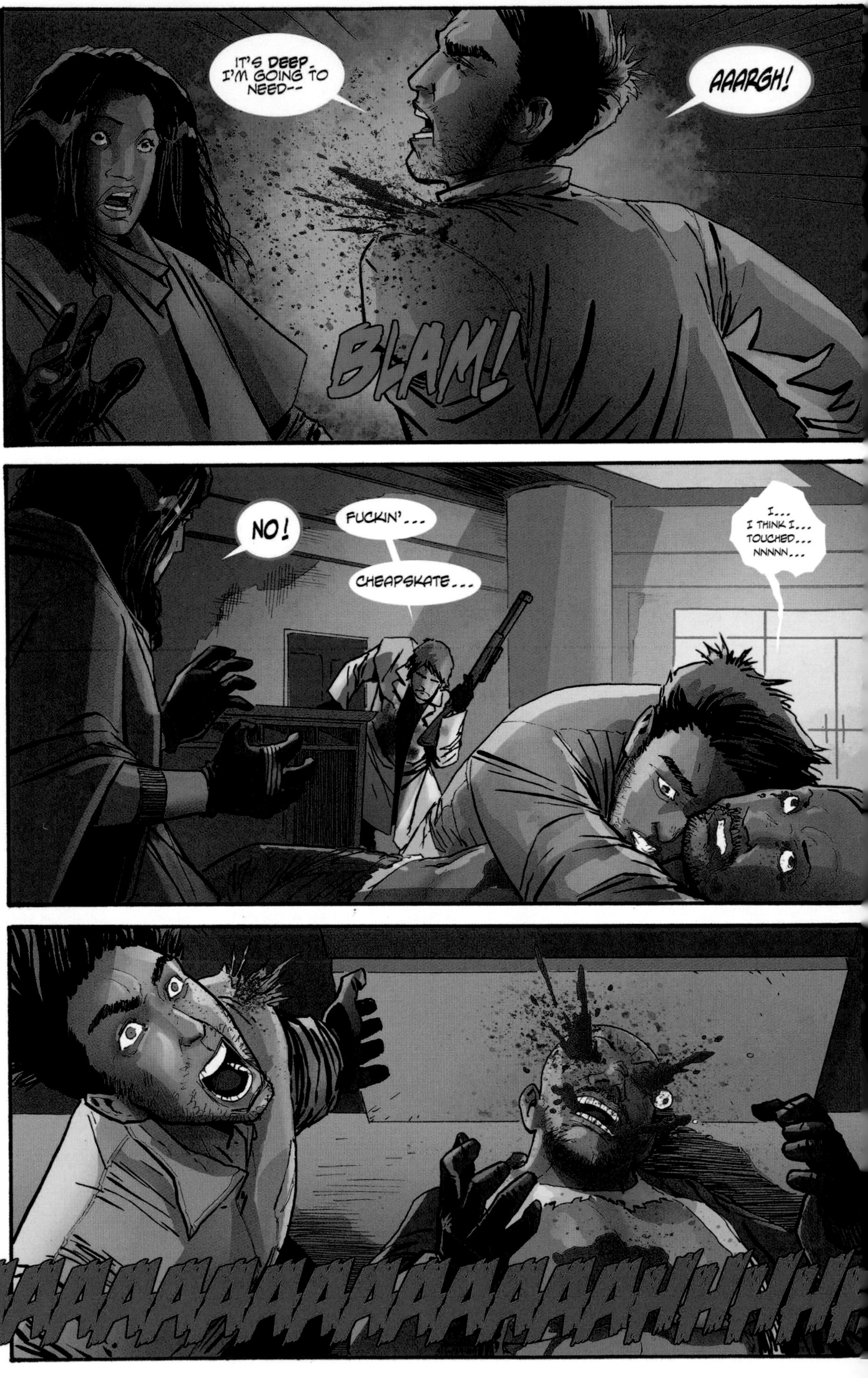
IT'S DEEP. I'M GOING TO NEED--
AAARGH!
BLAM!
NO!
FUCKIN'...
CHEAPSKATE...
I... I THINK I... TOUCHED... NNNNN...
AAAAAAAAAAAAAAAAHHHH

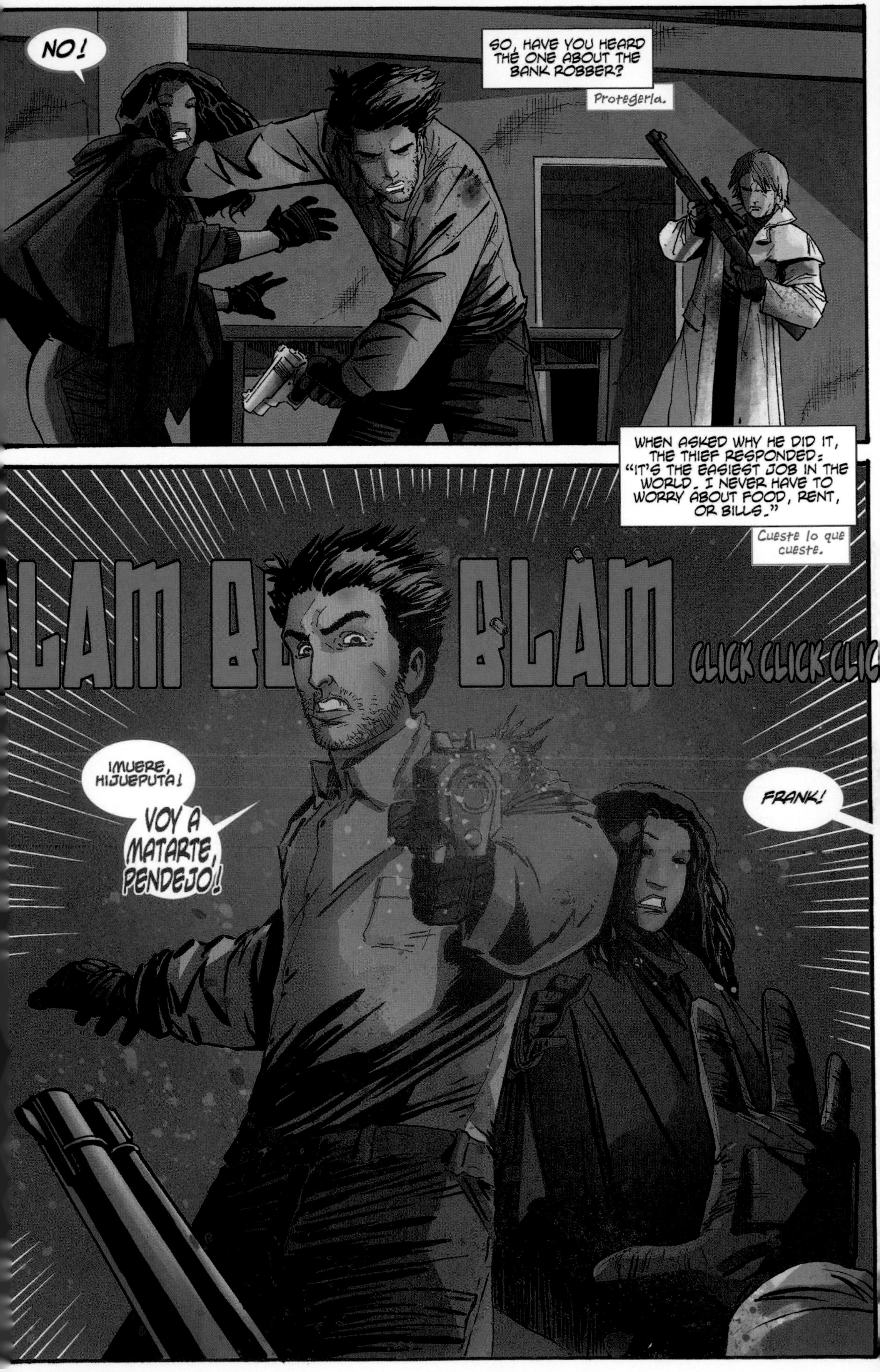
NO!
SO, HAVE YOU HEARD THE ONE ABOUT THE BANK ROBBER?
Protegería.
WHEN ASKED WHY HE DID IT, THE THIEF RESPONDED: "IT'S THE EASIEST JOB IN THE WORLD. I NEVER HAVE TO WORRY ABOUT FOOD, RENT, OR BILLS."
Cueste lo que cueste.
LAM BL BLAM
CLICK CLICK CLIC
¡MUERE, HIJUEPUTA!
VOY A MATARTE, PENDEJO!
FRANK!

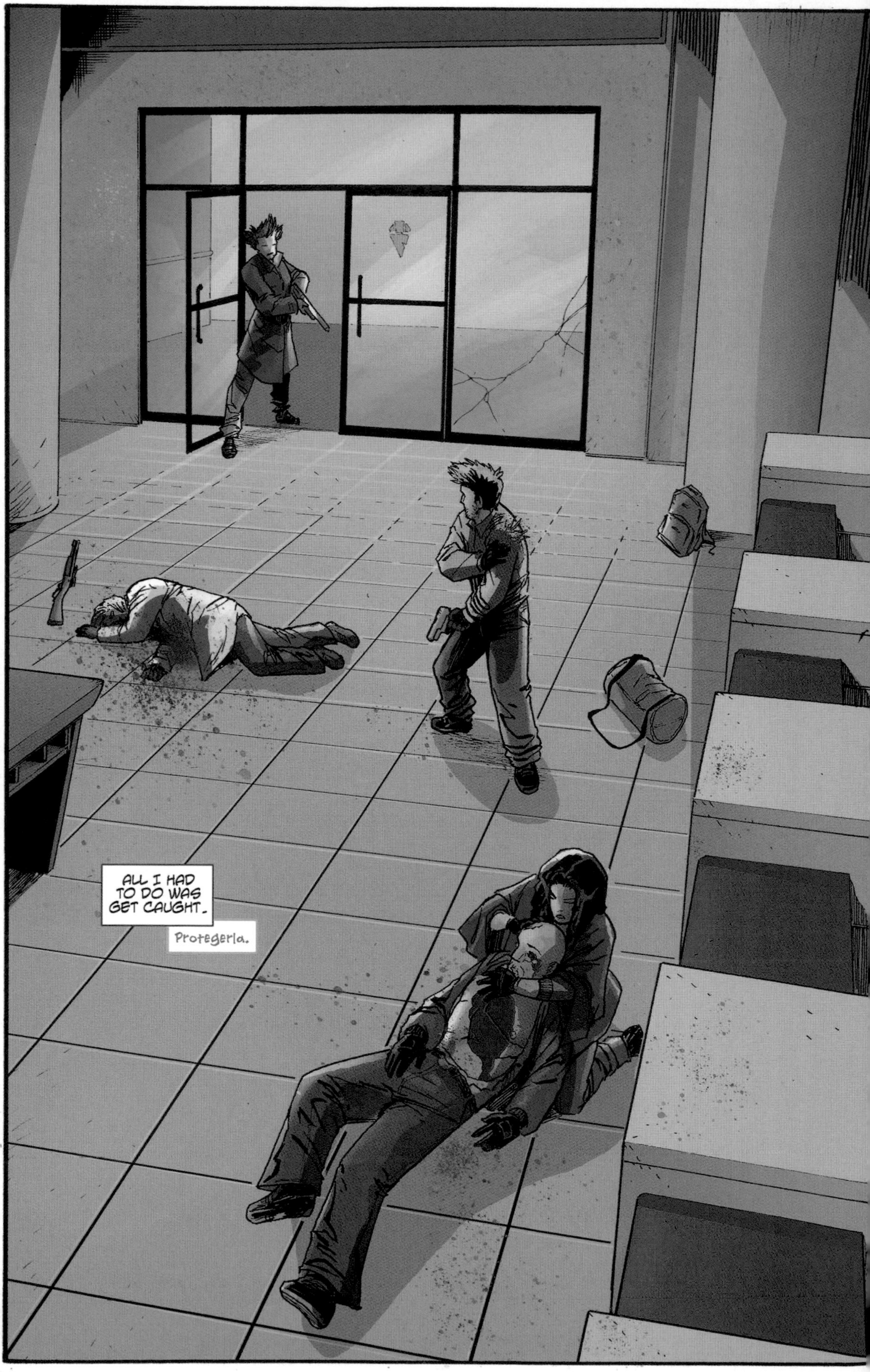
ALL I HAD TO DO WAS GET CAUGHT.
Protegerla.

CLASSIFIED

SECURITY LEVEL:
DOUBLE BLACK

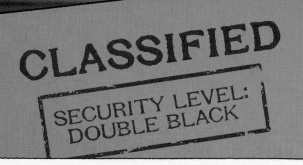

TelChan v0.78, Cpu Cycles: 3000, Frameskip 0, IRC restricted_research.gov

22:56:21 * VLS has joined the group. Security clearance confirmed. GPS link engaged.

23:02:12 <JCK> Victoria! Welcome back!

23:02:33 <ALG> You had us worried. It's been a week since the walkabout.

23:02:52 <VLS> Have you heard from any others?

23:03:04 <JCK> A few. Marcel checked in yesterday. We'd given up on anyone else.

23:03:21 <VLS> That was a bad one. I was out for nearly two days, and woke up in a hay field. I'm still picking straw out of my hair.

23:03:41 <ALG> "Bad one" is putting it mildly. If my predictive models for MRDF casualty rates are accurate, it cost us another 12-18% of the population. And those are conservative dehydraton estimates.

23:04:11 <VLS> Don't you ever feel like you're just studying the hands on a doomsday clock? Monitoring symptoms instead of seeking real answers?

23:04:15 <ALG> Back to this lecture already, Vic?

24:05:07 <JCK> Try telling my schitzopneuma patients that I shouldn't "waste" time evaluating their symptoms. Even a single absorbed consciousness results in dysgraphia and dyslexia, not to mention identity erosion. The psychological impact is devastating.

24:05:34 <VLS> I'm just hearing labels. Add those to the list with "Mass Recurring Dissociative Fugues" "Schitzopneuma" and "Dermadimak." They fix nothing.

24:05:51 <JCK> A new world needs a new vocabulary.

24:06:24 <VLS> But you're just describing HOW everything's gone to hell. I don't see any discussions about WHY.

24:06:30 <ALG> Nobody knows why.

23:06:39 <VLS> Not yet. But I've been running my own models. I still may not know why it started ...

23:07:01 <VLS> But I think I know WHERE.

23:07:04 * VLS has left the group. GPS link disengaged.

[Hvc] [SCREEN CAPTURE] [Ping] [Log] 23:07:13

For the desk of
Gen. Canter

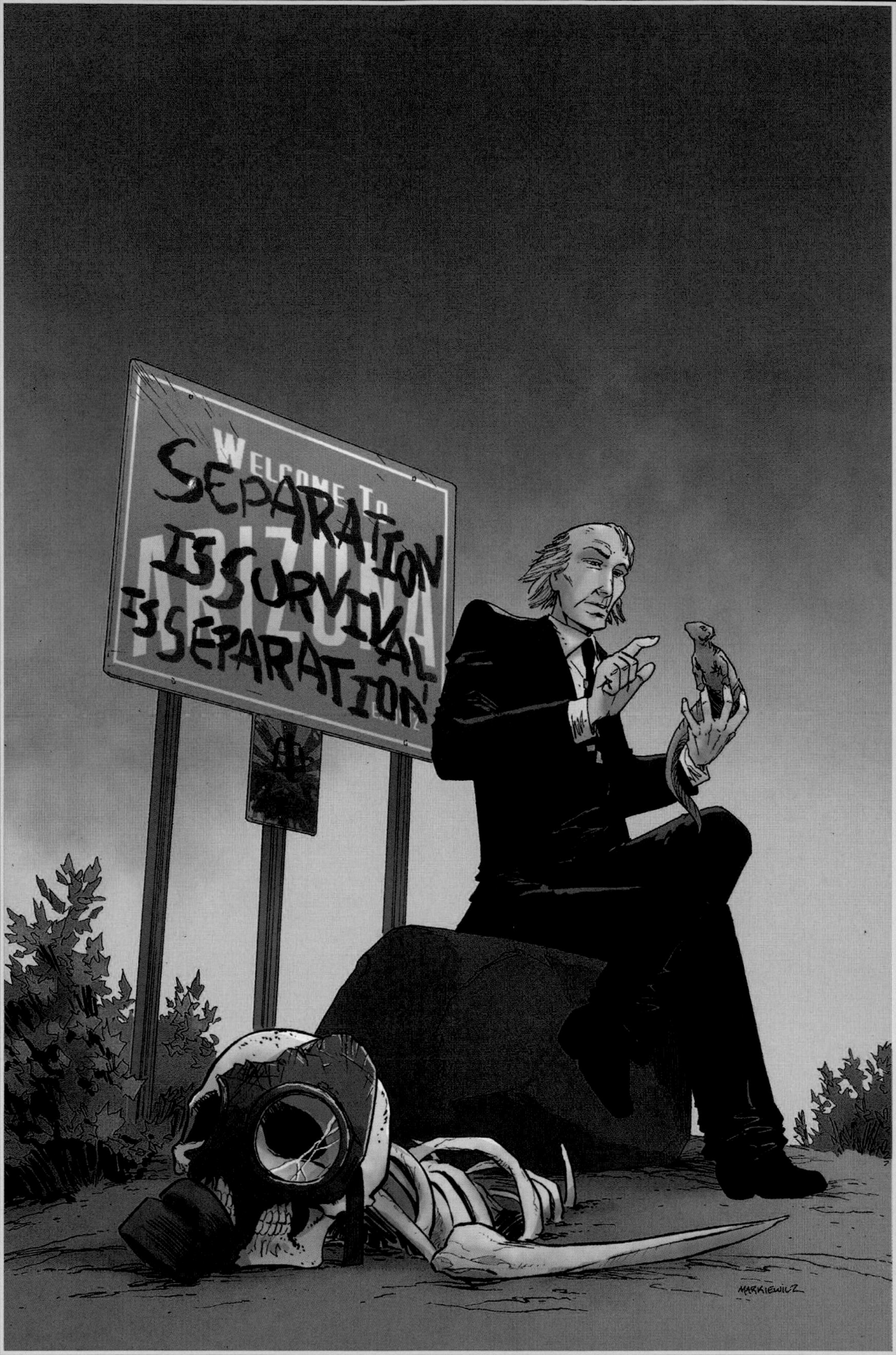
WELCOME TO
ARIZONA
SEPARATION IS SURVIVAL IS SEPARATION
MARKIEWICZ

ISSUE TWO
COVER ART BY ADAM MARKIEWICZ
COLORS BY MELANIE DARLING

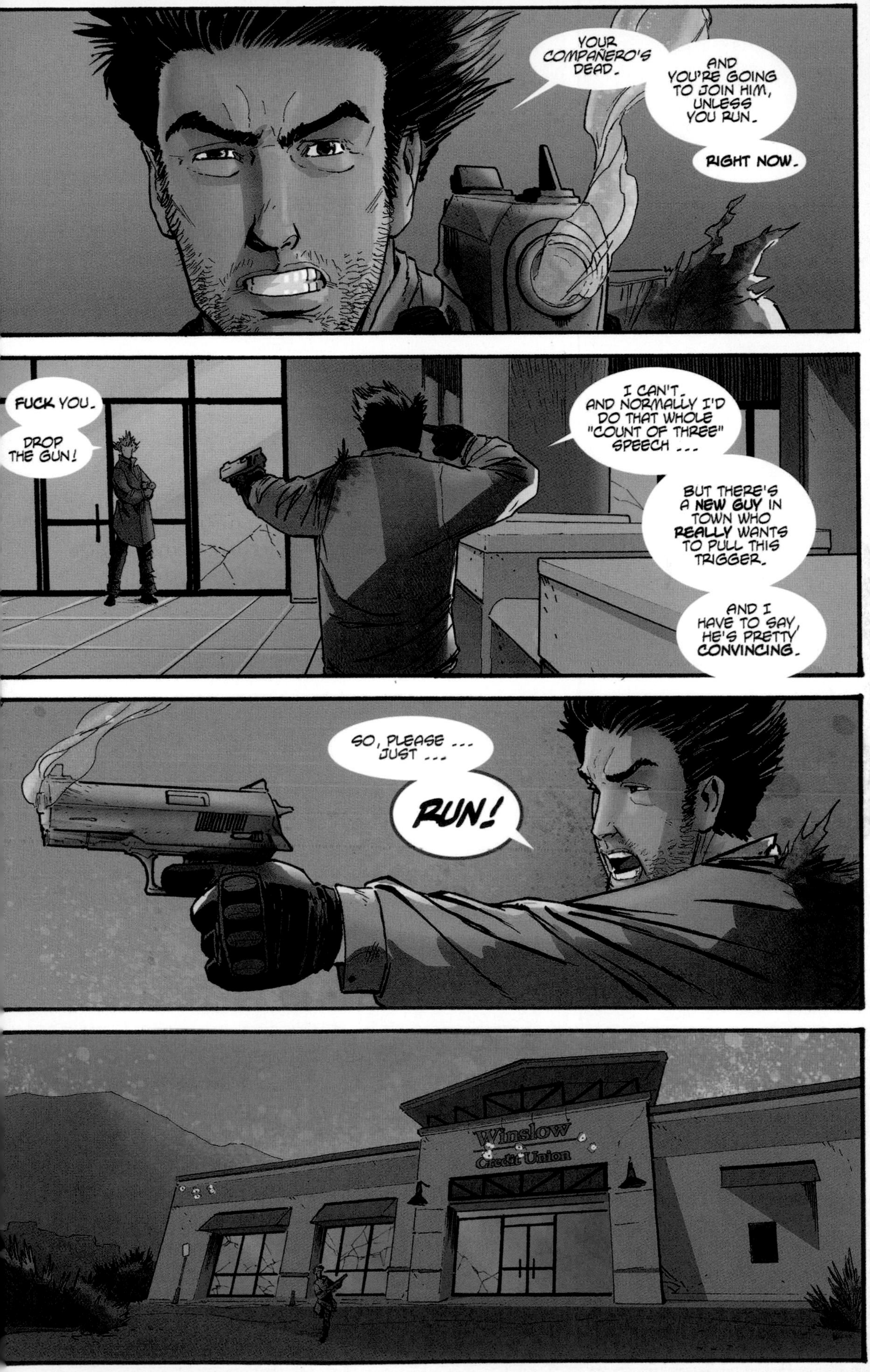
YOUR COMPAÑERO'S DEAD.
AND YOU'RE GOING TO JOIN HIM, UNLESS YOU RUN.
RIGHT NOW.
FUCK YOU.
DROP THE GUN!
I CAN'T. AND NORMALLY I'D DO THAT WHOLE "COUNT OF THREE" SPEECH ...
BUT THERE'S A NEW GUY IN TOWN WHO REALLY WANTS TO PULL THIS TRIGGER.
AND I HAVE TO SAY, HE'S PRETTY CONVINCING.
SO, PLEASE ... JUST ...
RUN!
Winslow
Credit Union

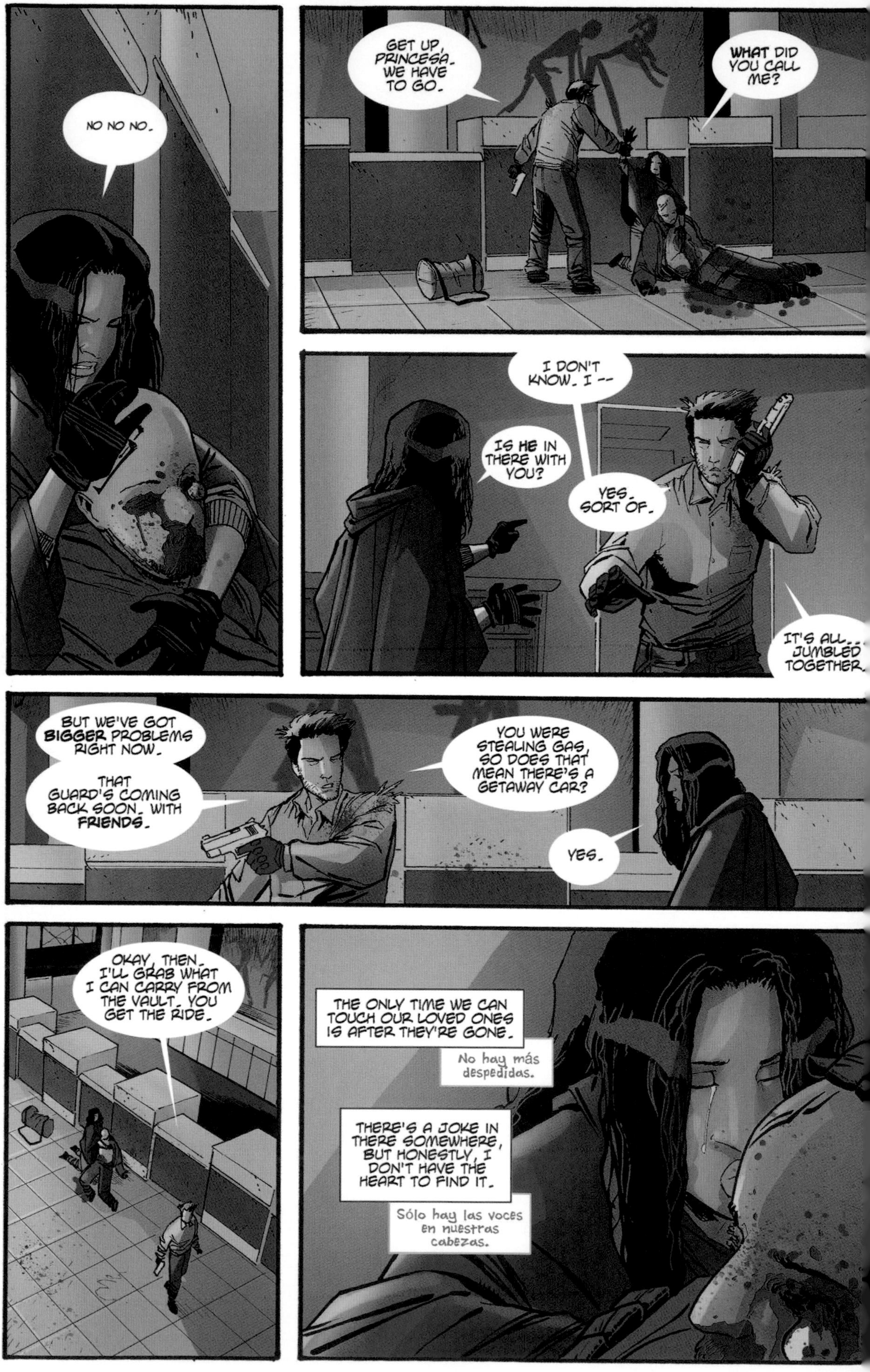
NO NO NO.
GET UP, PRINCESA. WE HAVE TO GO.
WHAT DID YOU CALL ME?
I DON'T KNOW. I --
IS HE IN THERE WITH YOU?
YES. SORT OF.
IT'S ALL... JUMBLED TOGETHER.
BUT WE'VE GOT BIGGER PROBLEMS RIGHT NOW.
THAT GUARD'S COMING BACK SOON. WITH FRIENDS.
YOU WERE STEALING GAS, SO DOES THAT MEAN THERE'S A GETAWAY CAR?
YES.
OKAY, THEN. I'LL GRAB WHAT I CAN CARRY FROM THE VAULT. YOU GET THE RIDE.
THE ONLY TIME WE CAN TOUCH OUR LOVED ONES IS AFTER THEY'RE GONE.
No hay más despedidas.
THERE'S A JOKE IN THERE SOMEWHERE, BUT HONESTLY, I DON'T HAVE THE HEART TO FIND IT.
Sólo hay las voces en nuestras cabezas.

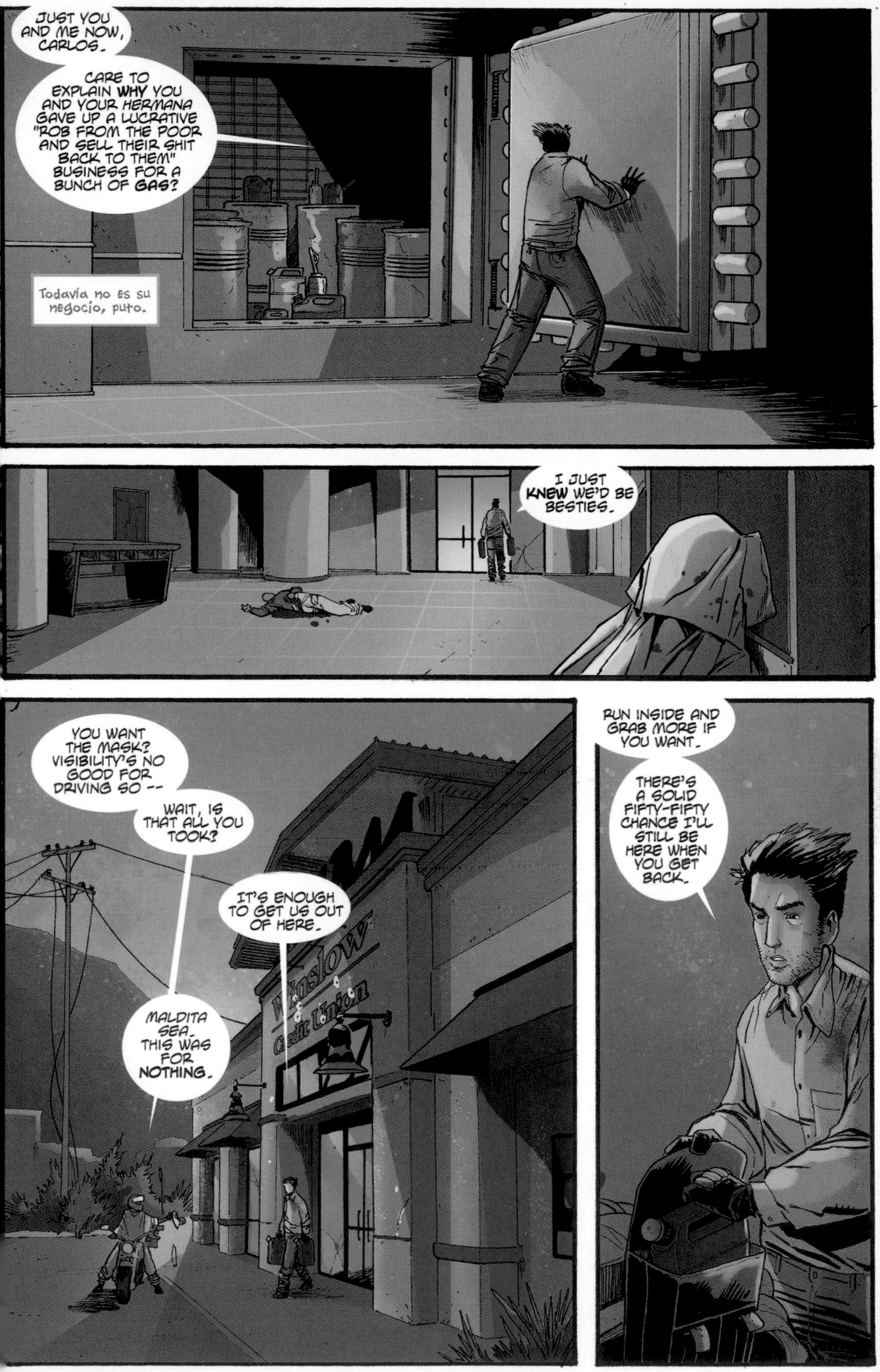
JUST YOU AND ME NOW, CARLOS.
CARE TO EXPLAIN WHY YOU AND YOUR HERMANA GAVE UP A LUCRATIVE "ROB FROM THE POOR AND SELL THEIR SHIT BACK TO THEM" BUSINESS FOR A BUNCH OF GAS?
Todavía no es su negocio, puto.
I JUST KNEW WE'D BE BESTIES.
YOU WANT THE MASK? VISIBILITY'S NO GOOD FOR DRIVING SO --
WAIT, IS THAT ALL YOU TOOK?
IT'S ENOUGH TO GET US OUT OF HERE.
MALDITA SEA. THIS WAS FOR NOTHING.
Winslow Credit Union
RUN INSIDE AND GRAB MORE IF YOU WANT.
THERE'S A SOLID FIFTY-FIFTY CHANCE I'LL STILL BE HERE WHEN YOU GET BACK.

MAYBE YOU SHOULD CATCH ANOTHER RIDE.

MAYBE I **SHOULD**. I COULD JUST EXPLAIN WHAT HAPPENED AND —

BAM!

BAM!

WWWRRRRRRRRRRRRRR

THEN AGAIN, I'VE ALWAYS **WANTED** TO BE IN A HIGH SPEED MOTORCYCLE CHASE WITH INADEQUATE HEADGEAR.

VROOOOOOM

SCHRACK!

SCHRACK!

SCHRACK!

SCHRACK!

BAM!

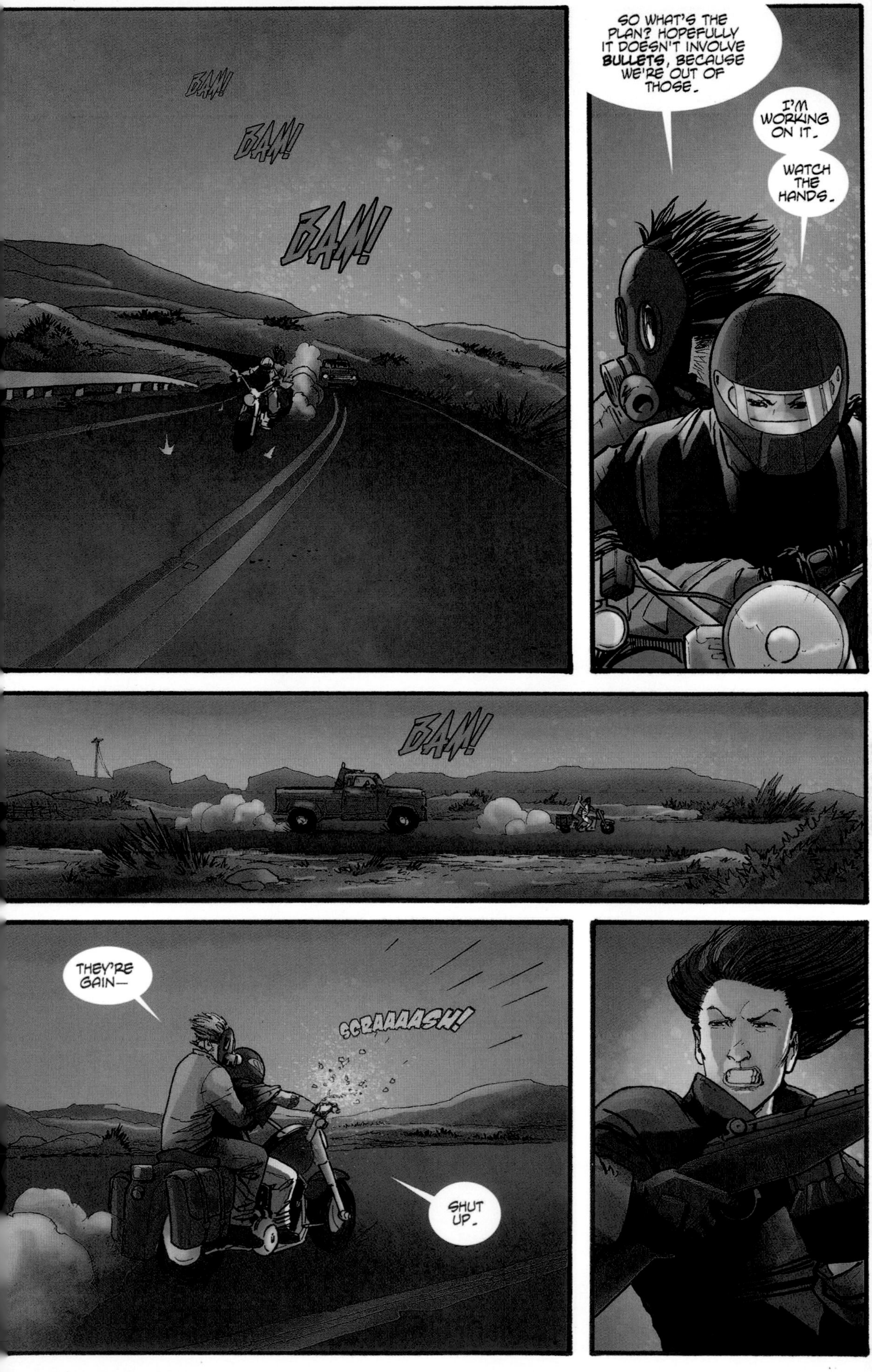
BAM!
BAM!
BAM!
SO WHAT'S THE PLAN? HOPEFULLY IT DOESN'T INVOLVE BULLETS, BECAUSE WE'RE OUT OF THOSE.
I'M WORKING ON IT.
WATCH THE HANDS.
BAM!
THEY'RE GAIN—
SCRAAAASH!
SHUT UP.

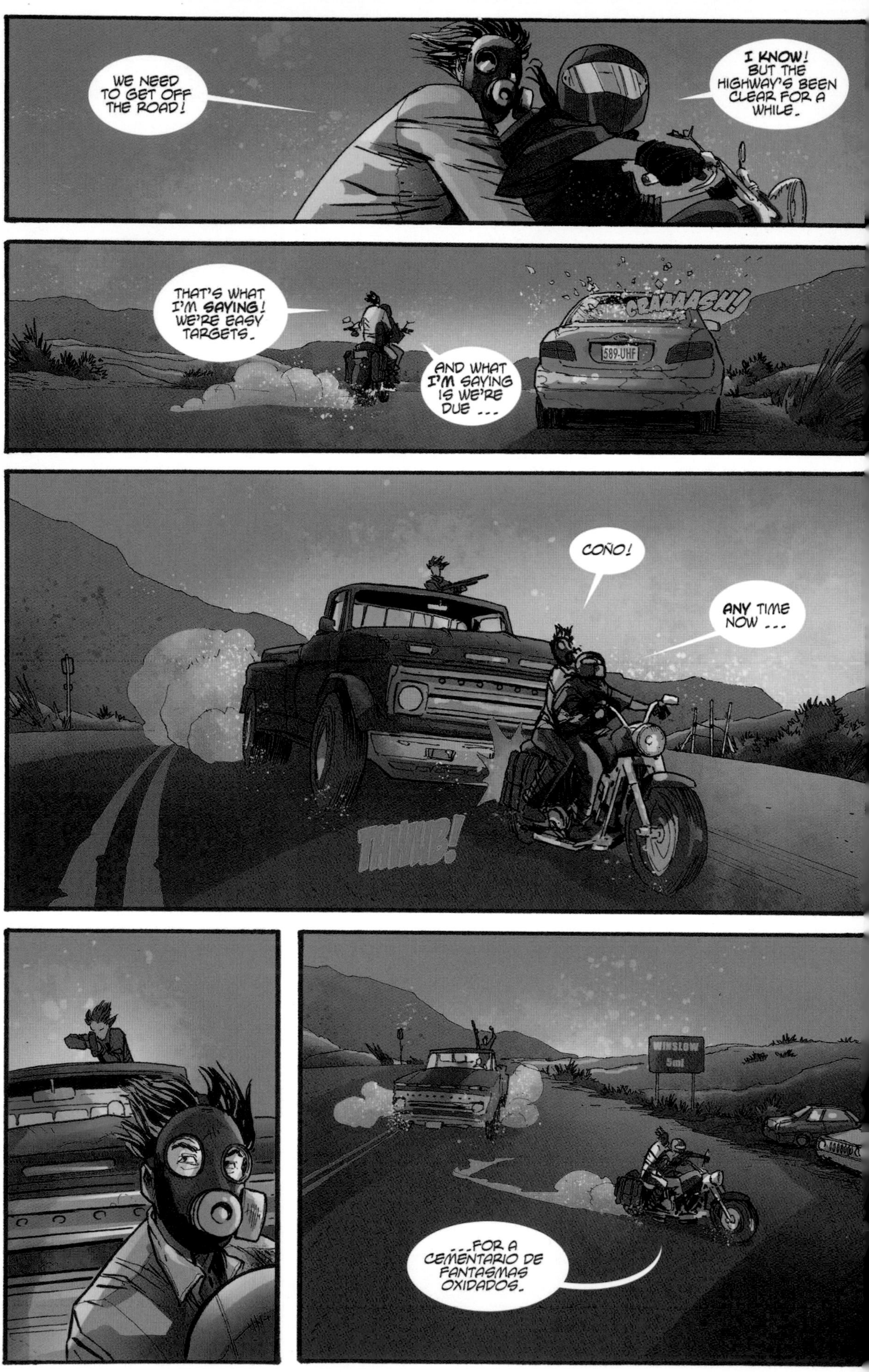
WE NEED TO GET OFF THE ROAD!
I KNOW! BUT THE HIGHWAY'S BEEN CLEAR FOR A WHILE.
THAT'S WHAT I'M SAYING! WE'RE EASY TARGETS.
AND WHAT I'M SAYING IS WE'RE DUE ...
CRAAAASH!
589-UHF
COÑO!
ANY TIME NOW ...
THWUB!
WINSLOW
5mi
...FOR A CEMENTARIO DE FANTASMAS OXIDADOS.

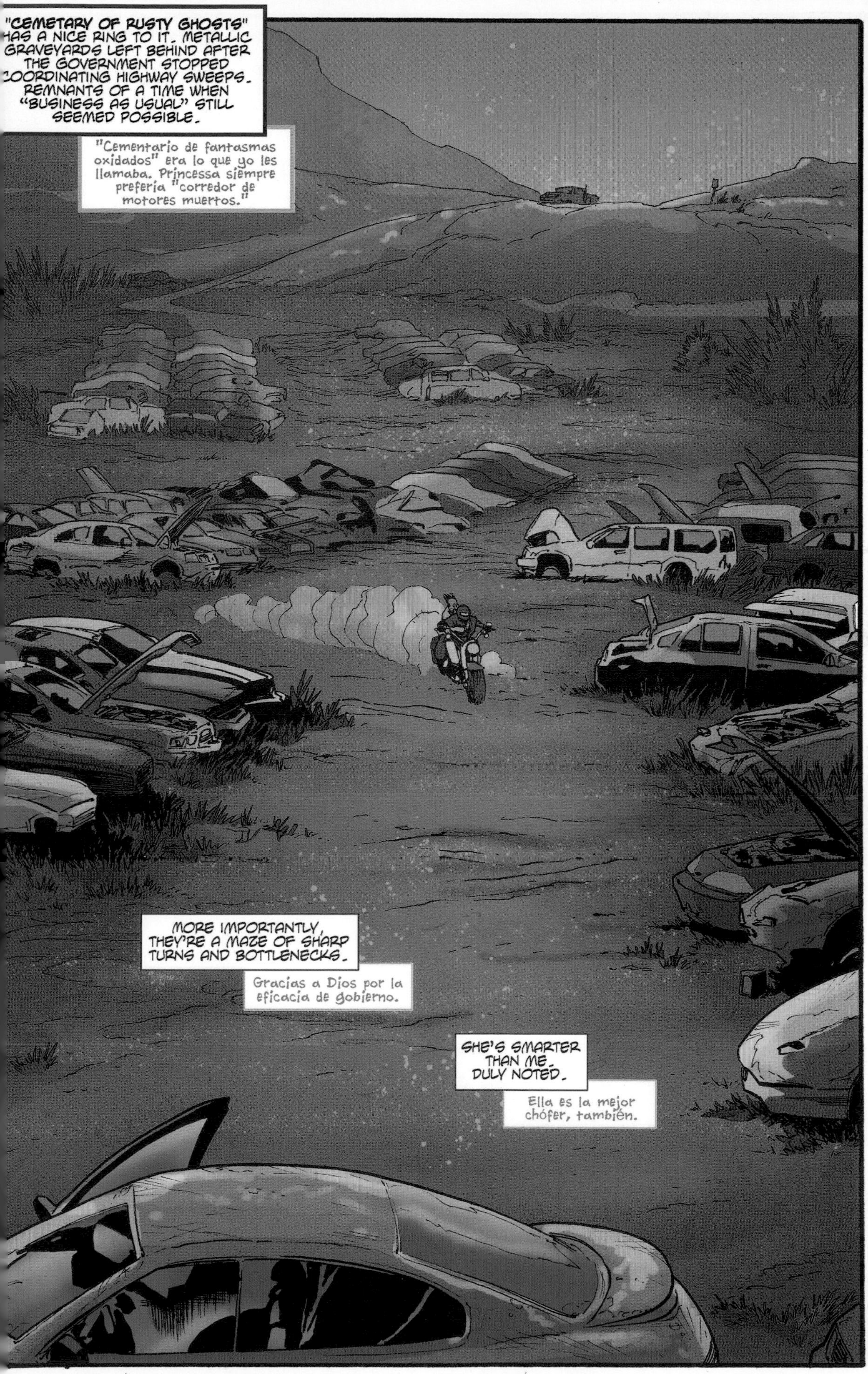
"CEMETARY OF RUSTY GHOSTS" HAS A NICE RING TO IT. METALLIC GRAVEYARDS LEFT BEHIND AFTER THE GOVERNMENT STOPPED COORDINATING HIGHWAY SWEEPS. REMNANTS OF A TIME WHEN "BUSINESS AS USUAL" STILL SEEMED POSSIBLE.
"Cementario de fantasmas oxidados" era lo que yo les llamaba. Princessa siempre prefería "corredor de motores muertos."
MORE IMPORTANTLY, THEY'RE A MAZE OF SHARP TURNS AND BOTTLENECKS.
Gracias a Dios por la eficacia de gobierno.
SHE'S SMARTER THAN ME. DULY NOTED.
Ella es la mejor chófer, también.

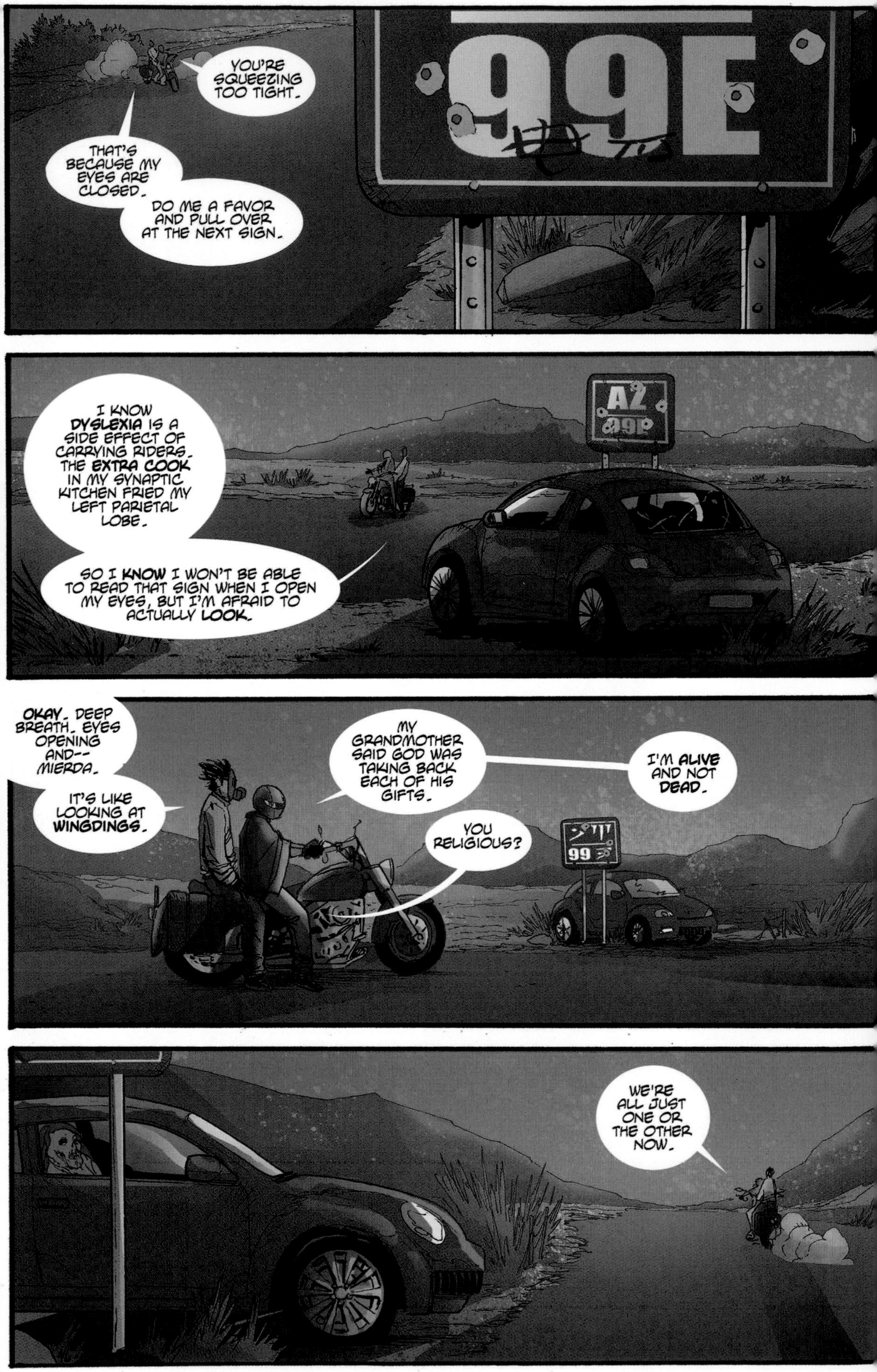
YOU'RE SQUEEZING TOO TIGHT.
THAT'S BECAUSE MY EYES ARE CLOSED.
DO ME A FAVOR AND PULL OVER AT THE NEXT SIGN.
I KNOW DYSLEXIA IS A SIDE EFFECT OF CARRYING RIDERS. THE EXTRA COOK IN MY SYNAPTIC KITCHEN FRIED MY LEFT PARIETAL LOBE.
SO I KNOW I WON'T BE ABLE TO READ THAT SIGN WHEN I OPEN MY EYES, BUT I'M AFRAID TO ACTUALLY LOOK.
OKAY. DEEP BREATH. EYES OPENING AND-- MIERDA.
IT'S LIKE LOOKING AT WINGDINGS.
MY GRANDMOTHER SAID GOD WAS TAKING BACK EACH OF HIS GIFTS.
I'M ALIVE AND NOT DEAD.
YOU RELIGIOUS?
WE'RE ALL JUST ONE OR THE OTHER NOW.

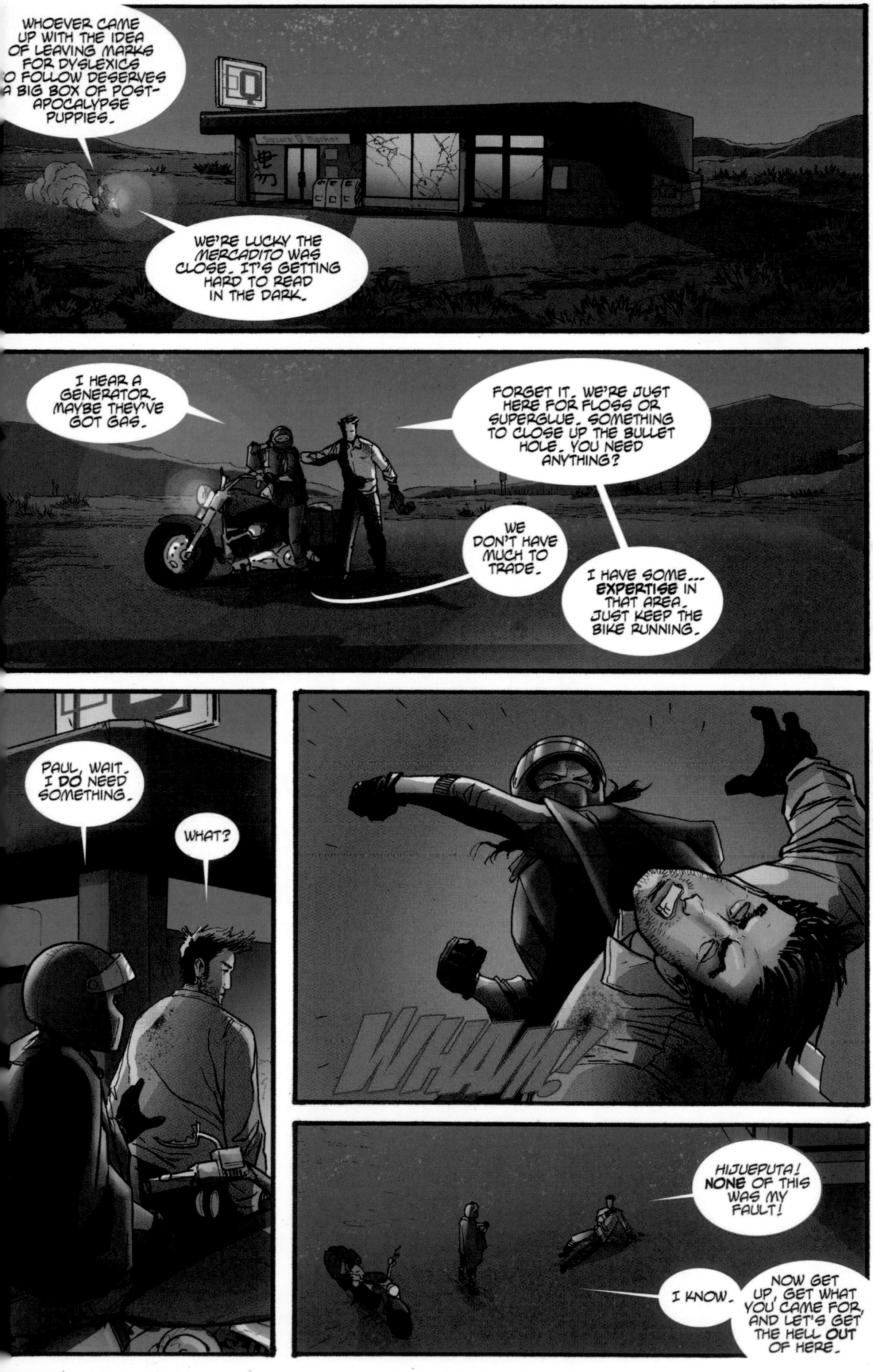
WHOEVER CAME UP WITH THE IDEA OF LEAVING MARKS FOR DYSLEXICS TO FOLLOW DESERVES A BIG BOX OF POST-APOCALYPSE PUPPIES.
WE'RE LUCKY THE MERCADITO WAS CLOSE. IT'S GETTING HARD TO READ IN THE DARK.
I HEAR A GENERATOR. MAYBE THEY'VE GOT GAS.
FORGET IT. WE'RE JUST HERE FOR FLOSS OR SUPERGLUE. SOMETHING TO CLOSE UP THE BULLET HOLE. YOU NEED ANYTHING?
WE DON'T HAVE MUCH TO TRADE.
I HAVE SOME... EXPERTISE IN THAT AREA. JUST KEEP THE BIKE RUNNING.
PAUL, WAIT. I DO NEED SOMETHING.
WHAT?
WHAM!
HIJUEPUTA! NONE OF THIS WAS MY FAULT!
I KNOW.
NOW GET UP, GET WHAT YOU CAME FOR, AND LET'S GET THE HELL OUT OF HERE.

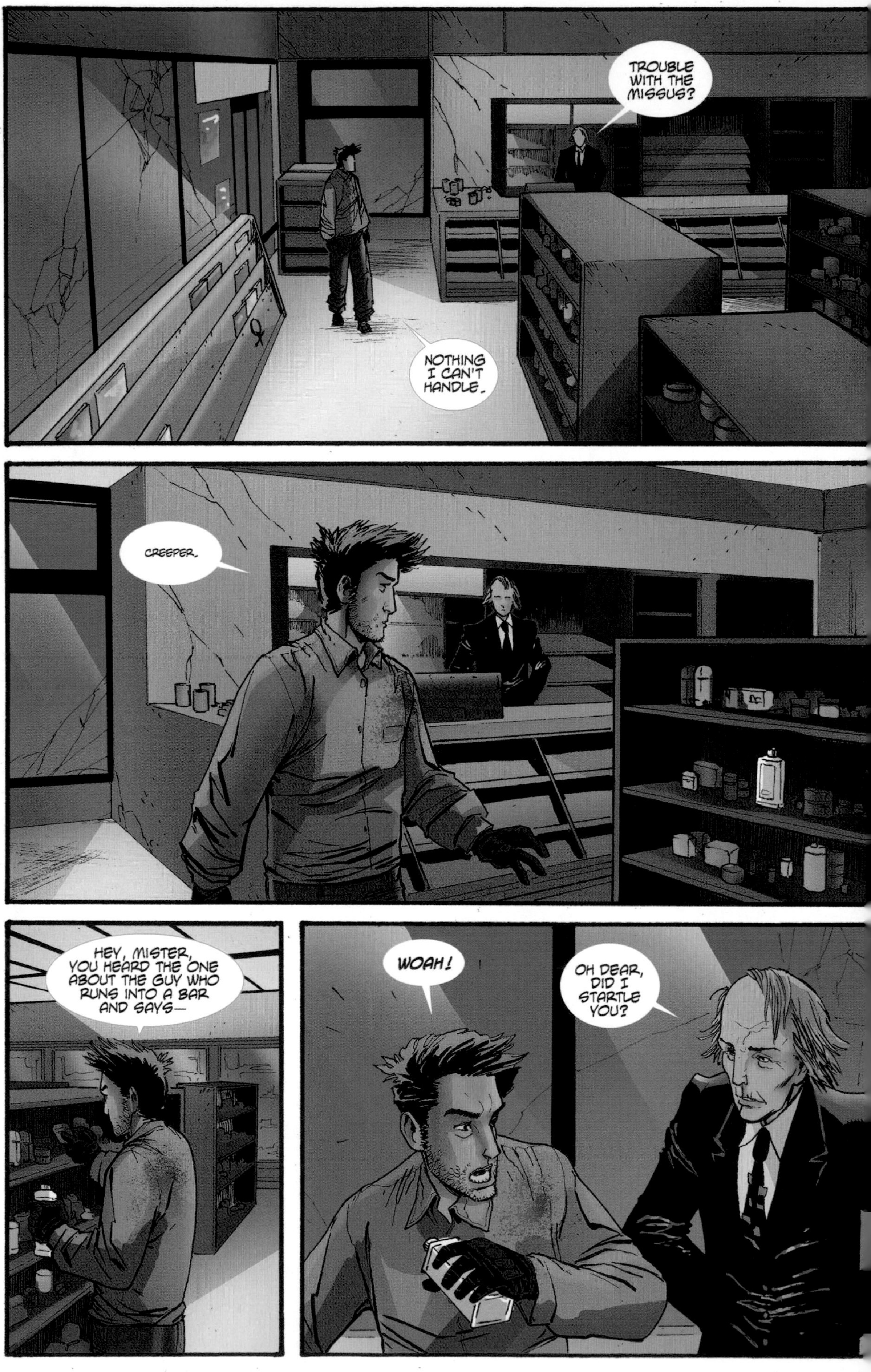
TROUBLE WITH THE MISSUS?
NOTHING I CAN'T HANDLE.
CREEPER.
HEY, MISTER, YOU HEARD THE ONE ABOUT THE GUY WHO RUNS INTO A BAR AND SAYS—
WOAH!
OH DEAR, DID I STARTLE YOU?

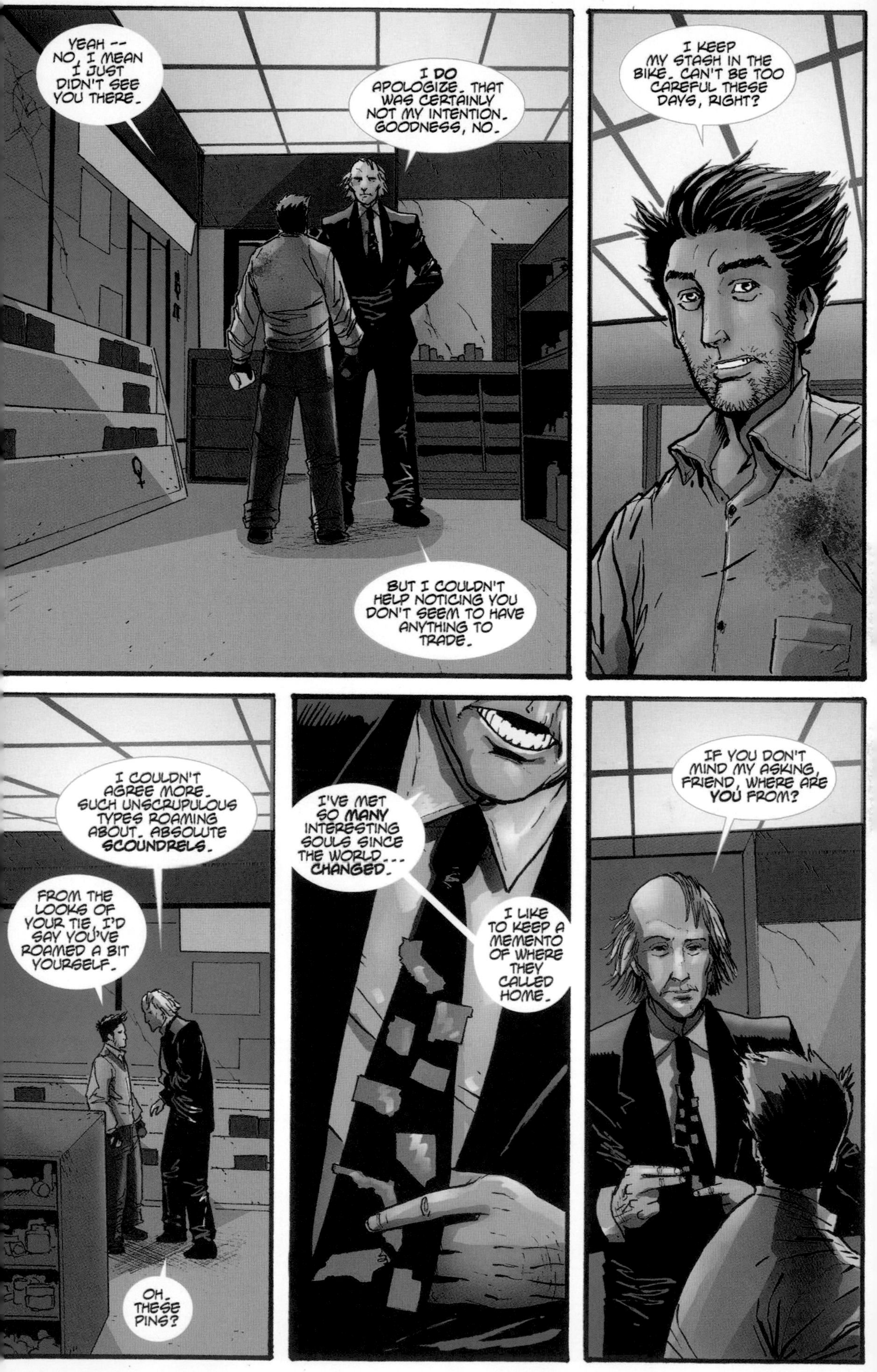
YEAH -- NO, I MEAN I JUST DIDN'T SEE YOU THERE.
I DO APOLOGIZE. THAT WAS CERTAINLY NOT MY INTENTION. GOODNESS, NO.
BUT I COULDN'T HELP NOTICING YOU DON'T SEEM TO HAVE ANYTHING TO TRADE.
I KEEP MY STASH IN THE BIKE. CAN'T BE TOO CAREFUL THESE DAYS, RIGHT?
I COULDN'T AGREE MORE. SUCH UNSCRUPULOUS TYPES ROAMING ABOUT. ABSOLUTE SCOUNDRELS.
FROM THE LOOKS OF YOUR TIE, I'D SAY YOU'VE ROAMED A BIT YOURSELF.
OH. THESE PINS?
I'VE MET SO MANY INTERESTING SOULS SINCE THE WORLD... CHANGED.
I LIKE TO KEEP A MEMENTO OF WHERE THEY CALLED HOME.
IF YOU DON'T MIND MY ASKING, FRIEND, WHERE ARE YOU FROM?

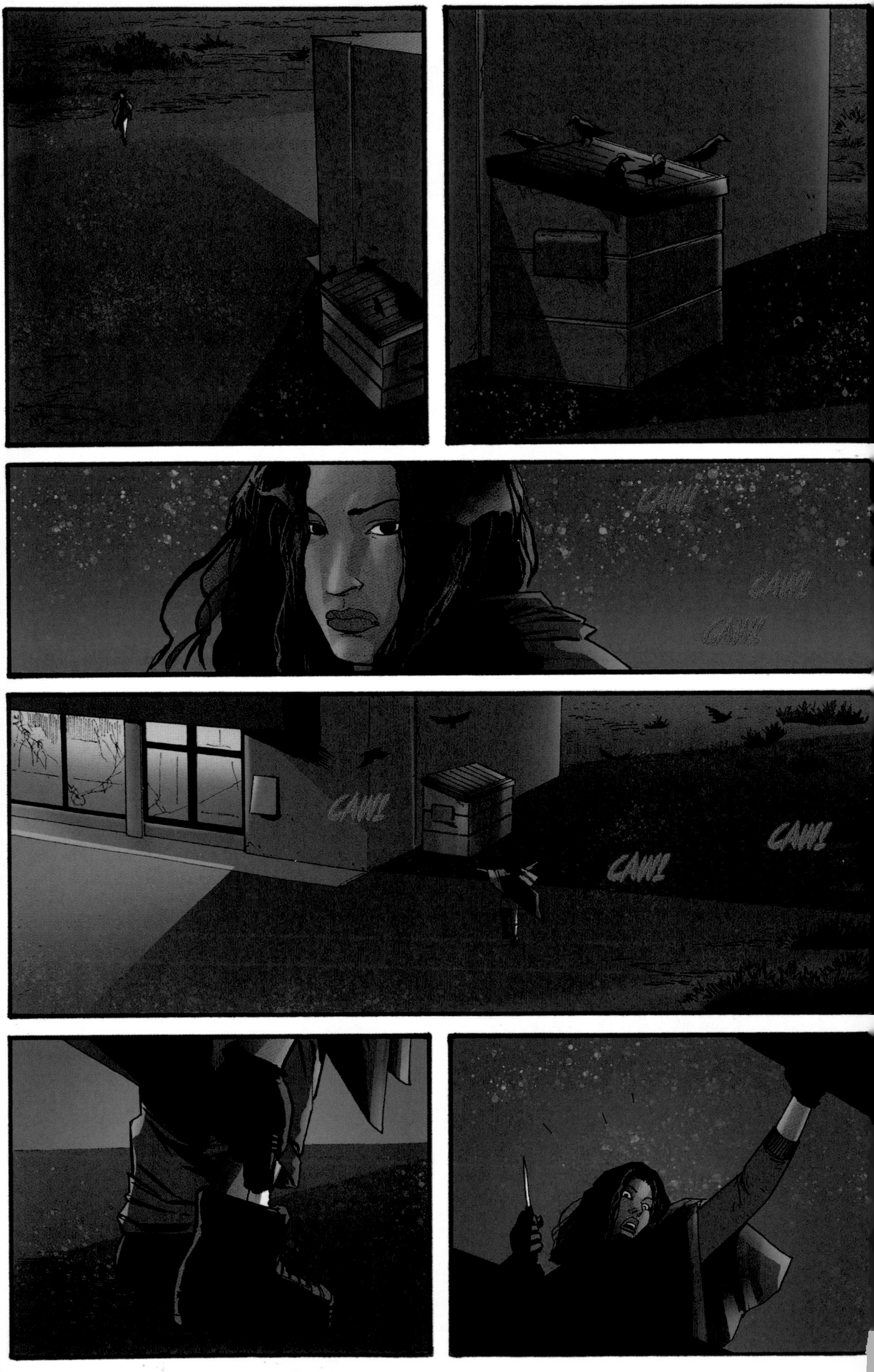
CAW!
CAW!
CAW!
CAW!
CAW!
CAW!

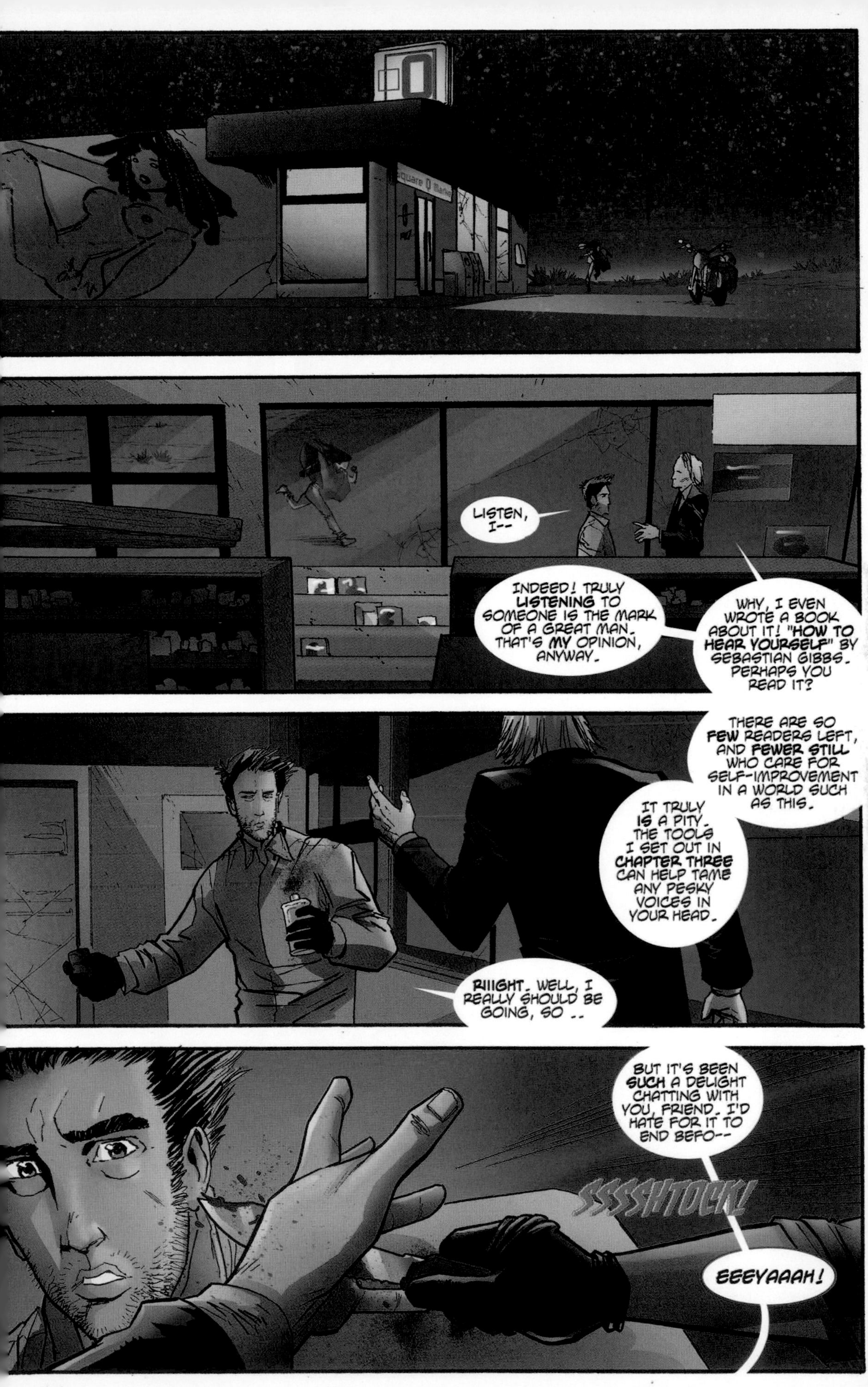
LISTEN, I--
INDEED! TRULY LISTENING TO SOMEONE IS THE MARK OF A GREAT MAN. THAT'S MY OPINION, ANYWAY.
WHY, I EVEN WROTE A BOOK ABOUT IT! "HOW TO HEAR YOURSELF" BY SEBASTIAN GIBBS. PERHAPS YOU READ IT?
THERE ARE SO FEW READERS LEFT, AND FEWER STILL WHO CARE FOR SELF-IMPROVEMENT IN A WORLD SUCH AS THIS.
IT TRULY IS A PITY. THE TOOLS I SET OUT IN CHAPTER THREE CAN HELP TAME ANY PESKY VOICES IN YOUR HEAD.
RIIIGHT. WELL, I REALLY SHOULD BE GOING, SO ..
BUT IT'S BEEN SUCH A DELIGHT CHATTING WITH YOU, FRIEND. I'D HATE FOR IT TO END BEFO--
SSSSHTOCK!
EEEYAAAH!

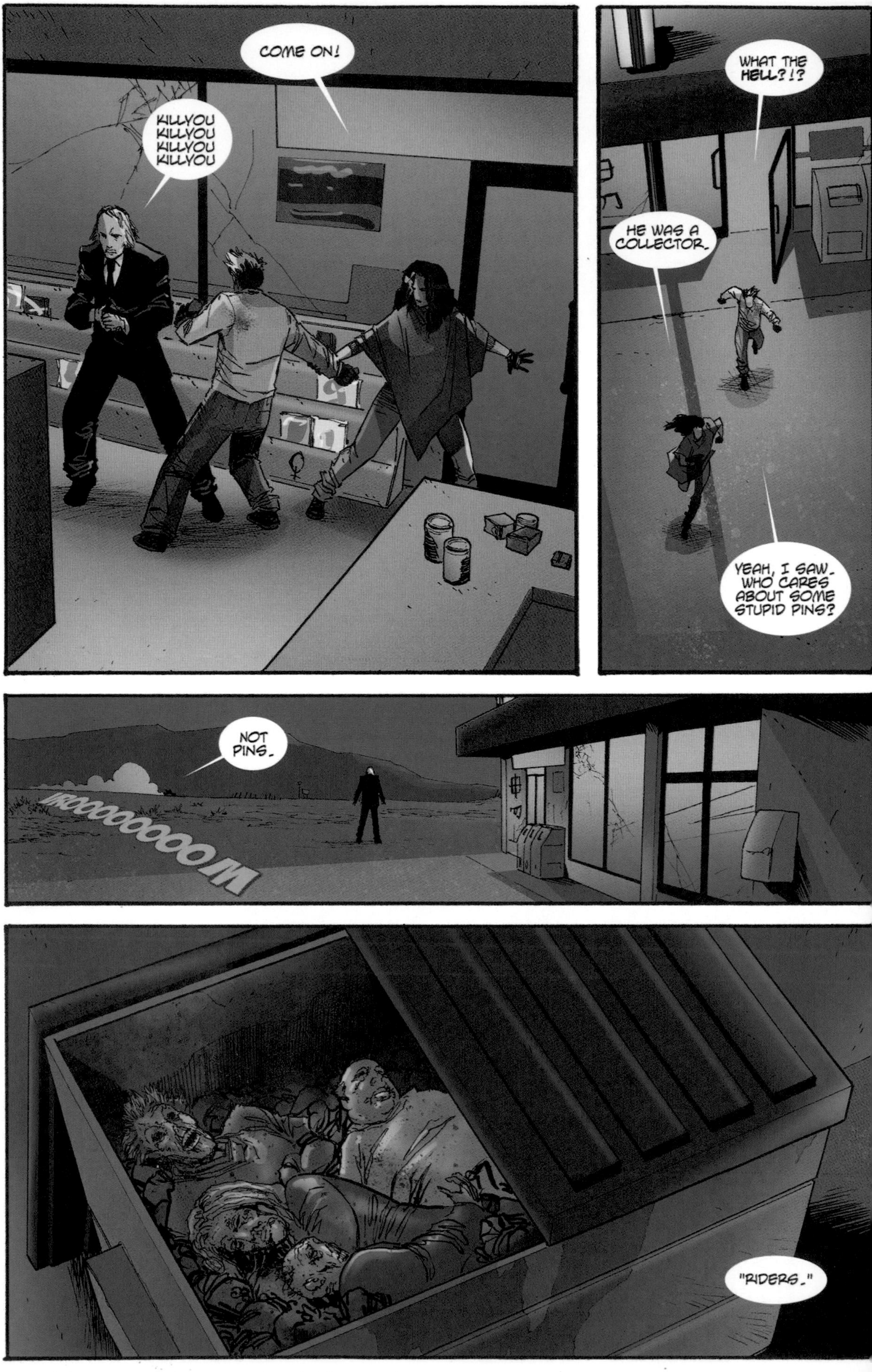
COME ON!
KILLYOU KILLYOU KILLYOU KILLYOU
WHAT THE HELL?!?
HE WAS A COLLECTOR.
YEAH, I SAW. WHO CARES ABOUT SOME STUPID PINS?
NOT PINS.
"RIDERS."

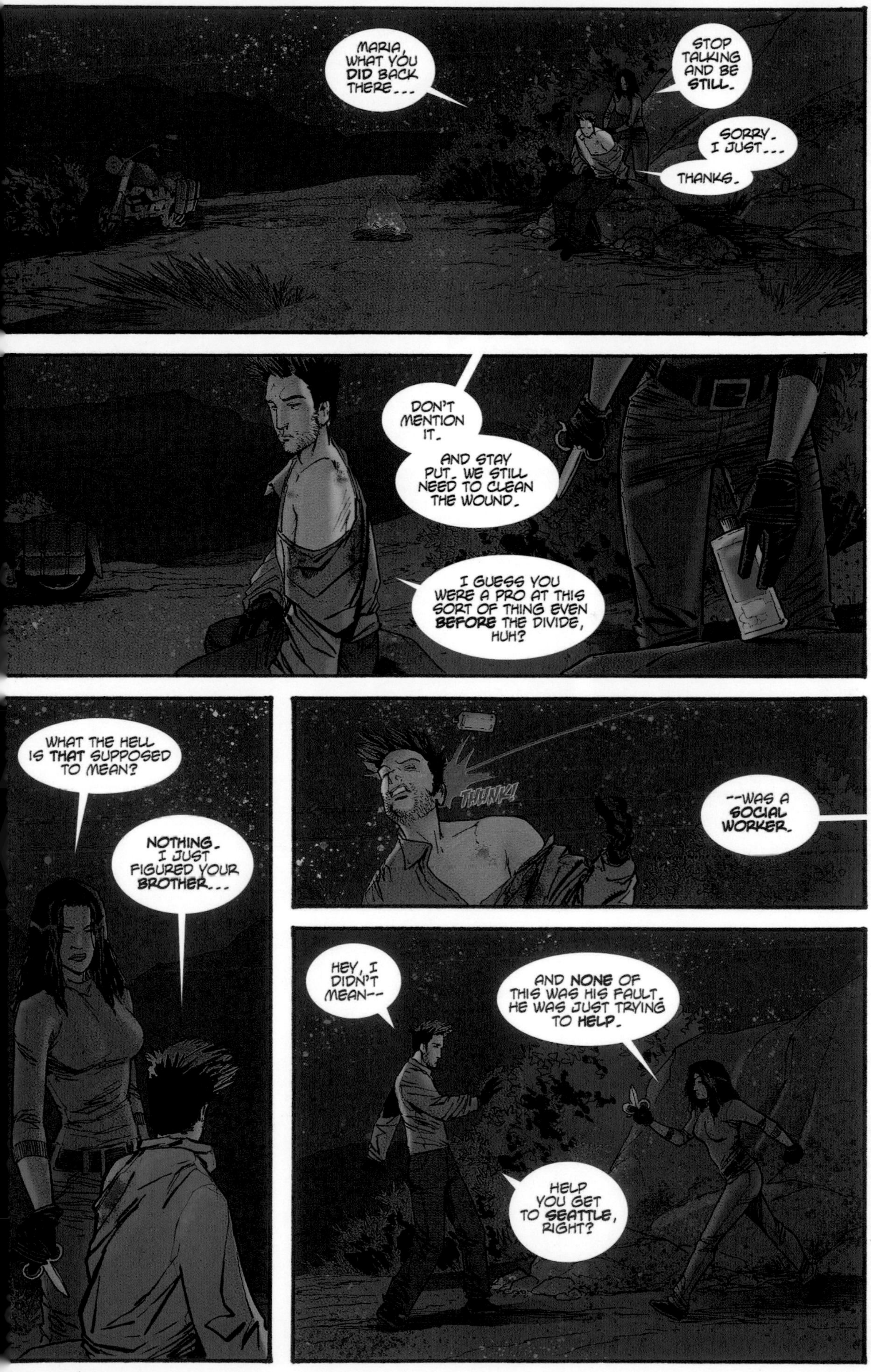
MARIA, WHAT YOU DID BACK THERE...
STOP TALKING AND BE STILL.
SORRY. I JUST...
THANKS.
DON'T MENTION IT.
AND STAY PUT. WE STILL NEED TO CLEAN THE WOUND.
I GUESS YOU WERE A PRO AT THIS SORT OF THING EVEN BEFORE THE DIVIDE, HUH?
WHAT THE HELL IS THAT SUPPOSED TO MEAN?
NOTHING. I JUST FIGURED YOUR BROTHER...
THUNK!
--WAS A SOCIAL WORKER.
HEY, I DIDN'T MEAN--
AND NONE OF THIS WAS HIS FAULT. HE WAS JUST TRYING TO HELP.
HELP YOU GET TO SEATTLE, RIGHT?

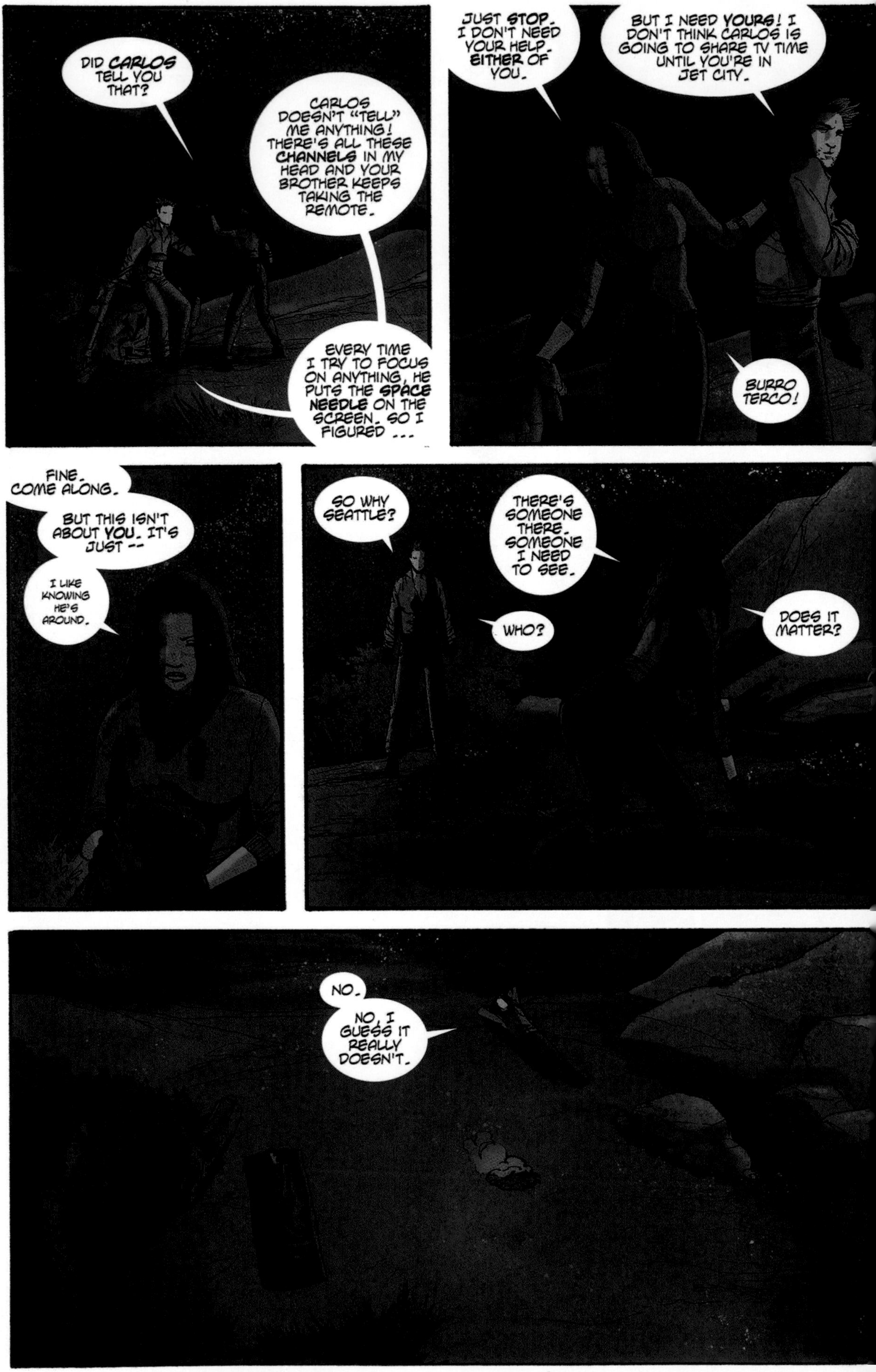
DID CARLOS TELL YOU THAT?
CARLOS DOESN'T "TELL" ME ANYTHING! THERE'S ALL THESE CHANNELS IN MY HEAD AND YOUR BROTHER KEEPS TAKING THE REMOTE.
EVERY TIME I TRY TO FOCUS ON ANYTHING, HE PUTS THE SPACE NEEDLE ON THE SCREEN. SO I FIGURED ...
JUST STOP. I DON'T NEED YOUR HELP. EITHER OF YOU.
BUT I NEED YOURS! I DON'T THINK CARLOS IS GOING TO SHARE TV TIME UNTIL YOU'RE IN JET CITY.
BURRO TERCO!
FINE. COME ALONG.
BUT THIS ISN'T ABOUT YOU. IT'S JUST --
I LIKE KNOWING HE'S AROUND.
SO WHY SEATTLE?
THERE'S SOMEONE THERE. SOMEONE I NEED TO SEE.
WHO?
DOES IT MATTER?
NO.
NO, I GUESS IT REALLY DOESN'T.

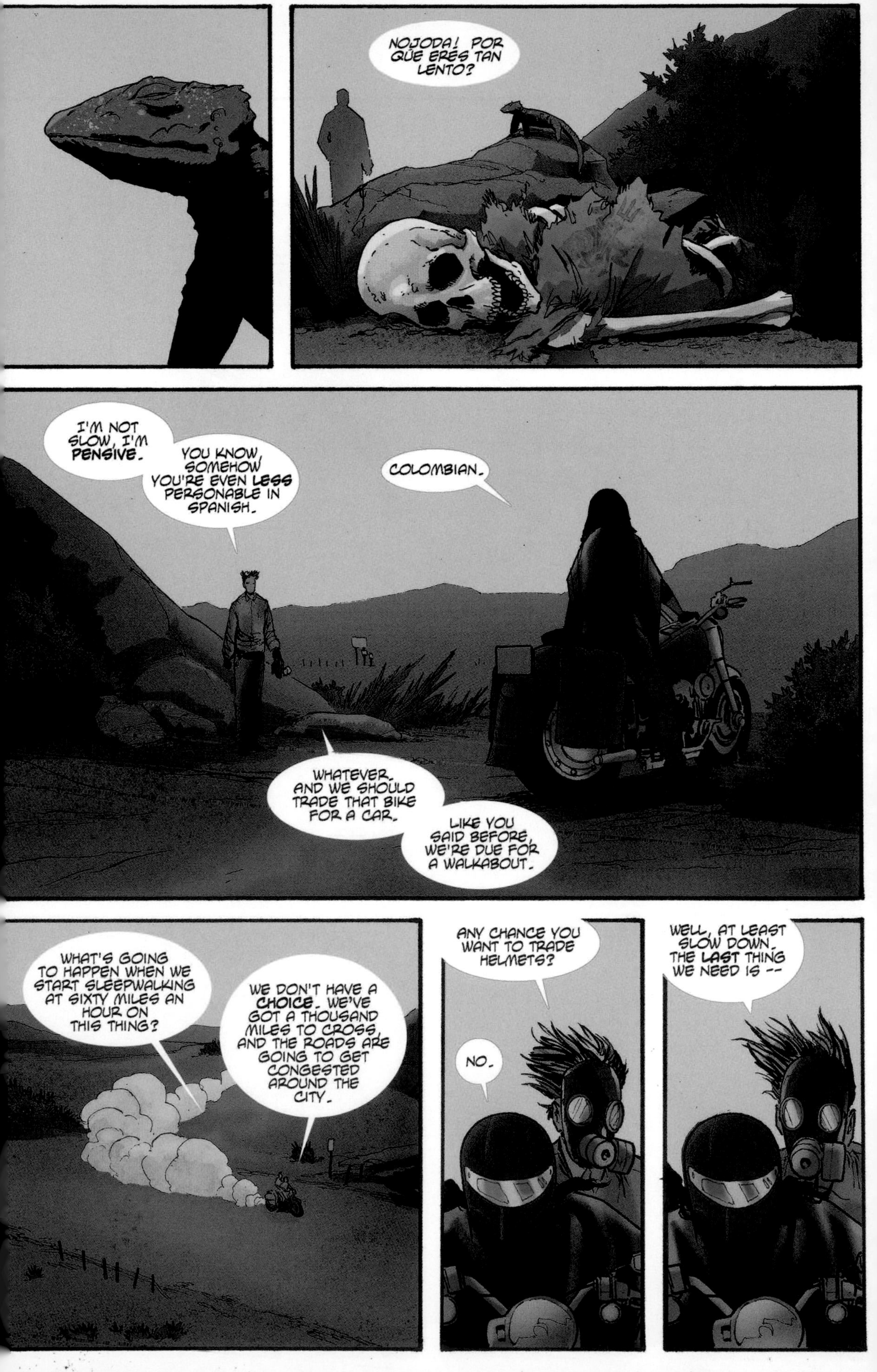
NOJODA! POR QUÉ ERES TAN LENTO?
I'M NOT SLOW, I'M PENSIVE.
YOU KNOW, SOMEHOW YOU'RE EVEN LESS PERSONABLE IN SPANISH.
COLOMBIAN.
WHATEVER. AND WE SHOULD TRADE THAT BIKE FOR A CAR.
LIKE YOU SAID BEFORE, WE'RE DUE FOR A WALKABOUT.
WHAT'S GOING TO HAPPEN WHEN WE START SLEEPWALKING AT SIXTY MILES AN HOUR ON THIS THING?
WE DON'T HAVE A CHOICE. WE'VE GOT A THOUSAND MILES TO CROSS, AND THE ROADS ARE GOING TO GET CONGESTED AROUND THE CITY.
ANY CHANCE YOU WANT TO TRADE HELMETS?
NO.
WELL, AT LEAST SLOW DOWN. THE LAST THING WE NEED IS --

SKREEEE-TANG!

THRUMP!

SCRUNCH!

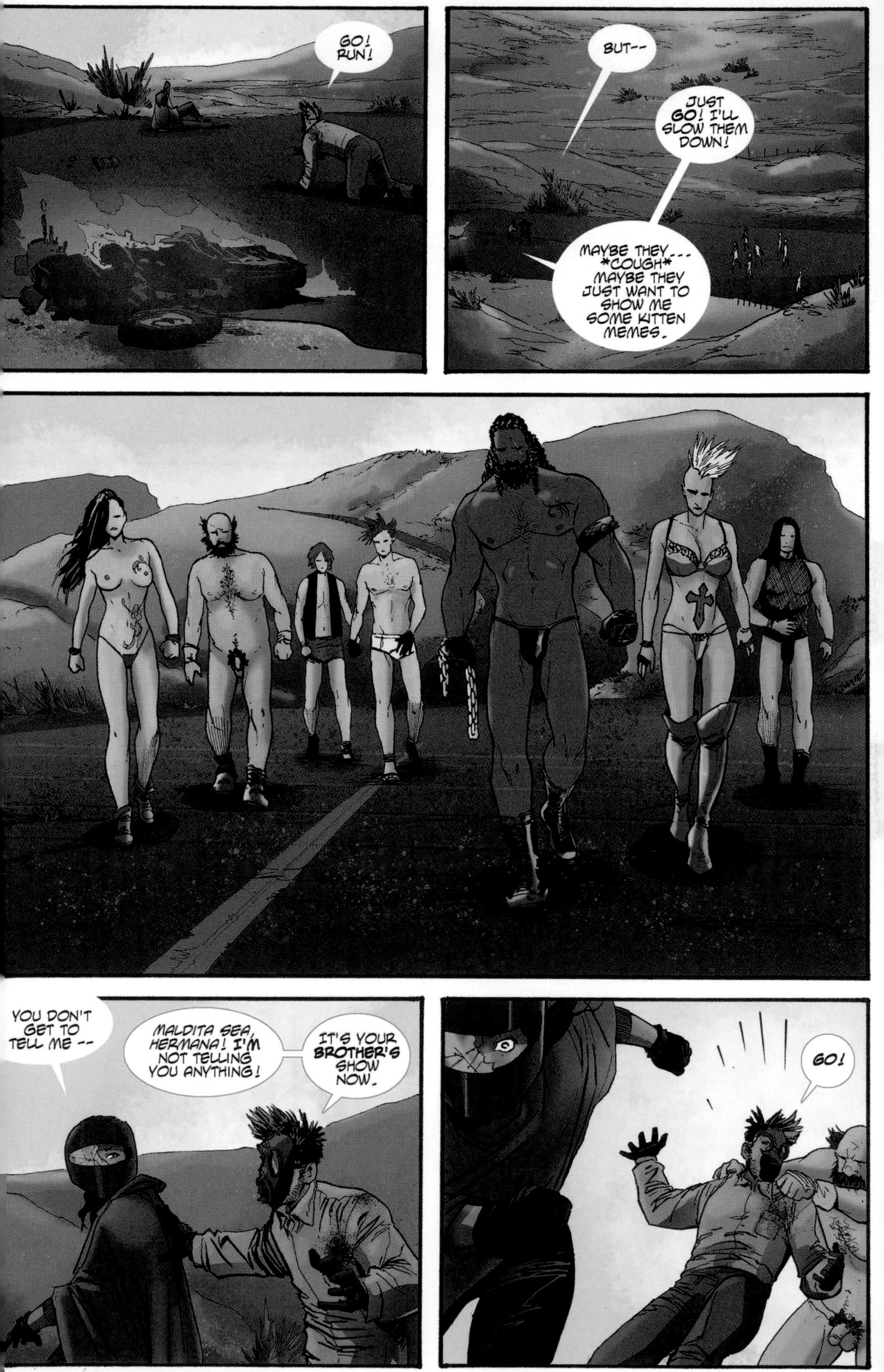
GO! RUN!
BUT--
JUST GO! I'LL SLOW THEM DOWN!
MAYBE THEY... *COUGH* MAYBE THEY JUST WANT TO SHOW ME SOME KITTEN MEMES.
YOU DON'T GET TO TELL ME --
MALDITA SEA, HERMANA! I'M NOT TELLING YOU ANYTHING!
IT'S YOUR BROTHER'S SHOW NOW.
GO!

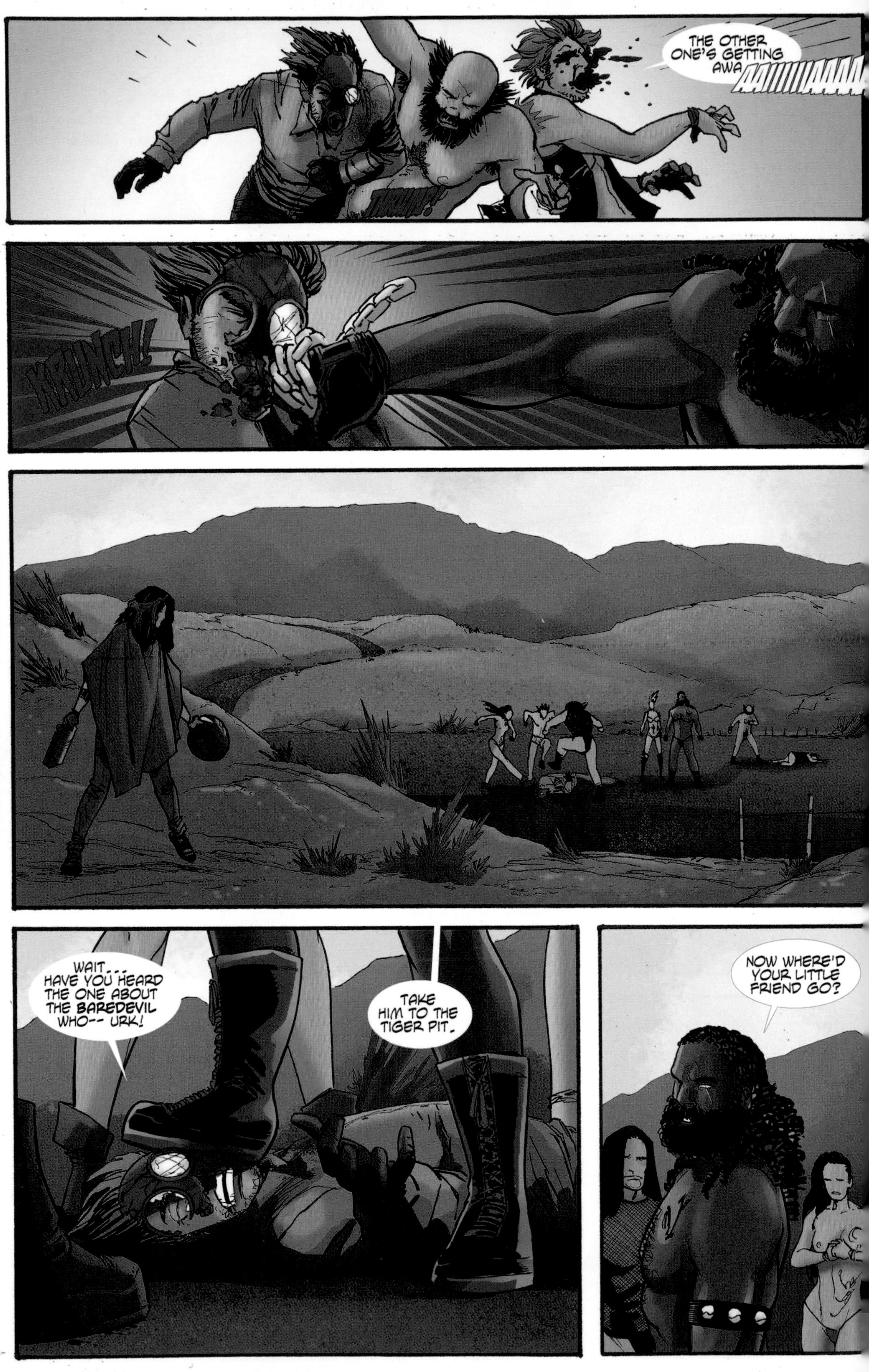
THE OTHER ONE'S GETTING AWA
AAIIIIIAAAA
THUNK!
KRUNCH!
WAIT... HAVE YOU HEARD THE ONE ABOUT THE BAREDEVIL WHO-- URK!
TAKE HIM TO THE TIGER PIT.
NOW WHERE'D YOUR LITTLE FRIEND GO?

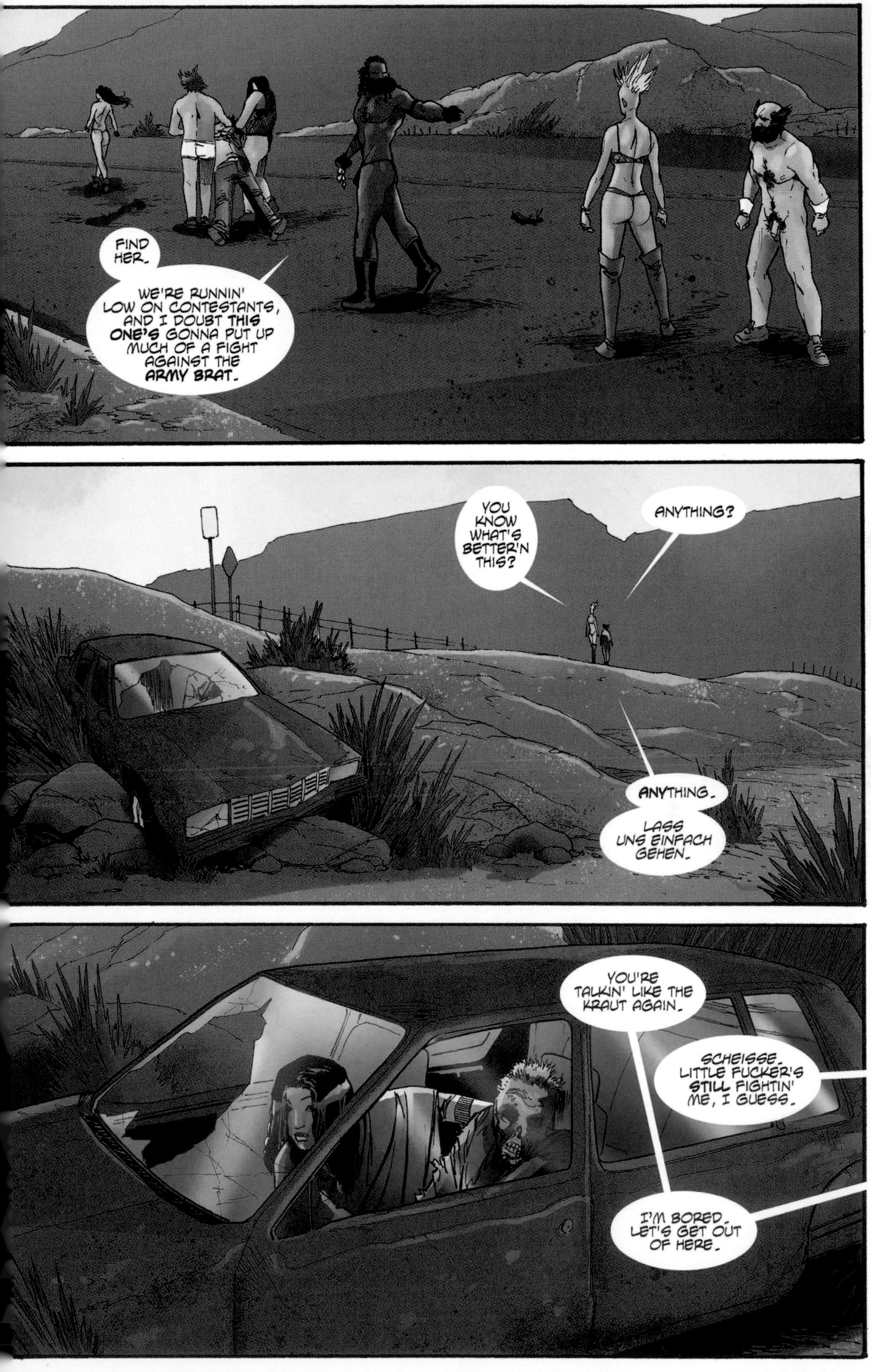
FIND HER.
WE'RE RUNNIN' LOW ON CONTESTANTS, AND I DOUBT THIS ONE'S GONNA PUT UP MUCH OF A FIGHT AGAINST THE ARMY BRAT.
YOU KNOW WHAT'S BETTER'N THIS?
ANYTHING?
ANYTHING.
LASS UNS EINFACH GEHEN.
YOU'RE TALKIN' LIKE THE KRAUT AGAIN.
SCHEISSE. LITTLE FUCKER'S STILL FIGHTIN' ME, I GUESS.
I'M BORED. LET'S GET OUT OF HERE.

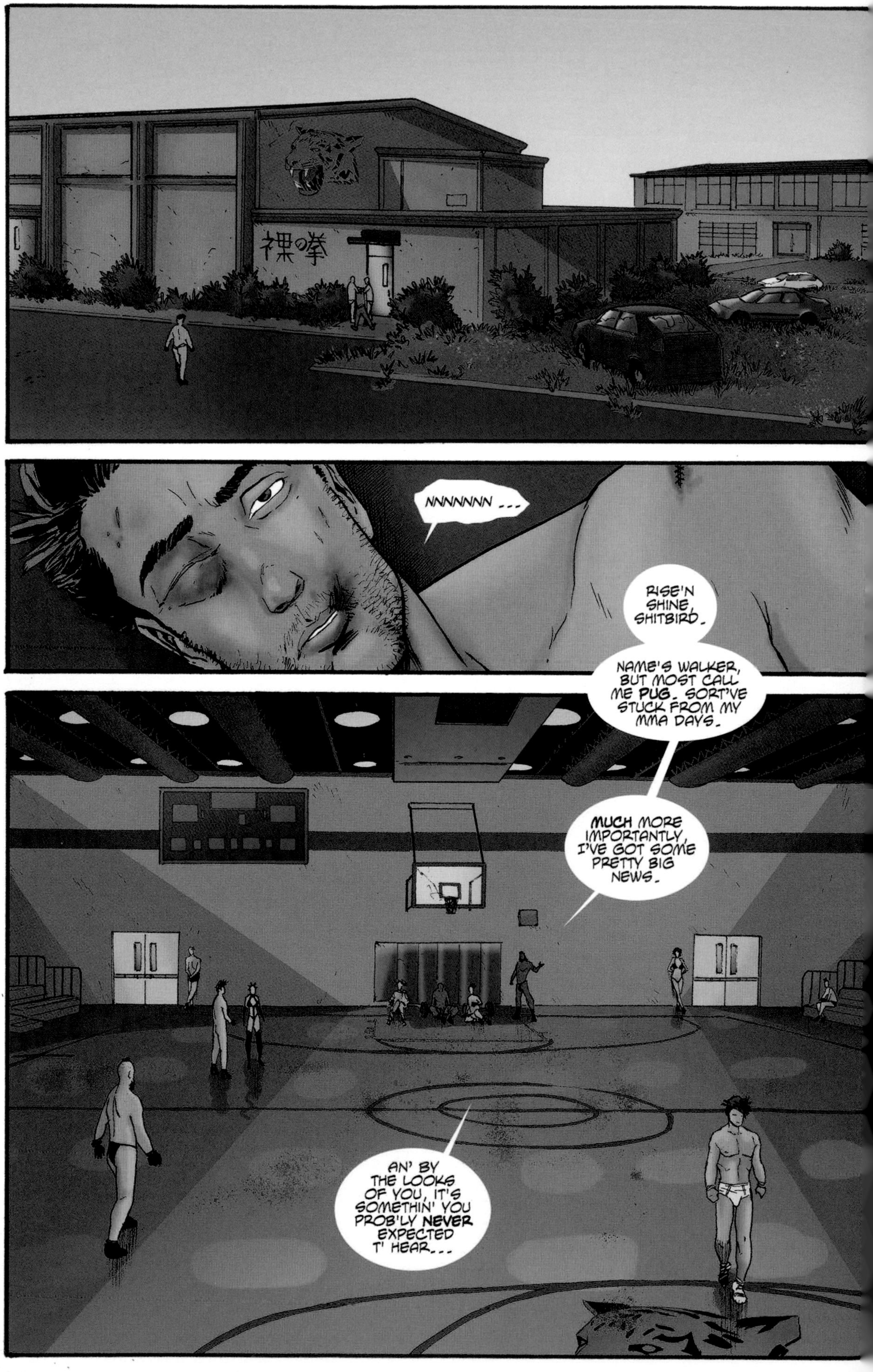

NNNNNNN...
RISE'N SHINE, SHITBIRD.
NAME'S WALKER, BUT MOST CALL ME PUG. SORT'VE STUCK FROM MY MMA DAYS.
MUCH MORE IMPORTANTLY, I'VE GOT SOME PRETTY BIG NEWS.
AN' BY THE LOOKS OF YOU, IT'S SOMETHIN' YOU PROB'LY NEVER EXPECTED T' HEAR...

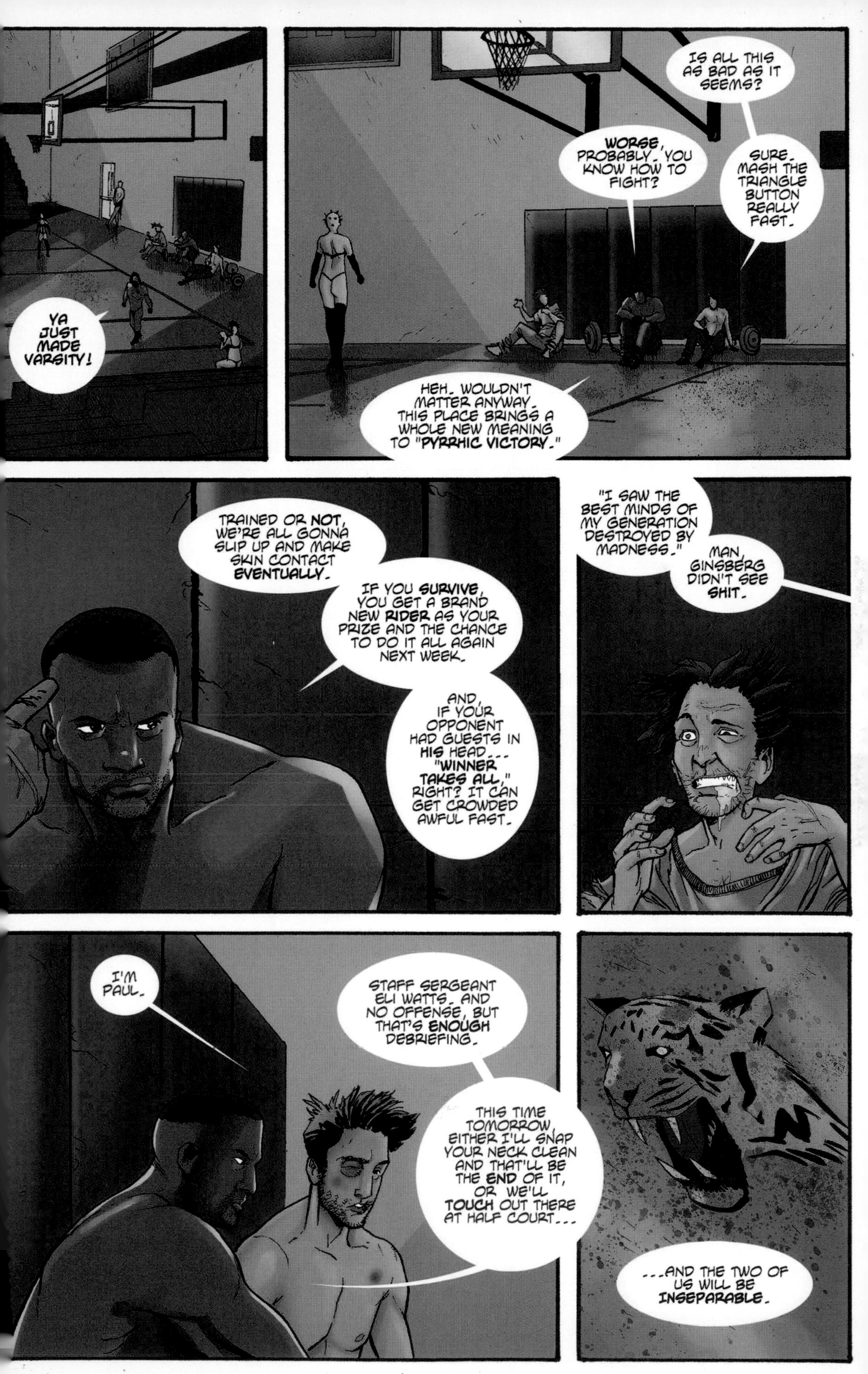
YA JUST MADE VARSITY!
IS ALL THIS AS BAD AS IT SEEMS?
WORSE, PROBABLY. YOU KNOW HOW TO FIGHT?
SURE. MASH THE TRIANGLE BUTTON REALLY FAST.
HEH. WOULDN'T MATTER ANYWAY. THIS PLACE BRINGS A WHOLE NEW MEANING TO "PYRRHIC VICTORY."
TRAINED OR NOT, WE'RE ALL GONNA SLIP UP AND MAKE SKIN CONTACT EVENTUALLY.
IF YOU SURVIVE, YOU GET A BRAND NEW RIDER AS YOUR PRIZE AND THE CHANCE TO DO IT ALL AGAIN NEXT WEEK.
AND, IF YOUR OPPONENT HAD GUESTS IN HIS HEAD... "WINNER TAKES ALL," RIGHT? IT CAN GET CROWDED AWFUL FAST.
"I SAW THE BEST MINDS OF MY GENERATION DESTROYED BY MADNESS."
MAN, GINSBERG DIDN'T SEE SHIT.
I'M PAUL.
STAFF SERGEANT ELI WATTS. AND NO OFFENSE, BUT THAT'S ENOUGH DEBRIEFING.
THIS TIME TOMORROW, EITHER I'LL SNAP YOUR NECK CLEAN AND THAT'LL BE THE END OF IT, OR WE'LL TOUCH OUT THERE AT HALF COURT...
...AND THE TWO OF US WILL BE INSEPARABLE.

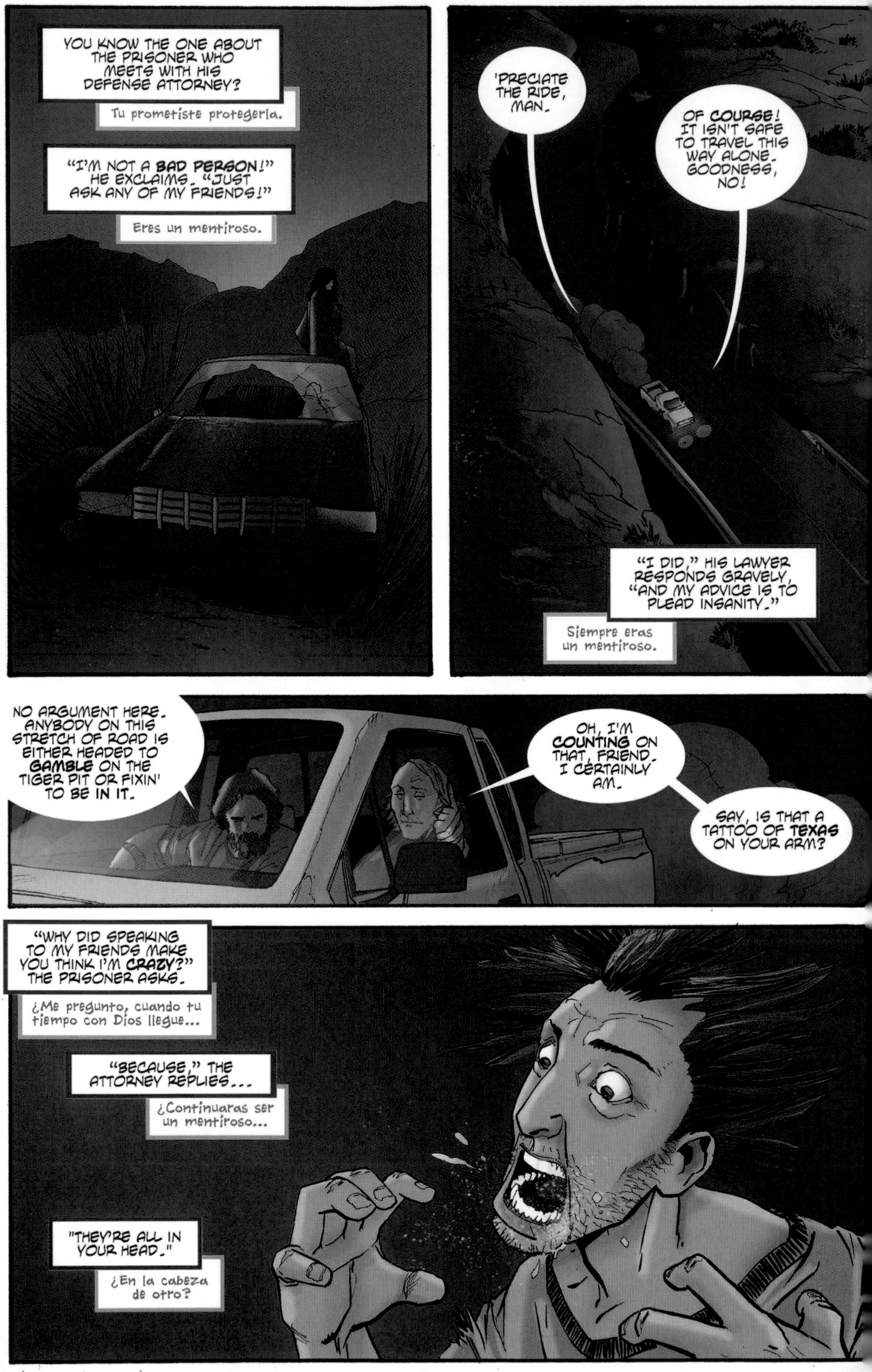

YOU KNOW THE ONE ABOUT THE PRISONER WHO MEETS WITH HIS DEFENSE ATTORNEY?
Tu prometiste protegerla.
"I'M NOT A BAD PERSON!" HE EXCLAIMS. "JUST ASK ANY OF MY FRIENDS!"
Eres un mentiroso.
'PRECIATE THE RIDE, MAN.
OF COURSE! IT ISN'T SAFE TO TRAVEL THIS WAY ALONE. GOODNESS, NO!
"I DID," HIS LAWYER RESPONDS GRAVELY, "AND MY ADVICE IS TO PLEAD INSANITY."
Siempre eras un mentiroso.
NO ARGUMENT HERE. ANYBODY ON THIS STRETCH OF ROAD IS EITHER HEADED TO GAMBLE ON THE TIGER PIT OR FIXIN' TO BE IN IT.
OH, I'M COUNTING ON THAT, FRIEND. I CERTAINLY AM.
SAY, IS THAT A TATTOO OF TEXAS ON YOUR ARM?
"WHY DID SPEAKING TO MY FRIENDS MAKE YOU THINK I'M CRAZY?" THE PRISONER ASKS.
¿Me pregunto, cuando tu tiempo con Dios llegue...
"BECAUSE," THE ATTORNEY REPLIES...
¿Continuaras ser un mentiroso...
"THEY'RE ALL IN YOUR HEAD."
¿En la cabeza de otro?

CLASSIFIED

SECURITY LEVEL: DOUBLE BLACK

For the desk of Gen. Canter

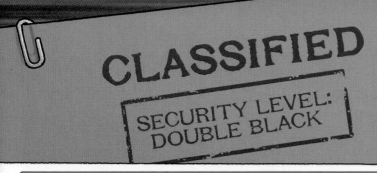

TelChan v0.78, Cpu Cycles: 3000, Frameskip 0, IRC restricted_research.gov

23:41:16 * ALG has joined the group. Security clearance confirmed. GPS link engaged.

23:41:21 <ALG> Sorry I'm late.

23:41:29 <MOL> No problem, Amy. We'll try to keep this short.

23:41:37 <JCK> Have you read any of the joint research that Marcel and I uploaded?

23:42:08 <ALG> Yeah. Linguistics, symbology, and psychology ... you guys are like the Frankenstein's monster of things that drive Vic crazy.

23:42:12 <ALG> Shit. She's not on here, is she?

23:42:19 <MOL> Ha. No, it's just you, me, and Josiah.

23:42:36 <JCK> So as you know, the purpose of our collaboration is to establish a set of unified logograms for schitzopneumatics.

23:42:51 <ALG> You're talking about a written language for people with riders.

23:43:24 <JCK> Exactly. In two years, there hasn't been a single reported instance of anyone recovering from the resultant dysgraphia and dyslexia. At this point, we have to assume the effect is permanent.

23:43:53 <MOL> We've witnessed a rapid adoption of replacement symbology by the afflicted. But it's geographic. On the West Coast, for example, we've seen the use of hyridized Asian characters. In the Southeast, thre's a Cherokee influence.

23:44:13 <JCK> This presents several long term concerns which could be mitigated by establishing a unified national system. Maybe even a gobal one.

23:44:28 <MOL> That's where you come in. Do you still have access to printers at the university?

23:44:41 <ALG> Sure. But it's pretty optimistic to be discussing long term goals, isn't it? You've both seen my predictive data -- It's a Greek tragedy on a Y axis.

23:45:33 <MOL> What choice do we have? Maybe our species is doomed. Or maybe the rumors are true and the Chinese are close to cracking petrie dish procreation. But if your models are accurate, what we DO know for sure is that these chatrooms share at least one thing in common with Sophocles.

23:45:39 <MOL> We're all using a dead language.

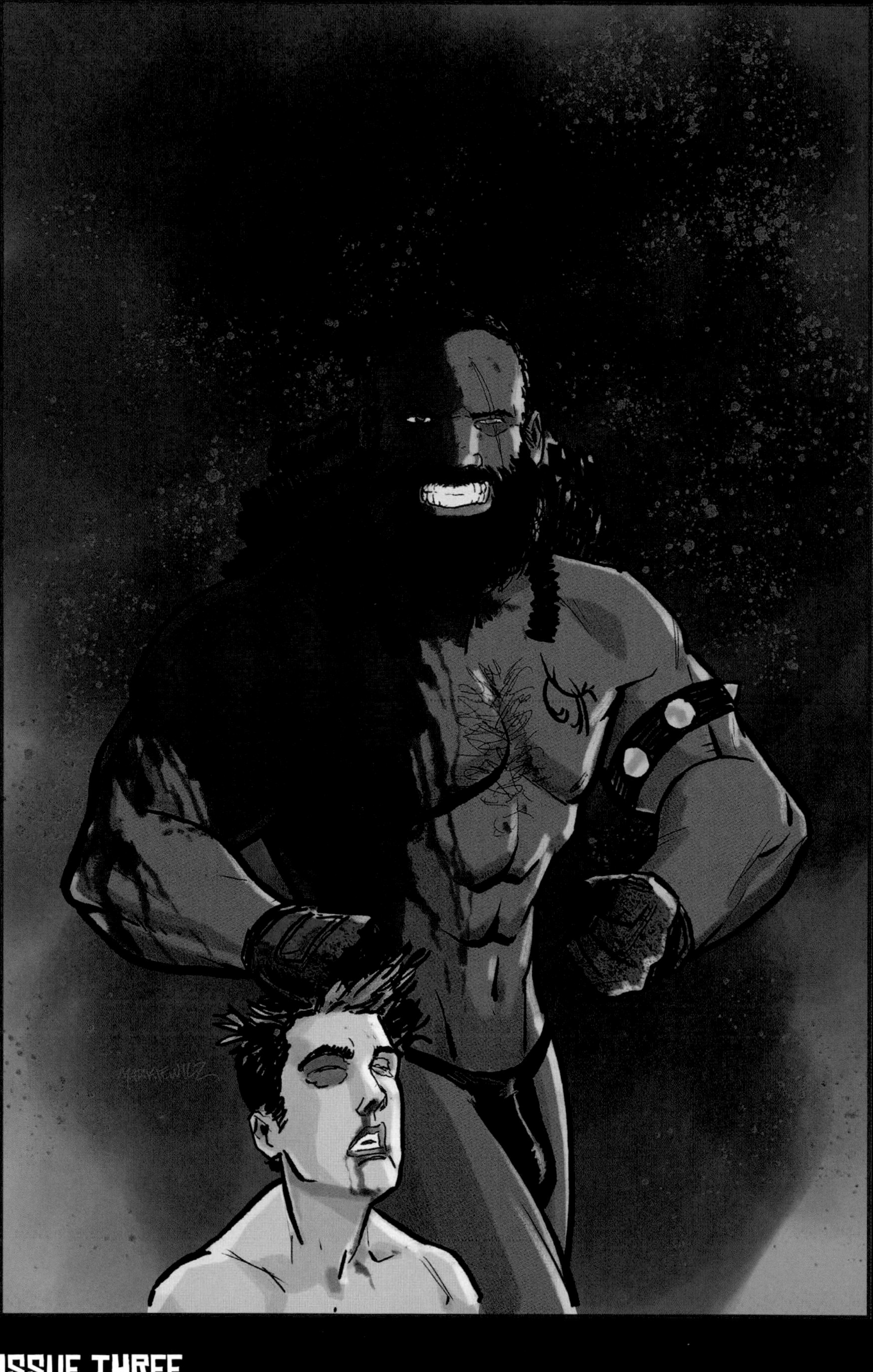

ISSUE THREE
COVER ART BY ADAM MARKIEWICZ
COLORS BY MELANIE DARLING

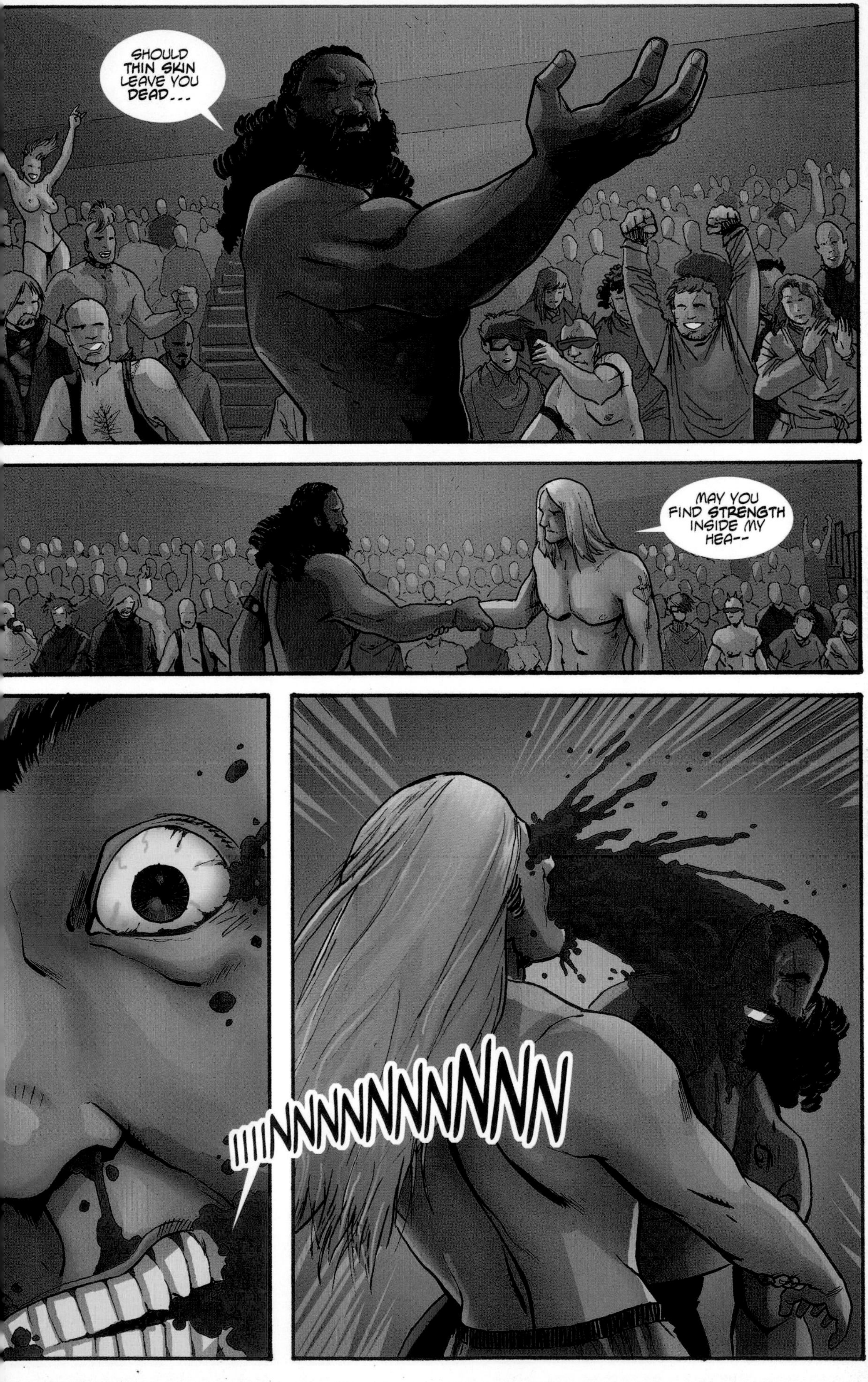
SHOULD THIN SKIN LEAVE YOU DEAD...
MAY YOU FIND STRENGTH INSIDE MY HEA--
IIIINNNNNNNNNNNN

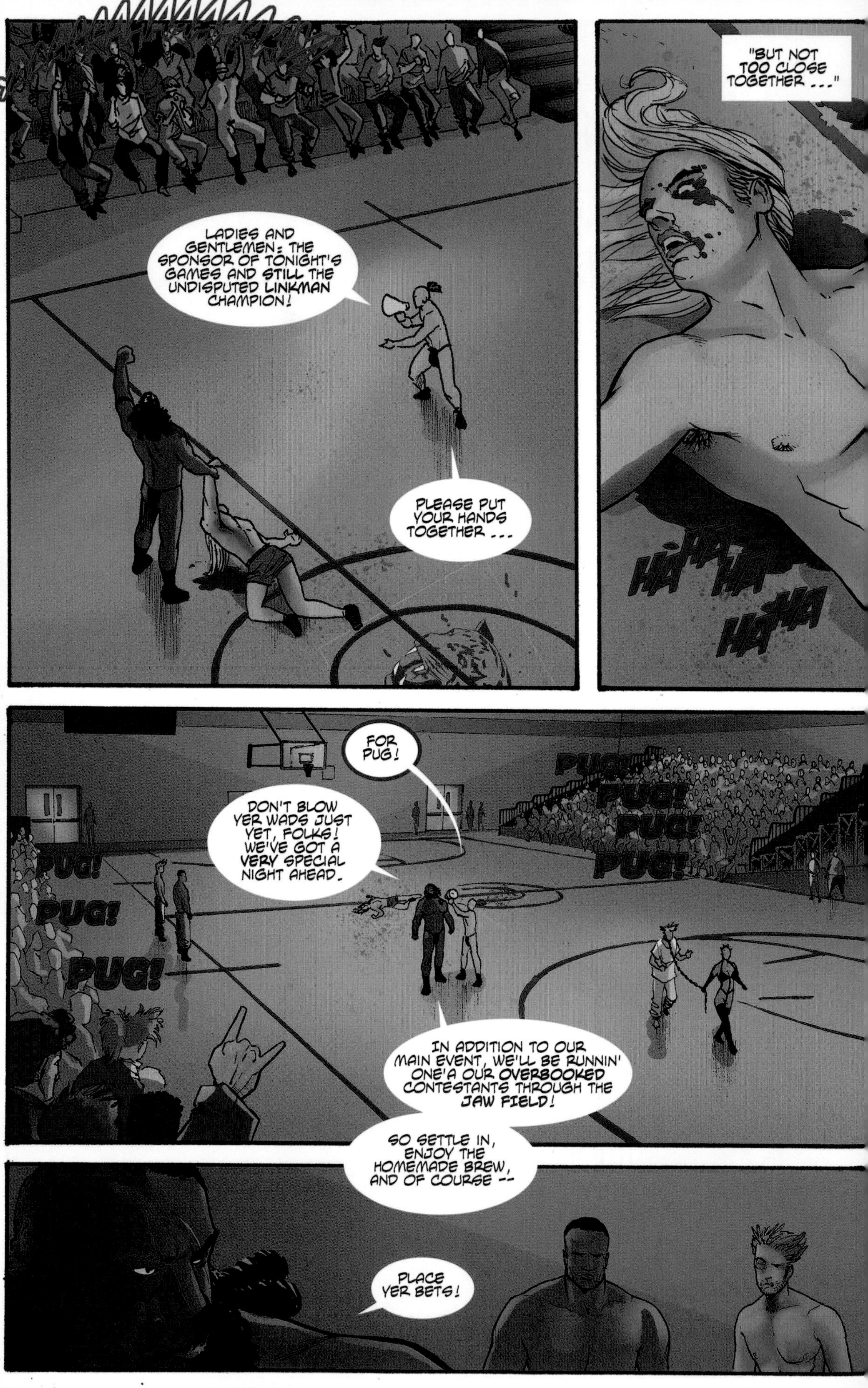
LADIES AND GENTLEMEN: THE SPONSOR OF TONIGHT'S GAMES AND STILL THE UNDISPUTED LINKMAN CHAMPION!
PLEASE PUT YOUR HANDS TOGETHER ...
"BUT NOT TOO CLOSE TOGETHER ..."
HA HA HA HA HA HA
FOR PUG!
DON'T BLOW YER WADS JUST YET, FOLKS! WE'VE GOT A VERY SPECIAL NIGHT AHEAD.
PUG! PUG! PUG! PUG!
PUG! PUG! PUG!
IN ADDITION TO OUR MAIN EVENT, WE'LL BE RUNNIN' ONE'A OUR OVERBOOKED CONTESTANTS THROUGH THE JAW FIELD!
SO SETTLE IN, ENJOY THE HOMEMADE BREW, AND OF COURSE --
PLACE YER BETS!

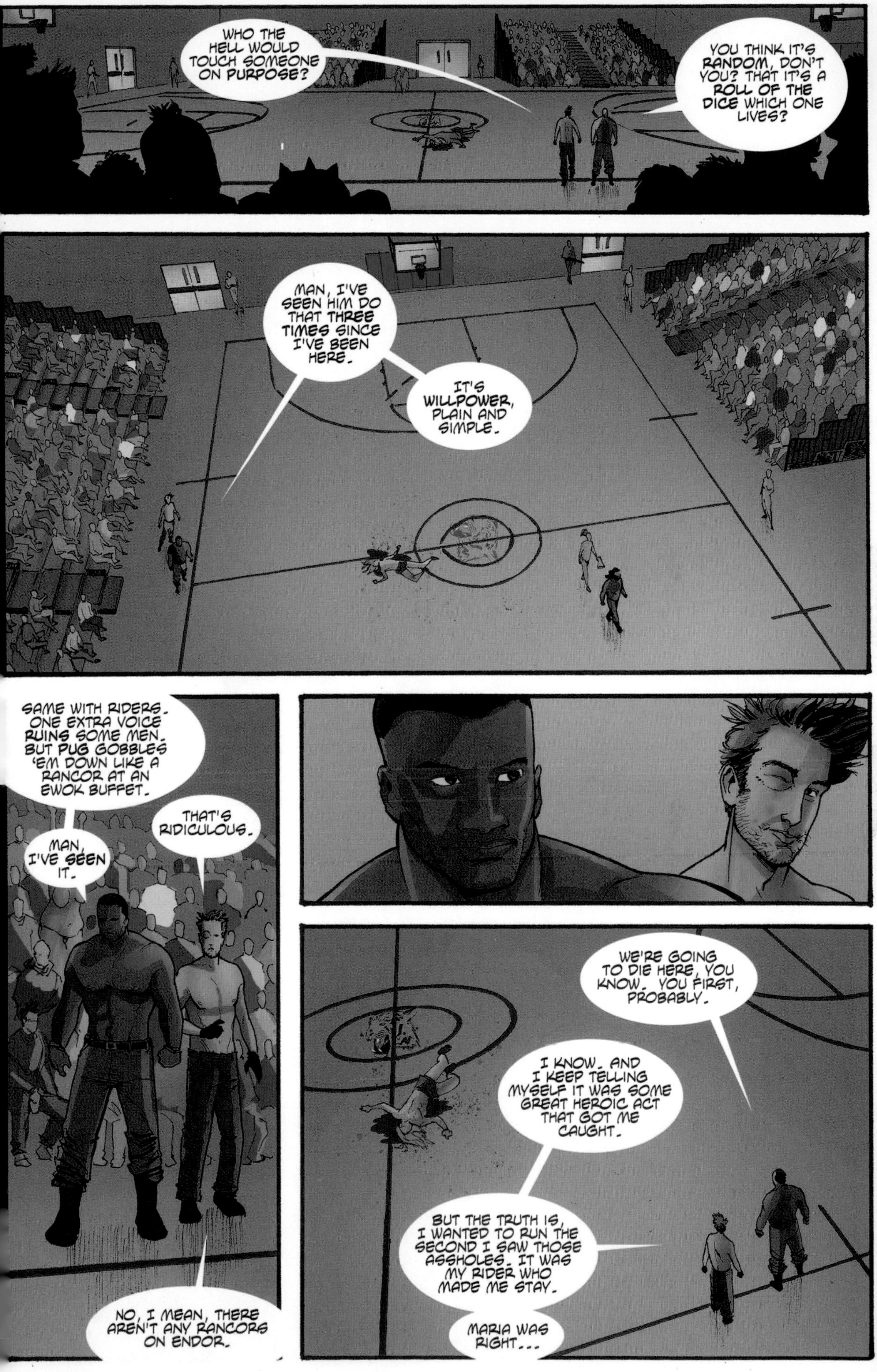
WHO THE HELL WOULD TOUCH SOMEONE ON PURPOSE?
YOU THINK IT'S RANDOM, DON'T YOU? THAT IT'S A ROLL OF THE DICE WHICH ONE LIVES?
MAN, I'VE SEEN HIM DO THAT THREE TIMES SINCE I'VE BEEN HERE.
IT'S WILLPOWER, PLAIN AND SIMPLE.
SAME WITH RIDERS. ONE EXTRA VOICE RUINS SOME MEN. BUT PUG GOBBLES 'EM DOWN LIKE A RANCOR AT AN EWOK BUFFET.
THAT'S RIDICULOUS.
MAN, I'VE SEEN IT.
NO, I MEAN, THERE AREN'T ANY RANCORS ON ENDOR.
WE'RE GOING TO DIE HERE, YOU KNOW. YOU FIRST, PROBABLY.
I KNOW. AND I KEEP TELLING MYSELF IT WAS SOME GREAT HEROIC ACT THAT GOT ME CAUGHT.
BUT THE TRUTH IS, I WANTED TO RUN THE SECOND I SAW THOSE ASSHOLES. IT WAS MY RIDER WHO MADE ME STAY.
MARIA WAS RIGHT...

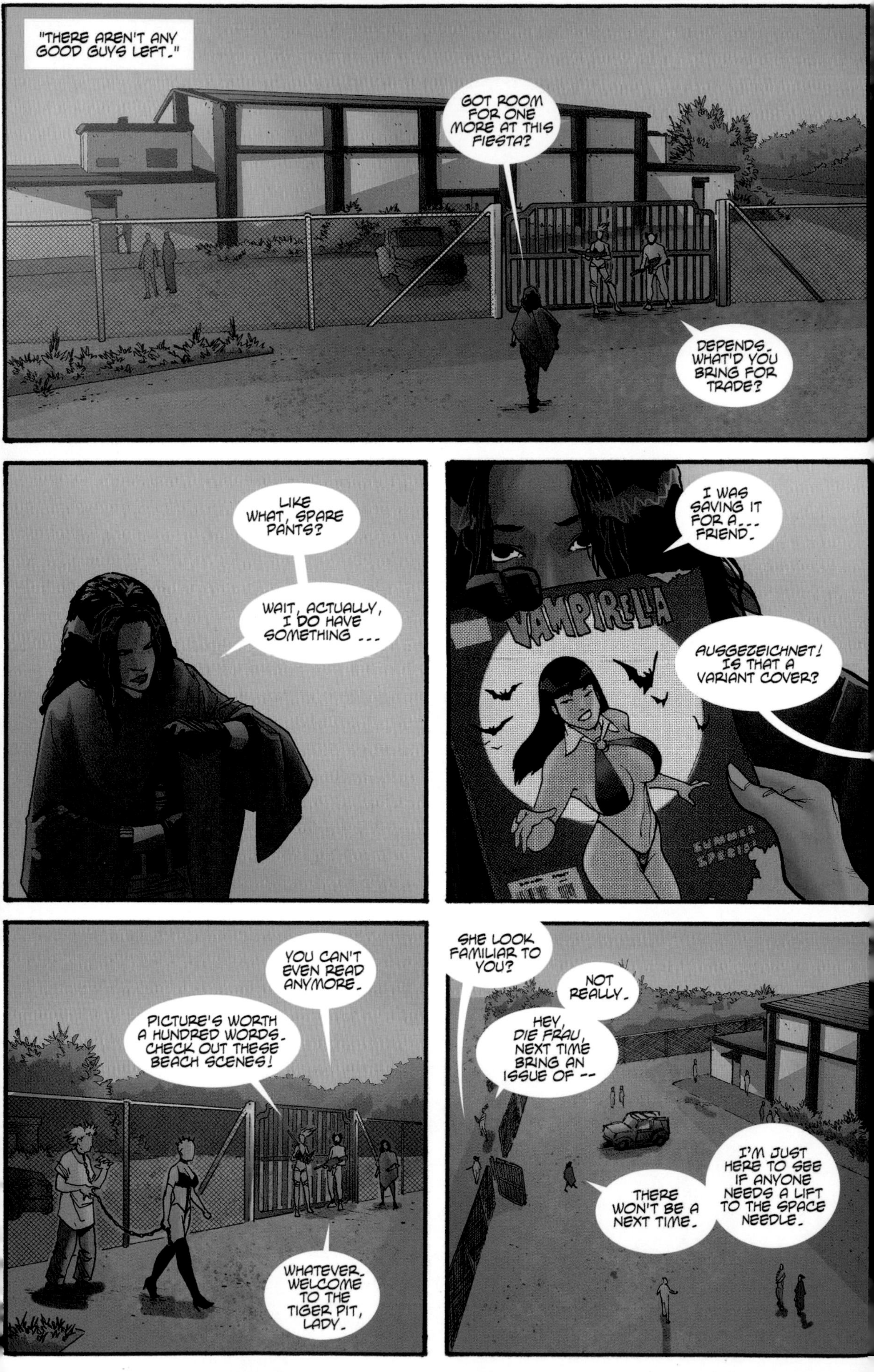
"THERE AREN'T ANY GOOD GUYS LEFT."
GOT ROOM FOR ONE MORE AT THIS FIESTA?
DEPENDS. WHAT'D YOU BRING FOR TRADE?
LIKE WHAT, SPARE PANTS?
WAIT, ACTUALLY, I DO HAVE SOMETHING ...
I WAS SAVING IT FOR A... FRIEND.
VAMPIRELLA
SUMMER SPECIAL
AUSGEZEICHNET! IS THAT A VARIANT COVER?
YOU CAN'T EVEN READ ANYMORE.
PICTURE'S WORTH A HUNDRED WORDS. CHECK OUT THESE BEACH SCENES!
WHATEVER. WELCOME TO THE TIGER PIT, LADY.
SHE LOOK FAMILIAR TO YOU?
NOT REALLY.
HEY, DIE FRAU, NEXT TIME BRING AN ISSUE OF --
THERE WON'T BE A NEXT TIME.
I'M JUST HERE TO SEE IF ANYONE NEEDS A LIFT TO THE SPACE NEEDLE.

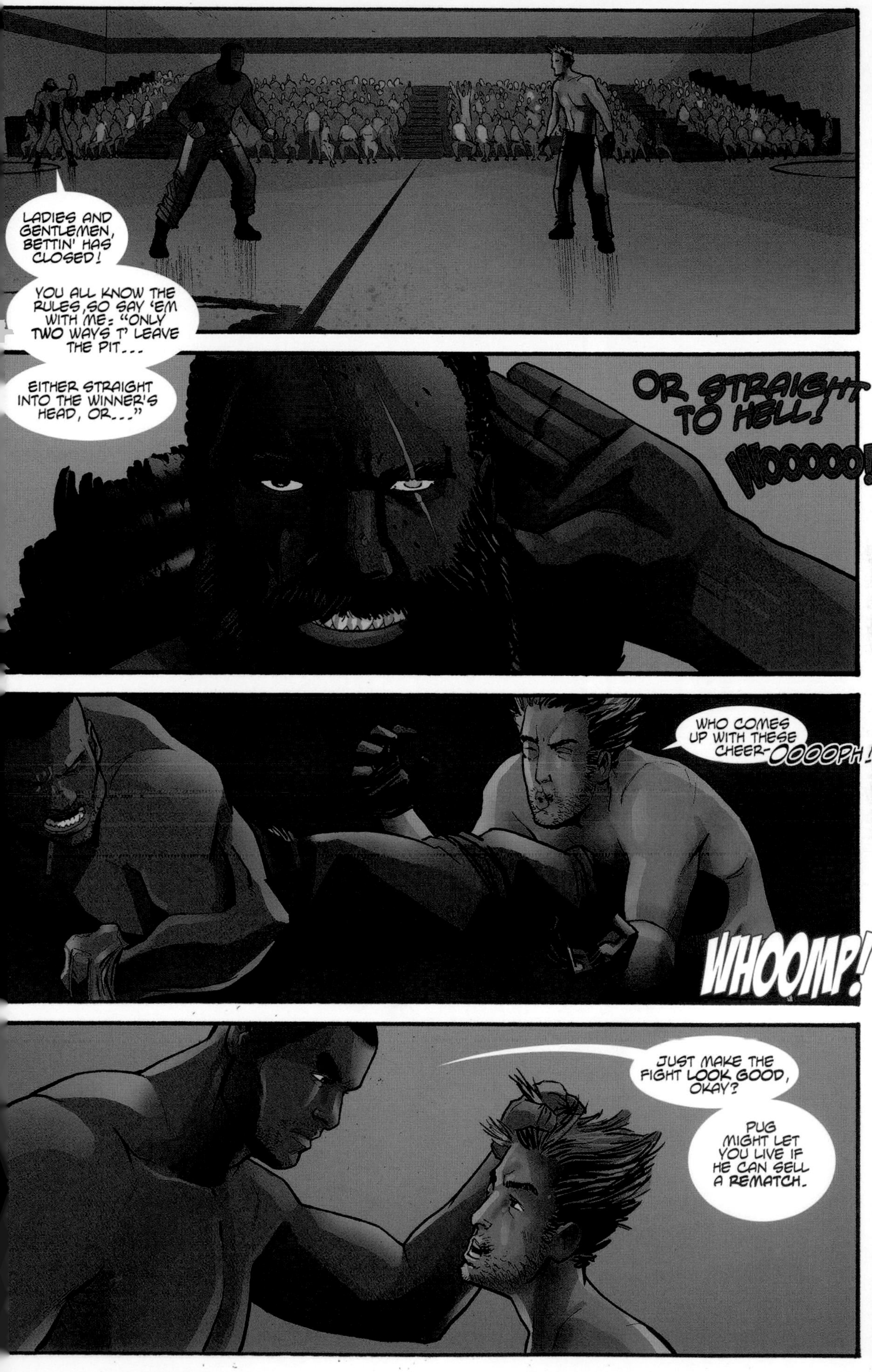
LADIES AND GENTLEMEN, BETTIN' HAS CLOSED!
YOU ALL KNOW THE RULES, SO SAY 'EM WITH ME: "ONLY TWO WAYS T' LEAVE THE PIT...
EITHER STRAIGHT INTO THE WINNER'S HEAD, OR..."
OR STRAIGHT TO HELL!
WOOOOOO!
WHO COMES UP WITH THESE CHEER-OOOOPH!
WHOOMP!
JUST MAKE THE FIGHT LOOK GOOD, OKAY?
PUG MIGHT LET YOU LIVE IF HE CAN SELL A REMATCH.

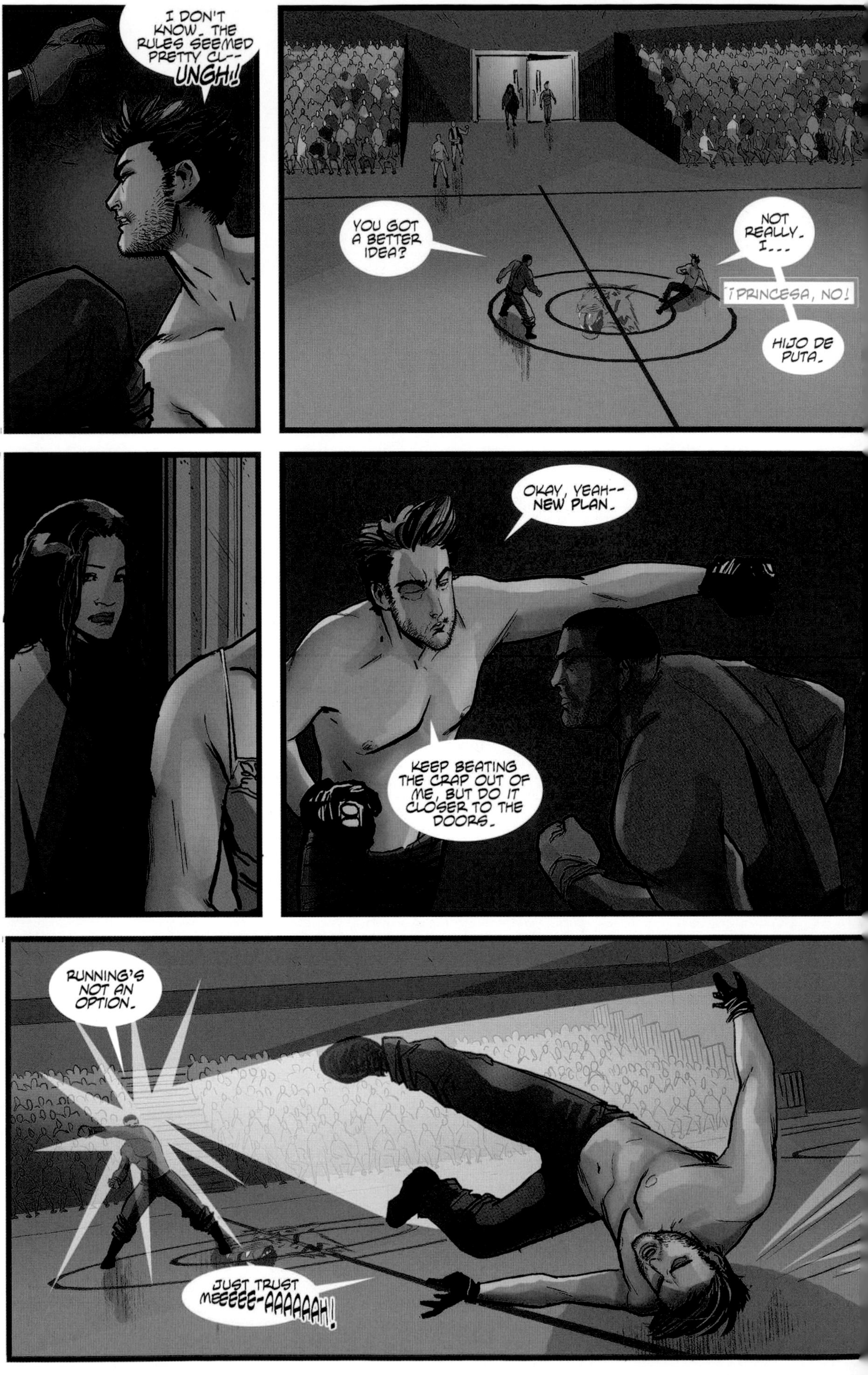
I DON'T KNOW. THE RULES SEEMED PRETTY CL-- UNGH!
YOU GOT A BETTER IDEA?
NOT REALLY. I...
¡PRINCESA, NO!
HIJO DE PUTA.
OKAY, YEAH-- NEW PLAN.
KEEP BEATING THE CRAP OUT OF ME, BUT DO IT CLOSER TO THE DOORS.
RUNNING'S NOT AN OPTION.
JUST TRUST MEEEEE-AAAAAAH!

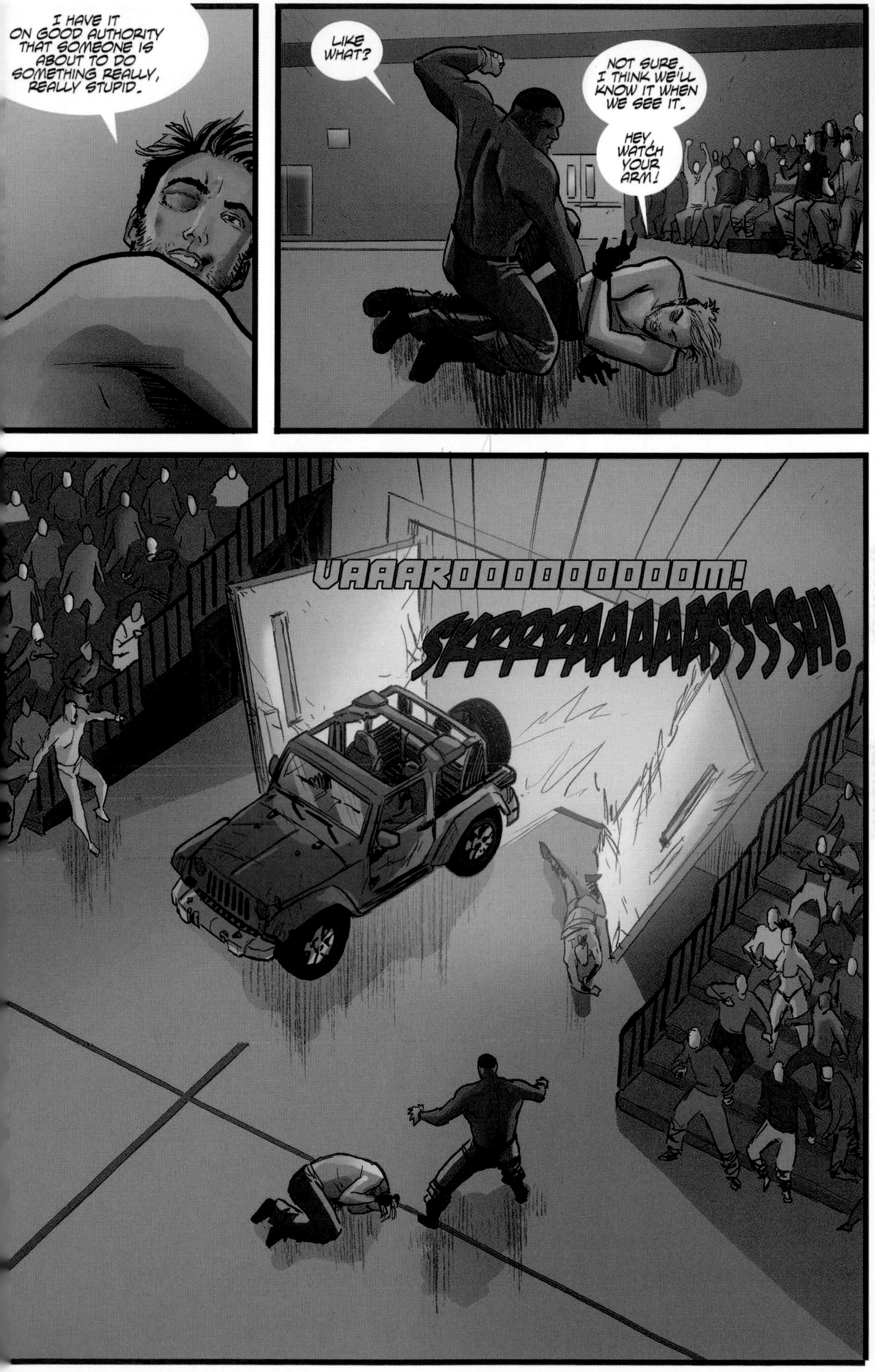
I HAVE IT ON GOOD AUTHORITY THAT SOMEONE IS ABOUT TO DO SOMETHING REALLY, REALLY STUPID.
LIKE WHAT?
NOT SURE. I THINK WE'LL KNOW IT WHEN WE SEE IT.
HEY, WATCH YOUR ARM!
VAAAROOOOOOOOOOM!
SKRRRAAAAAASSSSH!

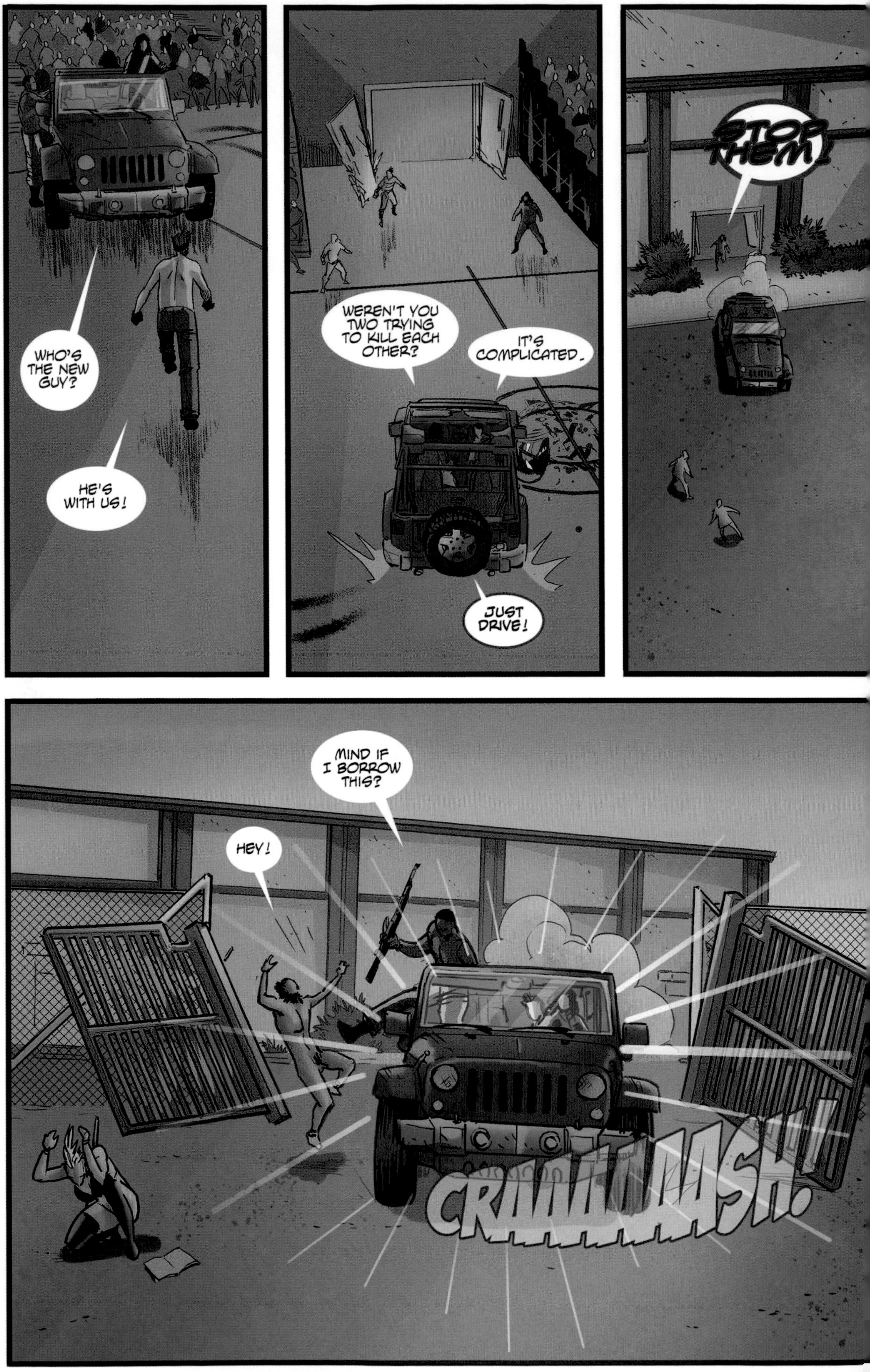
WHO'S THE NEW GUY?
HE'S WITH US!
WEREN'T YOU TWO TRYING TO KILL EACH OTHER?
IT'S COMPLICATED...
JUST DRIVE!
STOP THEM!
MIND IF I BORROW THIS?
HEY!
CRAAAAASH!

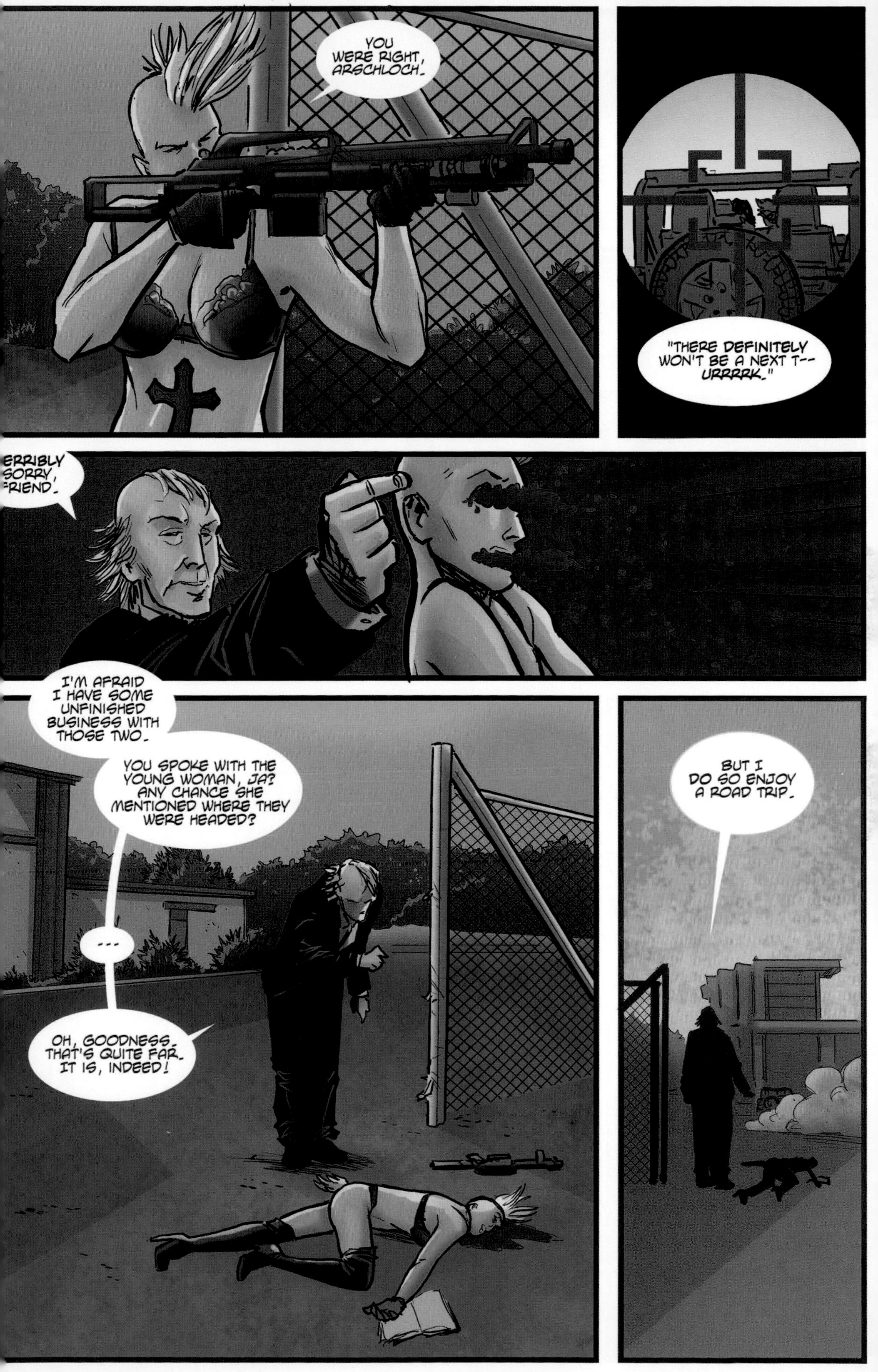
YOU WERE RIGHT, ARSCHLOCH.
"THERE DEFINITELY WON'T BE A NEXT T-- URRRRK."
ERRIBLY SORRY, FRIEND.
I'M AFRAID I HAVE SOME UNFINISHED BUSINESS WITH THOSE TWO.
YOU SPOKE WITH THE YOUNG WOMAN, JA? ANY CHANCE SHE MENTIONED WHERE THEY WERE HEADED?
...
OH, GOODNESS. THAT'S QUITE FAR. IT IS, INDEED!
BUT I DO SO ENJOY A ROAD TRIP.

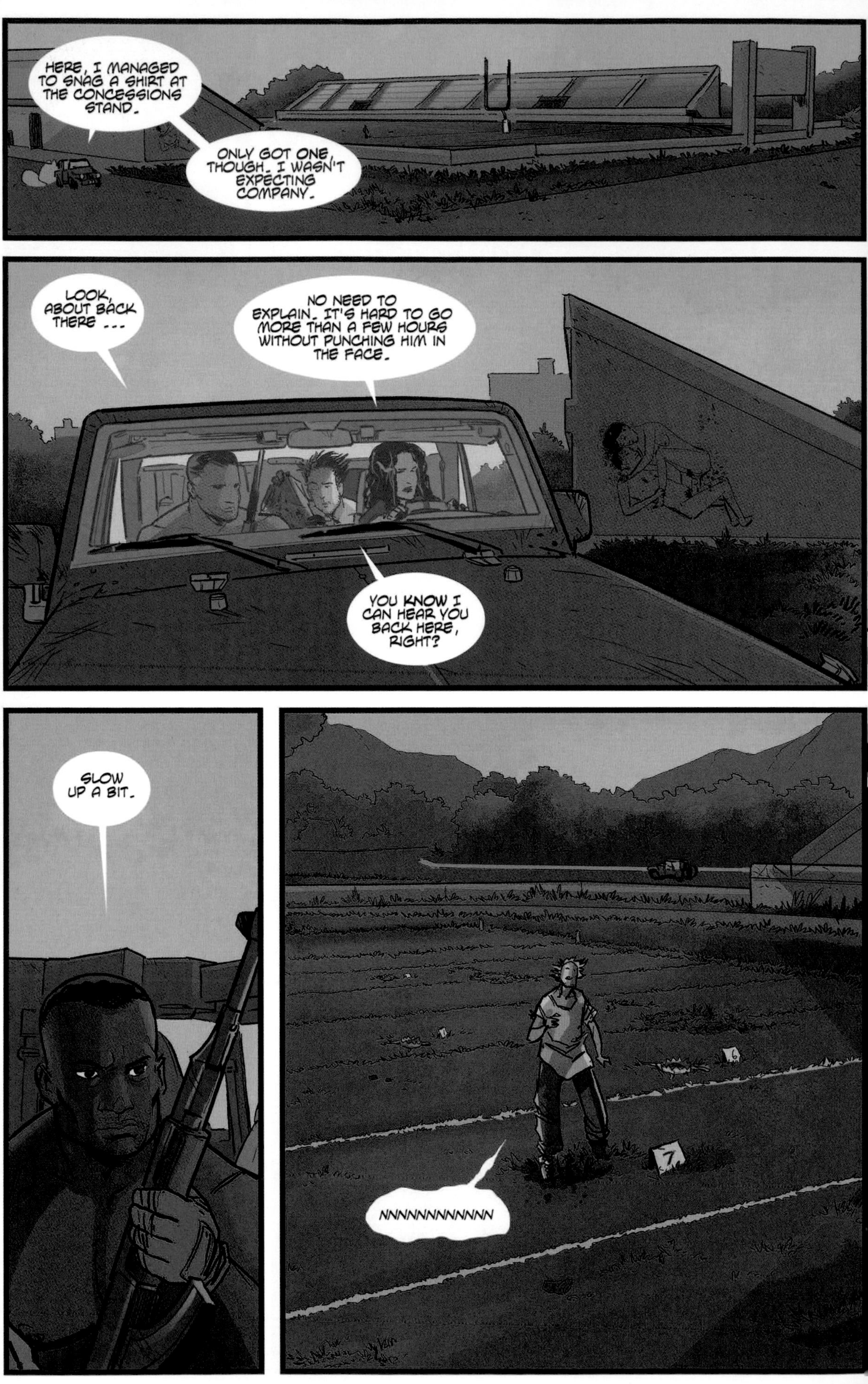
HERE, I MANAGED TO SNAG A SHIRT AT THE CONCESSIONS STAND.
ONLY GOT ONE, THOUGH. I WASN'T EXPECTING COMPANY.
LOOK, ABOUT BACK THERE ...
NO NEED TO EXPLAIN. IT'S HARD TO GO MORE THAN A FEW HOURS WITHOUT PUNCHING HIM IN THE FACE.
YOU KNOW I CAN HEAR YOU BACK HERE, RIGHT?
SLOW UP A BIT.
NNNNNNNNNNN

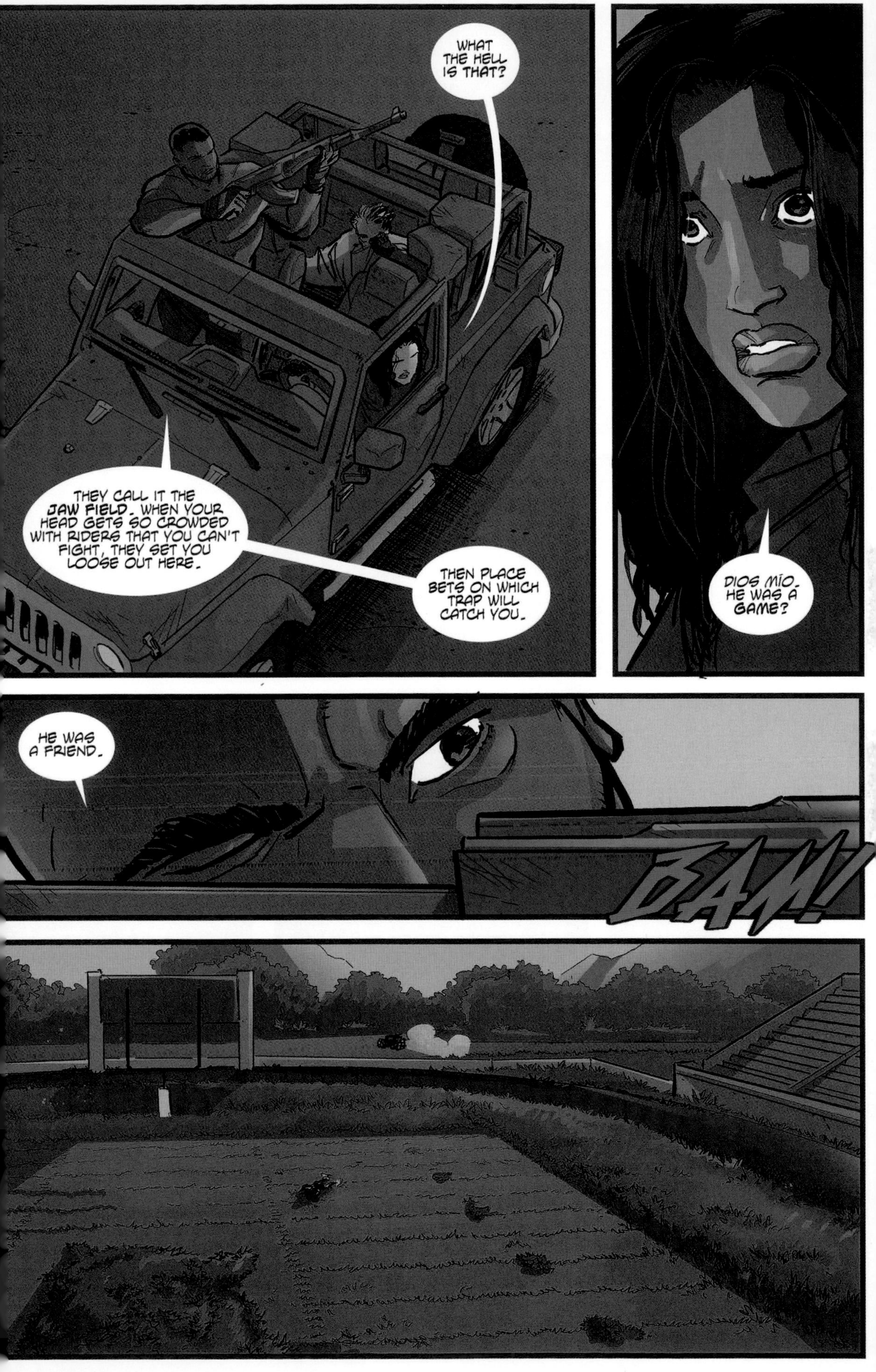
WHAT THE HELL IS THAT?
THEY CALL IT THE JAW FIELD. WHEN YOUR HEAD GETS SO CROWDED WITH RIDERS THAT YOU CAN'T FIGHT, THEY SET YOU LOOSE OUT HERE.
THEN PLACE BETS ON WHICH TRAP WILL CATCH YOU.
DIOS MÍO. HE WAS A GAME?
HE WAS A FRIEND.
BAM!

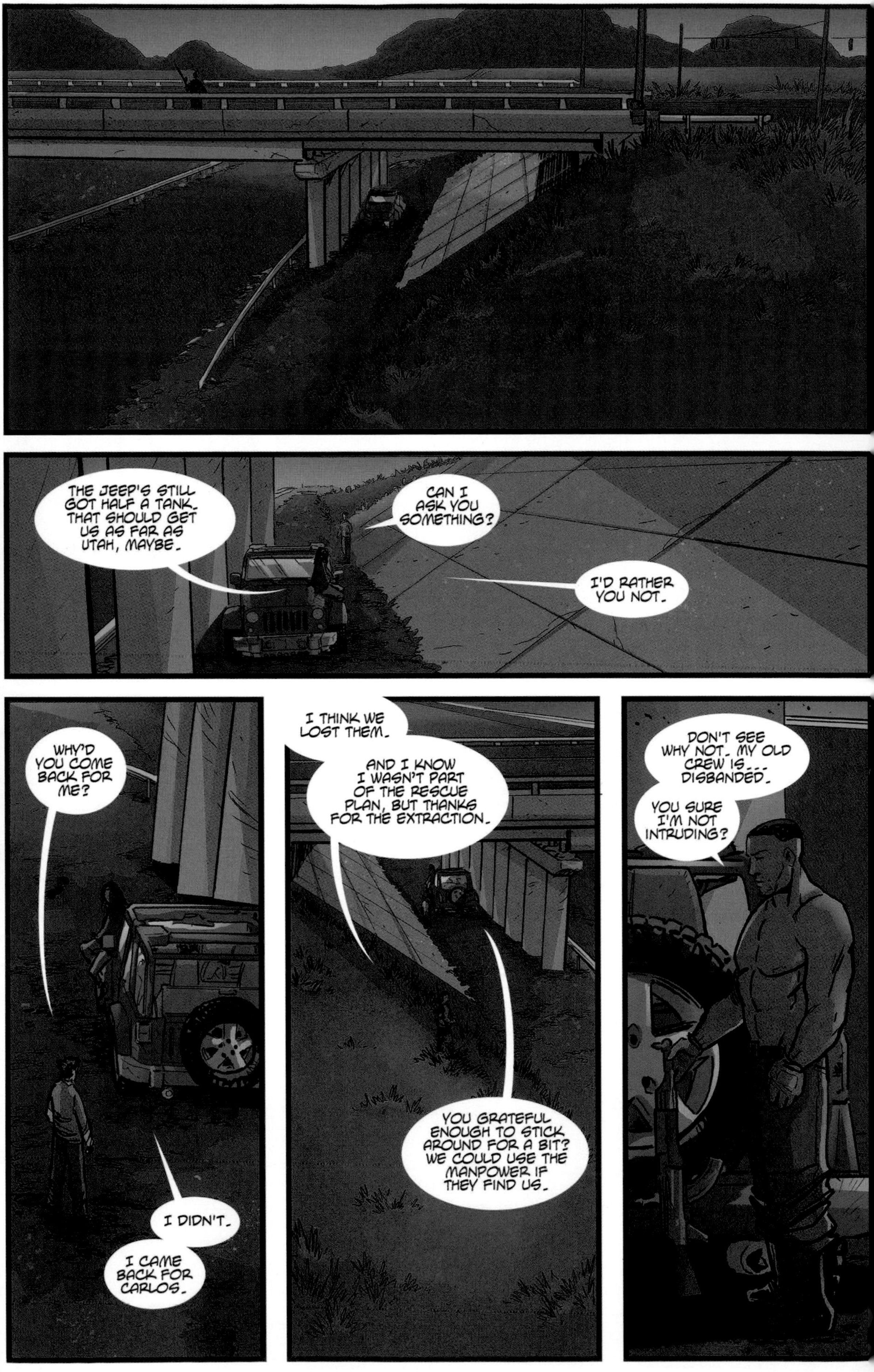
THE JEEP'S STILL GOT HALF A TANK. THAT SHOULD GET US AS FAR AS UTAH, MAYBE.
CAN I ASK YOU SOMETHING?
I'D RATHER YOU NOT.
WHY'D YOU COME BACK FOR ME?
I DIDN'T.
I CAME BACK FOR CARLOS.
I THINK WE LOST THEM.
AND I KNOW I WASN'T PART OF THE RESCUE PLAN, BUT THANKS FOR THE EXTRACTION.
YOU GRATEFUL ENOUGH TO STICK AROUND FOR A BIT? WE COULD USE THE MANPOWER IF THEY FIND US.
DON'T SEE WHY NOT. MY OLD CREW IS... DISBANDED.
YOU SURE I'M NOT INTRUDING?

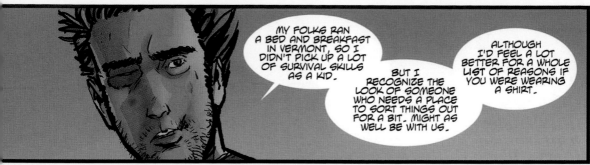

MY FOLKS RAN A BED AND BREAKFAST IN VERMONT, SO I DIDN'T PICK UP A LOT OF SURVIVAL SKILLS AS A KID.

BUT I RECOGNIZE THE LOOK OF SOMEONE WHO NEEDS A PLACE TO SORT THINGS OUT FOR A BIT. MIGHT AS WELL BE WITH US.

ALTHOUGH I'D FEEL A LOT BETTER FOR A WHOLE LIST OF REASONS IF YOU WERE WEARING A SHIRT.

YOUR BOYFRIEND'S GOT A POINT. YOU FIND ANYTHING TO WEAR IN HERE?

JUST A FEW CANNED GOODS. WE'LL SCROUNGE UP SOME CLOTHES TOMORROW.

AND HE'S NOT MY BOYFRIEND.

ROGER THAT.

YOU TWO GET SOME SHUT-EYE. I'LL TAKE FIRST WATCH.

I DOUBT THEY'LL WASTE THE RESOURCES ON A SEARCH PERIMETER THIS WIDE, BUT WE SHOULD PLAY IT SAFE.

SURE DIDN'T TAKE HIM LONG TO REACH FULL ARMY MODE.

AIR FORCE.

WHATEVER. I JUST HOPE HE DOESN'T START BARKING ORDERS.

"HE NEEDS TO REMEMBER THAT HIS 'CREW' IS LONG GONE."

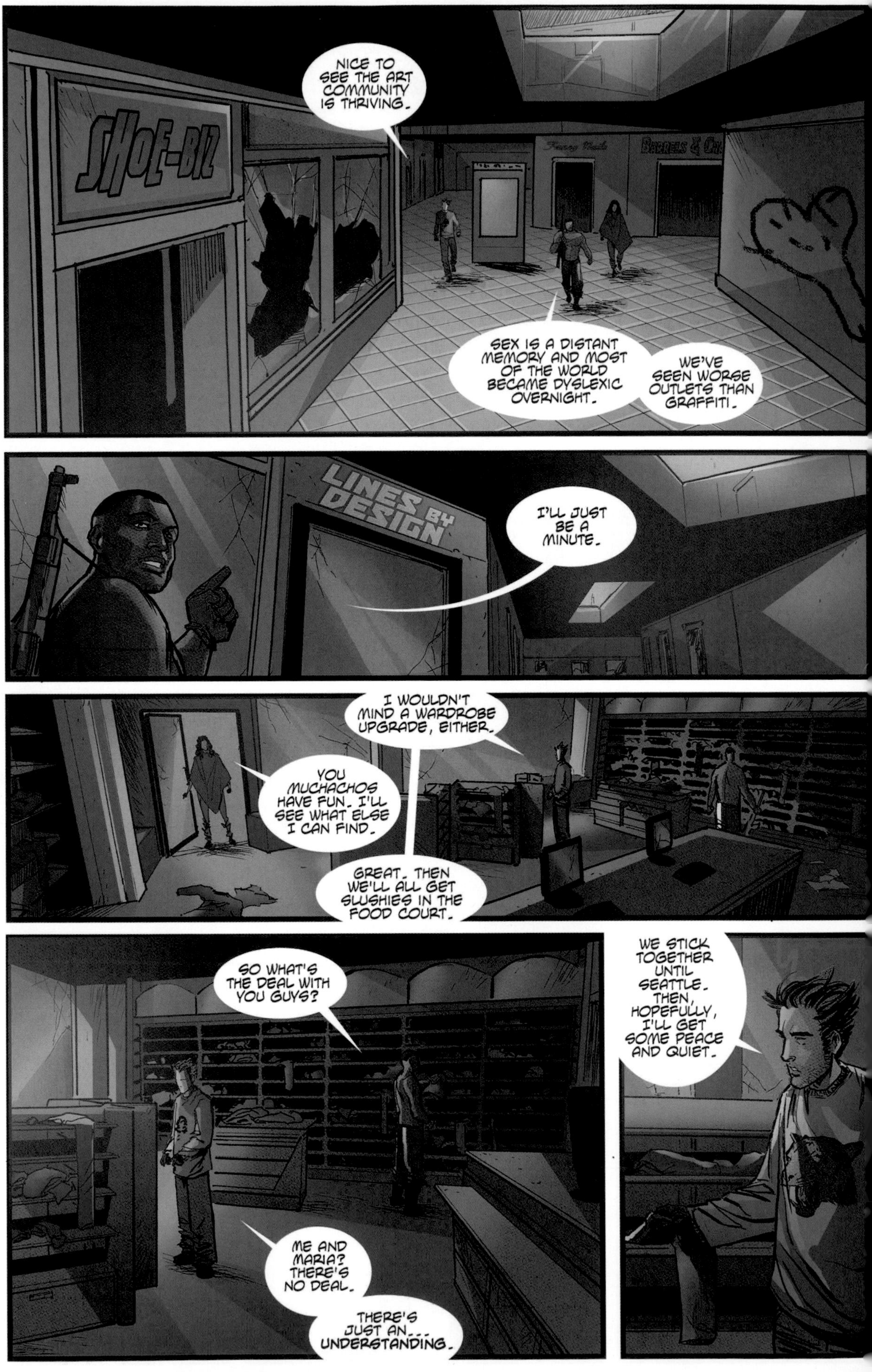
SHOE-BIZ
NICE TO SEE THE ART COMMUNITY IS THRIVING.
SEX IS A DISTANT MEMORY AND MOST OF THE WORLD BECAME DYSLEXIC OVERNIGHT.
WE'VE SEEN WORSE OUTLETS THAN GRAFFITI.
LINES BY DESIGN
I'LL JUST BE A MINUTE.
I WOULDN'T MIND A WARDROBE UPGRADE, EITHER.
YOU MUCHACHOS HAVE FUN. I'LL SEE WHAT ELSE I CAN FIND.
GREAT. THEN WE'LL ALL GET SLUSHIES IN THE FOOD COURT.
SO WHAT'S THE DEAL WITH YOU GUYS?
ME AND MARIA? THERE'S NO DEAL.
THERE'S JUST AN... UNDERSTANDING.
WE STICK TOGETHER UNTIL SEATTLE. THEN, HOPEFULLY, I'LL GET SOME PEACE AND QUIET.

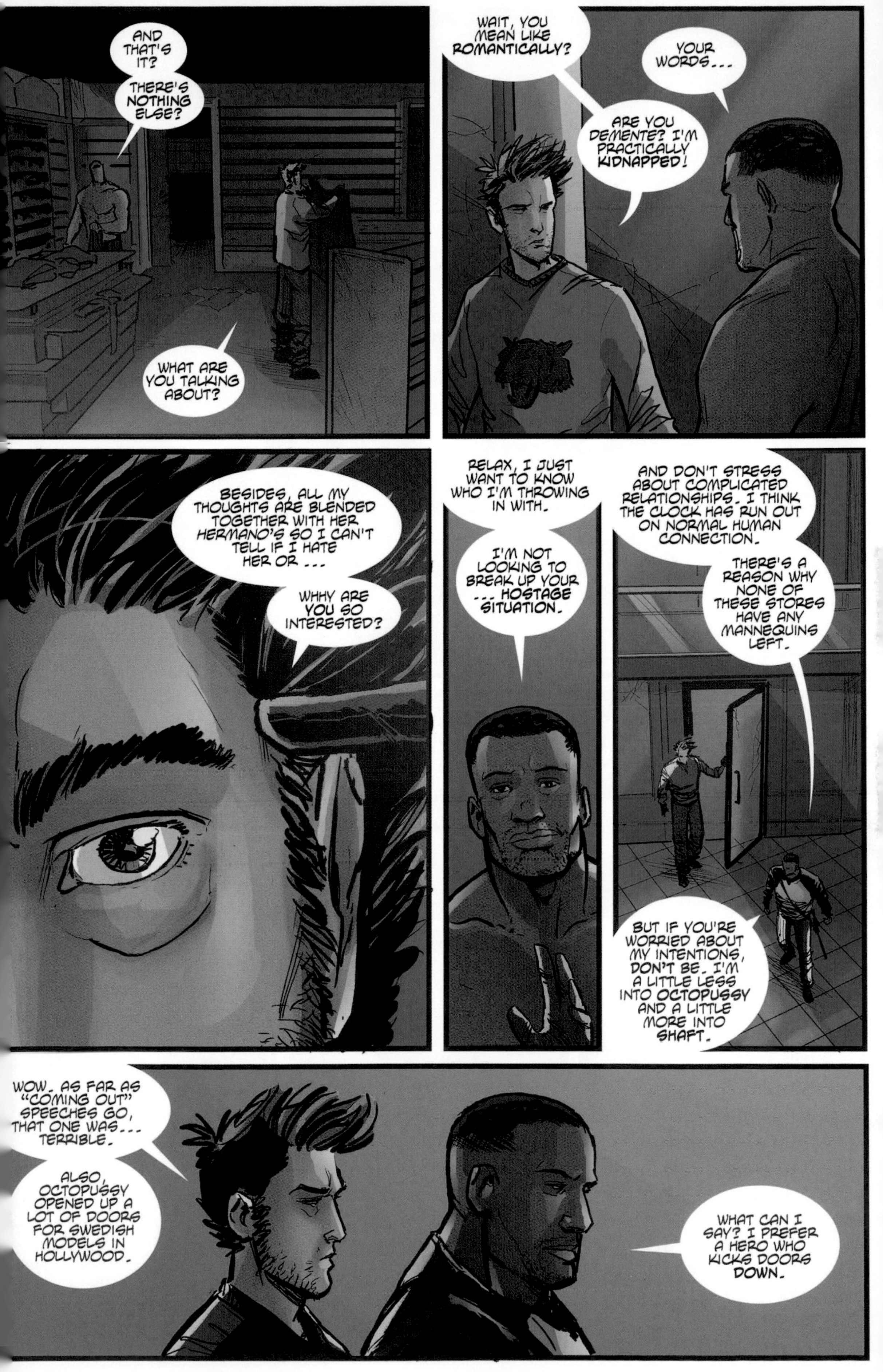
AND THAT'S IT?
THERE'S NOTHING ELSE?
WHAT ARE YOU TALKING ABOUT?
WAIT, YOU MEAN LIKE ROMANTICALLY?
YOUR WORDS...
ARE YOU DEMENTE? I'M PRACTICALLY KIDNAPPED!
BESIDES, ALL MY THOUGHTS ARE BLENDED TOGETHER WITH HER HERMANO'S SO I CAN'T TELL IF I HATE HER OR...
WHHY ARE YOU SO INTERESTED?
RELAX, I JUST WANT TO KNOW WHO I'M THROWING IN WITH.
I'M NOT LOOKING TO BREAK UP YOUR... HOSTAGE SITUATION.
AND DON'T STRESS ABOUT COMPLICATED RELATIONSHIPS. I THINK THE CLOCK HAS RUN OUT ON NORMAL HUMAN CONNECTION.
THERE'S A REASON WHY NONE OF THESE STORES HAVE ANY MANNEQUINS LEFT.
BUT IF YOU'RE WORRIED ABOUT MY INTENTIONS, DON'T BE. I'M A LITTLE LESS INTO OCTOPUSSY AND A LITTLE MORE INTO SHAFT.
WOW. AS FAR AS "COMING OUT" SPEECHES GO, THAT ONE WAS... TERRIBLE.
ALSO, OCTOPUSSY OPENED UP A LOT OF DOORS FOR SWEDISH MODELS IN HOLLYWOOD.
WHAT CAN I SAY? I PREFER A HERO WHO KICKS DOORS DOWN.

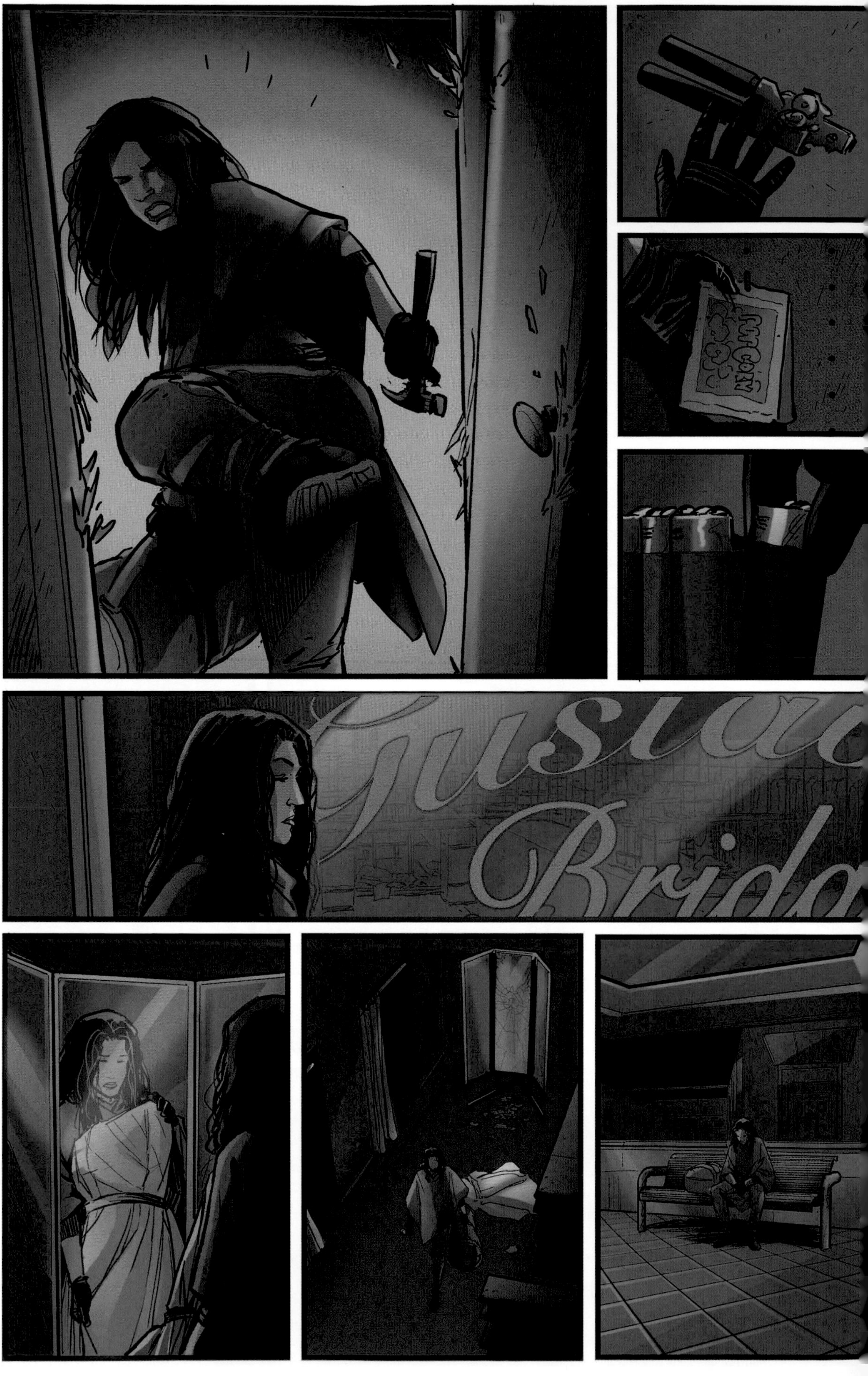

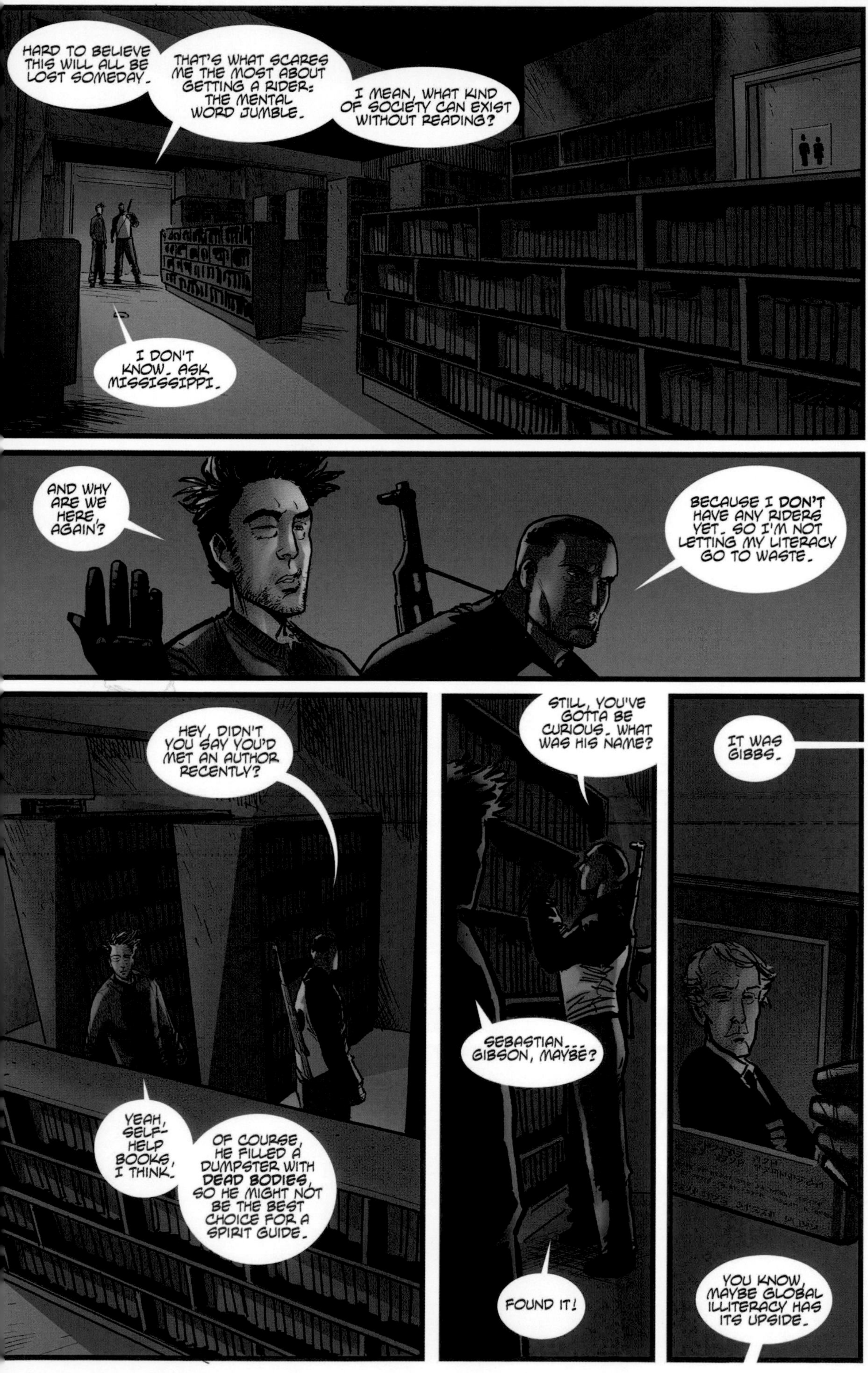
HARD TO BELIEVE THIS WILL ALL BE LOST SOMEDAY.
THAT'S WHAT SCARES ME THE MOST ABOUT GETTING A RIDER: THE MENTAL WORD JUMBLE.
I MEAN, WHAT KIND OF SOCIETY CAN EXIST WITHOUT READING?
I DON'T KNOW. ASK MISSISSIPPI.
AND WHY ARE WE HERE, AGAIN?
BECAUSE I DON'T HAVE ANY RIDERS YET. SO I'M NOT LETTING MY LITERACY GO TO WASTE.
HEY, DIDN'T YOU SAY YOU'D MET AN AUTHOR RECENTLY?
YEAH, SELF-HELP BOOKS, I THINK.
OF COURSE, HE FILLED A DUMPSTER WITH DEAD BODIES, SO HE MIGHT NOT BE THE BEST CHOICE FOR A SPIRIT GUIDE.
STILL, YOU'VE GOTTA BE CURIOUS. WHAT WAS HIS NAME?
SEBASTIAN... GIBSON, MAYBE?
FOUND IT!
IT WAS GIBBS.
YOU KNOW, MAYBE GLOBAL ILLITERACY HAS ITS UPSIDE.

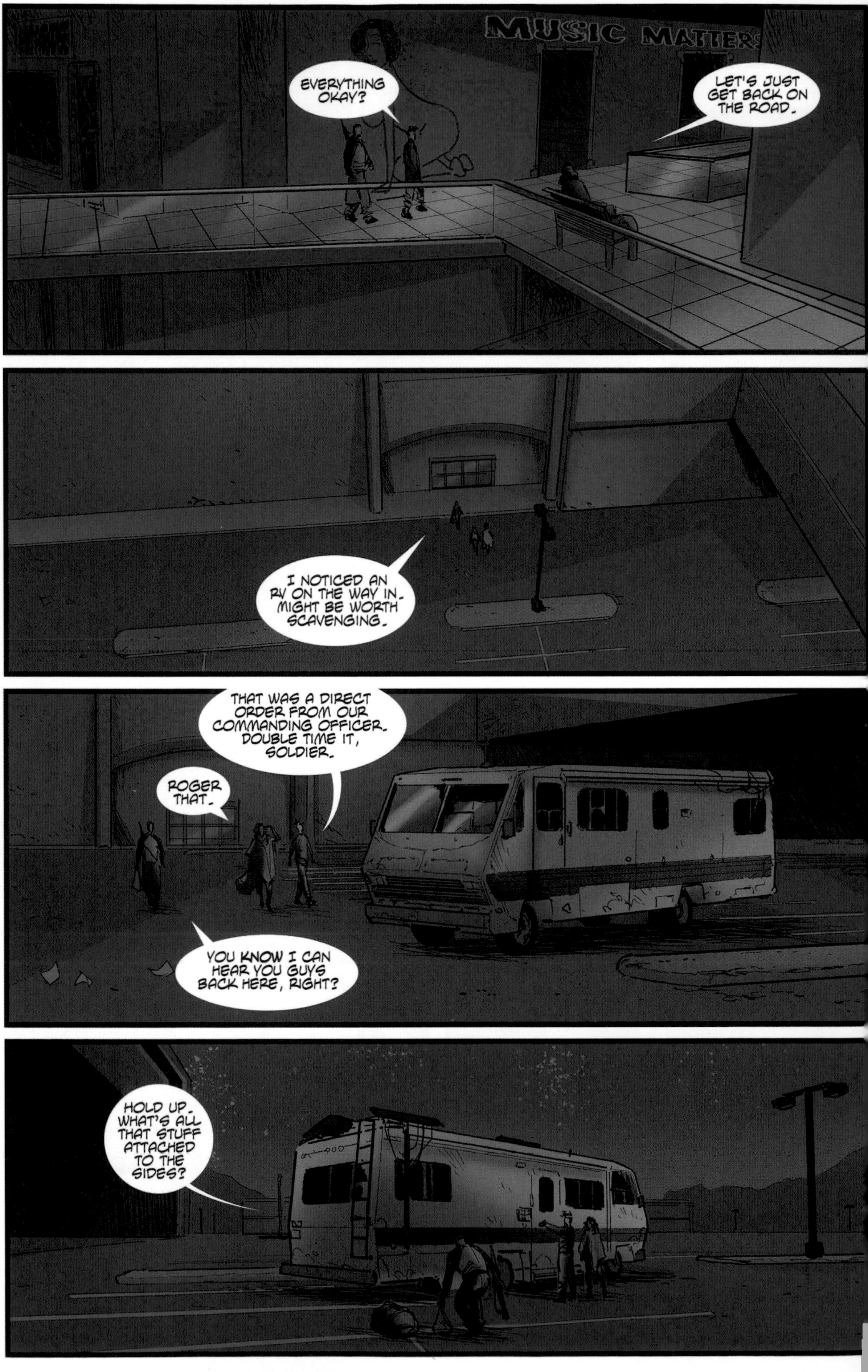
MUSIC MATTERS
EVERYTHING OKAY?
LET'S JUST GET BACK ON THE ROAD.
I NOTICED AN RV ON THE WAY IN. MIGHT BE WORTH SCAVENGING.
THAT WAS A DIRECT ORDER FROM OUR COMMANDING OFFICER. DOUBLE TIME IT, SOLDIER.
ROGER THAT.
YOU KNOW I CAN HEAR YOU GUYS BACK HERE, RIGHT?
HOLD UP. WHAT'S ALL THAT STUFF ATTACHED TO THE SIDES?

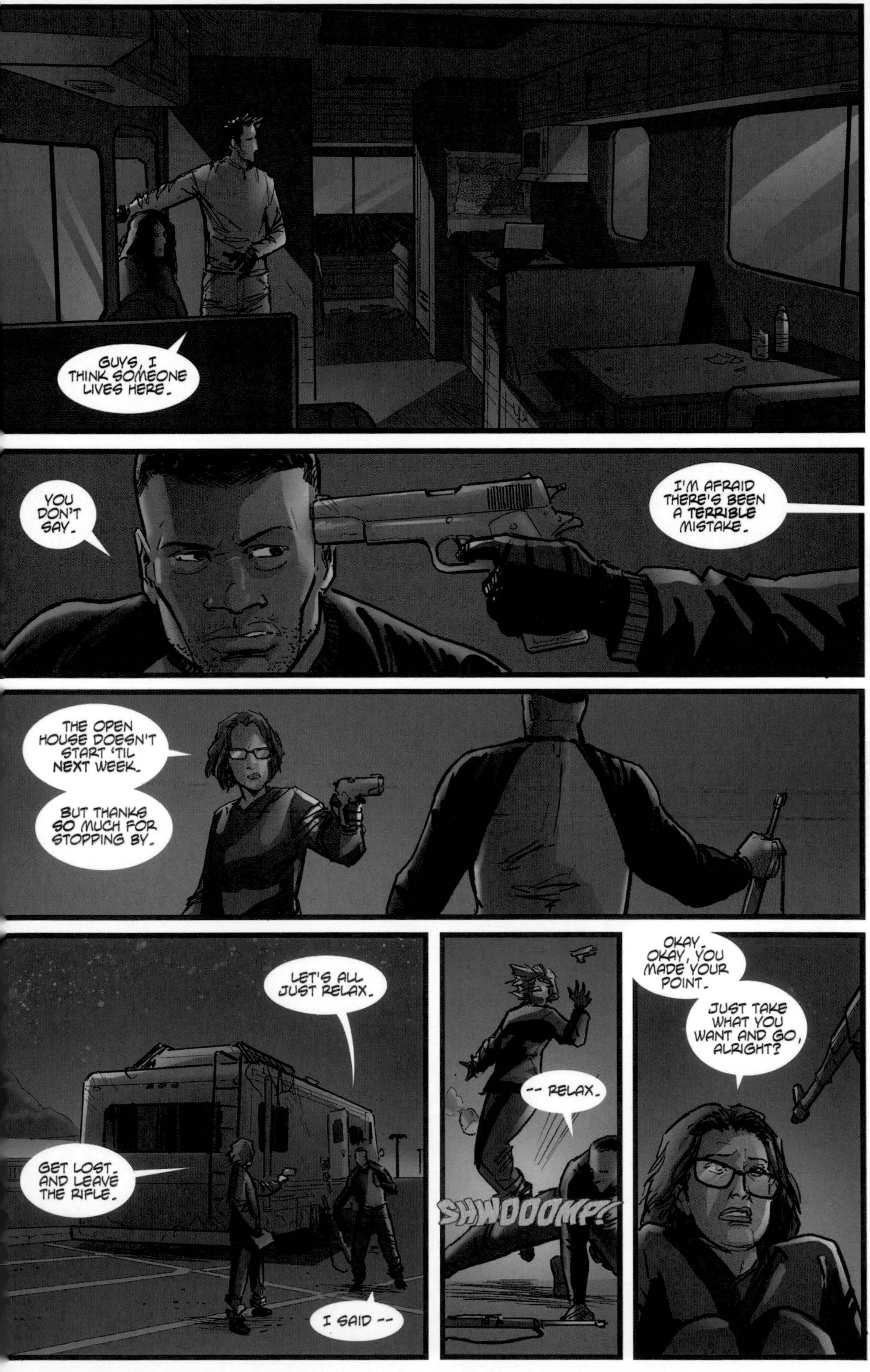
GUYS, I THINK SOMEONE LIVES HERE.
YOU DON'T SAY.
I'M AFRAID THERE'S BEEN A TERRIBLE MISTAKE.
THE OPEN HOUSE DOESN'T START 'TIL NEXT WEEK.
BUT THANKS SO MUCH FOR STOPPING BY.
LET'S ALL JUST RELAX.
GET LOST. AND LEAVE THE RIFLE.
I SAID --
-- RELAX.
SHWOOOMP!
OKAY. OKAY, YOU MADE YOUR POINT.
JUST TAKE WHAT YOU WANT AND GO, ALRIGHT?

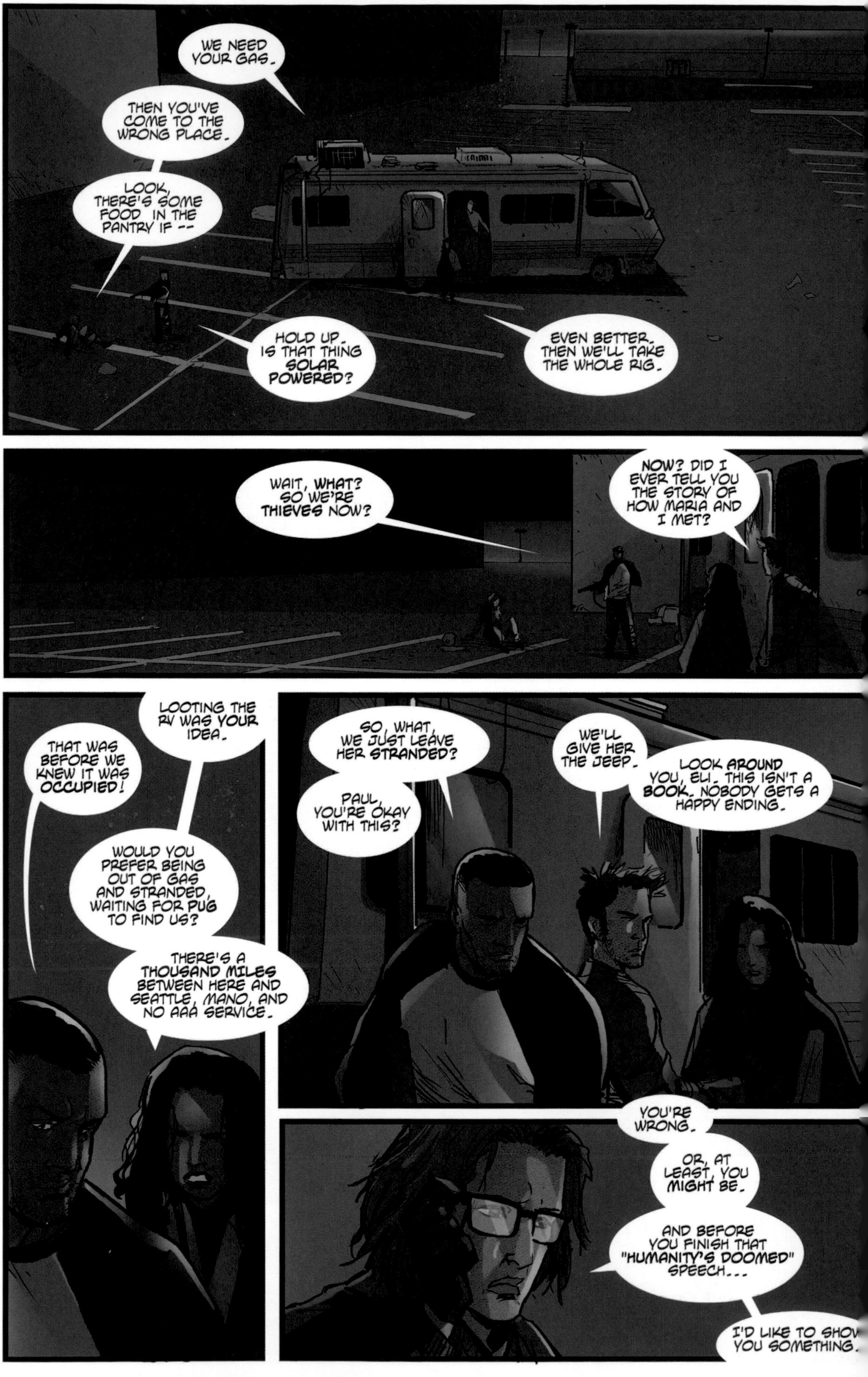

WE NEED YOUR GAS.
THEN YOU'VE COME TO THE WRONG PLACE.
LOOK, THERE'S SOME FOOD IN THE PANTRY IF --
HOLD UP. IS THAT THING SOLAR POWERED?
EVEN BETTER. THEN WE'LL TAKE THE WHOLE RIG.
WAIT, WHAT? SO WE'RE THIEVES NOW?
NOW? DID I EVER TELL YOU THE STORY OF HOW MARIA AND I MET?
THAT WAS BEFORE WE KNEW IT WAS OCCUPIED!
LOOTING THE RV WAS YOUR IDEA.
WOULD YOU PREFER BEING OUT OF GAS AND STRANDED, WAITING FOR PUG TO FIND US?
THERE'S A THOUSAND MILES BETWEEN HERE AND SEATTLE, MANO, AND NO AAA SERVICE.
SO, WHAT, WE JUST LEAVE HER STRANDED?
PAUL, YOU'RE OKAY WITH THIS?
WE'LL GIVE HER THE JEEP.
LOOK AROUND YOU, ELI. THIS ISN'T A BOOK. NOBODY GETS A HAPPY ENDING.
YOU'RE WRONG.
OR, AT LEAST, YOU MIGHT BE.
AND BEFORE YOU FINISH THAT "HUMANITY'S DOOMED" SPEECH...
I'D LIKE TO SHOW YOU SOMETHING.

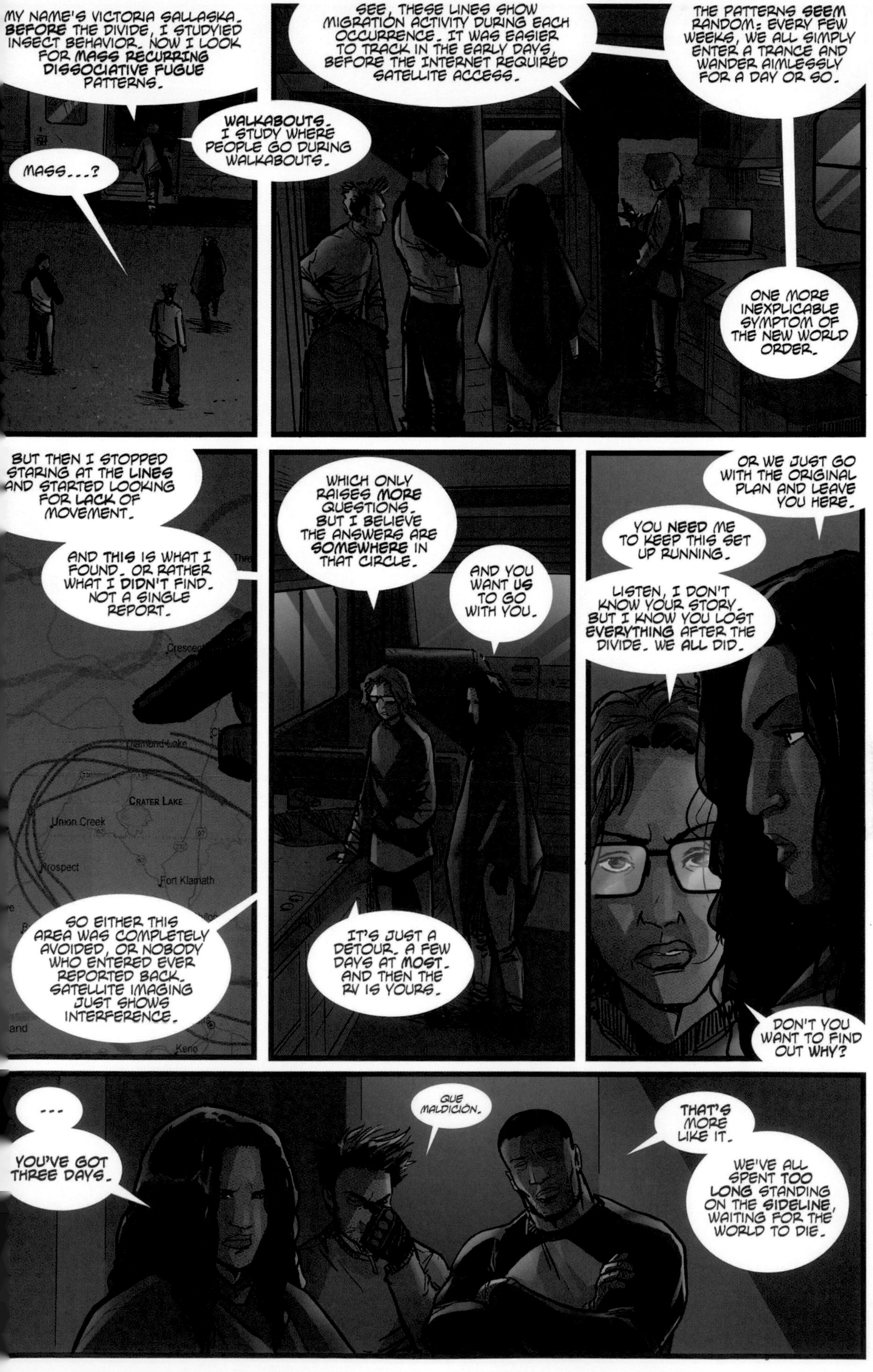
MY NAME'S VICTORIA SALLASKA. BEFORE THE DIVIDE, I STUDYIED INSECT BEHAVIOR. NOW I LOOK FOR MASS RECURRING DISSOCIATIVE FUGUE PATTERNS.
MASS...?
WALKABOUTS. I STUDY WHERE PEOPLE GO DURING WALKABOUTS.
SEE, THESE LINES SHOW MIGRATION ACTIVITY DURING EACH OCCURRENCE. IT WAS EASIER TO TRACK IN THE EARLY DAYS, BEFORE THE INTERNET REQUIRED SATELLITE ACCESS.
THE PATTERNS SEEM RANDOM: EVERY FEW WEEKS, WE ALL SIMPLY ENTER A TRANCE AND WANDER AIMLESSLY FOR A DAY OR SO.
ONE MORE INEXPLICABLE SYMPTOM OF THE NEW WORLD ORDER.
BUT THEN I STOPPED STARING AT THE LINES AND STARTED LOOKING FOR LACK OF MOVEMENT.
AND THIS IS WHAT I FOUND. OR RATHER WHAT I DIDN'T FIND. NOT A SINGLE REPORT.
Crater Lake
Union Creek
Prospect
Fort Klamath
Diamond Lake
Keno
SO EITHER THIS AREA WAS COMPLETELY AVOIDED, OR NOBODY WHO ENTERED EVER REPORTED BACK. SATELLITE IMAGING JUST SHOWS INTERFERENCE.
WHICH ONLY RAISES MORE QUESTIONS. BUT I BELIEVE THE ANSWERS ARE SOMEWHERE IN THAT CIRCLE.
AND YOU WANT US TO GO WITH YOU.
IT'S JUST A DETOUR. A FEW DAYS AT MOST. AND THEN THE RV IS YOURS.
OR WE JUST GO WITH THE ORIGINAL PLAN AND LEAVE YOU HERE.
YOU NEED ME TO KEEP THIS SET UP RUNNING.
LISTEN, I DON'T KNOW YOUR STORY. BUT I KNOW YOU LOST EVERYTHING AFTER THE DIVIDE. WE ALL DID.
DON'T YOU WANT TO FIND OUT WHY?
...
YOU'VE GOT THREE DAYS.
QUE MALDICIÓN.
THAT'S MORE LIKE IT.
WE'VE ALL SPENT TOO LONG STANDING ON THE SIDELINE, WAITING FOR THE WORLD TO DIE.

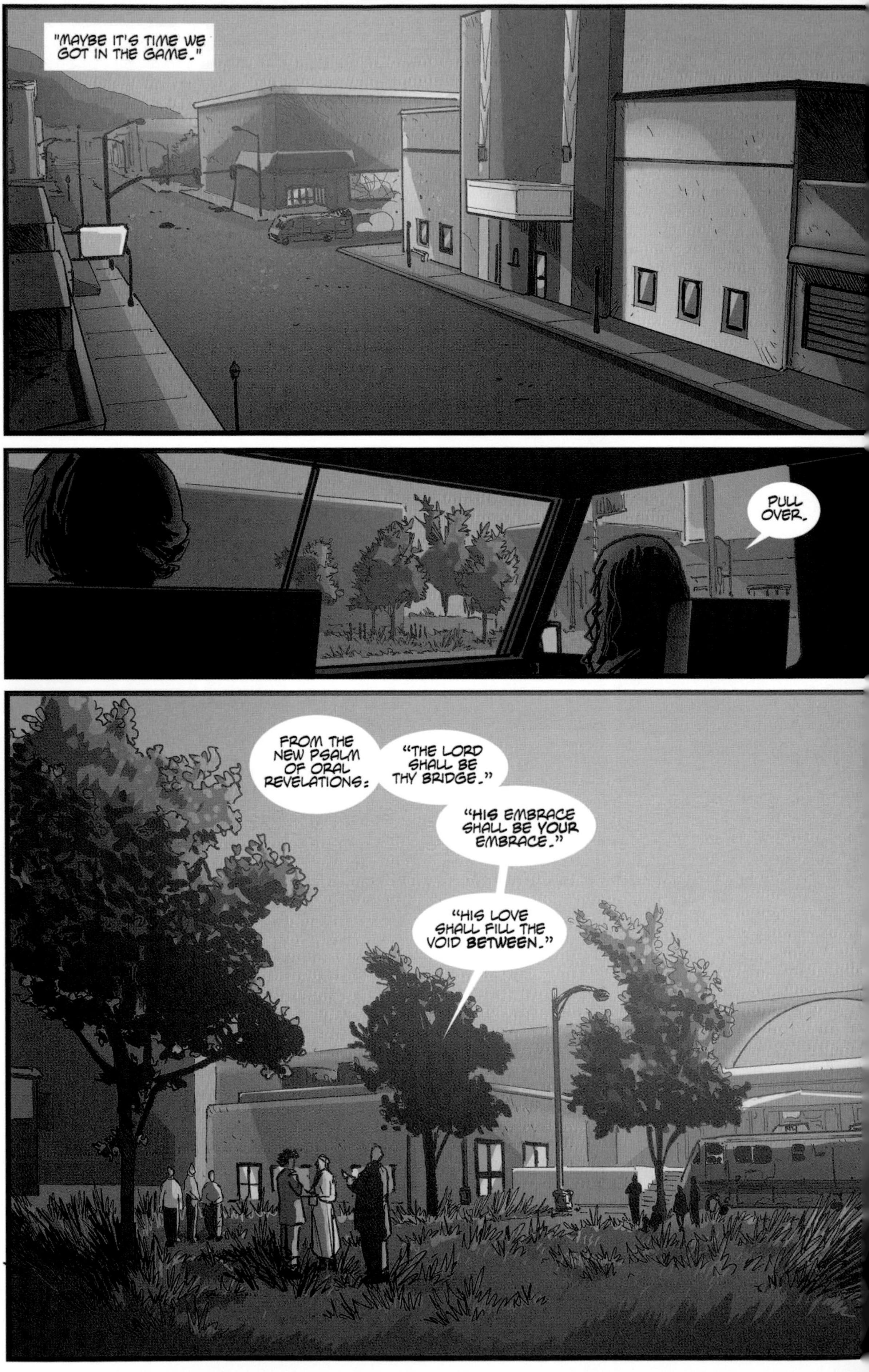
"MAYBE IT'S TIME WE GOT IN THE GAME."
PULL OVER.
FROM THE NEW PSALM OF ORAL REVELATIONS:
"THE LORD SHALL BE THY BRIDGE."
"HIS EMBRACE SHALL BE YOUR EMBRACE."
"HIS LOVE SHALL FILL THE VOID BETWEEN."

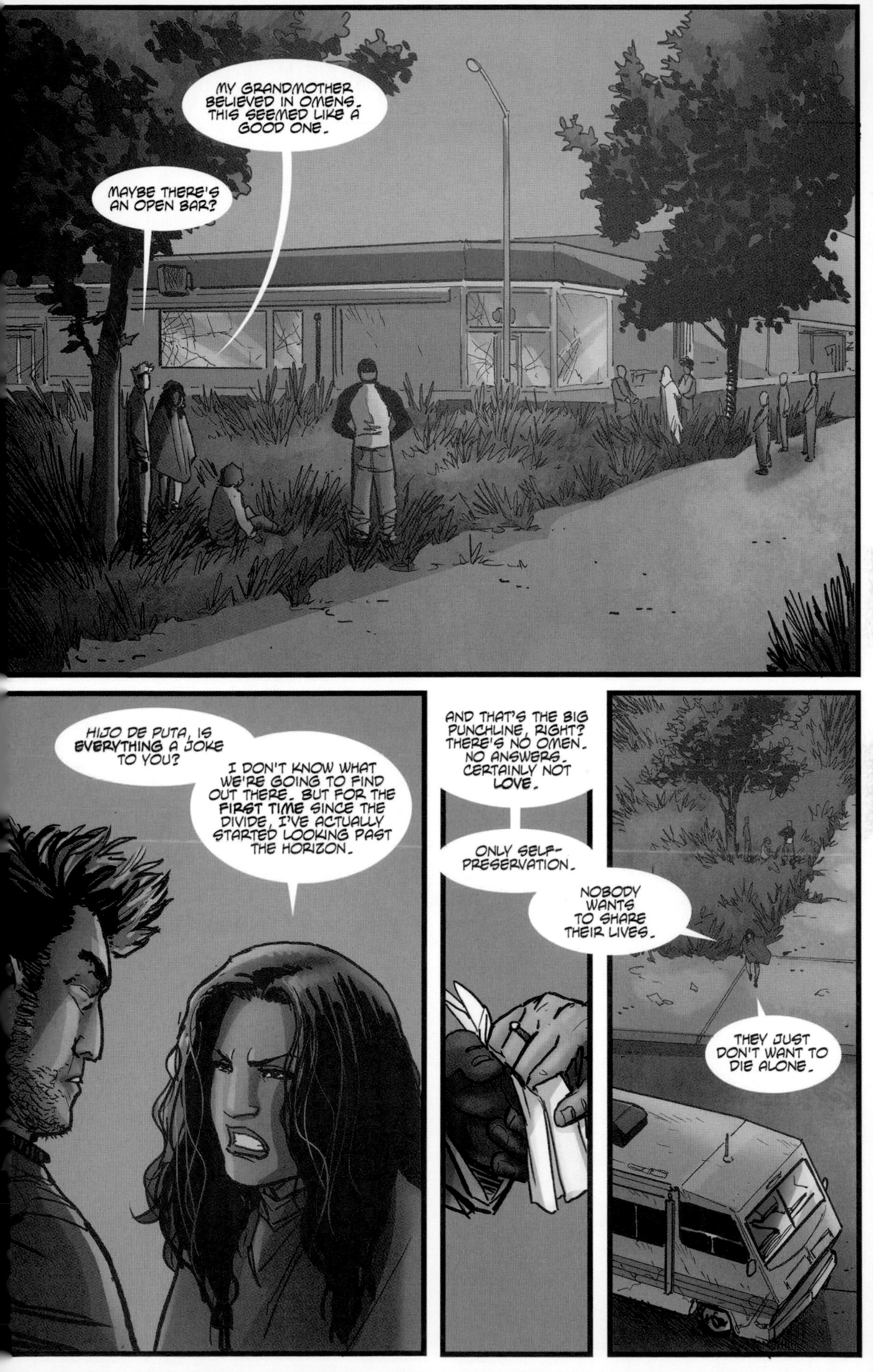
MAYBE THERE'S AN OPEN BAR?
MY GRANDMOTHER BELIEVED IN OMENS. THIS SEEMED LIKE A GOOD ONE.
HIJO DE PUTA, IS EVERYTHING A JOKE TO YOU?
I DON'T KNOW WHAT WE'RE GOING TO FIND OUT THERE. BUT FOR THE FIRST TIME SINCE THE DIVIDE, I'VE ACTUALLY STARTED LOOKING PAST THE HORIZON.
AND THAT'S THE BIG PUNCHLINE, RIGHT? THERE'S NO OMEN. NO ANSWERS. CERTAINLY NOT LOVE.
ONLY SELF-PRESERVATION.
NOBODY WANTS TO SHARE THEIR LIVES.
THEY JUST DON'T WANT TO DIE ALONE.

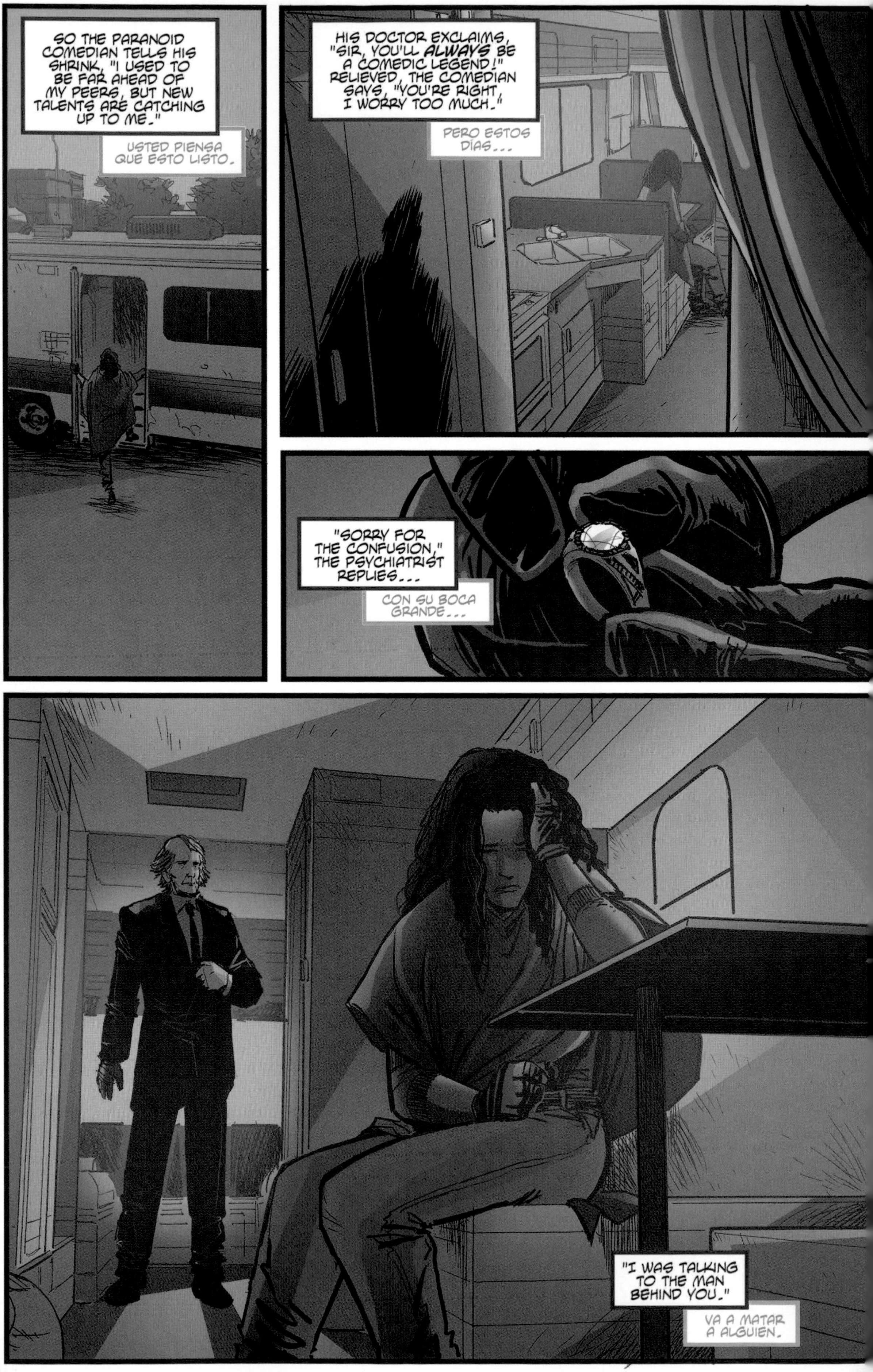
SO THE PARANOID COMEDIAN TELLS HIS SHRINK, "I USED TO BE FAR AHEAD OF MY PEERS, BUT NEW TALENTS ARE CATCHING UP TO ME."
USTED PIENSA QUE ESTO LISTO.
HIS DOCTOR EXCLAIMS, "SIR, YOU'LL ALWAYS BE A COMEDIC LEGEND!" RELIEVED, THE COMEDIAN SAYS, "YOU'RE RIGHT, I WORRY TOO MUCH."
PERO ESTOS DÍAS...
"SORRY FOR THE CONFUSION," THE PSYCHIATRIST REPLIES...
CON SU BOCA GRANDE...
"I WAS TALKING TO THE MAN BEHIND YOU."
VA A MATAR A ALGUIEN.

CLASSIFIED

SECURITY LEVEL:
DOUBLE BLACK

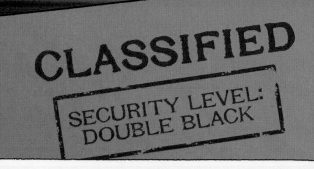

TelChan v0.78, Cpu Cycles: 3000, Frameskip 0, IRC restricted_research.gov

23:02:44 * VLS has joined the group. Security clearance confirmed. GPS link engaged.

23:02:49 <VLS> So how was everyone's day?

23:03:13 <ALG> Just crunching some new data from the last walkabout. Processing is a chore on solar, but I found a Lost DVD box set for my laptop while I wait.

23:03:20 <VLS> It turns out they're all at church.

23:03:26 <ALG> Spoilers!

23:03:46 <VLS> Sorry, but I wasn't really interested in your day. I just wanted someone to ask about MINE so I could say I've been hijacked by thieves.

23:03:54 <JCK> Jesus. You okay?

23:04:16 <VLS> I'm fine. We sort of made a truce. But I watend to touch base with everyone while one of them was driving.

23:04:29 <ALG> Your truce includes chauffeur service?

23:04:39 <VLS> My "truce" is that they're going to ditch me in Seattle.
But first, we're going to save the world.

23:04:56 <JCK> The city's still population controlled. My office is in a free zone, though, so you can stay with me. And maybe discuss your messiah complex.

23:04:39 <VLS> Very funny. Although I do think one of my companions could use your help. I get the impression his rider isn't playing nice.

23:05:04 <JCK> Identity erosion varies wildly between patients, but if there's a power struggle in his head, the situation could escalate. Be careful, Vic

23:05:51 <VLS> I always am. In fact, I'm about to carefully yank Big Brother's GPS unit out of the SatCom. Because I'm on to something big here, Josiah. And I don't know if the military's really been sitting hebind the wheel this whole time like the conspiracy theorists say.

23:06:08 <VLS> But just in case, I have no intention of handing them a roadmap.

23:07:01 * !ERROR! VLS GPS not found !ERROR!

23:07:09 * VLS has left the group.

For the desk of
Gen. Canter

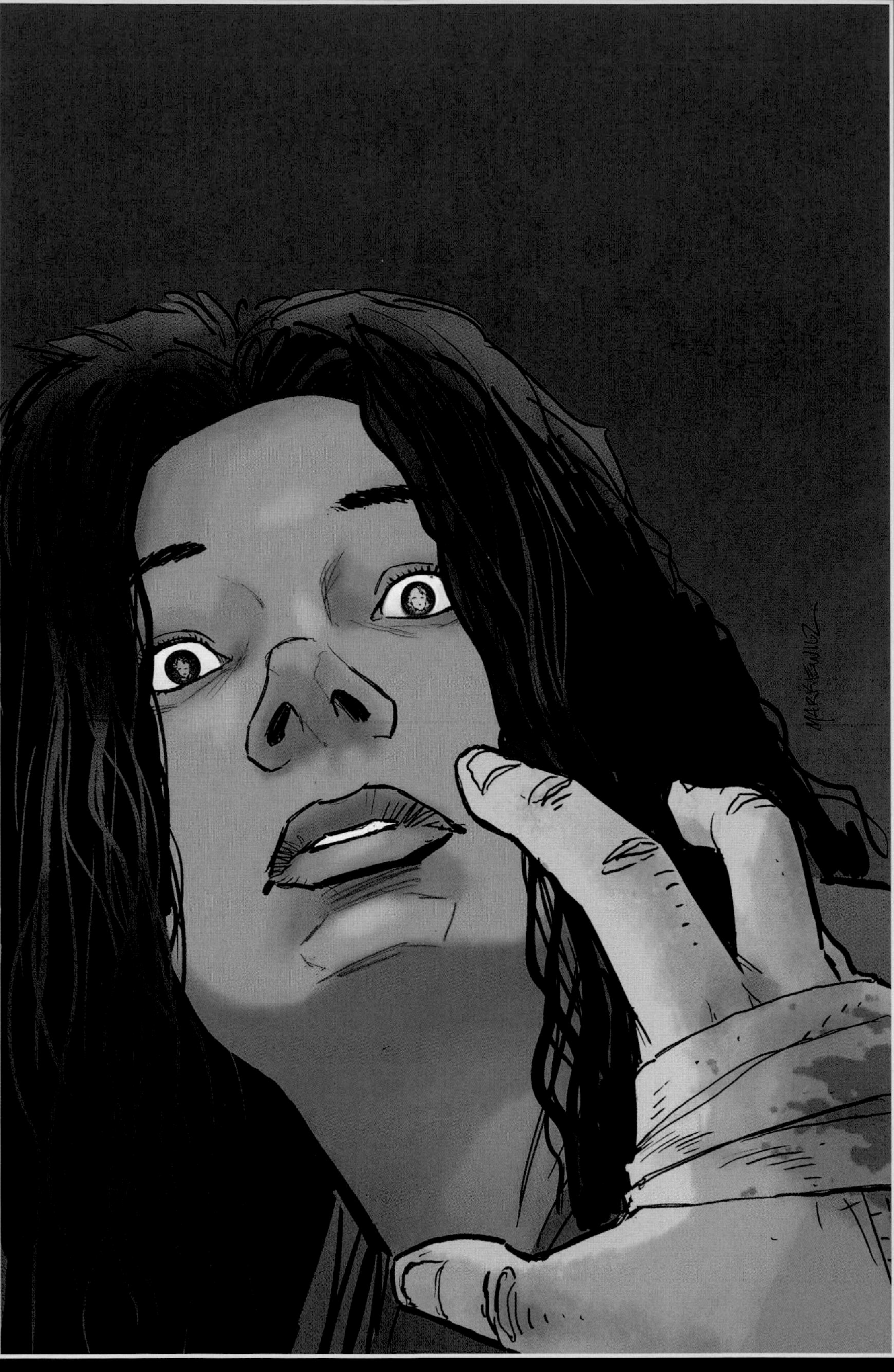

ISSUE FOUR
COVER ART BY ADAM MARKIEWICZ
COLORS BY MELANIE DARLING

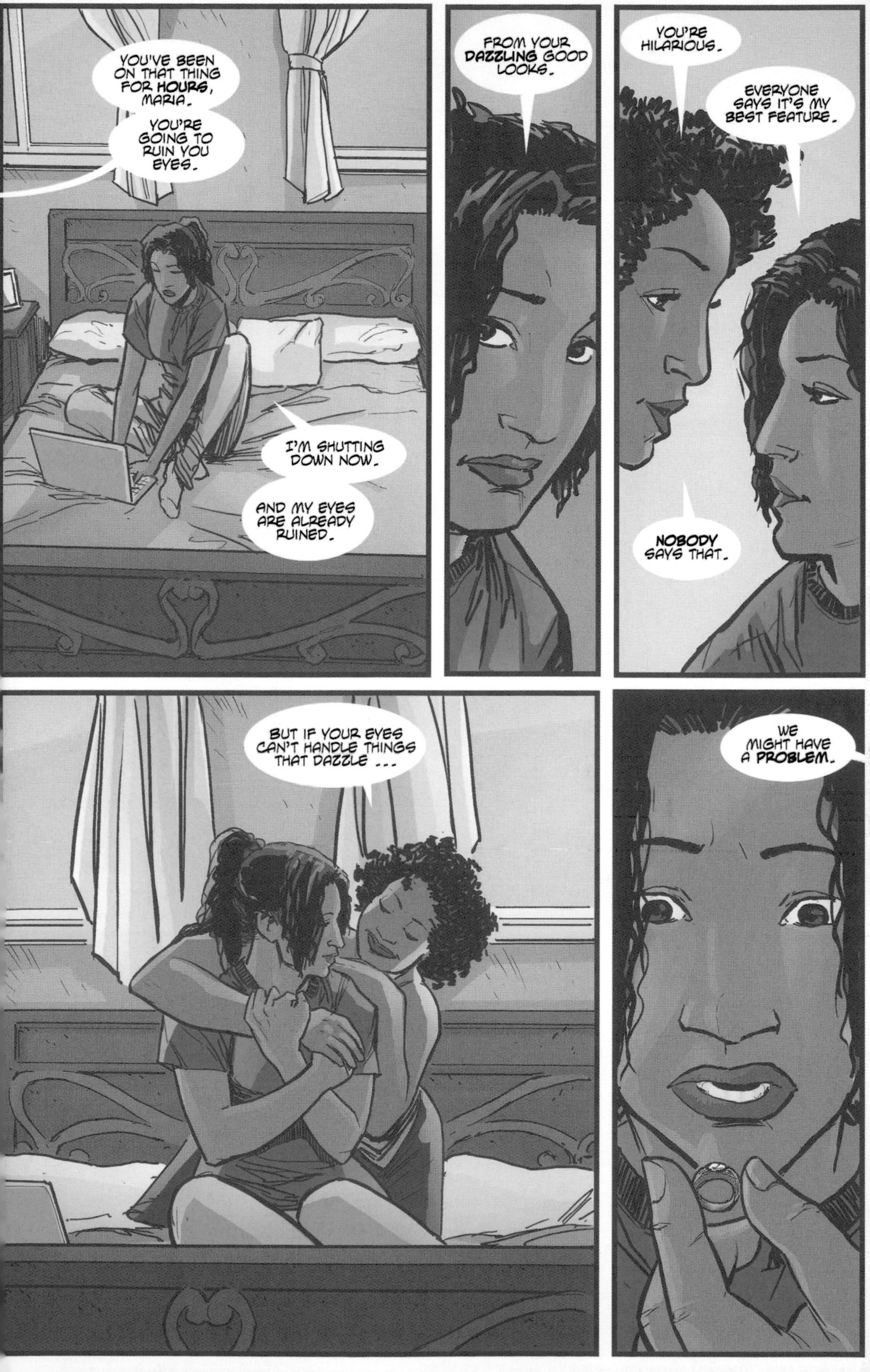
YOU'VE BEEN ON THAT THING FOR **HOURS**, MARIA.
YOU'RE GOING TO RUIN YOU EYES.
I'M SHUTTING DOWN NOW.
AND MY EYES ARE ALREADY RUINED.
FROM YOUR **DAZZLING** GOOD LOOKS.
YOU'RE HILARIOUS.
EVERYONE SAYS IT'S MY BEST FEATURE.
NOBODY SAYS THAT.
BUT IF YOUR EYES CAN'T HANDLE THINGS THAT DAZZLE ...
WE MIGHT HAVE A **PROBLEM**.

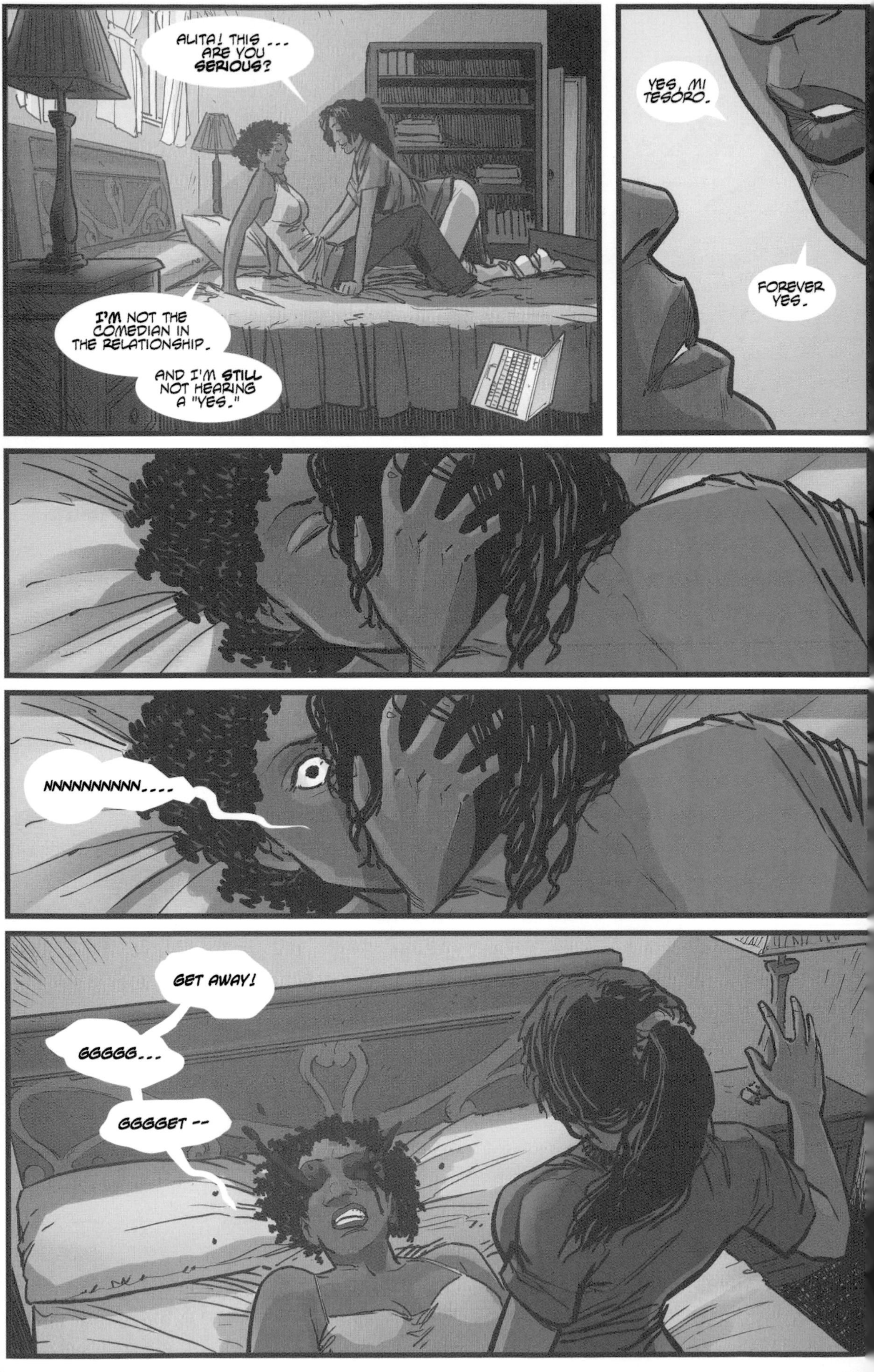
ALITA! THIS ... ARE YOU SERIOUS?
I'M NOT THE COMEDIAN IN THE RELATIONSHIP.
AND I'M STILL NOT HEARING A "YES."
YES, MI TESORO.
FOREVER YES.
NNNNNNNNNN....
GET AWAY!
GGGGG...
GGGGET --

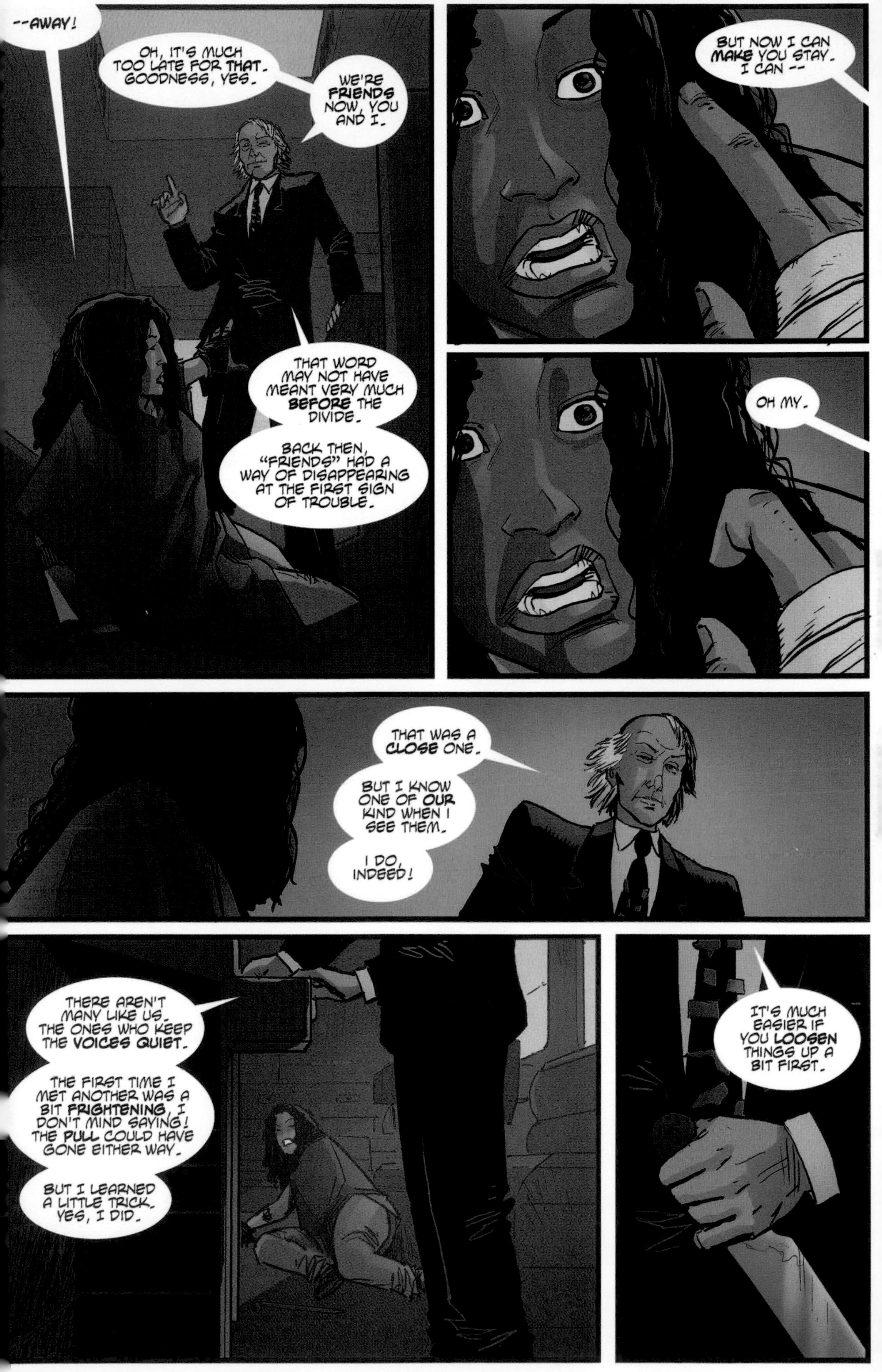
--AWAY!
OH, IT'S MUCH TOO LATE FOR THAT. GOODNESS, YES.
WE'RE FRIENDS NOW, YOU AND I.
THAT WORD MAY NOT HAVE MEANT VERY MUCH BEFORE THE DIVIDE.
BACK THEN, "FRIENDS" HAD A WAY OF DISAPPEARING AT THE FIRST SIGN OF TROUBLE.
BUT NOW I CAN MAKE YOU STAY. I CAN --
OH MY.
THAT WAS A CLOSE ONE.
BUT I KNOW ONE OF OUR KIND WHEN I SEE THEM.
I DO, INDEED!
THERE AREN'T MANY LIKE US. THE ONES WHO KEEP THE VOICES QUIET.
THE FIRST TIME I MET ANOTHER WAS A BIT FRIGHTENING, I DON'T MIND SAYING! THE PULL COULD HAVE GONE EITHER WAY.
BUT I LEARNED A LITTLE TRICK. YES, I DID.
IT'S MUCH EASIER IF YOU LOOSEN THINGS UP A BIT FIRST.

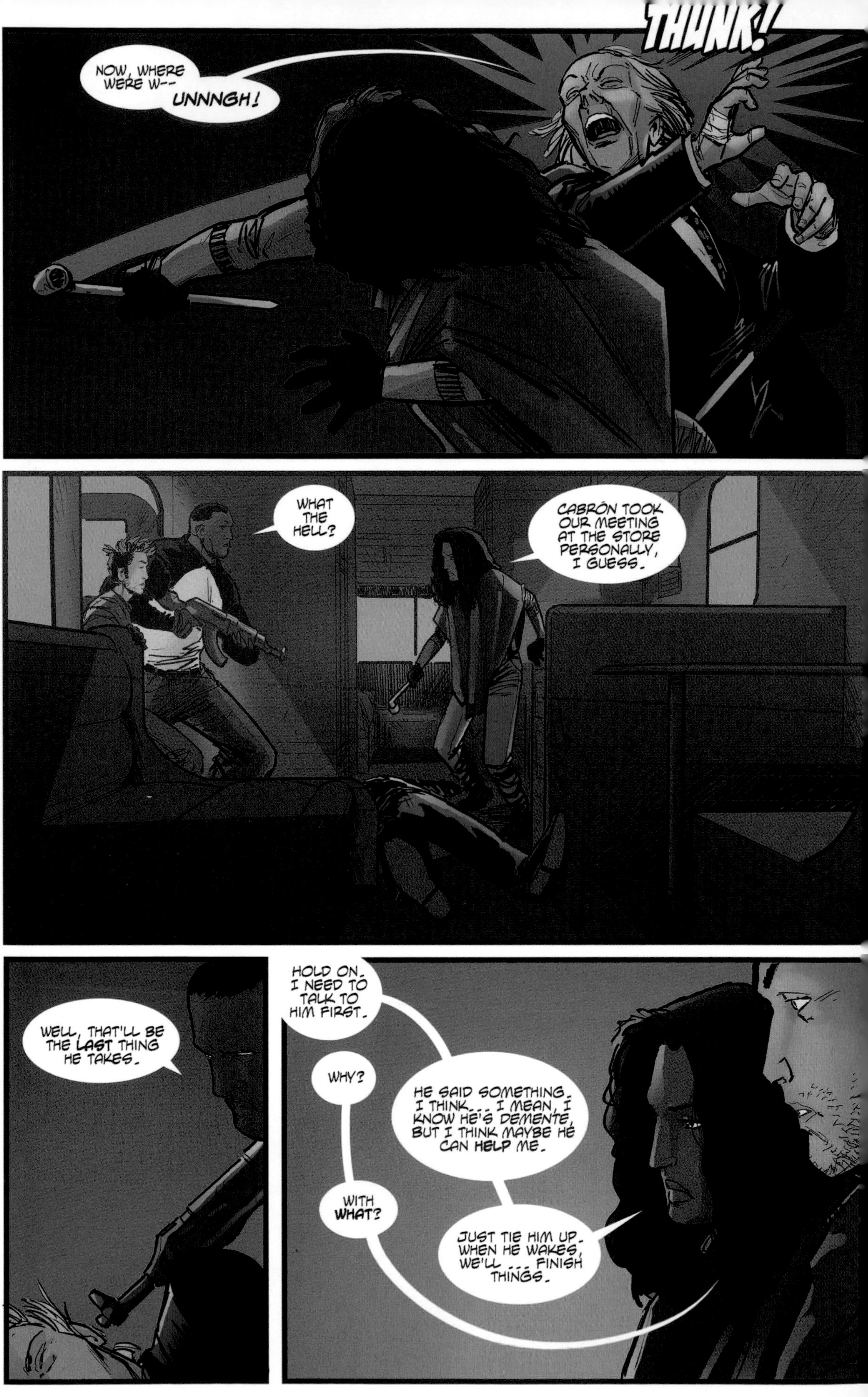
THUNK!
NOW, WHERE WERE W-- UNNNGH!
WHAT THE HELL?
CABRÓN TOOK OUR MEETING AT THE STORE PERSONALLY, I GUESS.
WELL, THAT'LL BE THE **LAST** THING HE TAKES.
HOLD ON. I NEED TO TALK TO HIM FIRST.
WHY?
HE SAID SOMETHING. I THINK... I MEAN, I KNOW HE'S DEMENTE, BUT I THINK MAYBE HE CAN **HELP** ME.
WITH **WHAT?**
JUST TIE HIM UP. WHEN HE WAKES, WE'LL ... FINISH THINGS.

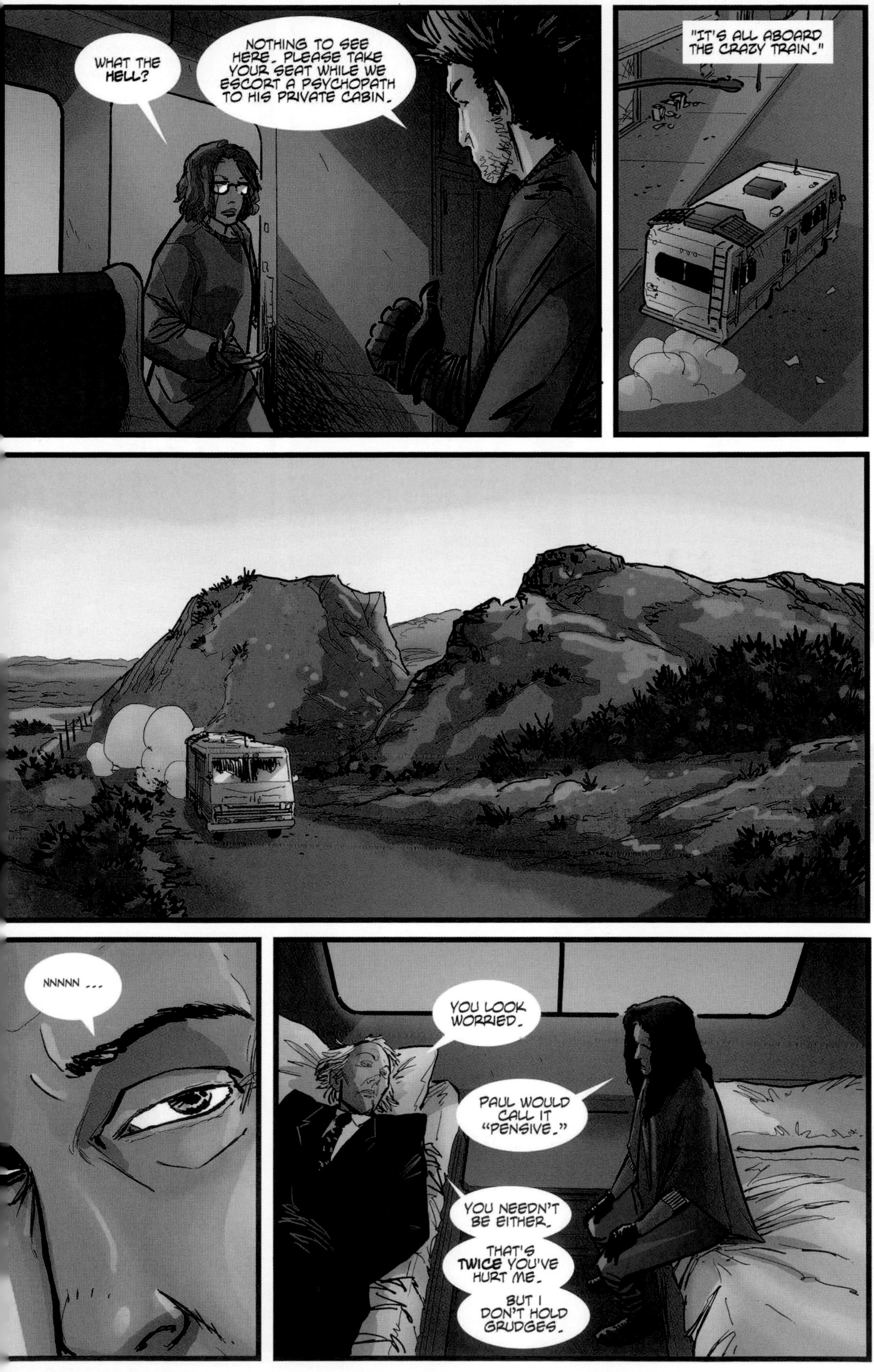
WHAT THE HELL?
NOTHING TO SEE HERE. PLEASE TAKE YOUR SEAT WHILE WE ESCORT A PSYCHOPATH TO HIS PRIVATE CABIN.
"IT'S ALL ABOARD THE CRAZY TRAIN."
NNNNN ...
YOU LOOK WORRIED.
PAUL WOULD CALL IT "PENSIVE."
YOU NEEDN'T BE EITHER.
THAT'S TWICE YOU'VE HURT ME.
BUT I DON'T HOLD GRUDGES.

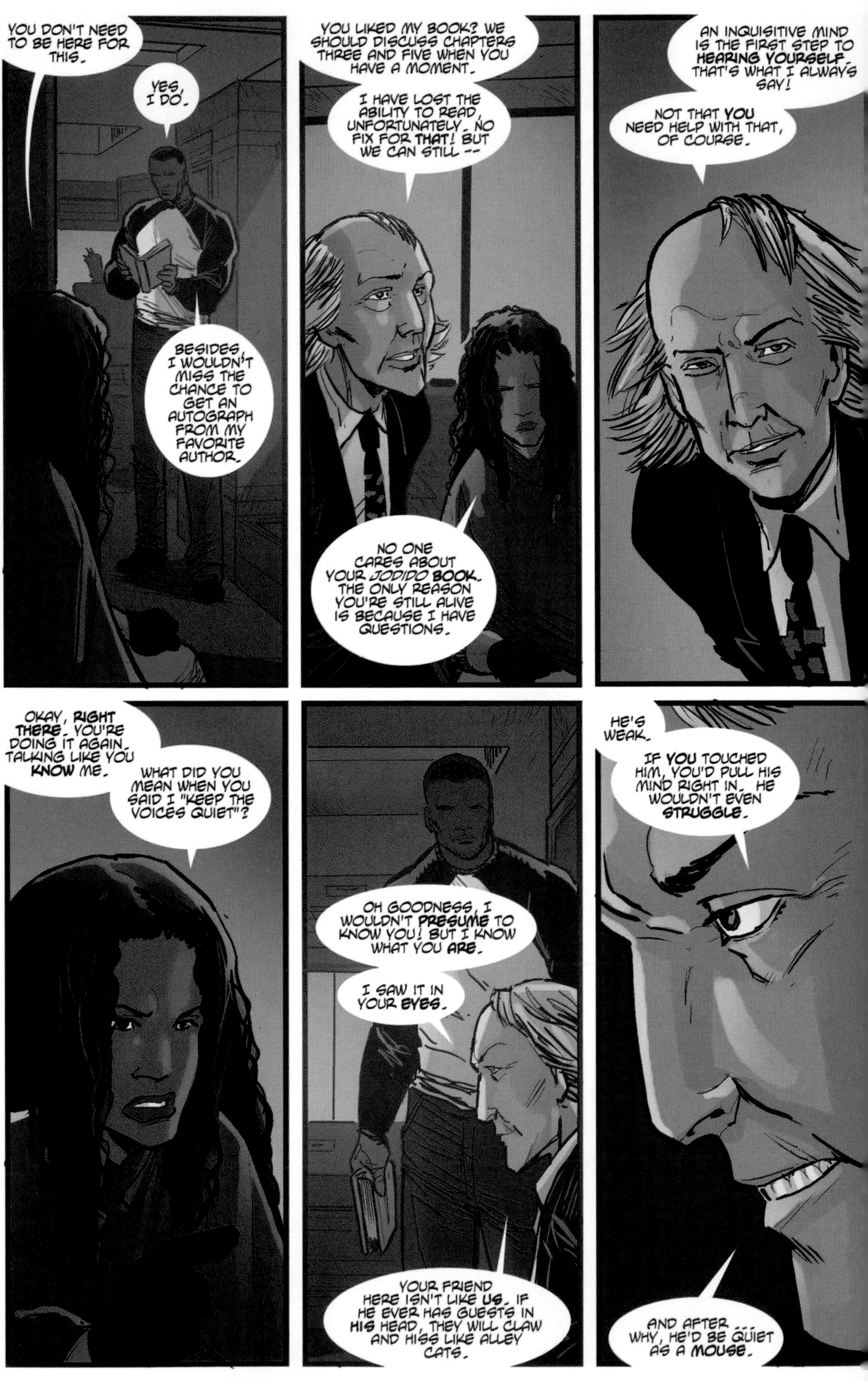
YOU DON'T NEED TO BE HERE FOR THIS.
YES, I DO.
BESIDES, I WOULDN'T MISS THE CHANCE TO GET AN AUTOGRAPH FROM MY FAVORITE AUTHOR.
YOU LIKED MY BOOK? WE SHOULD DISCUSS CHAPTERS THREE AND FIVE WHEN YOU HAVE A MOMENT.
I HAVE LOST THE ABILITY TO READ, UNFORTUNATELY. NO FIX FOR THAT! BUT WE CAN STILL --
NO ONE CARES ABOUT YOUR JODIDO BOOK. THE ONLY REASON YOU'RE STILL ALIVE IS BECAUSE I HAVE QUESTIONS.
AN INQUISITIVE MIND IS THE FIRST STEP TO HEARING YOURSELF. THAT'S WHAT I ALWAYS SAY!
NOT THAT YOU NEED HELP WITH THAT, OF COURSE.
OKAY, RIGHT THERE. YOU'RE DOING IT AGAIN. TALKING LIKE YOU KNOW ME.
WHAT DID YOU MEAN WHEN YOU SAID I "KEEP THE VOICES QUIET"?
OH GOODNESS, I WOULDN'T PRESUME TO KNOW YOU! BUT I KNOW WHAT YOU ARE.
I SAW IT IN YOUR EYES.
YOUR FRIEND HERE ISN'T LIKE US. IF HE EVER HAS GUESTS IN HIS HEAD, THEY WILL CLAW AND HISS LIKE ALLEY CATS.
HE'S WEAK.
IF YOU TOUCHED HIM, YOU'D PULL HIS MIND RIGHT IN. HE WOULDN'T EVEN STRUGGLE.
AND AFTER... WHY, HE'D BE QUIET AS A MOUSE.

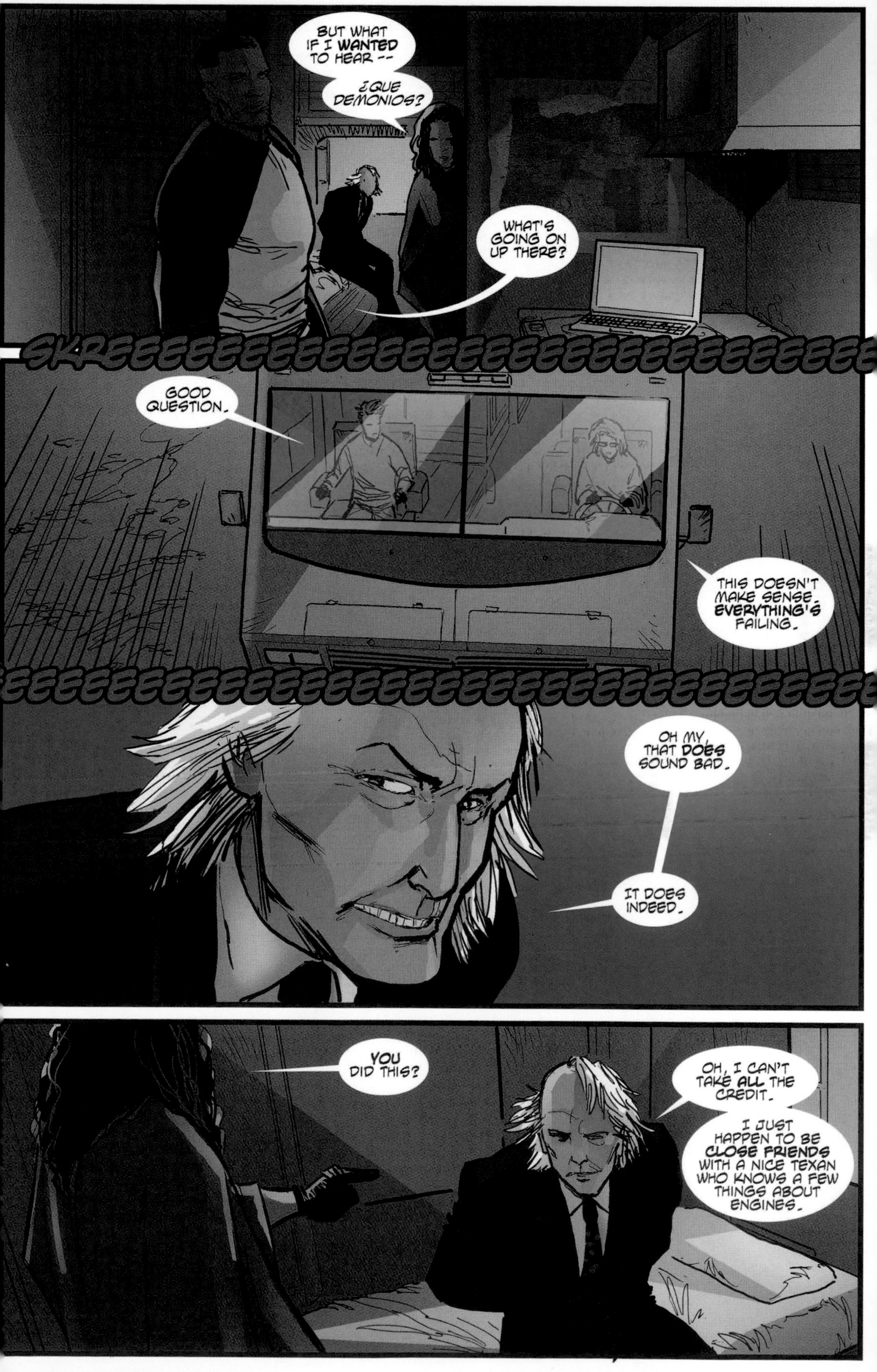
BUT WHAT IF I WANTED TO HEAR --
¿QUE DEMONIOS?
WHAT'S GOING ON UP THERE?
SKREEEEEEEEEEEEEEEEEEEEEEEEEEEEEEEEEEEEEEEEEEEEEEEEEEEEEEEEEEEEEEEEEE
GOOD QUESTION.
THIS DOESN'T MAKE SENSE. EVERYTHING'S FAILING.
OH MY, THAT DOES SOUND BAD.
IT DOES INDEED.
YOU DID THIS?
OH, I CAN'T TAKE ALL THE CREDIT.
I JUST HAPPEN TO BE CLOSE FRIENDS WITH A NICE TEXAN WHO KNOWS A FEW THINGS ABOUT ENGINES.

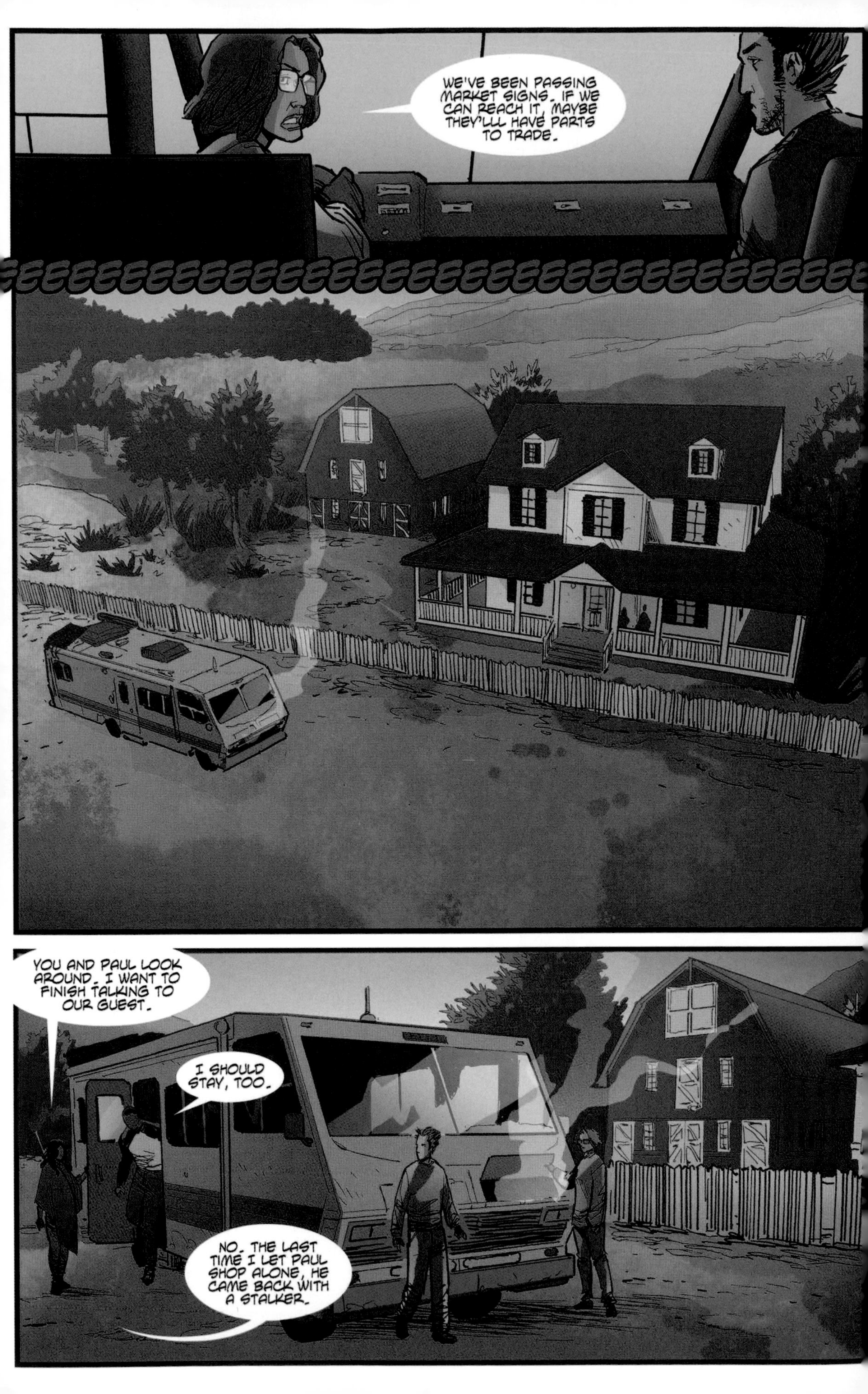
WE'VE BEEN PASSING MARKET SIGNS. IF WE CAN REACH IT, MAYBE THEY'LLL HAVE PARTS TO TRADE.
EEEEEEEEEEEEEEEEEEEEEEEEEEEEEEEEEEEEEEEEE
YOU AND PAUL LOOK AROUND. I WANT TO FINISH TALKING TO OUR GUEST.
I SHOULD STAY, TOO.
NO. THE LAST TIME I LET PAUL SHOP ALONE, HE CAME BACK WITH A STALKER.

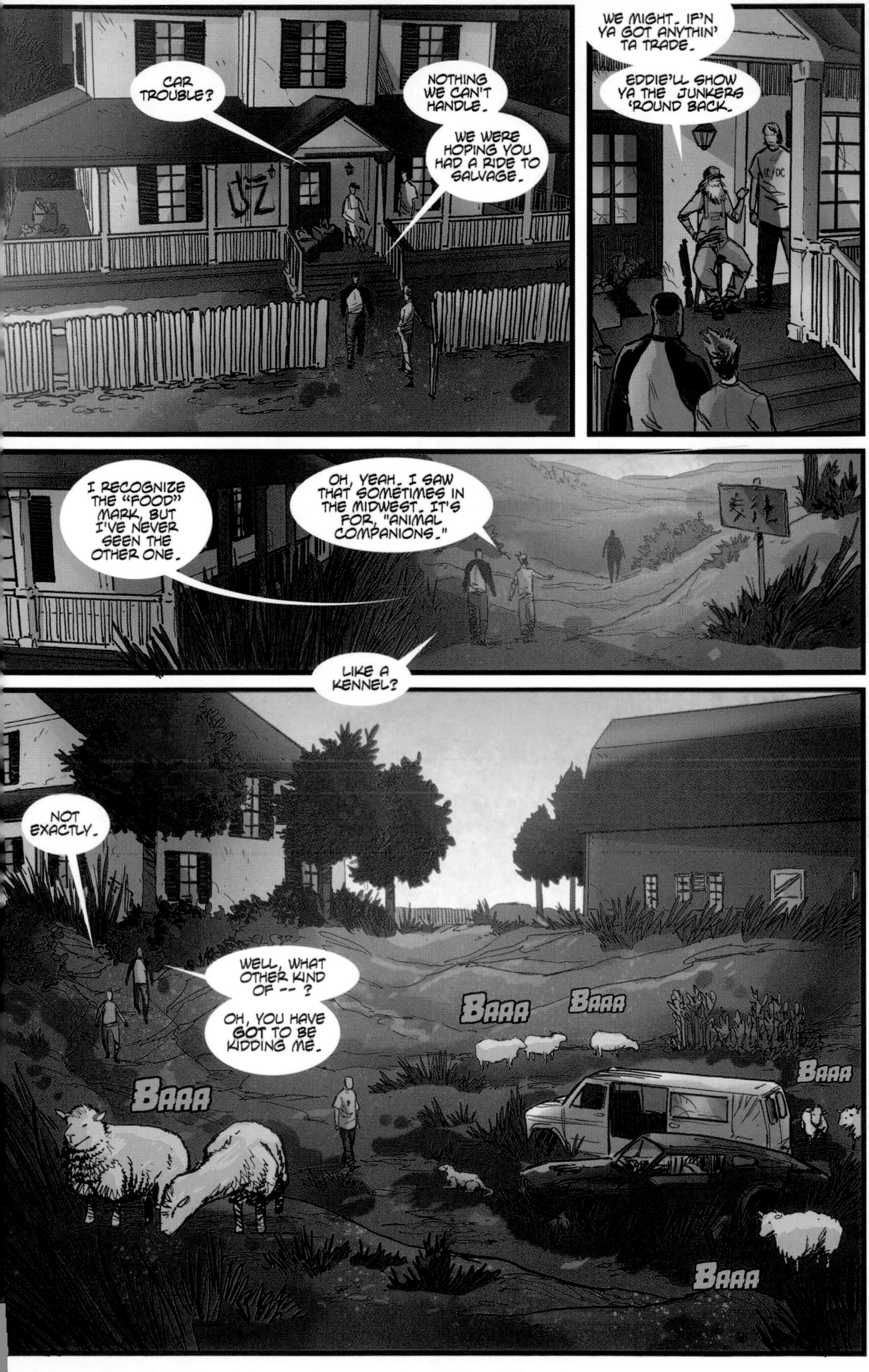
CAR TROUBLE?
NOTHING WE CAN'T HANDLE.
WE WERE HOPING YOU HAD A RIDE TO SALVAGE.
WE MIGHT. IF'N YA GOT ANYTHIN' TA TRADE.
EDDIE'LL SHOW YA THE JUNKERS 'ROUND BACK.
I RECOGNIZE THE "FOOD" MARK, BUT I'VE NEVER SEEN THE OTHER ONE.
OH, YEAH. I SAW THAT SOMETIMES IN THE MIDWEST. IT'S FOR, "ANIMAL COMPANIONS."
LIKE A KENNEL?
NOT EXACTLY.
WELL, WHAT OTHER KIND OF -- ?
OH, YOU HAVE GOT TO BE KIDDING ME.
BAAA
BAAA
BAAA
BAAA
BAAA

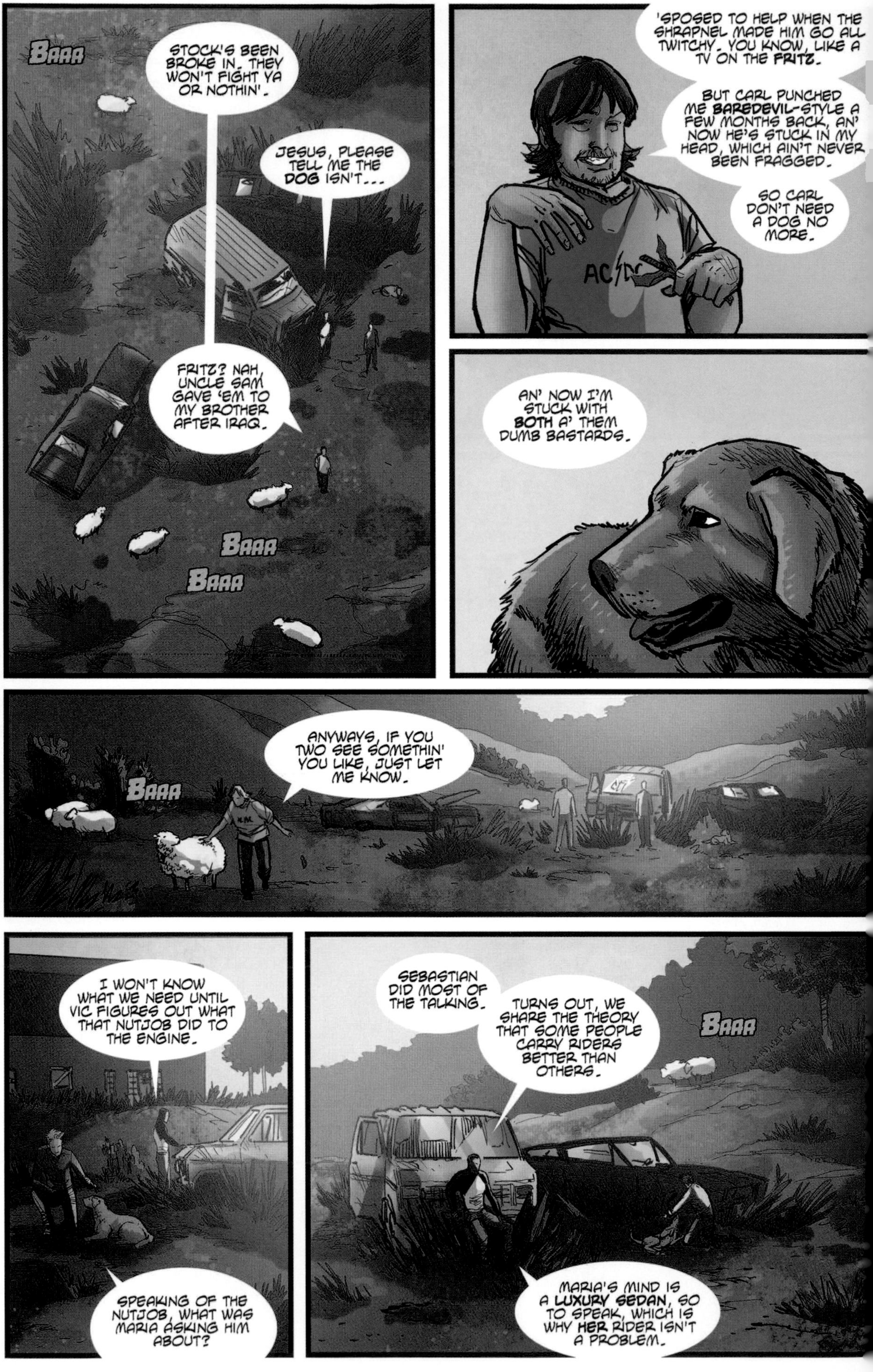
BAAA
STOCK'S BEEN BROKE IN. THEY WON'T FIGHT YA OR NOTHIN'.
JESUS, PLEASE TELL ME THE DOG ISN'T...
FRITZ? NAH, UNCLE SAM GAVE 'EM TO MY BROTHER AFTER IRAQ.
BAAA
BAAA
'SPOSED TO HELP WHEN THE SHRAPNEL MADE HIM GO ALL TWITCHY. YOU KNOW, LIKE A TV ON THE FRITZ.
BUT CARL PUNCHED ME BAREDEVIL-STYLE A FEW MONTHS BACK, AN' NOW HE'S STUCK IN MY HEAD, WHICH AIN'T NEVER BEEN FRAGGED.
SO CARL DON'T NEED A DOG NO MORE.
AC/DC
AN' NOW I'M STUCK WITH BOTH A' THEM DUMB BASTARDS.
BAAA
ANYWAYS, IF YOU TWO SEE SOMETHIN' YOU LIKE, JUST LET ME KNOW.
I WON'T KNOW WHAT WE NEED UNTIL VIC FIGURES OUT WHAT THAT NUTJOB DID TO THE ENGINE.
SPEAKING OF THE NUTJOB, WHAT WAS MARIA ASKING HIM ABOUT?
SEBASTIAN DID MOST OF THE TALKING.
TURNS OUT, WE SHARE THE THEORY THAT SOME PEOPLE CARRY RIDERS BETTER THAN OTHERS.
BAAA
MARIA'S MIND IS A LUXURY SEDAN, SO TO SPEAK, WHICH IS WHY HER RIDER ISN'T A PROBLEM.

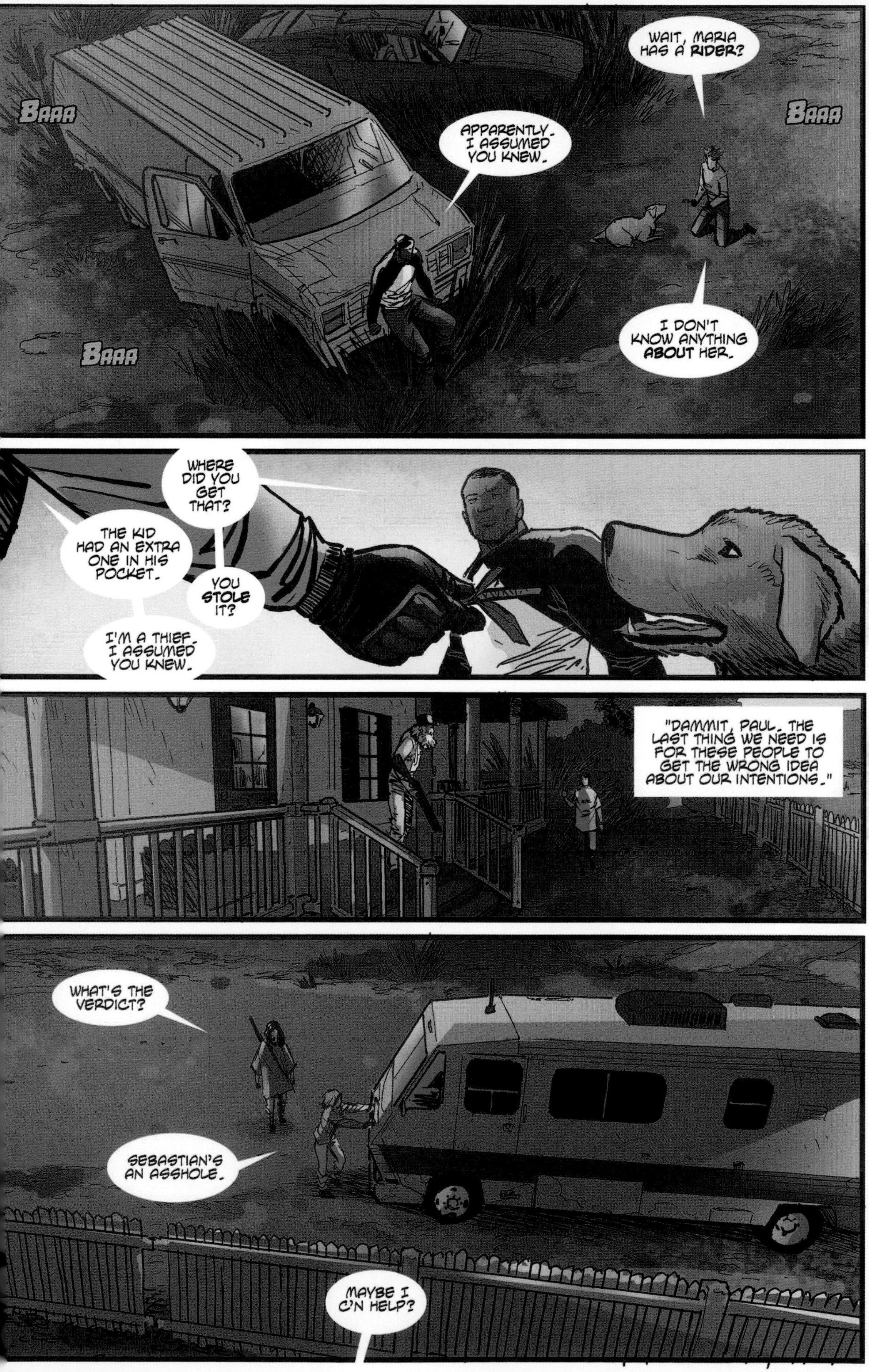
BAAA
WAIT, MARIA HAS A RIDER?
BAAA
APPARENTLY. I ASSUMED YOU KNEW.
I DON'T KNOW ANYTHING ABOUT HER.
BAAA
WHERE DID YOU GET THAT?
THE KID HAD AN EXTRA ONE IN HIS POCKET.
YOU STOLE IT?
I'M A THIEF. I ASSUMED YOU KNEW.
"DAMMIT, PAUL. THE LAST THING WE NEED IS FOR THESE PEOPLE TO GET THE WRONG IDEA ABOUT OUR INTENTIONS."
WHAT'S THE VERDICT?
SEBASTIAN'S AN ASSHOLE.
MAYBE I C'N HELP?

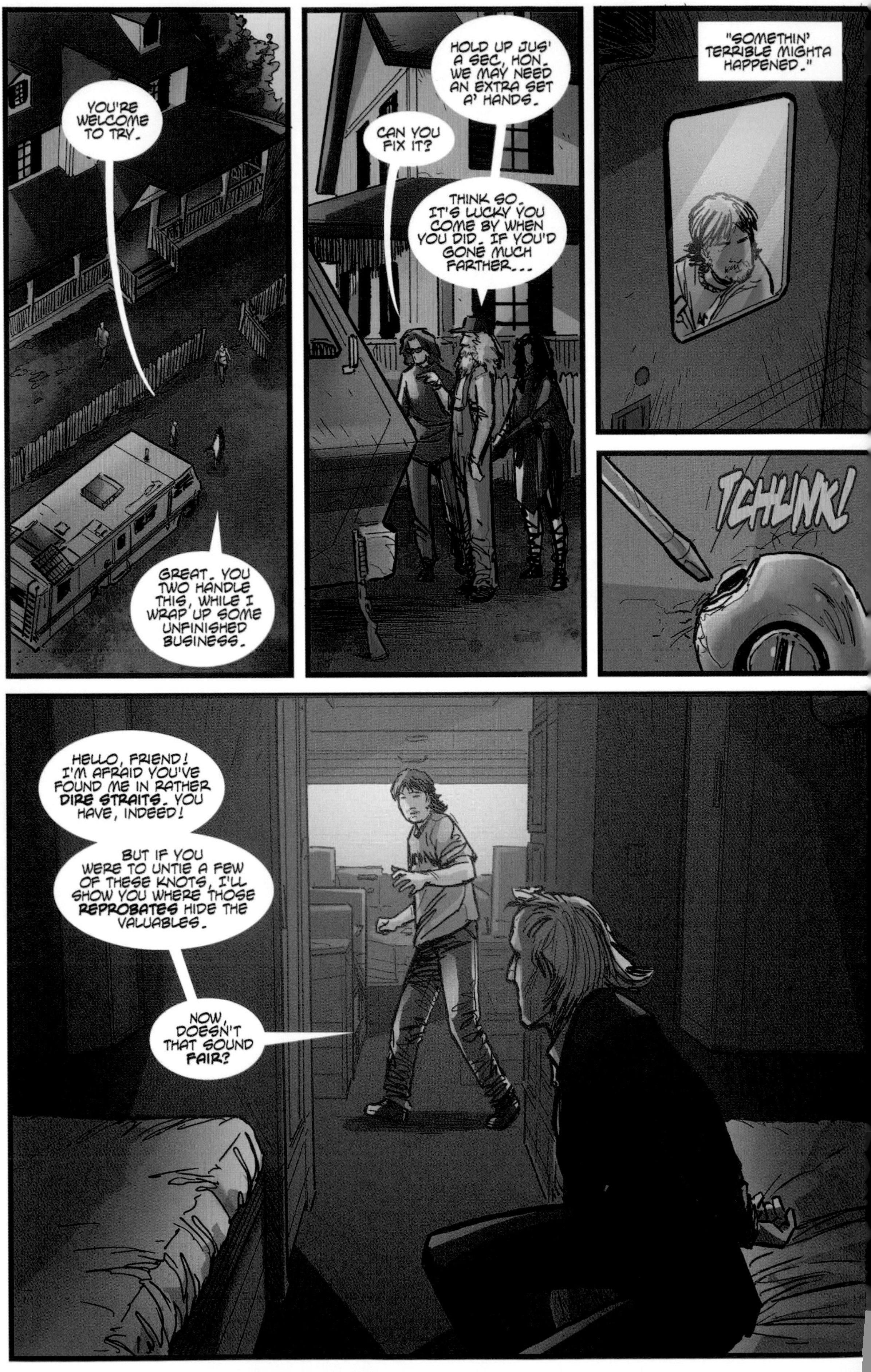
YOU'RE WELCOME TO TRY.
GREAT. YOU TWO HANDLE THIS, WHILE I WRAP UP SOME UNFINISHED BUSINESS.
CAN YOU FIX IT?
HOLD UP JUS' A SEC, HON. WE MAY NEED AN EXTRA SET A' HANDS.
THINK SO. IT'S LUCKY YOU COME BY WHEN YOU DID. IF YOU'D GONE MUCH FARTHER...
"SOMETHIN' TERRIBLE MIGHTA HAPPENED."
TCHLINK!
HELLO, FRIEND! I'M AFRAID YOU'VE FOUND ME IN RATHER DIRE STRAITS. YOU HAVE, INDEED!
BUT IF YOU WERE TO UNTIE A FEW OF THESE KNOTS, I'LL SHOW YOU WHERE THOSE REPROBATES HIDE THE VALUABLES.
NOW, DOESN'T THAT SOUND FAIR?

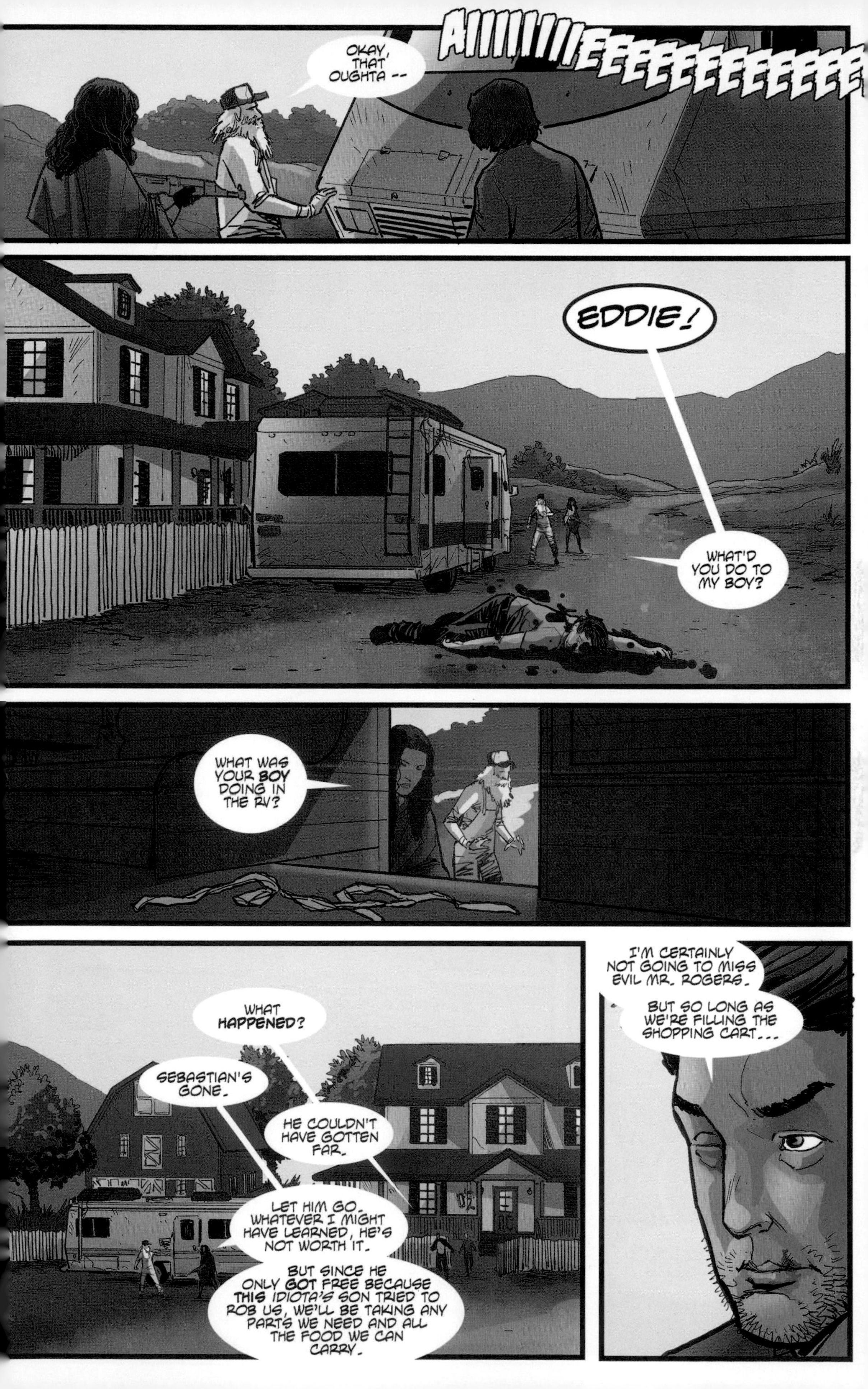

AIIIIIIIEEEEEEEEEEEEEE
OKAY, THAT OUGHTA --
EDDIE!
WHAT'D YOU DO TO MY BOY?
WHAT WAS YOUR BOY DOING IN THE RV?
WHAT HAPPENED?
SEBASTIAN'S GONE.
HE COULDN'T HAVE GOTTEN FAR.
LET HIM GO. WHATEVER I MIGHT HAVE LEARNED, HE'S NOT WORTH IT.
BUT SINCE HE ONLY GOT FREE BECAUSE THIS IDIOTA'S SON TRIED TO ROB US, WE'LL BE TAKING ANY PARTS WE NEED AND ALL THE FOOD WE CAN CARRY.
I'M CERTAINLY NOT GOING TO MISS EVIL MR. ROGERS.
BUT SO LONG AS WE'RE FILLING THE SHOPPING CART...

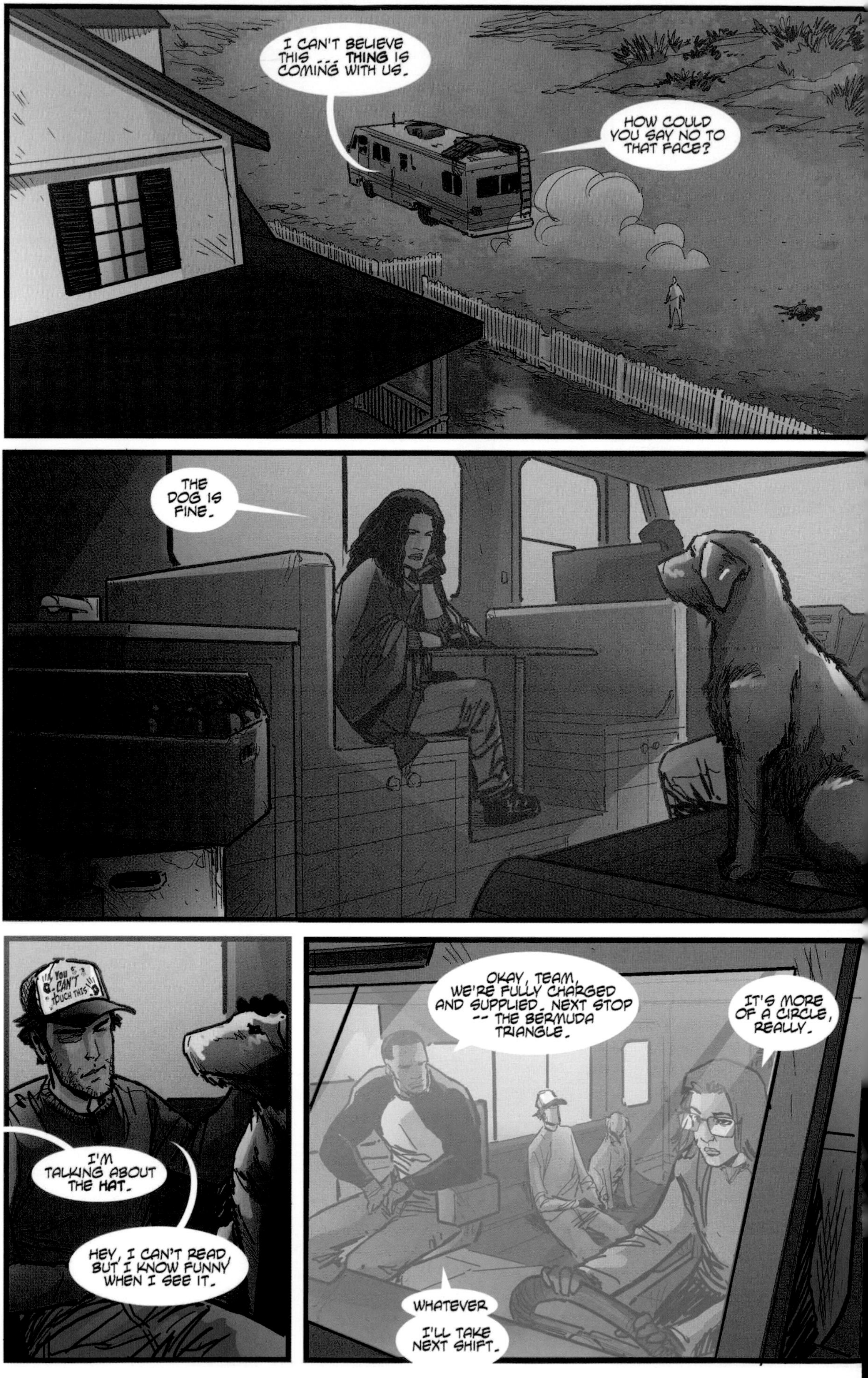
I CAN'T BELIEVE THIS ... THING IS COMING WITH US.
HOW COULD YOU SAY NO TO THAT FACE?
THE DOG IS FINE.
YOU CAN'T TOUCH THIS
I'M TALKING ABOUT THE HAT.
HEY, I CAN'T READ BUT I KNOW FUNNY WHEN I SEE IT.
OKAY, TEAM, WE'RE FULLY CHARGED AND SUPPLIED. NEXT STOP -- THE BERMUDA TRIANGLE.
IT'S MORE OF A CIRCLE, REALLY.
WHATEVER
I'LL TAKE NEXT SHIFT.

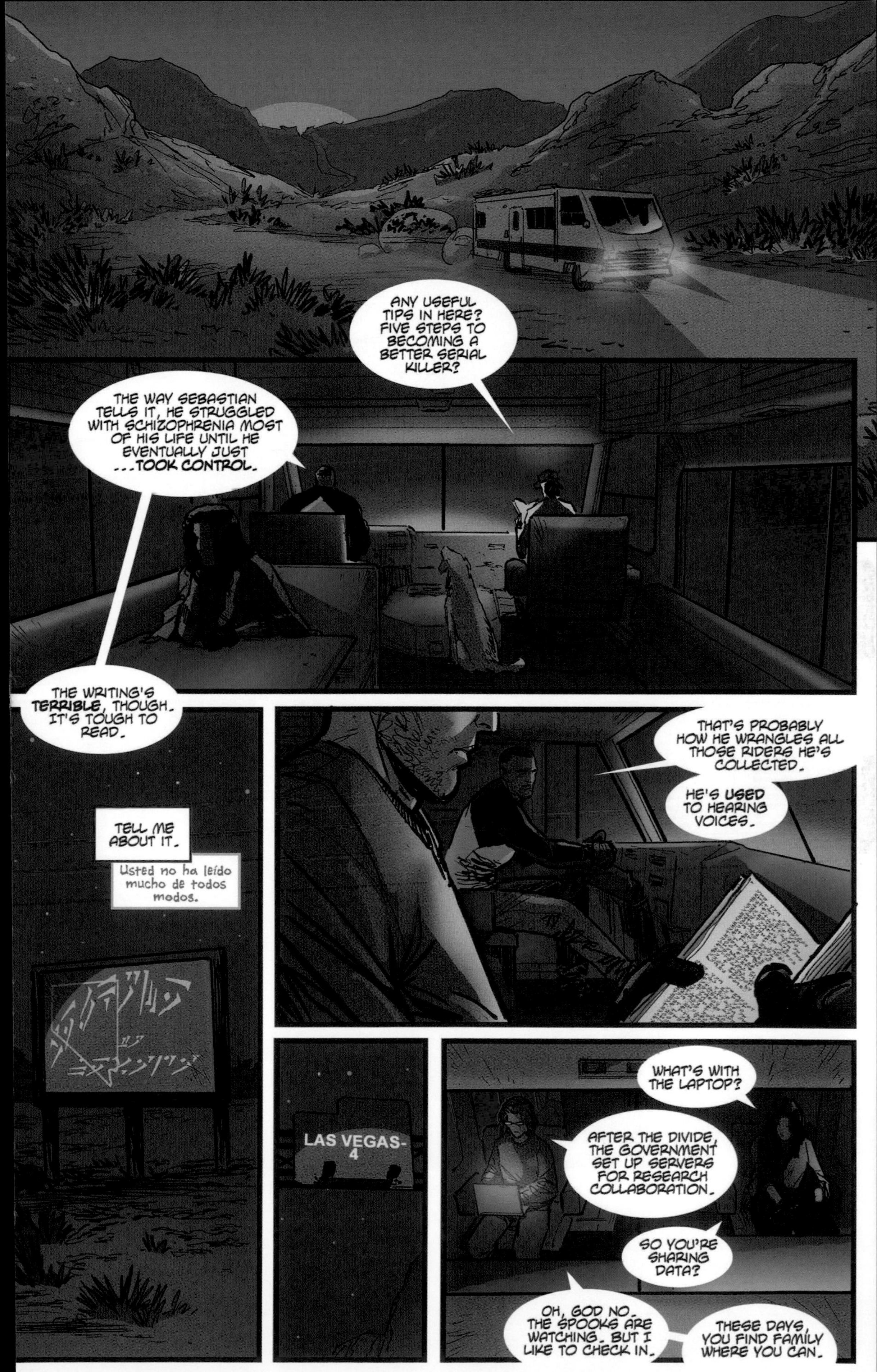
ANY USEFUL TIPS IN HERE? FIVE STEPS TO BECOMING A BETTER SERIAL KILLER?
THE WAY SEBASTIAN TELLS IT, HE STRUGGLED WITH SCHIZOPHRENIA MOST OF HIS LIFE UNTIL HE EVENTUALLY JUST ...TOOK CONTROL.
THE WRITING'S TERRIBLE, THOUGH. IT'S TOUGH TO READ.
TELL ME ABOUT IT.
Usted no ha leído mucho de todos modos.
THAT'S PROBABLY HOW HE WRANGLES ALL THOSE RIDERS HE'S COLLECTED.
HE'S USED TO HEARING VOICES.
LAS VEGAS-
4
WHAT'S WITH THE LAPTOP?
AFTER THE DIVIDE, THE GOVERNMENT SET UP SERVERS FOR RESEARCH COLLABORATION.
SO YOU'RE SHARING DATA?
OH, GOD NO. THE SPOOKS ARE WATCHING. BUT I LIKE TO CHECK IN.
THESE DAYS, YOU FIND FAMILY WHERE YOU CAN.

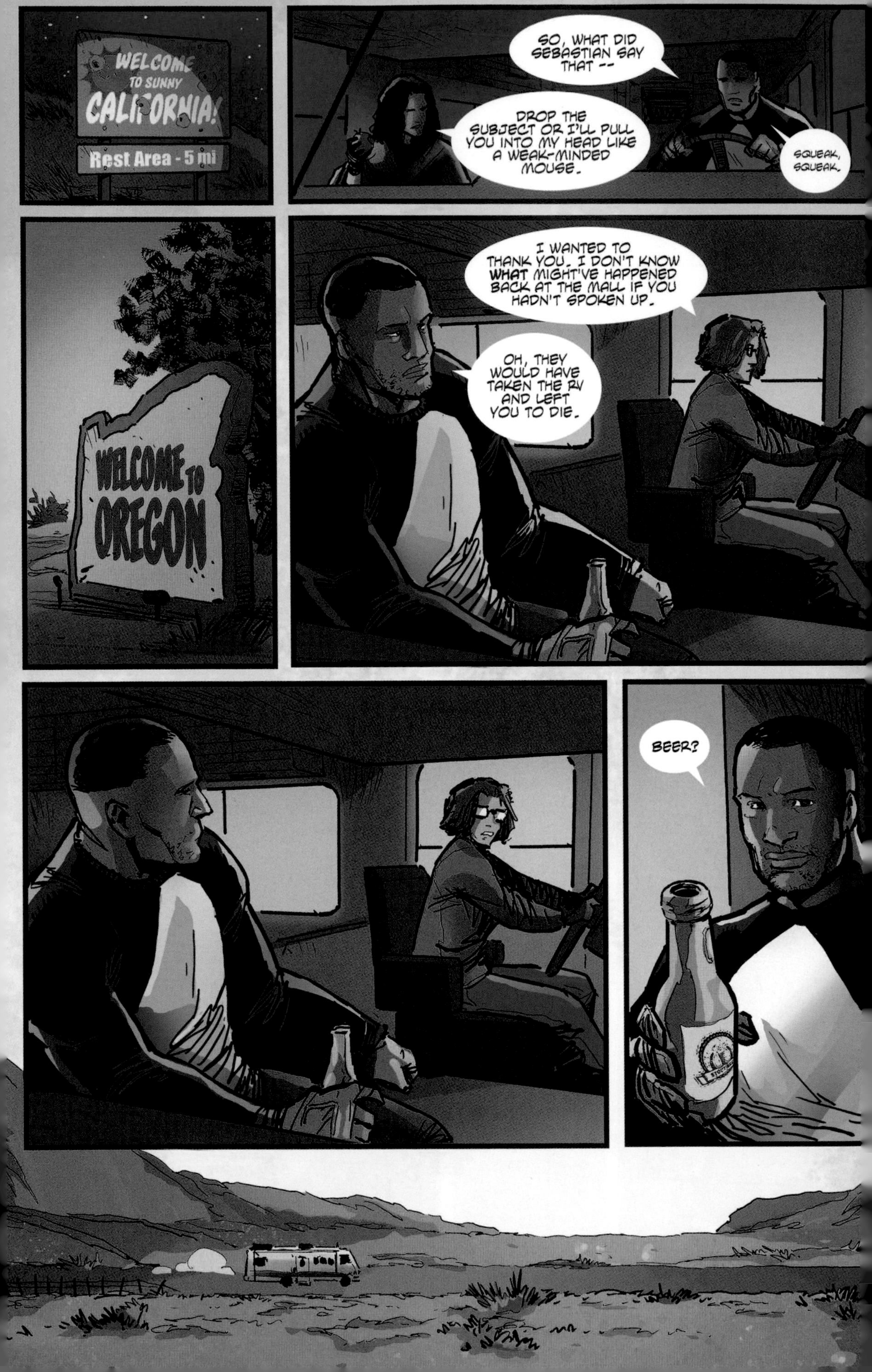
WELCOME TO SUNNY CALIFORNIA!
Rest Area - 5 mi
SO, WHAT DID SEBASTIAN SAY THAT --
DROP THE SUBJECT OR I'LL PULL YOU INTO MY HEAD LIKE A WEAK-MINDED MOUSE.
SQUEAK, SQUEAK.
WELCOME TO OREGON
I WANTED TO THANK YOU. I DON'T KNOW **WHAT** MIGHT'VE HAPPENED BACK AT THE MALL IF YOU HADN'T SPOKEN UP.
OH, THEY WOULD HAVE TAKEN THE RV AND LEFT YOU TO DIE.
BEER?

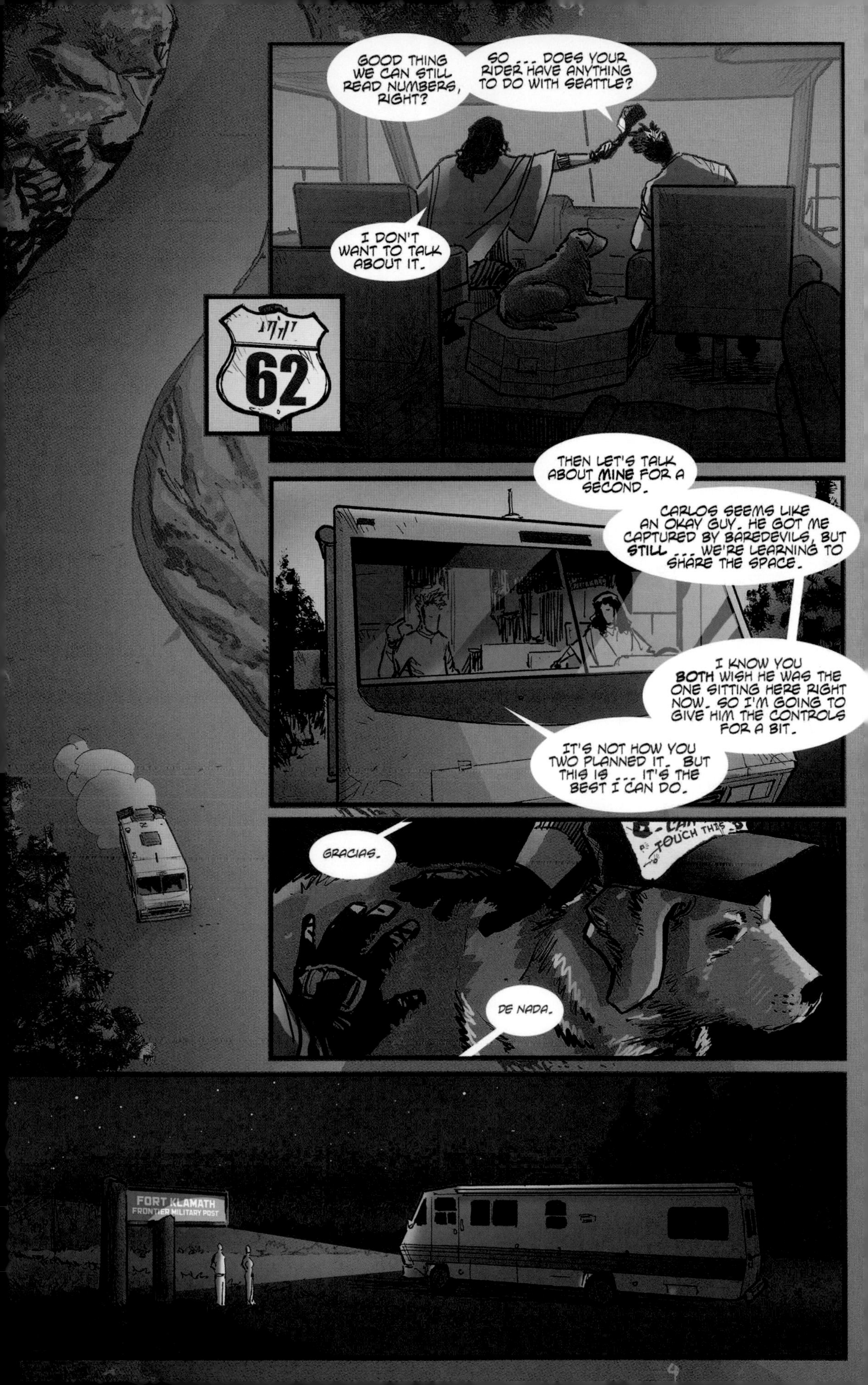
GOOD THING WE CAN STILL READ NUMBERS, RIGHT?
SO ... DOES YOUR RIDER HAVE ANYTHING TO DO WITH SEATTLE?
I DON'T WANT TO TALK ABOUT IT.
62
THEN LET'S TALK ABOUT **MINE** FOR A SECOND.
CARLOS SEEMS LIKE AN OKAY GUY. HE GOT ME CAPTURED BY BAREDEVILS, BUT **STILL** ... WE'RE LEARNING TO SHARE THE SPACE.
I KNOW YOU **BOTH** WISH HE WAS THE ONE SITTING HERE RIGHT NOW. SO I'M GOING TO GIVE HIM THE CONTROLS FOR A BIT.
IT'S NOT HOW YOU TWO PLANNED IT. BUT THIS IS ... IT'S THE BEST I CAN DO.
GRACIAS.
TOUCH THIS
DE NADA.
FORT KLAMATH
FRONTIER MILITARY POST

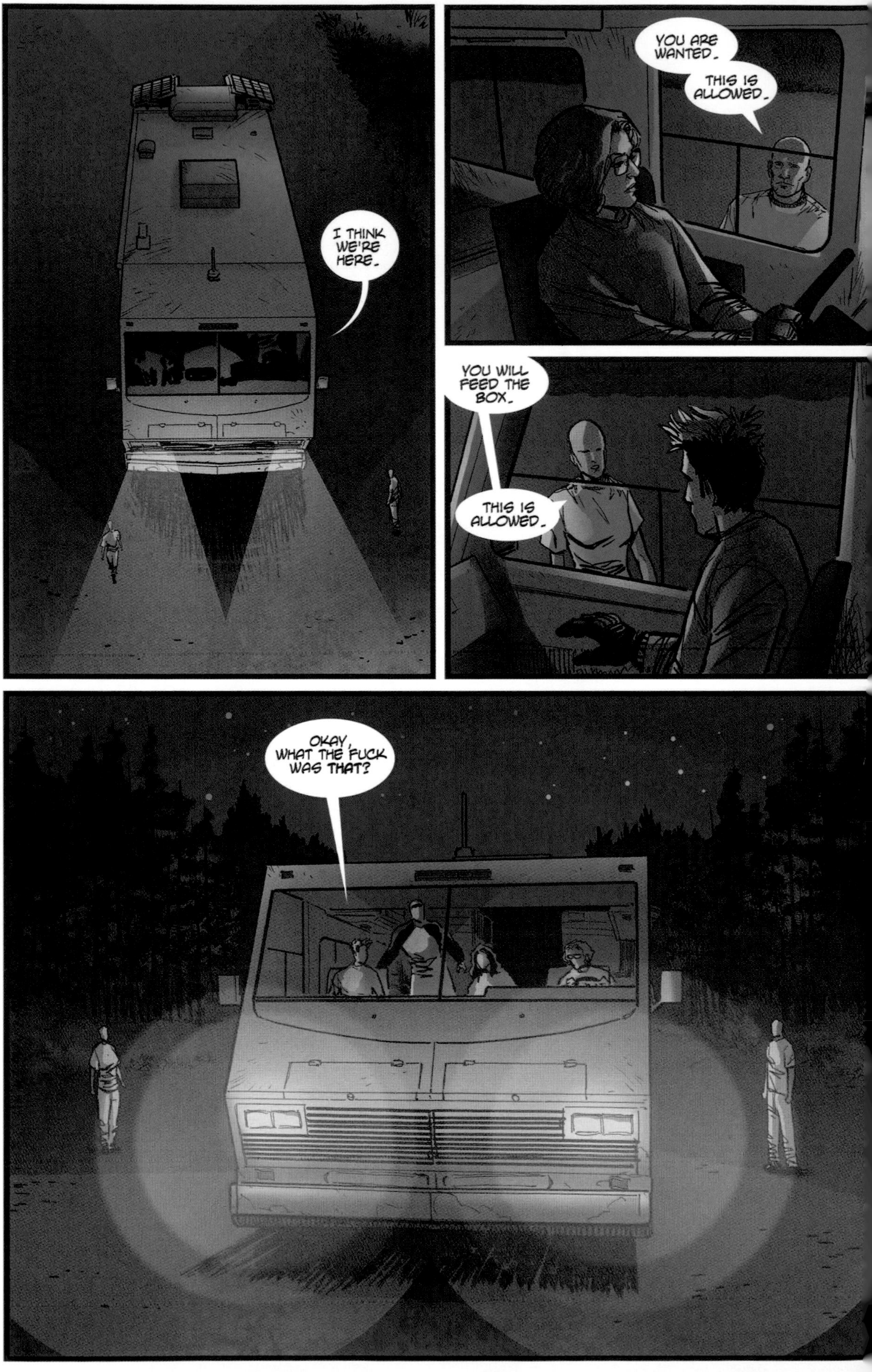
I THINK WE'RE HERE.
YOU ARE WANTED.
THIS IS ALLOWED.
YOU WILL FEED THE BOX.
THIS IS ALLOWED.
OKAY, WHAT THE FUCK WAS THAT?

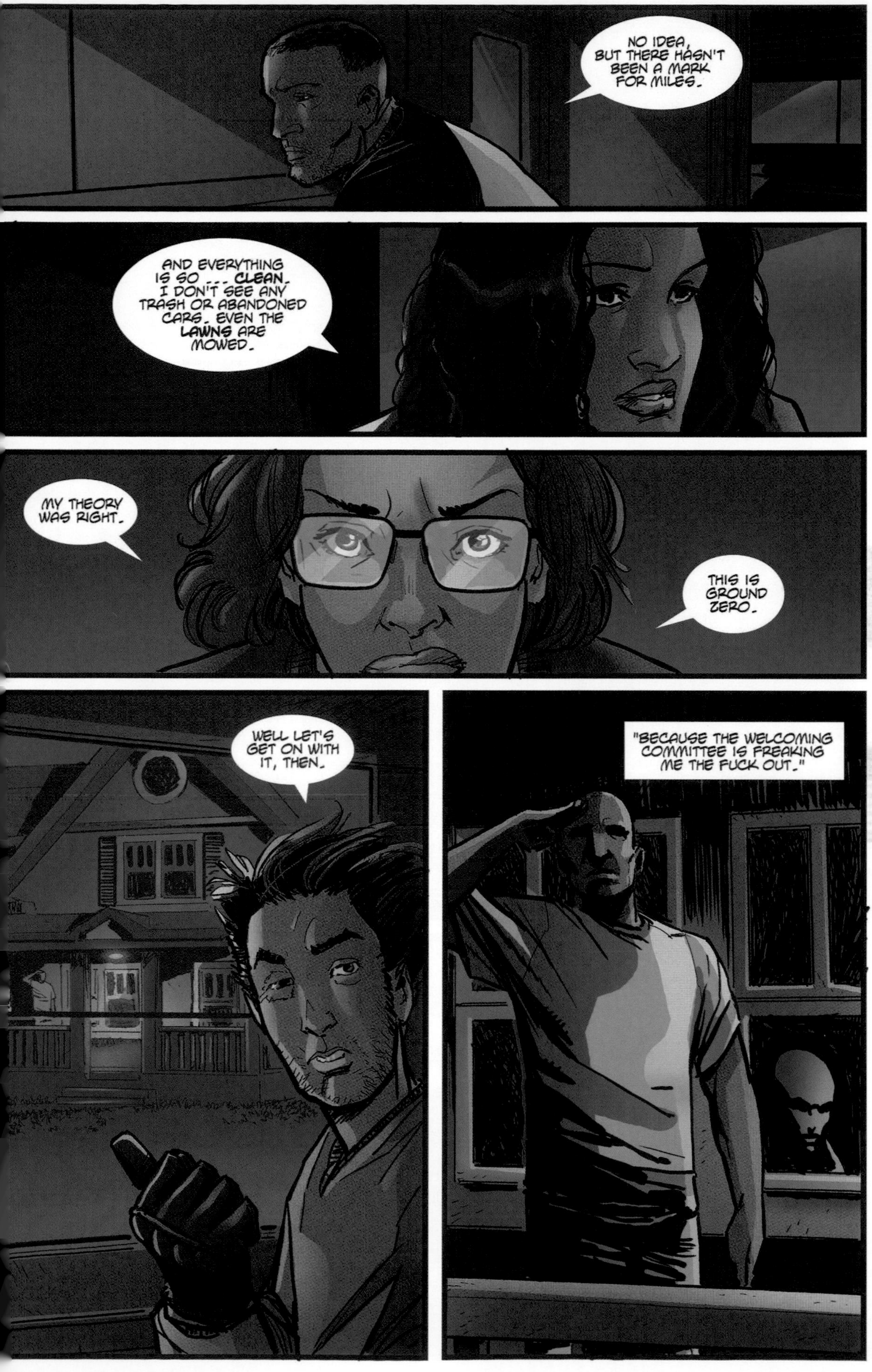
NO IDEA, BUT THERE HASN'T BEEN A MARK FOR MILES.
AND EVERYTHING IS SO ... CLEAN. I DON'T SEE ANY TRASH OR ABANDONED CARS. EVEN THE LAWNS ARE MOWED.
MY THEORY WAS RIGHT.
THIS IS GROUND ZERO.
WELL LET'S GET ON WITH IT, THEN.
"BECAUSE THE WELCOMING COMMITTEE IS FREAKING ME THE FUCK OUT."

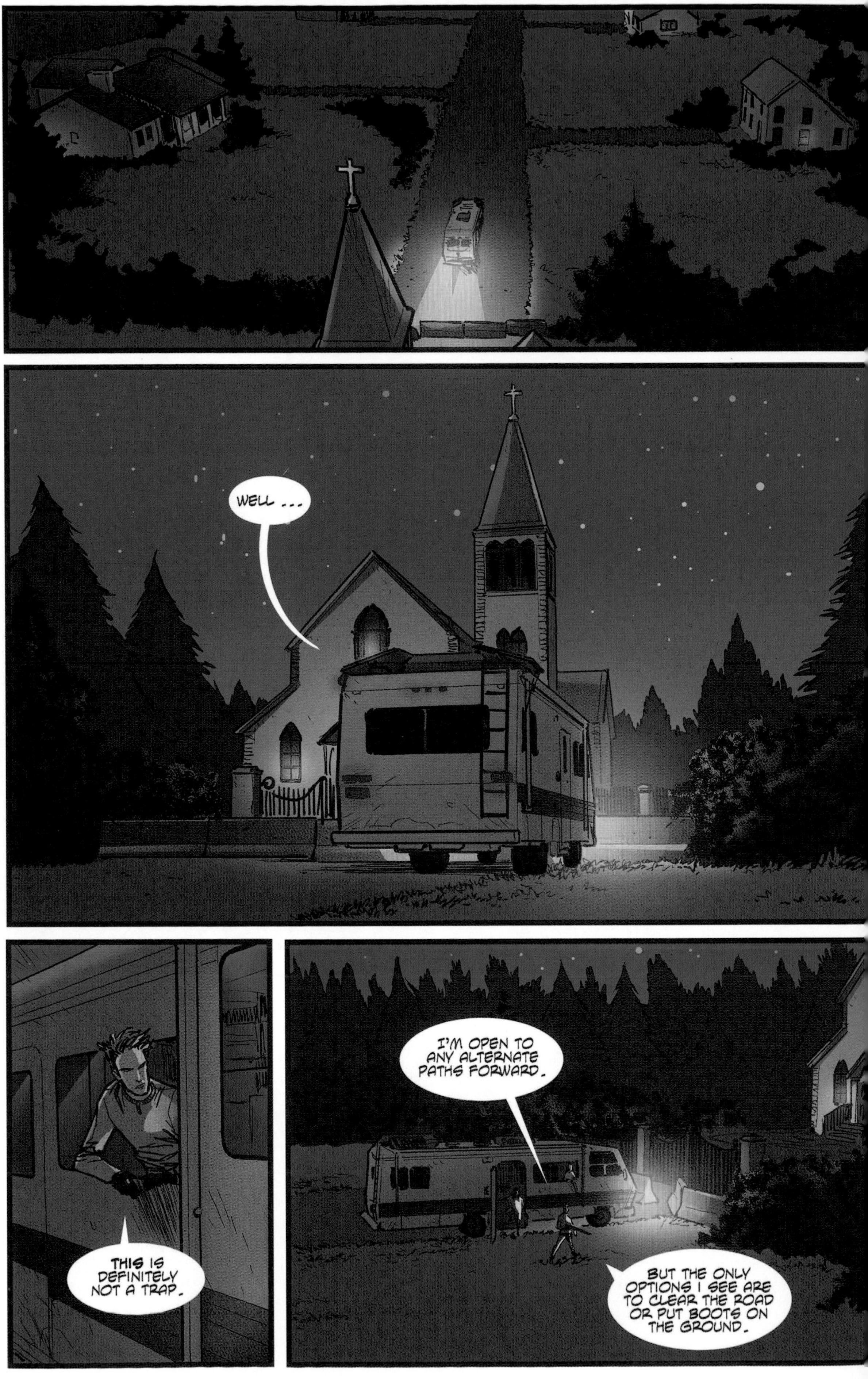
WELL . . .
THIS IS DEFINITELY NOT A TRAP.
I'M OPEN TO ANY ALTERNATE PATHS FORWARD.
BUT THE ONLY OPTIONS I SEE ARE TO CLEAR THE ROAD OR PUT BOOTS ON THE GROUND.

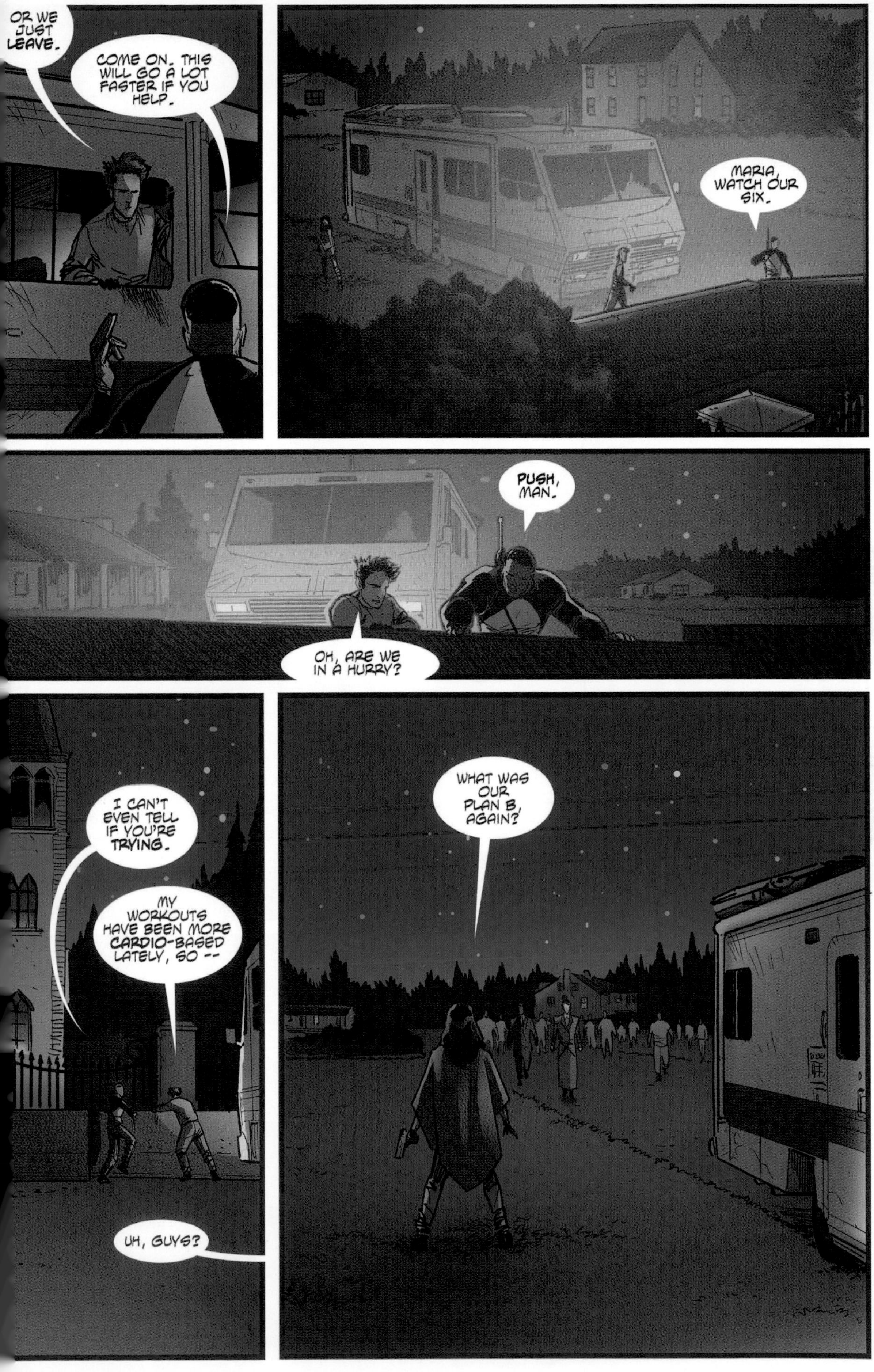
OR WE JUST LEAVE.
COME ON. THIS WILL GO A LOT FASTER IF YOU HELP.
MARIA, WATCH OUR SIX.
PUSH, MAN.
OH, ARE WE IN A HURRY?
I CAN'T EVEN TELL IF YOU'RE TRYING.
MY WORKOUTS HAVE BEEN MORE CARDIO-BASED LATELY, SO --
UH, GUYS?
WHAT WAS OUR PLAN B, AGAIN?

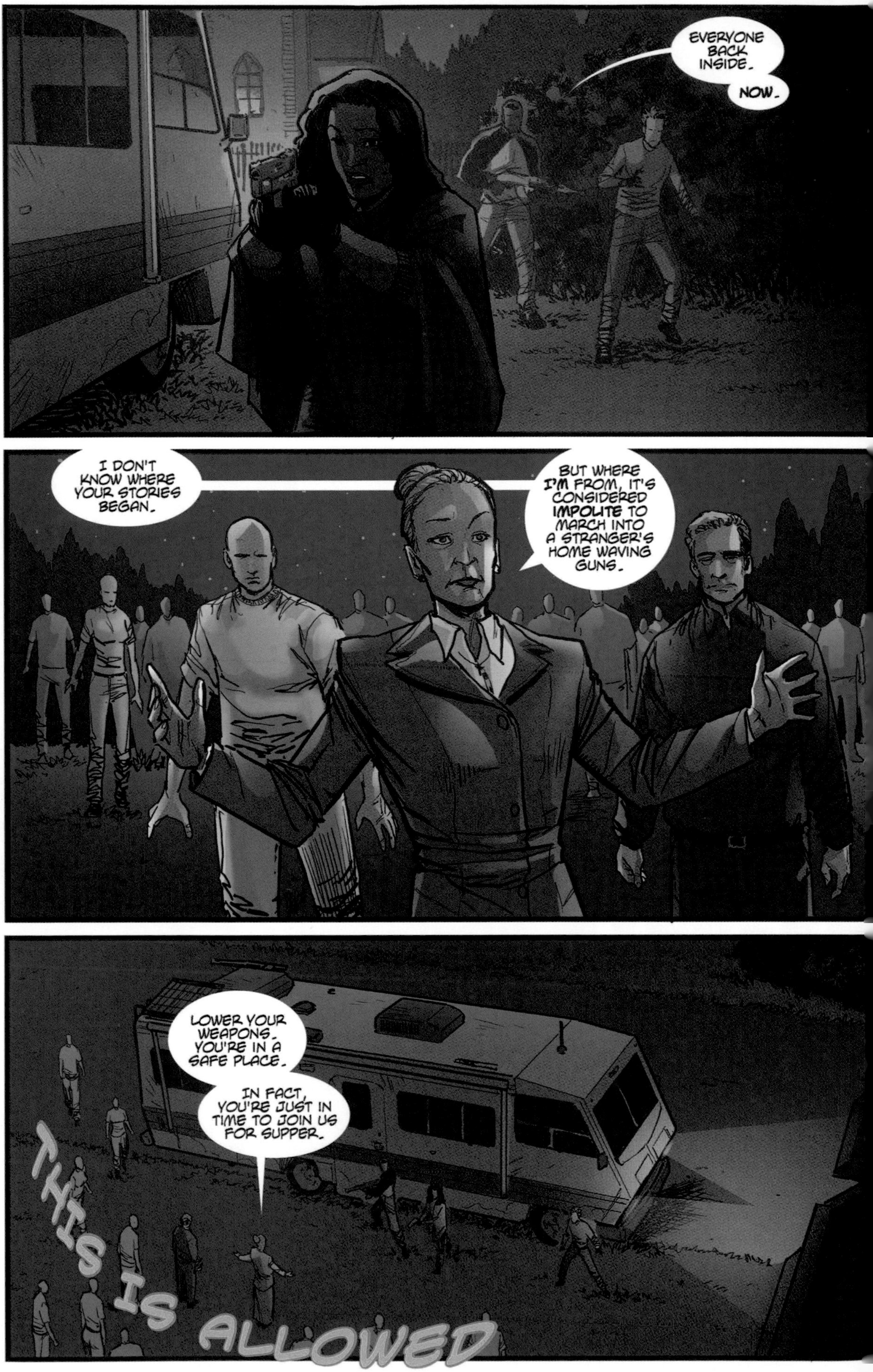
EVERYONE BACK INSIDE.
NOW.
I DON'T KNOW WHERE YOUR STORIES BEGAN.
BUT WHERE I'M FROM, IT'S CONSIDERED IMPOLITE TO MARCH INTO A STRANGER'S HOME WAVING GUNS.
LOWER YOUR WEAPONS. YOU'RE IN A SAFE PLACE.
IN FACT, YOU'RE JUST IN TIME TO JOIN US FOR SUPPER.
THIS IS ALLOWED

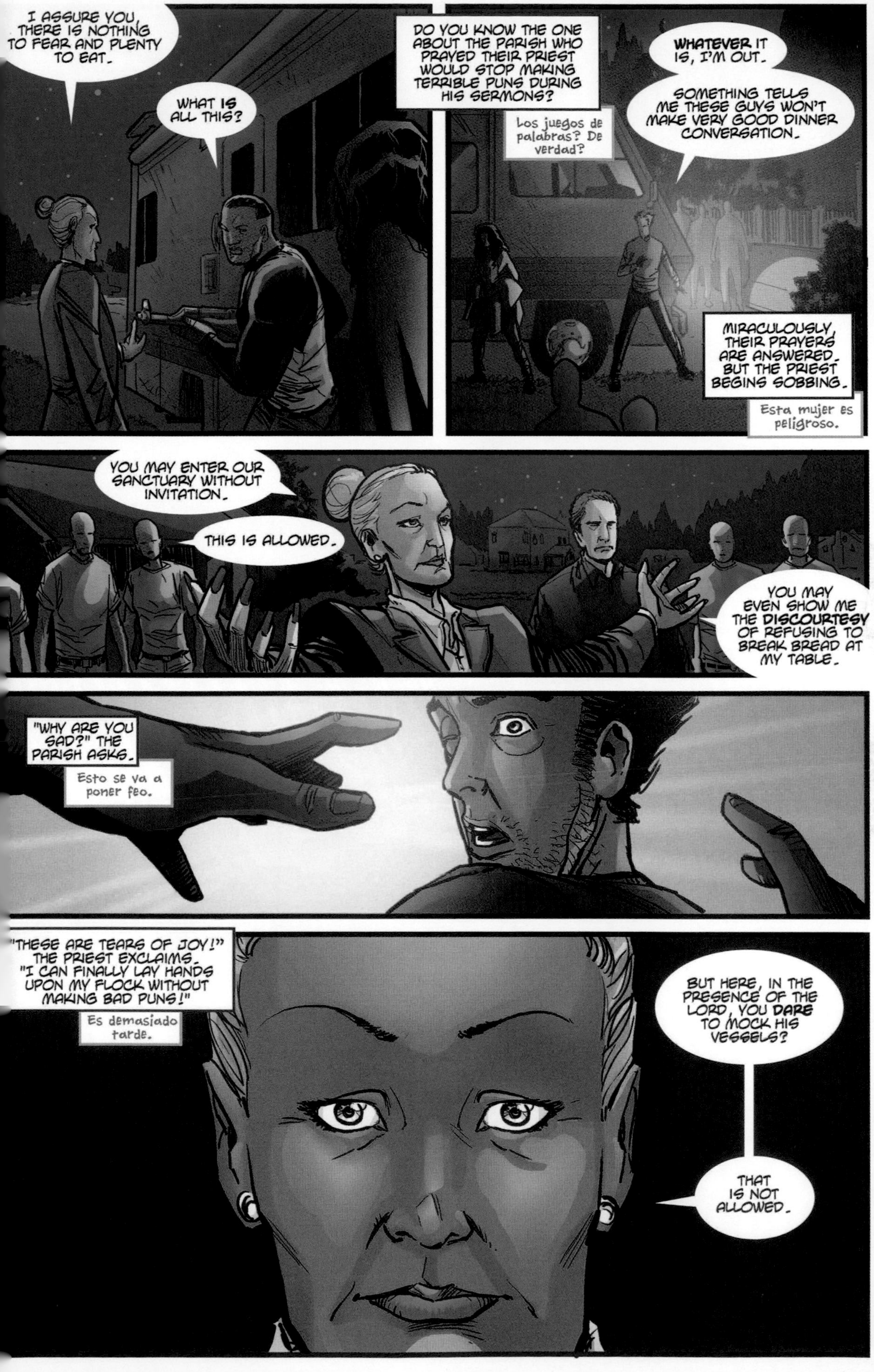

I ASSURE YOU, THERE IS NOTHING TO FEAR AND PLENTY TO EAT.
WHAT IS ALL THIS?
DO YOU KNOW THE ONE ABOUT THE PARISH WHO PRAYED THEIR PRIEST WOULD STOP MAKING TERRIBLE PUNS DURING HIS SERMONS?
Los juegos de palabras? De verdad?
WHATEVER IT IS, I'M OUT.
SOMETHING TELLS ME THESE GUYS WON'T MAKE VERY GOOD DINNER CONVERSATION.
MIRACULOUSLY, THEIR PRAYERS ARE ANSWERED. BUT THE PRIEST BEGINS SOBBING.
Esta mujer es peligroso.
YOU MAY ENTER OUR SANCTUARY WITHOUT INVITATION.
THIS IS ALLOWED.
YOU MAY EVEN SHOW ME THE DISCOURTESY OF REFUSING TO BREAK BREAD AT MY TABLE.
"WHY ARE YOU SAD?" THE PARISH ASKS.
Esto se va a poner feo.
"THESE ARE TEARS OF JOY!" THE PRIEST EXCLAIMS. "I CAN FINALLY LAY HANDS UPON MY FLOCK WITHOUT MAKING BAD PUNS!"
Es demasiado tarde.
BUT HERE, IN THE PRESENCE OF THE LORD, YOU DARE TO MOCK HIS VESSELS?
THAT IS NOT ALLOWED.

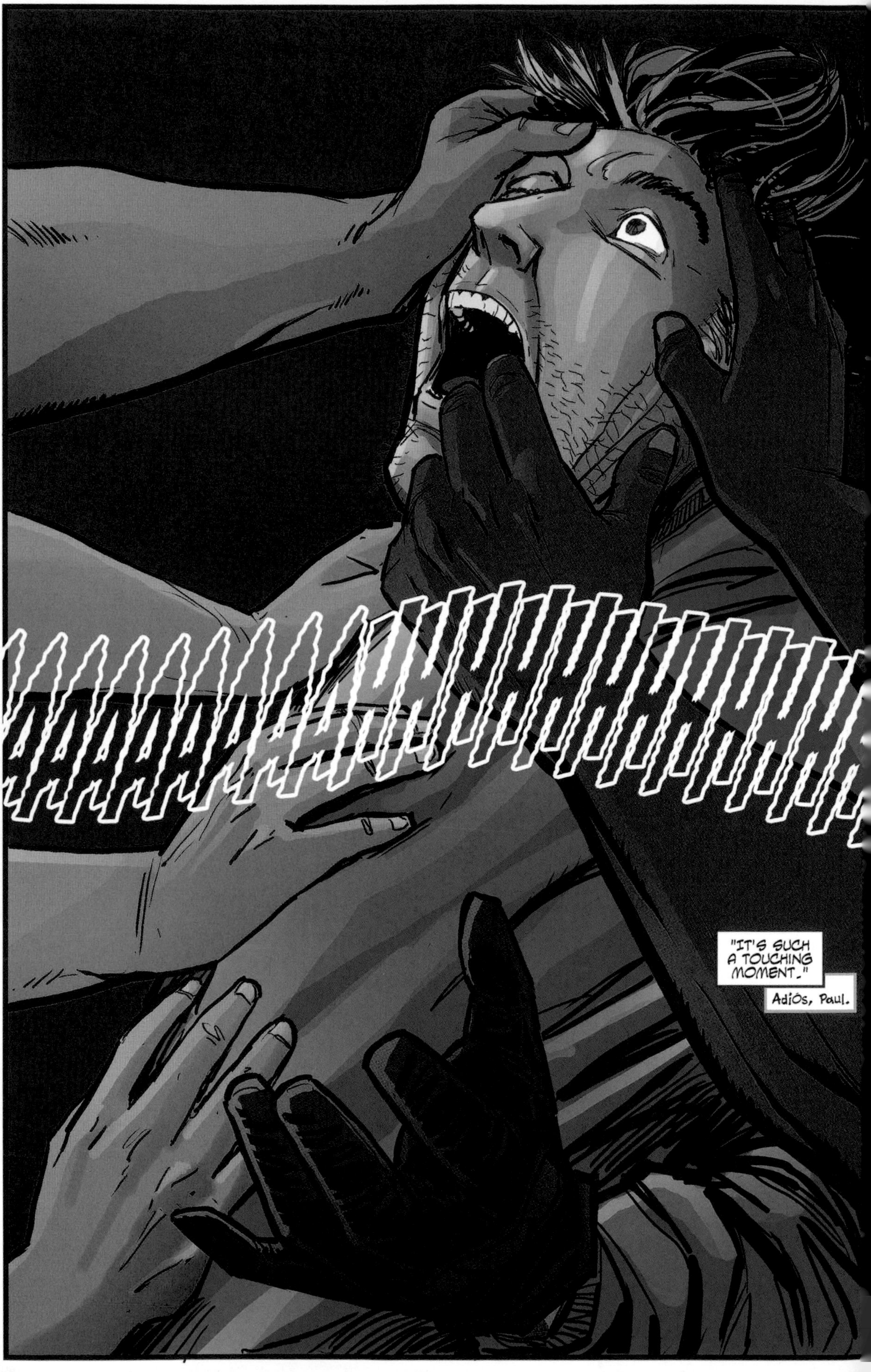
AAAAAAAAAAAAHHHHHHHHHHHHHH
"IT'S SUCH A TOUCHING MOMENT."
AdiOs, Paul.

CLASSIFIED

SECURITY LEVEL:
DOUBLE BLACK

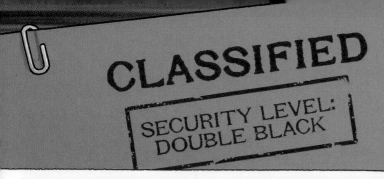

TelChan v0.78, Cpu Cycles: 3000, Frameskip 0, IRC restricted_research.gov

23:02:44 * VLS has joined the group. Security clearance confirmed.
!ERROR! GPS not found !ERROR!

23:02:49 <VLS> Hello!

23:03:54 <JCK> Vic! Are you okay?

23:03:20 <VLS> As far as kidnappings go, mine hasn't been so bad.

23:03:26 <ALG> Well, keep us informed. And is now a good time to ask what the HELL the last episode of Lost was about?

23:03:46 <VLS> I tried to warn you. Turns out the title was referring to its plot threads.

23:04:56 <ALG> Wait, is developing a sense of humor a symptom of Stockholm Syndrome?

23:04:16 <VLS> Actually, tying up loose ends is why I'm online. We're about to cross over into No Man's Land, and in case I don't make it back, I just wanted to thank you both for your help.

23:04:56 <JCK> You're thanking us? Now we KNOW you're under duress.

23:04:39 <VLS> I disagree with how you've applied your research, true. It's a waste of time and resources.

23:04:56 <ALG> Aaaand she's back.

23:04:39 <VLS> But the data itself was invaluable. Josiah, your study of the effect riders have on walkabout patterns was critical to my analysis. And I relied extensively on Amy's calculation of the increased walkabout fatality rates among populations residing near deep water.

23:04:29 <ALG> It's not just water. The odds of suriving an MRFD event are exponentially higher for those residing more than 50 miles from dramatic elevation shifts. The Grand Canyon isn't a nice place to visit in your sleep.

23:06:08 <VLS> Anyway, I wanted to give you both credit while I can. And if you wake up soon to find the world a better place ... do me a favor and try to keep the graffiti off all the statues erected in my honor.

23:07:09 * VLS has left the group.

For the desk of
Gen. Canter

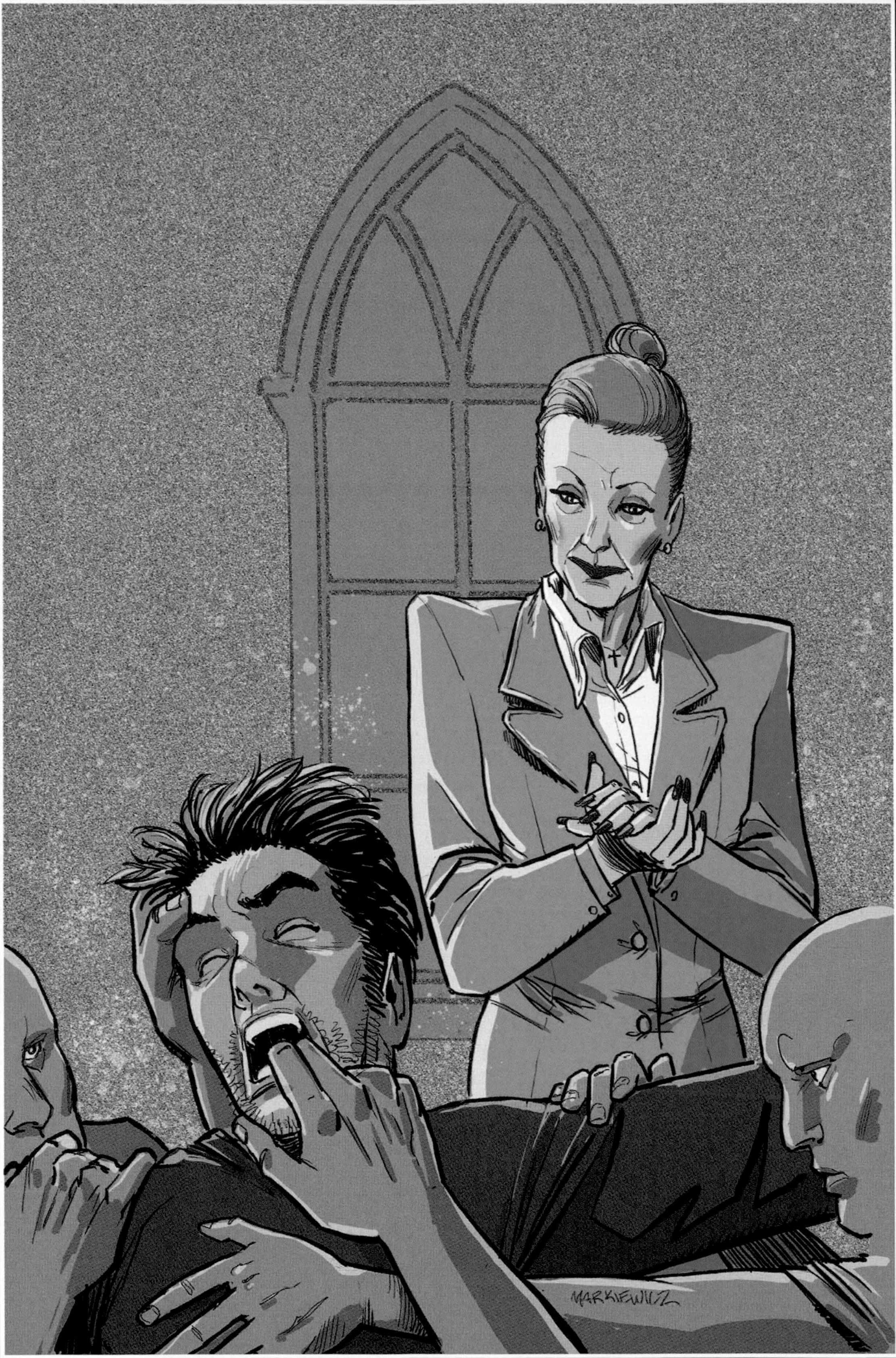
MARKIEWICZ

ISSUE FIVE
COVER ART BY ADAM MARKIEWICZ
COLORS BY MELANIE DARLING

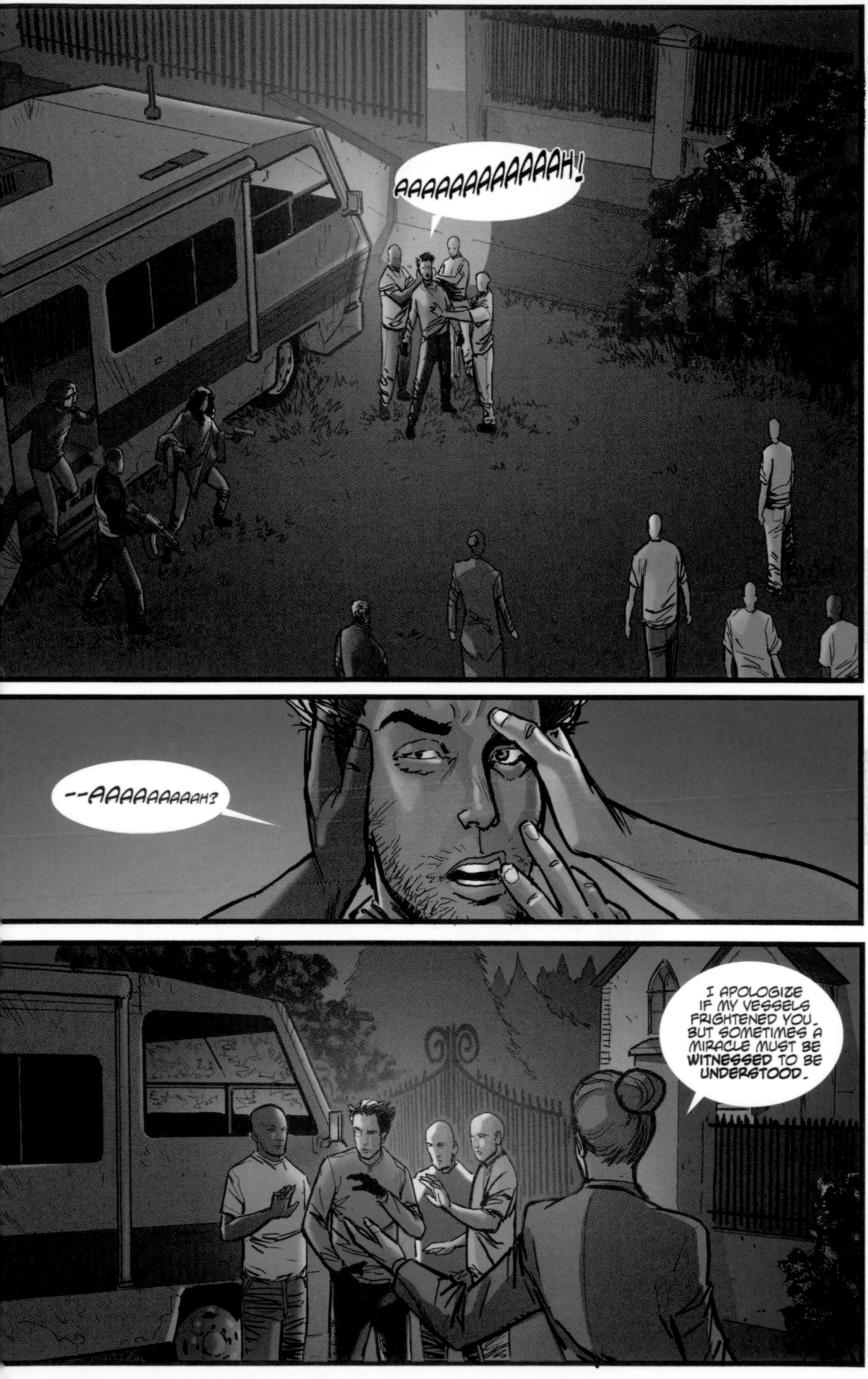
AAAAAAAAAAAAH!
--AAAAAAAAAH?
I APOLOGIZE IF MY VESSELS FRIGHTENED YOU. BUT SOMETIMES A MIRACLE MUST BE WITNESSED TO BE UNDERSTOOD.

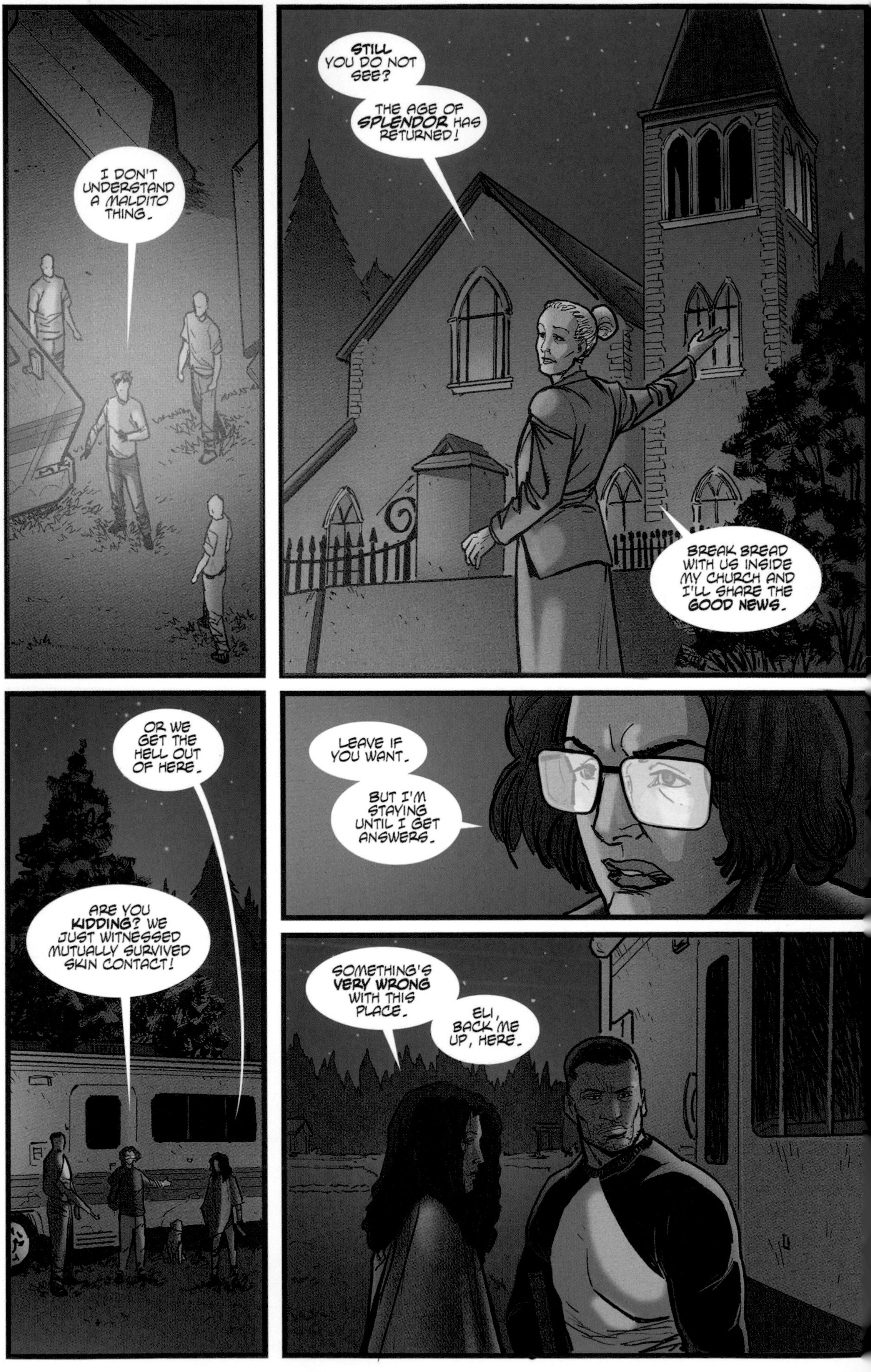
I DON'T UNDERSTAND A MALDITO THING.
STILL YOU DO NOT SEE?
THE AGE OF SPLENDOR HAS RETURNED!
BREAK BREAD WITH US INSIDE MY CHURCH AND I'LL SHARE THE GOOD NEWS.
OR WE GET THE HELL OUT OF HERE.
ARE YOU KIDDING? WE JUST WITNESSED MUTUALLY SURVIVED SKIN CONTACT!
LEAVE IF YOU WANT.
BUT I'M STAYING UNTIL I GET ANSWERS.
SOMETHING'S VERY WRONG WITH THIS PLACE.
ELI, BACK ME UP, HERE.

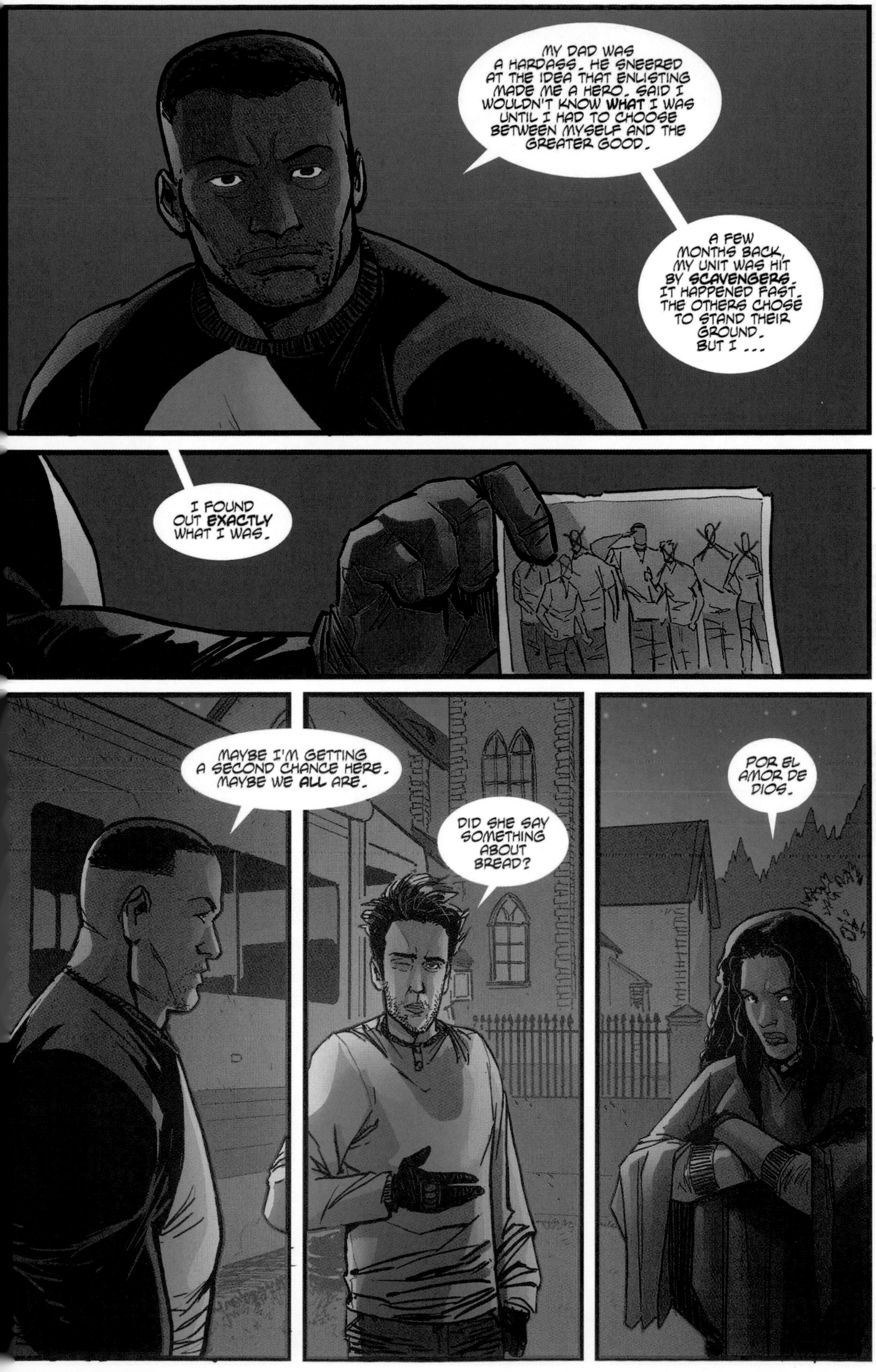
MY DAD WAS A HARDASS. HE SNEERED AT THE IDEA THAT ENLISTING MADE ME A HERO. SAID I WOULDN'T KNOW WHAT I WAS UNTIL I HAD TO CHOOSE BETWEEN MYSELF AND THE GREATER GOOD.
A FEW MONTHS BACK, MY UNIT WAS HIT BY SCAVENGERS. IT HAPPENED FAST. THE OTHERS CHOSE TO STAND THEIR GROUND. BUT I...
I FOUND OUT EXACTLY WHAT I WAS.
MAYBE I'M GETTING A SECOND CHANCE HERE. MAYBE WE ALL ARE.
DID SHE SAY SOMETHING ABOUT BREAD?
POR EL AMOR DE DIOS.

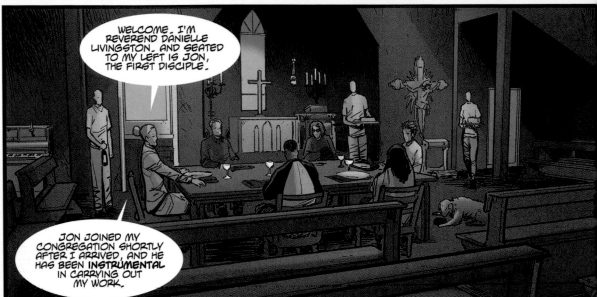

WELCOME. I'M REVEREND DANIELLE LIVINGSTON. AND SEATED TO MY LEFT IS JON, THE FIRST DISCIPLE.

JON JOINED MY CONGREGATION SHORTLY AFTER I ARRIVED, AND HE HAS BEEN INSTRUMENTAL IN CARRYING OUT MY WORK.

YOU MIND IF I FILM THIS?

CLICK

AS YOU WISH.

CAREFUL, CHILD! YOU'RE SPILLING!

THEY MEAN WELL, MY VESSELS.

BUT SOME RESPOND TO JON'S... PROGRAMMING BETTER THAN OTHERS.

NOW, YOU HAVE QUESTIONS, I'M SURE.

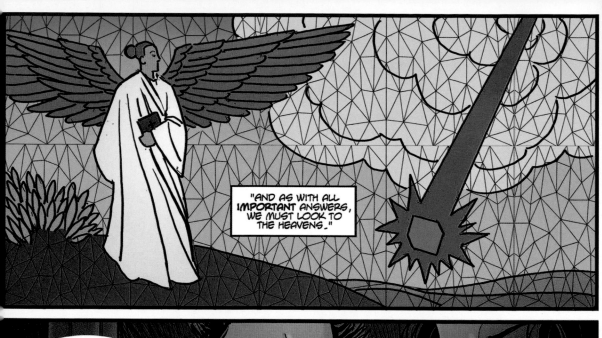

"AND AS WITH ALL IMPORTANT ANSWERS, WE MUST LOOK TO THE HEAVENS."

ONCE, JUST ONCE, I'D LIKE TO MEET SOMEONE ON THIS TRIP WHO ISN'T BATSHIT INSANE.

I TRIED TO TELL YOU.

DURING THE FIRST WALKABOUT, I WAS PULLED DOWN FROM THE SKIES TO BEHOLD GOD'S WILL.

"AND THEN THE SOUL BOX WAS REVEALED UNTO ME."

"AT FIRST I DID NOT UNDERSTAND. I WATCHED THE LOST SOULS POUR THEIR SINS INSIDE, BUT I COULD NOT FATHOM ITS PURPOSE."

"THEN, GUIDED BY THE HAND OF GOD, DISCIPLE JON ARRIVED. TOGETHER, WE DECIPHERED THE BOX'S MYSTERIES, AND SO TOO WE CAME TO REALIZE MY TRUE CALLING."

"I WOULD FILL THESE EMPTY VESSELS WITH ALL THE LOVE AND OBEDIENCE THAT THEIR PRIOR LIVES HAD LACKED."

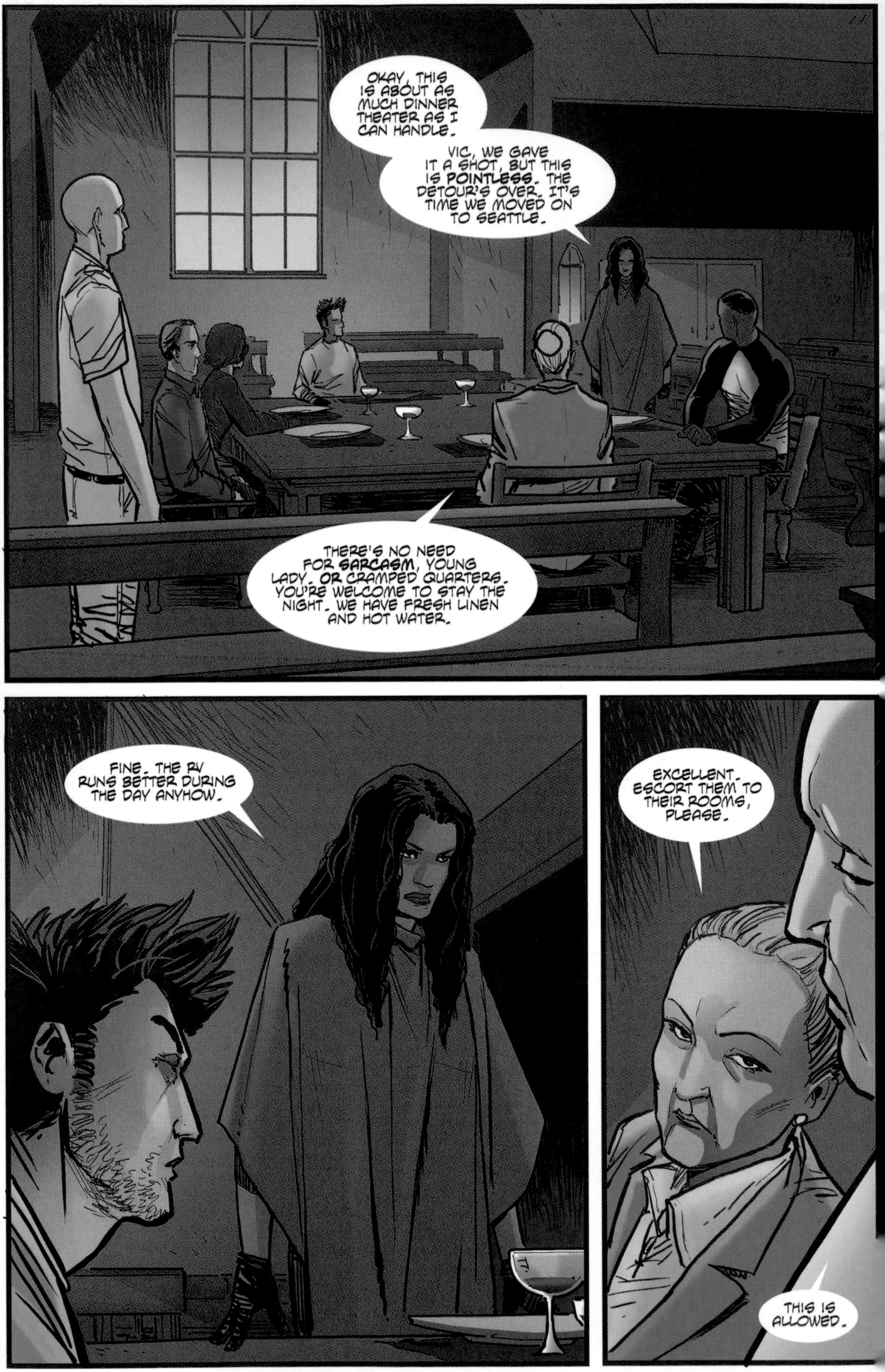
OKAY, THIS IS ABOUT AS MUCH DINNER THEATER AS I CAN HANDLE.
VIC, WE GAVE IT A SHOT, BUT THIS IS POINTLESS. THE DETOUR'S OVER. IT'S TIME WE MOVED ON TO SEATTLE.
THERE'S NO NEED FOR SARCASM, YOUNG LADY. OR CRAMPED QUARTERS. YOU'RE WELCOME TO STAY THE NIGHT. WE HAVE FRESH LINEN AND HOT WATER.
FINE. THE RV RUNS BETTER DURING THE DAY ANYHOW.
EXCELLENT. ESCORT THEM TO THEIR ROOMS, PLEASE.
THIS IS ALLOWED.

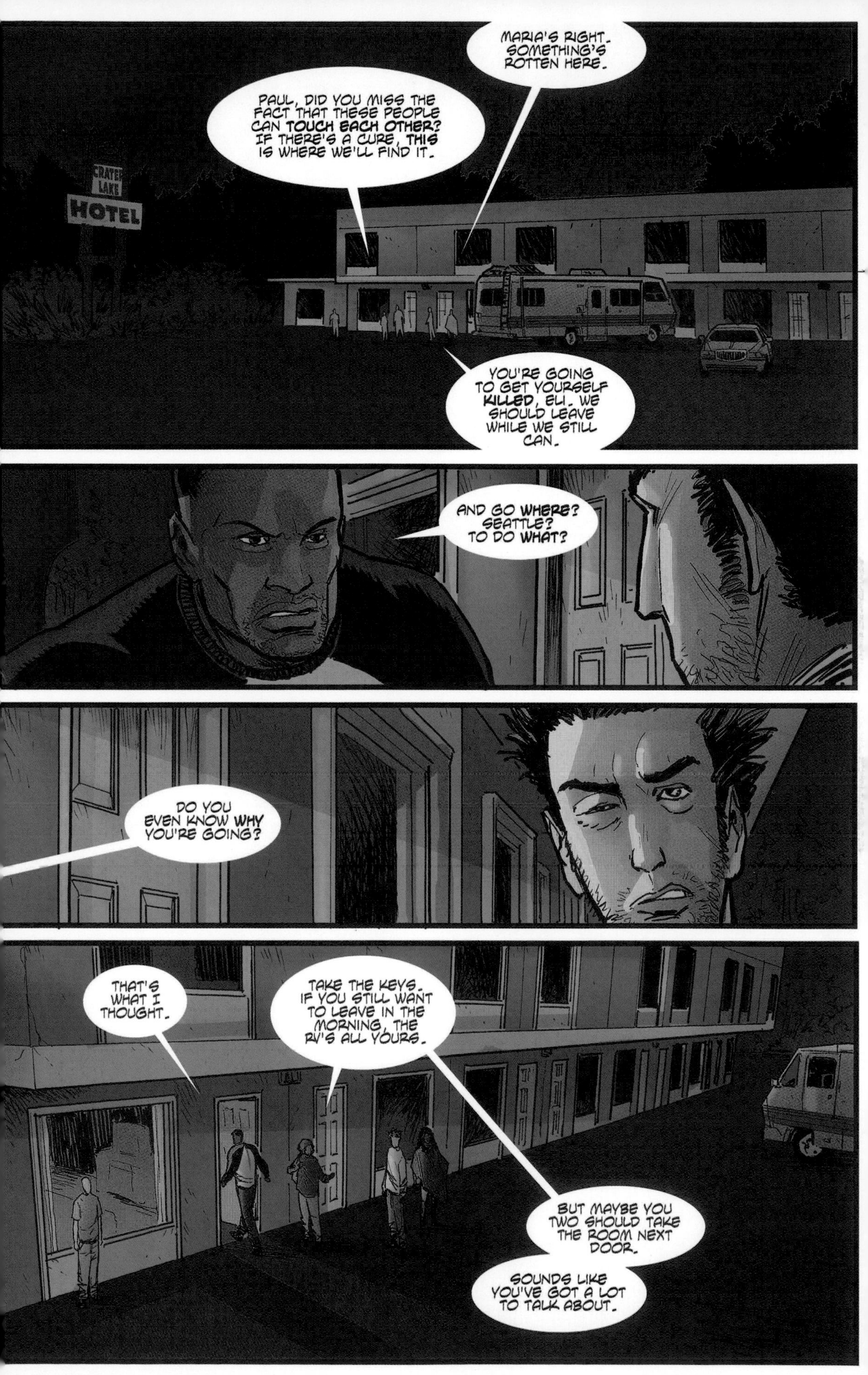
PAUL, DID YOU MISS THE FACT THAT THESE PEOPLE CAN TOUCH EACH OTHER? IF THERE'S A CURE, THIS IS WHERE WE'LL FIND IT.
MARIA'S RIGHT. SOMETHING'S ROTTEN HERE.
CRATER LAKE HOTEL
YOU'RE GOING TO GET YOURSELF KILLED, ELI. WE SHOULD LEAVE WHILE WE STILL CAN.
AND GO WHERE? SEATTLE? TO DO WHAT?
DO YOU EVEN KNOW WHY YOU'RE GOING?
THAT'S WHAT I THOUGHT.
TAKE THE KEYS. IF YOU STILL WANT TO LEAVE IN THE MORNING, THE RV'S ALL YOURS.
BUT MAYBE YOU TWO SHOULD TAKE THE ROOM NEXT DOOR.
SOUNDS LIKE YOU'VE GOT A LOT TO TALK ABOUT.

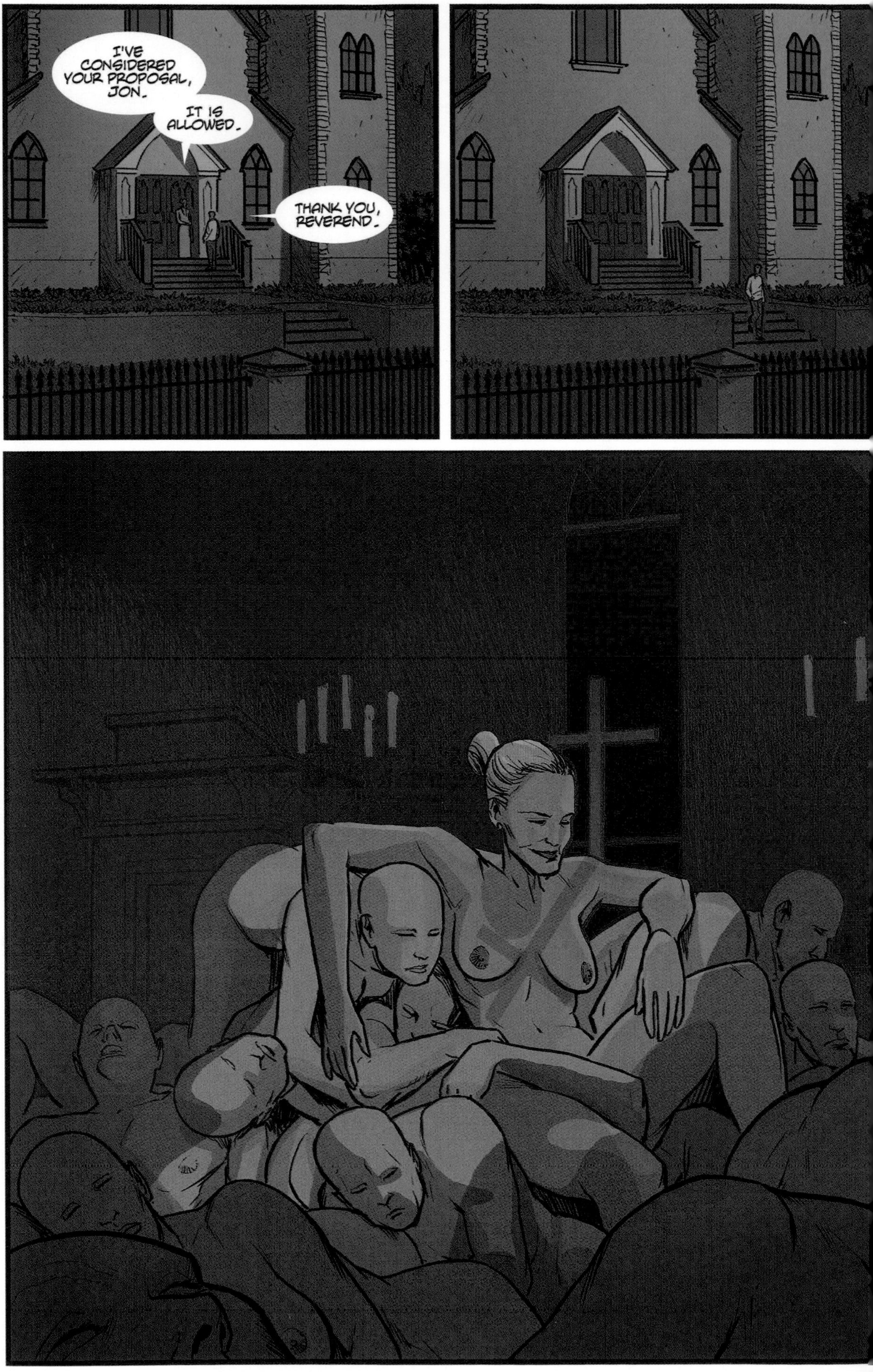
I'VE CONSIDERED YOUR PROPOSAL, JON.
IT IS ALLOWED.
THANK YOU, REVEREND.

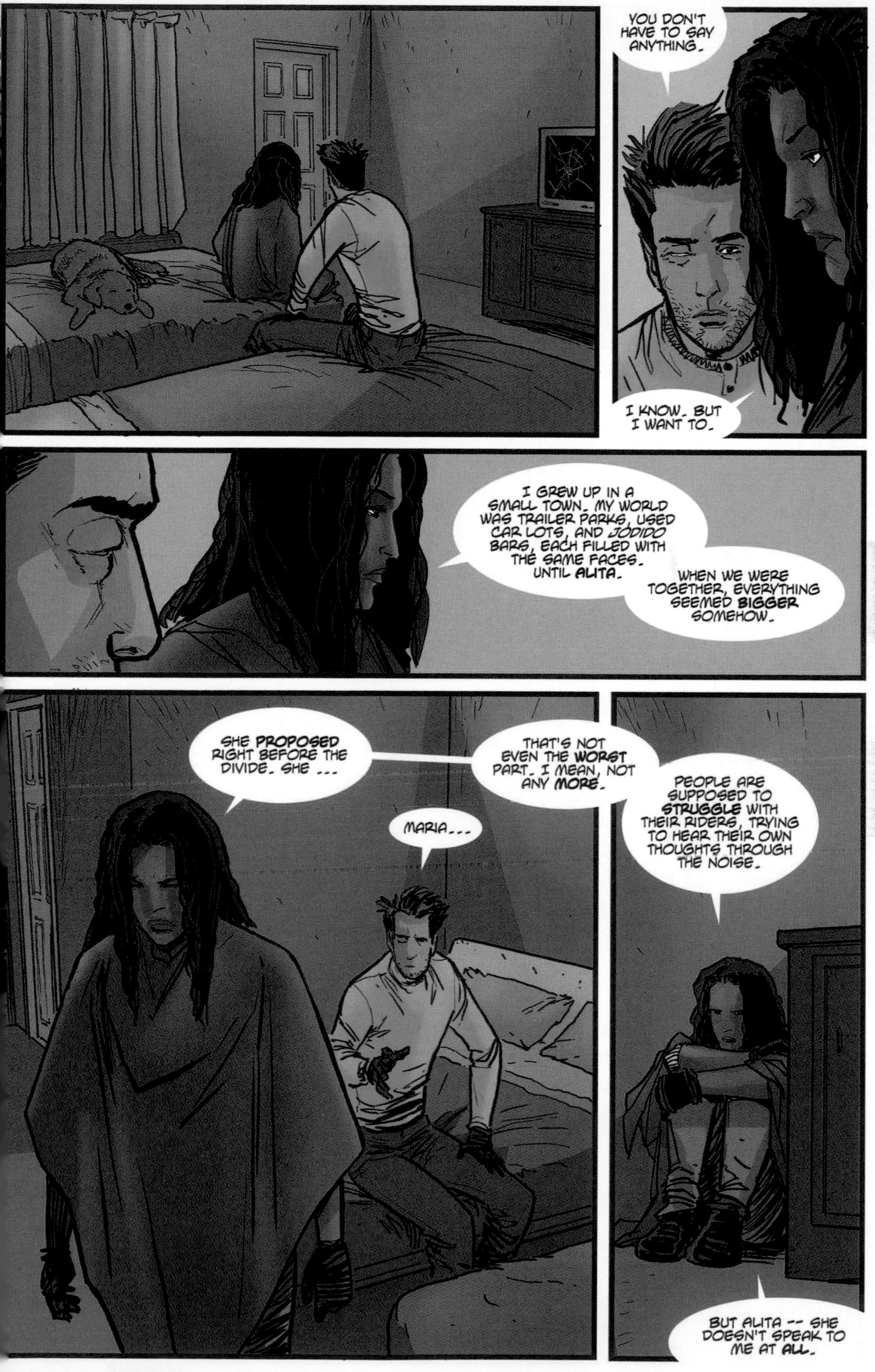
YOU DON'T HAVE TO SAY ANYTHING.
I KNOW. BUT I WANT TO.
I GREW UP IN A SMALL TOWN. MY WORLD WAS TRAILER PARKS, USED CAR LOTS, AND JODIDO BARS, EACH FILLED WITH THE SAME FACES. UNTIL ALITA.
WHEN WE WERE TOGETHER, EVERYTHING SEEMED BIGGER SOMEHOW.
SHE PROPOSED RIGHT BEFORE THE DIVIDE. SHE ...
THAT'S NOT EVEN THE WORST PART. I MEAN, NOT ANY MORE.
MARIA...
PEOPLE ARE SUPPOSED TO STRUGGLE WITH THEIR RIDERS, TRYING TO HEAR THEIR OWN THOUGHTS THROUGH THE NOISE.
BUT ALITA -- SHE DOESN'T SPEAK TO ME AT ALL.

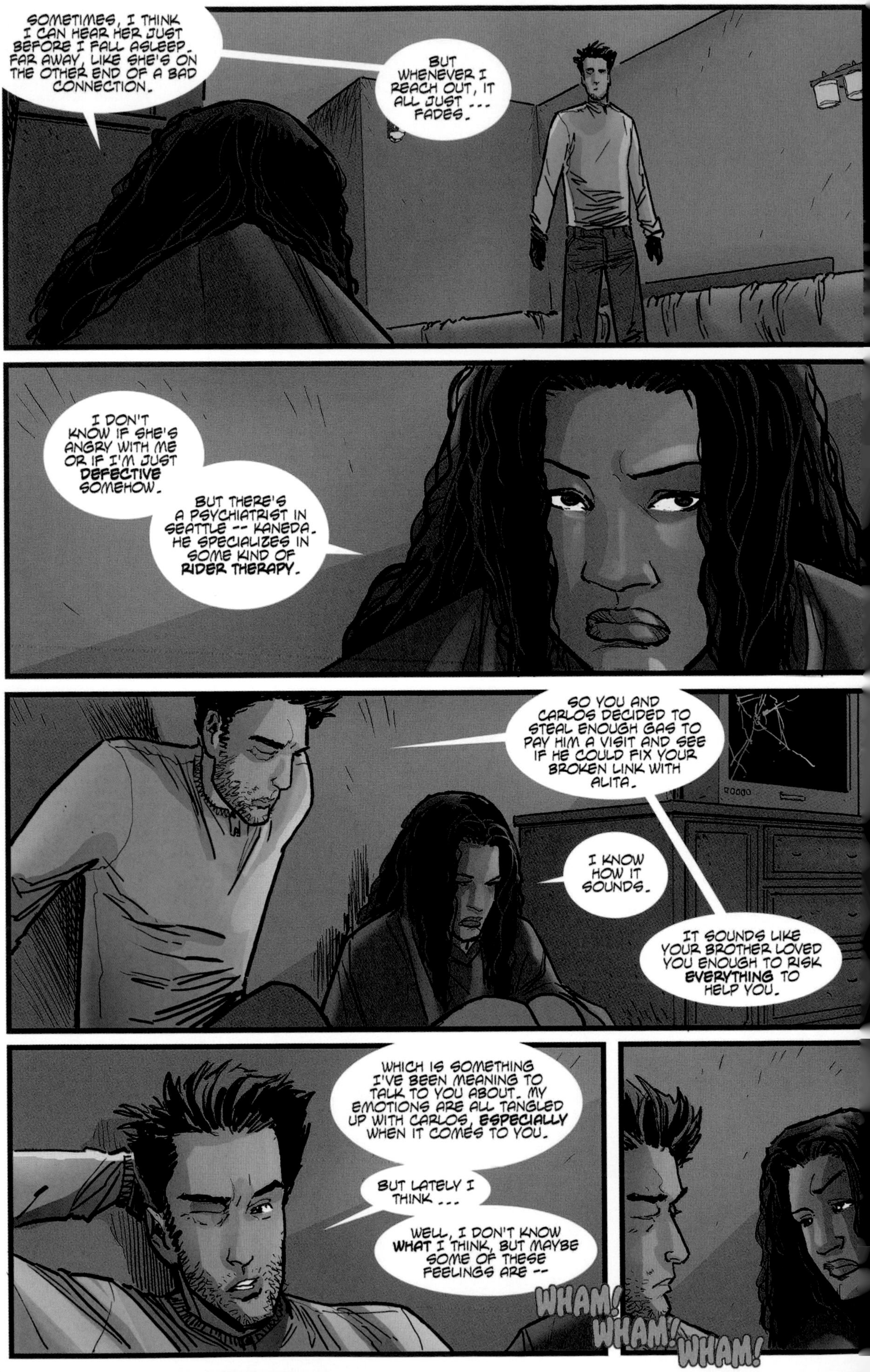
SOMETIMES, I THINK I CAN HEAR HER JUST BEFORE I FALL ASLEEP. FAR AWAY, LIKE SHE'S ON THE OTHER END OF A BAD CONNECTION.
BUT WHENEVER I REACH OUT, IT ALL JUST --- FADES.
I DON'T KNOW IF SHE'S ANGRY WITH ME OR IF I'M JUST **DEFECTIVE** SOMEHOW.
BUT THERE'S A PSYCHIATRIST IN SEATTLE -- KANEDA. HE SPECIALIZES IN SOME KIND OF **RIDER THERAPY**.
SO YOU AND CARLOS DECIDED TO STEAL ENOUGH GAS TO PAY HIM A VISIT AND SEE IF HE COULD FIX YOUR BROKEN LINK WITH ALITA.
I KNOW HOW IT SOUNDS.
IT SOUNDS LIKE YOUR BROTHER LOVED YOU ENOUGH TO RISK **EVERYTHING** TO HELP YOU.
WHICH IS SOMETHING I'VE BEEN MEANING TO TALK TO YOU ABOUT. MY EMOTIONS ARE ALL TANGLED UP WITH CARLOS, **ESPECIALLY** WHEN IT COMES TO YOU.
BUT LATELY I THINK ---
WELL, I DON'T KNOW **WHAT** I THINK, BUT MAYBE SOME OF THESE FEELINGS ARE --
WHAM! WHAM! WHAM!

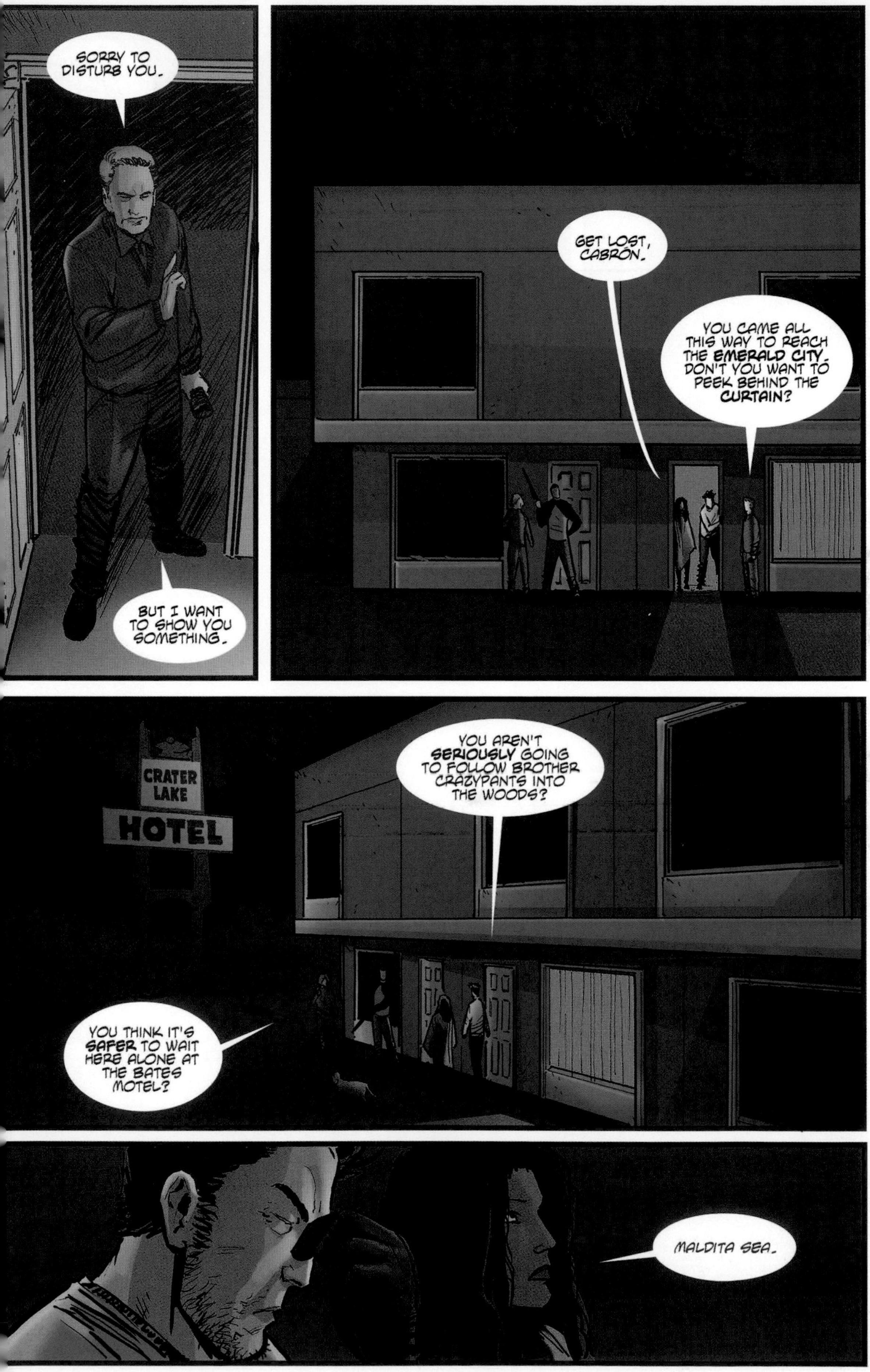
SORRY TO DISTURB YOU.
BUT I WANT TO SHOW YOU SOMETHING.
GET LOST, CABRÓN.
YOU CAME ALL THIS WAY TO REACH THE EMERALD CITY. DON'T YOU WANT TO PEEK BEHIND THE CURTAIN?
CRATER LAKE HOTEL
YOU AREN'T SERIOUSLY GOING TO FOLLOW BROTHER CRAZYPANTS INTO THE WOODS?
YOU THINK IT'S SAFER TO WAIT HERE ALONE AT THE BATES MOTEL?
MALDITA SEA.

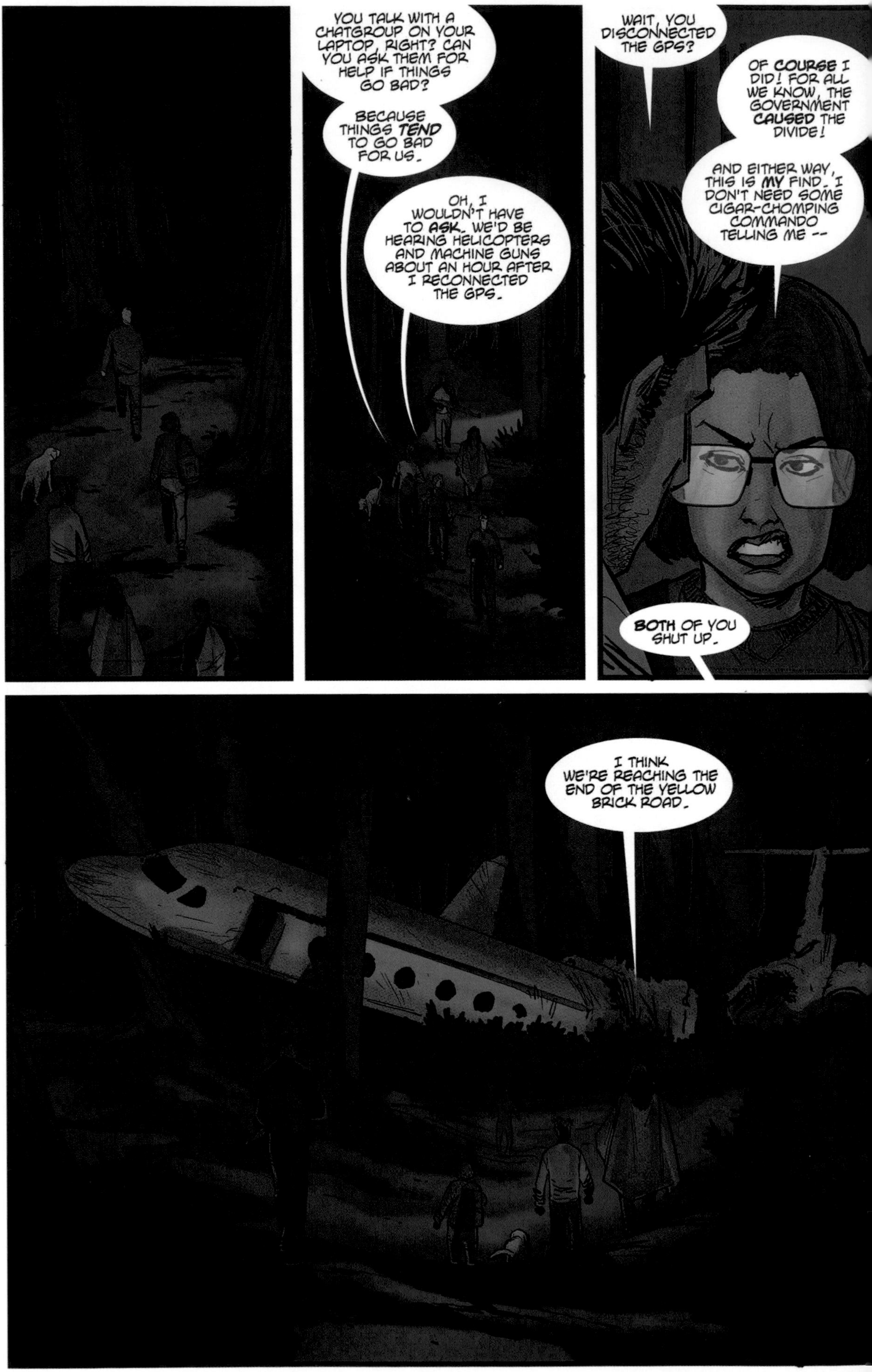
YOU TALK WITH A CHATGROUP ON YOUR LAPTOP, RIGHT? CAN YOU ASK THEM FOR HELP IF THINGS GO BAD?
BECAUSE THINGS TEND TO GO BAD FOR US.
OH, I WOULDN'T HAVE TO ASK. WE'D BE HEARING HELICOPTERS AND MACHINE GUNS ABOUT AN HOUR AFTER I RECONNECTED THE GPS.
WAIT, YOU DISCONNECTED THE GPS?
OF COURSE I DID! FOR ALL WE KNOW, THE GOVERNMENT CAUSED THE DIVIDE!
AND EITHER WAY, THIS IS MY FIND. I DON'T NEED SOME CIGAR-CHOMPING COMMANDO TELLING ME --
BOTH OF YOU SHUT UP.
I THINK WE'RE REACHING THE END OF THE YELLOW BRICK ROAD.

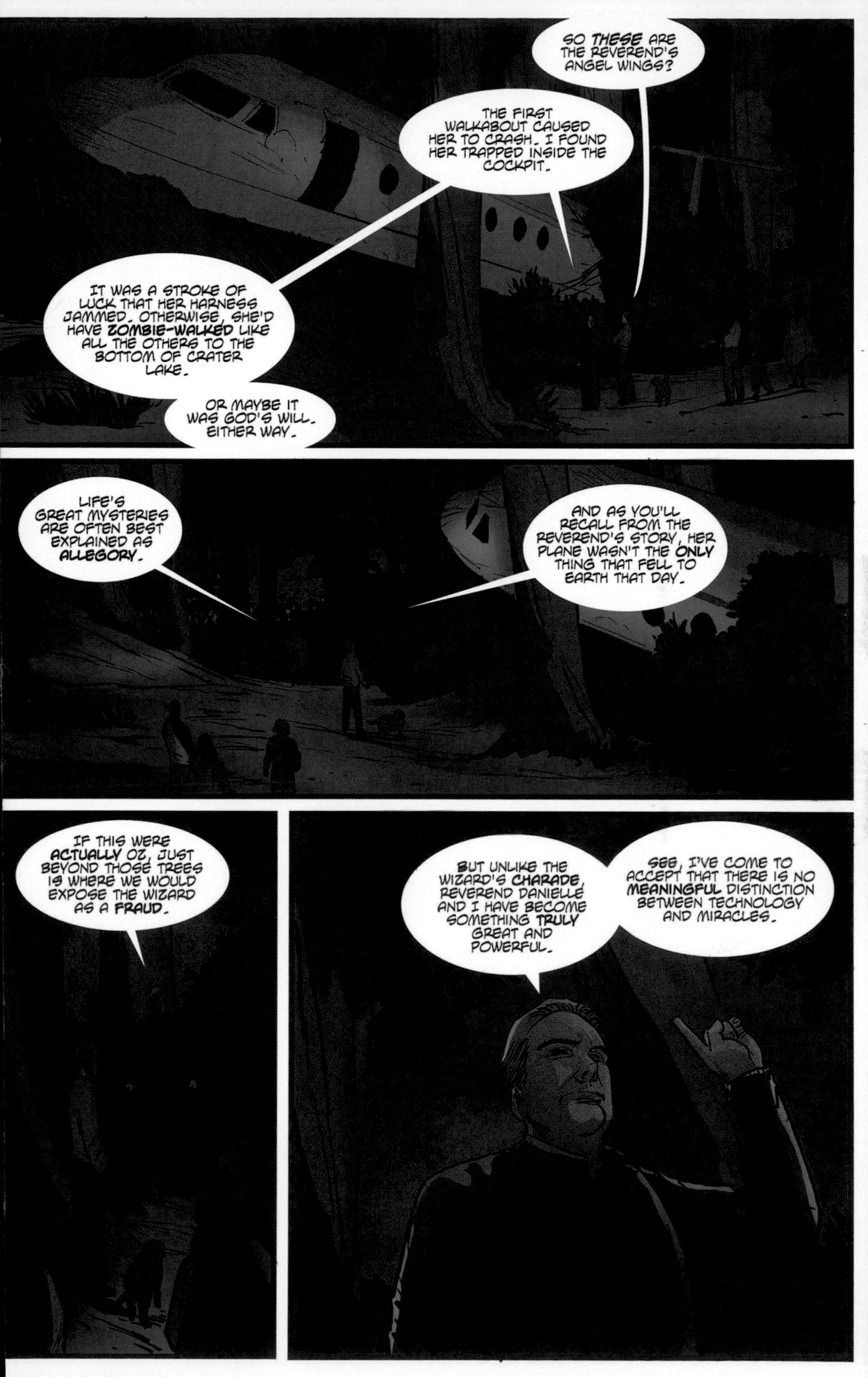

SO THESE ARE THE REVEREND'S ANGEL WINGS?
THE FIRST WALKABOUT CAUSED HER TO CRASH. I FOUND HER TRAPPED INSIDE THE COCKPIT.
IT WAS A STROKE OF LUCK THAT HER HARNESS JAMMED. OTHERWISE, SHE'D HAVE ZOMBIE-WALKED LIKE ALL THE OTHERS TO THE BOTTOM OF CRATER LAKE.
OR MAYBE IT WAS GOD'S WILL. EITHER WAY.
LIFE'S GREAT MYSTERIES ARE OFTEN BEST EXPLAINED AS ALLEGORY.
AND AS YOU'LL RECALL FROM THE REVEREND'S STORY, HER PLANE WASN'T THE ONLY THING THAT FELL TO EARTH THAT DAY.
IF THIS WERE ACTUALLY OZ, JUST BEYOND THOSE TREES IS WHERE WE WOULD EXPOSE THE WIZARD AS A FRAUD.
BUT UNLIKE THE WIZARD'S CHARADE, REVEREND DANIELLE AND I HAVE BECOME SOMETHING TRULY GREAT AND POWERFUL.
SEE, I'VE COME TO ACCEPT THAT THERE IS NO MEANINGFUL DISTINCTION BETWEEN TECHNOLOGY AND MIRACLES.

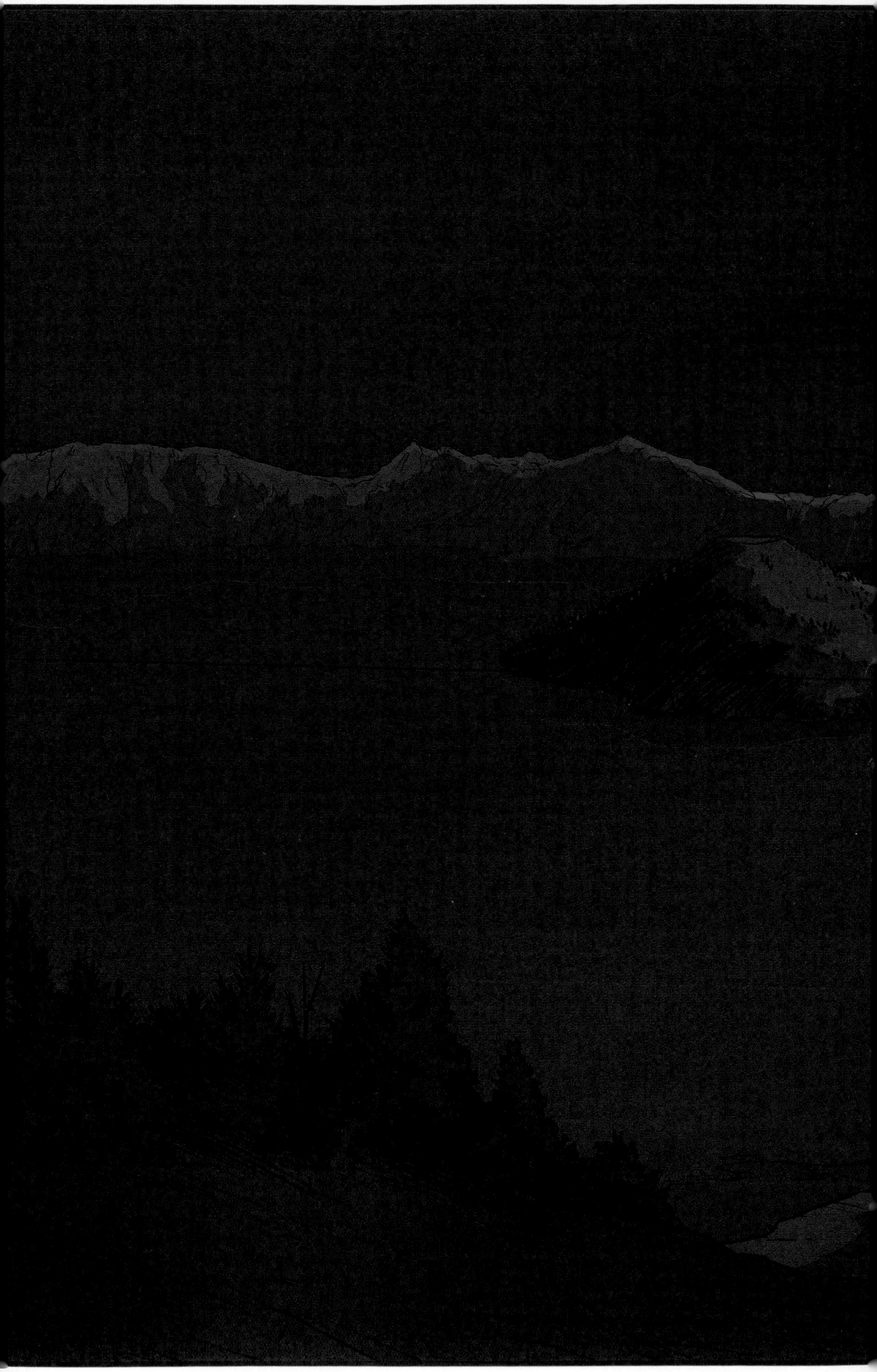

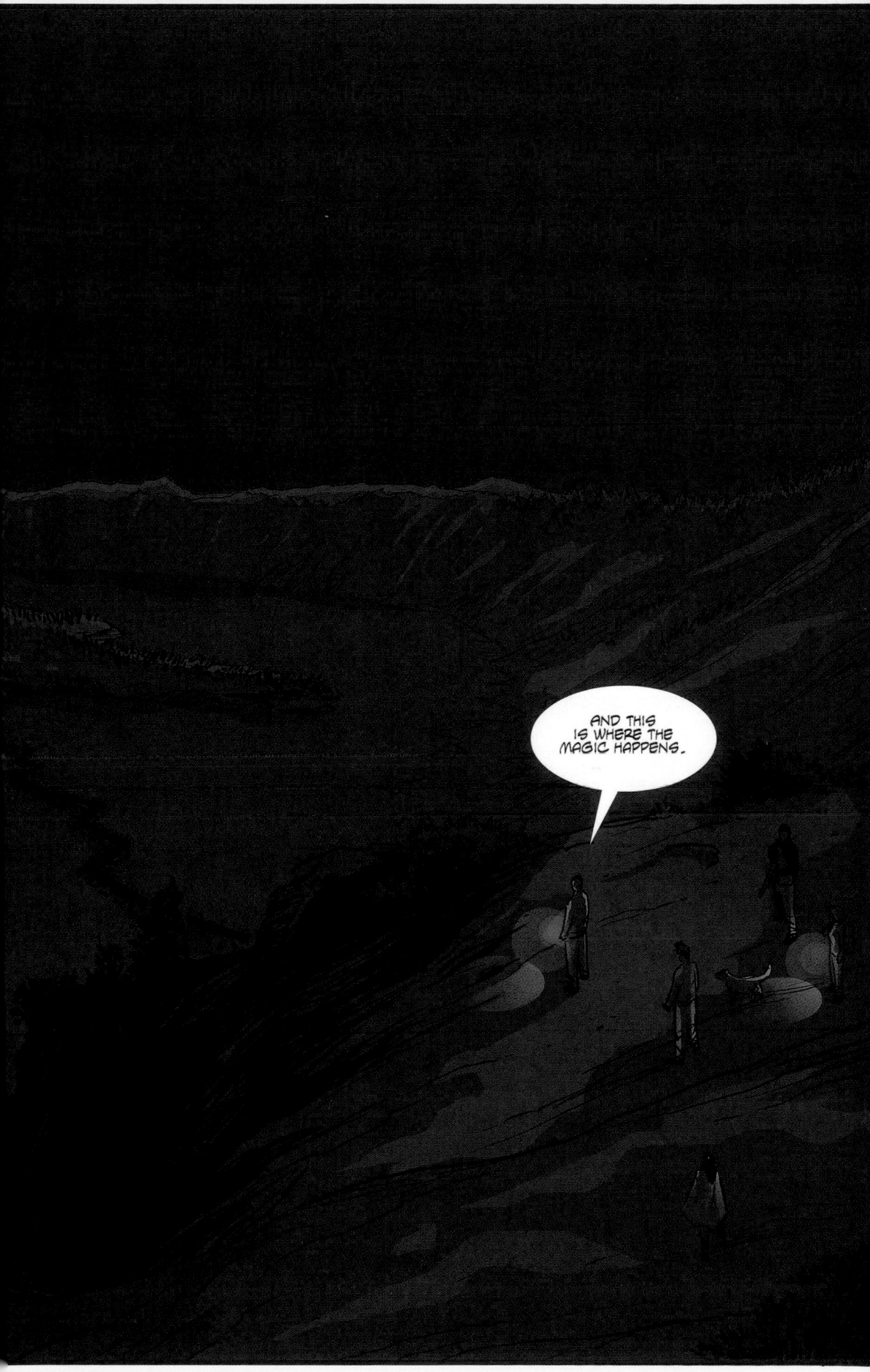
AND THIS IS WHERE THE MAGIC HAPPENS.

LEAVE YOUR GUNS. WE CAN'T RISK DAMAGING THE BOX.

NO CHANCE.

THEN TURN AROUND AND LEARN NOTHING.

YOUR CHOICE.

IT'S FINE, ELI. WHATEVER'S GOING ON HERE --

I DON'T THINK BULLETS WILL HELP.

WHAT HAPPENED TO THESE PEOPLE?

THEY COME DURING WALKABOUTS. ANYONE WITHIN A FIVE MILE RADIUS IS DRAWN DIRECTLY TO THIS SPOT.

SO MY DATA WAS RIGHT.

BEFORE THE DIVIDE, I WAS ON THE FOREFRONT OF DRONE RESEARCH. AS IT TURNS OUT, A BRAIN WITH NO MEMORIES HAS A SIMILAR CODING STRUCTURE. YOU START WITH BASIC FUNCTIONALITY, AND ADD INSTRUCTIONAL LAYERS.

SUCH AS THE SKILLS NECESSARY TO CONSTRUCT THIS BRIDGE.

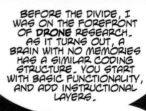

BUT ENOUGH SHOP TALK. IT'S TIME TO INTRODUCE THE MAIN ATTRACTION.

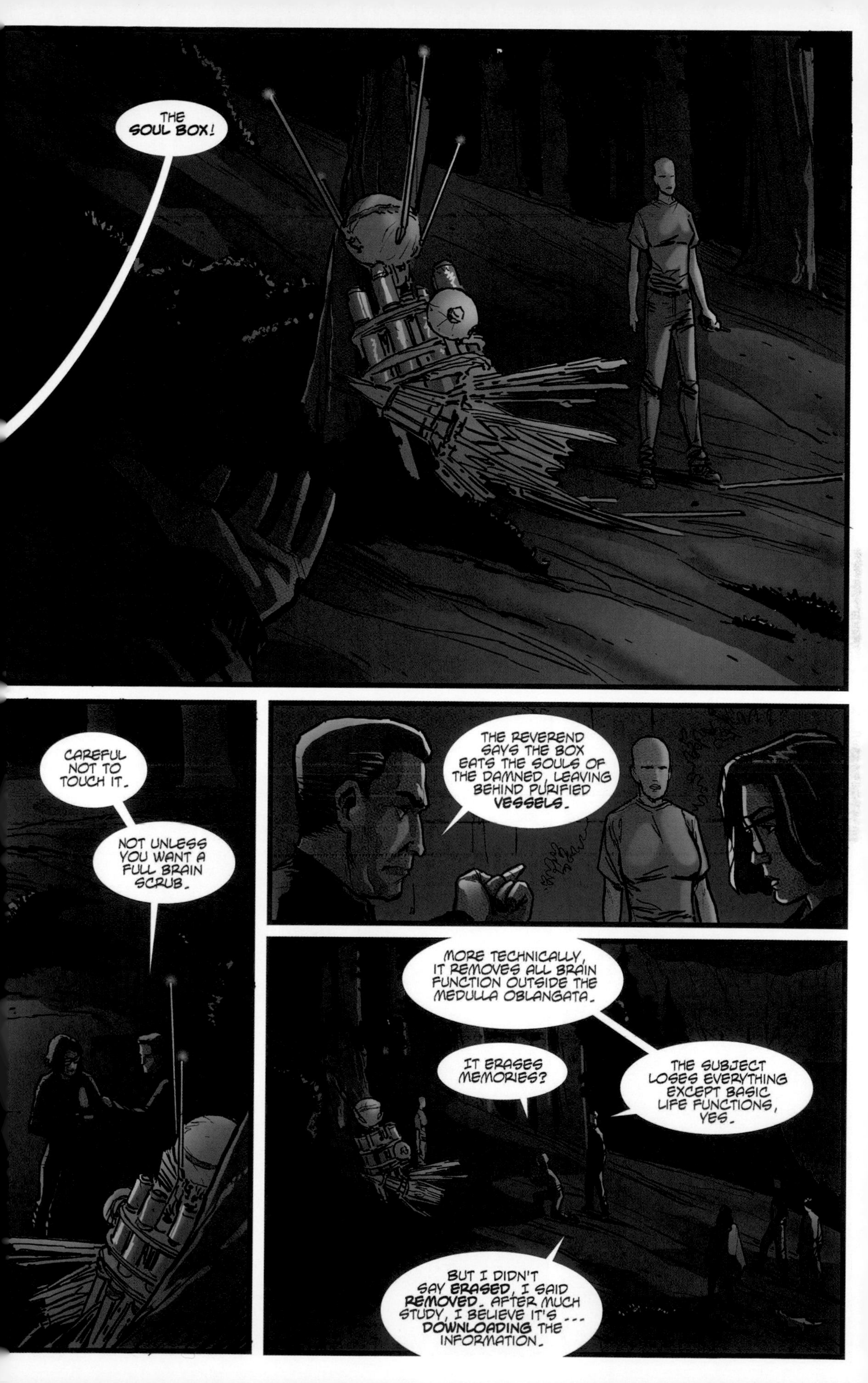
THE SOUL BOX!
CAREFUL NOT TO TOUCH IT.
NOT UNLESS YOU WANT A FULL BRAIN SCRUB.
THE REVEREND SAYS THE BOX EATS THE SOULS OF THE DAMNED, LEAVING BEHIND PURIFIED VESSELS.
MORE TECHNICALLY, IT REMOVES ALL BRAIN FUNCTION OUTSIDE THE MEDULLA OBLANGATA.
IT ERASES MEMORIES?
THE SUBJECT LOSES EVERYTHING EXCEPT BASIC LIFE FUNCTIONS, YES.
BUT I DIDN'T SAY ERASED, I SAID REMOVED. AFTER MUCH STUDY, I BELIEVE IT'S... DOWNLOADING THE INFORMATION.

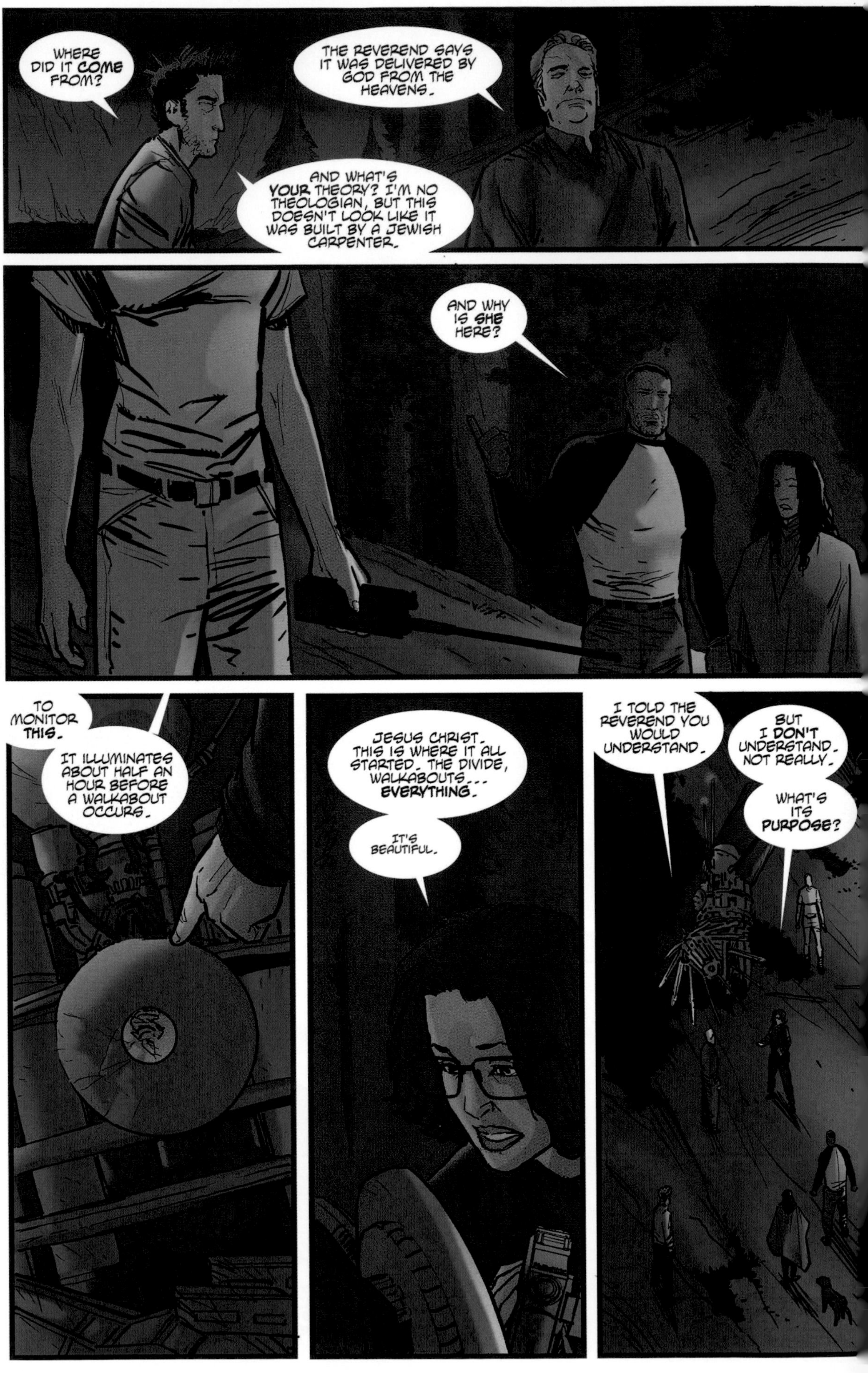
WHERE DID IT COME FROM?
THE REVEREND SAYS IT WAS DELIVERED BY GOD FROM THE HEAVENS.
AND WHAT'S YOUR THEORY? I'M NO THEOLOGIAN, BUT THIS DOESN'T LOOK LIKE IT WAS BUILT BY A JEWISH CARPENTER.
AND WHY IS SHE HERE?
TO MONITOR THIS.
IT ILLUMINATES ABOUT HALF AN HOUR BEFORE A WALKABOUT OCCURS.
JESUS CHRIST. THIS IS WHERE IT ALL STARTED. THE DIVIDE, WALKABOUTS... EVERYTHING.
IT'S BEAUTIFUL.
I TOLD THE REVEREND YOU WOULD UNDERSTAND.
BUT I DON'T UNDERSTAND. NOT REALLY.
WHAT'S ITS PURPOSE?

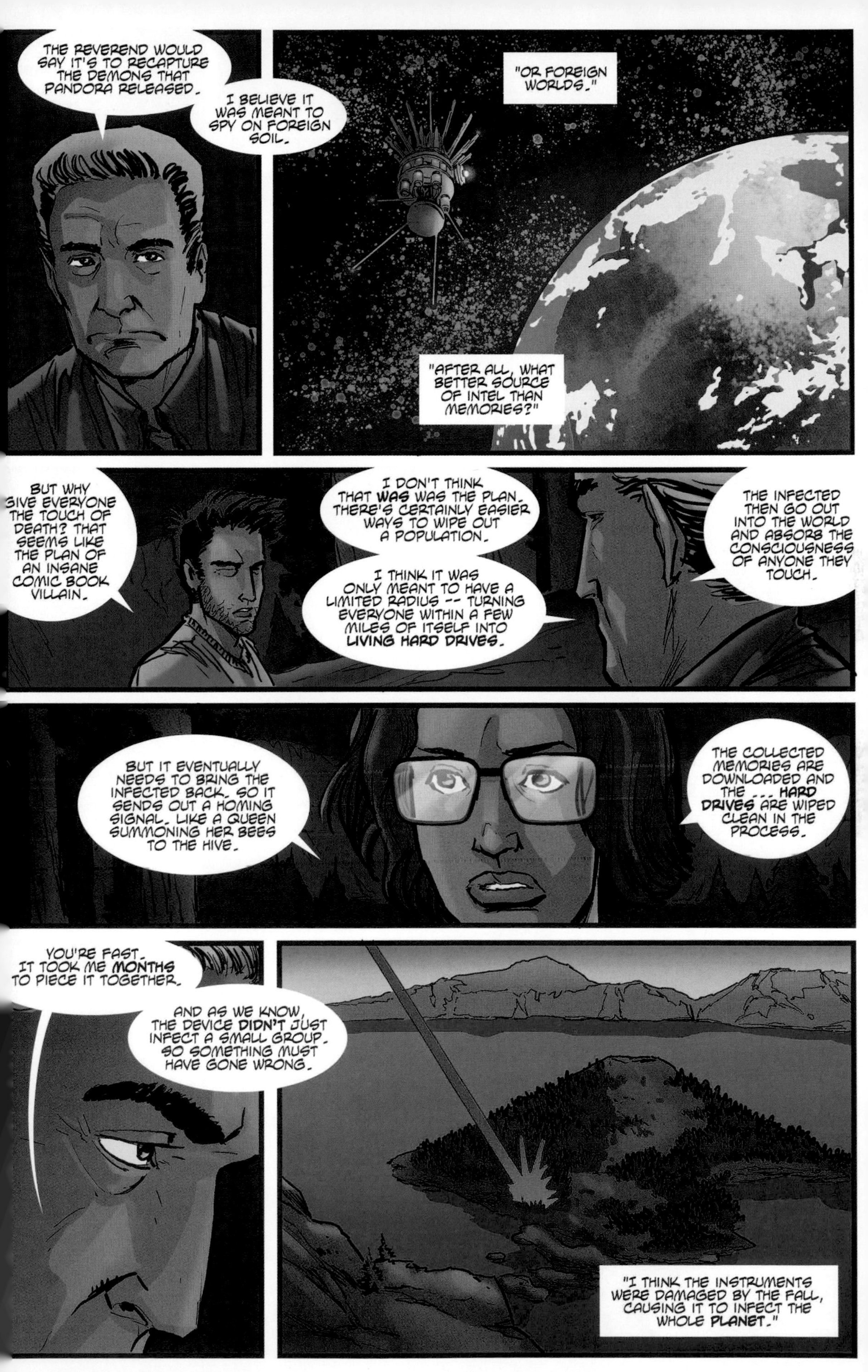
THE REVEREND WOULD SAY IT'S TO RECAPTURE THE DEMONS THAT PANDORA RELEASED.
I BELIEVE IT WAS MEANT TO SPY ON FOREIGN SOIL.
"OR FOREIGN WORLDS."
"AFTER ALL, WHAT BETTER SOURCE OF INTEL THAN MEMORIES?"
BUT WHY GIVE EVERYONE THE TOUCH OF DEATH? THAT SEEMS LIKE THE PLAN OF AN INSANE COMIC BOOK VILLAIN.
I DON'T THINK THAT WAS WAS THE PLAN. THERE'S CERTAINLY EASIER WAYS TO WIPE OUT A POPULATION.
I THINK IT WAS ONLY MEANT TO HAVE A LIMITED RADIUS -- TURNING EVERYONE WITHIN A FEW MILES OF ITSELF INTO LIVING HARD DRIVES.
THE INFECTED THEN GO OUT INTO THE WORLD AND ABSORB THE CONSCIOUSNESS OF ANYONE THEY TOUCH.
BUT IT EVENTUALLY NEEDS TO BRING THE INFECTED BACK, SO IT SENDS OUT A HOMING SIGNAL. LIKE A QUEEN SUMMONING HER BEES TO THE HIVE.
THE COLLECTED MEMORIES ARE DOWNLOADED AND THE ... HARD DRIVES ARE WIPED CLEAN IN THE PROCESS.
YOU'RE FAST. IT TOOK ME MONTHS TO PIECE IT TOGETHER.
AND AS WE KNOW, THE DEVICE DIDN'T JUST INFECT A SMALL GROUP. SO SOMETHING MUST HAVE GONE WRONG.
"I THINK THE INSTRUMENTS WERE DAMAGED BY THE FALL, CAUSING IT TO INFECT THE WHOLE PLANET."

AND IF THE HOMING BEACON TRIGGERS EVERYONE WHO'S INFECTED, THAT WOULD EXPLAIN THE GLOBAL WALKABOUTS.

EXACTLY. BUT ITS "SUMMONING" RANGE IS LIMITED, EITHER BY DESIGN OR DAMAGE. ONLY PEOPLE NEARBY ARE DRAWN BACK TO THE BOX WHEN IT ACTIVATES. EVERYONE ELSE JUST WANDERS AIMLESSLY.

LIKE DRONES WITHOUT A GUIDING SEQUENCE.

OR BEES WITH FAULTY PHEROMONES.

SO THE WORLD ENDED BECAUSE OF A GLITCH?

MAYBE. IT'S AN INTERESTING THEORY.

CAN YOU FIX IT?

I DON'T KNOW. I'D NEED TIME TO STUDY IT. MAYBE IF --

"FIX" IT? NO, I'M AFRAID THAT'S NOT ALLOWED.

I CONVINCED THE REVEREND THAT A FELLOW SCIENTIST'S MIND WAS WORTH SAVING. AND I WAS OBVIOUSLY RIGHT.

BUT THAT BARGAIN CAME AT A PRICE.

THE OTHERS WILL HAVE TO FEED THE BOX.

WHY ARE YOU DOING THIS? THAT LADY'S INSANE.

THE REVEREND AND I MAY HAVE DIFFERENT OPINIONS ABOUT HOW THE SOUL BOX **WORKS**, BUT WE SHARE THE SAME VISION.

WE'RE REMAKING THE WORLD INTO BETTER PLACE, CAN'T YOU SEE THAT?

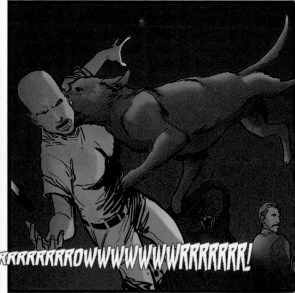

GRRRRRRRRRRRRRRRRRRROWWWWWWWRRRRRRR!

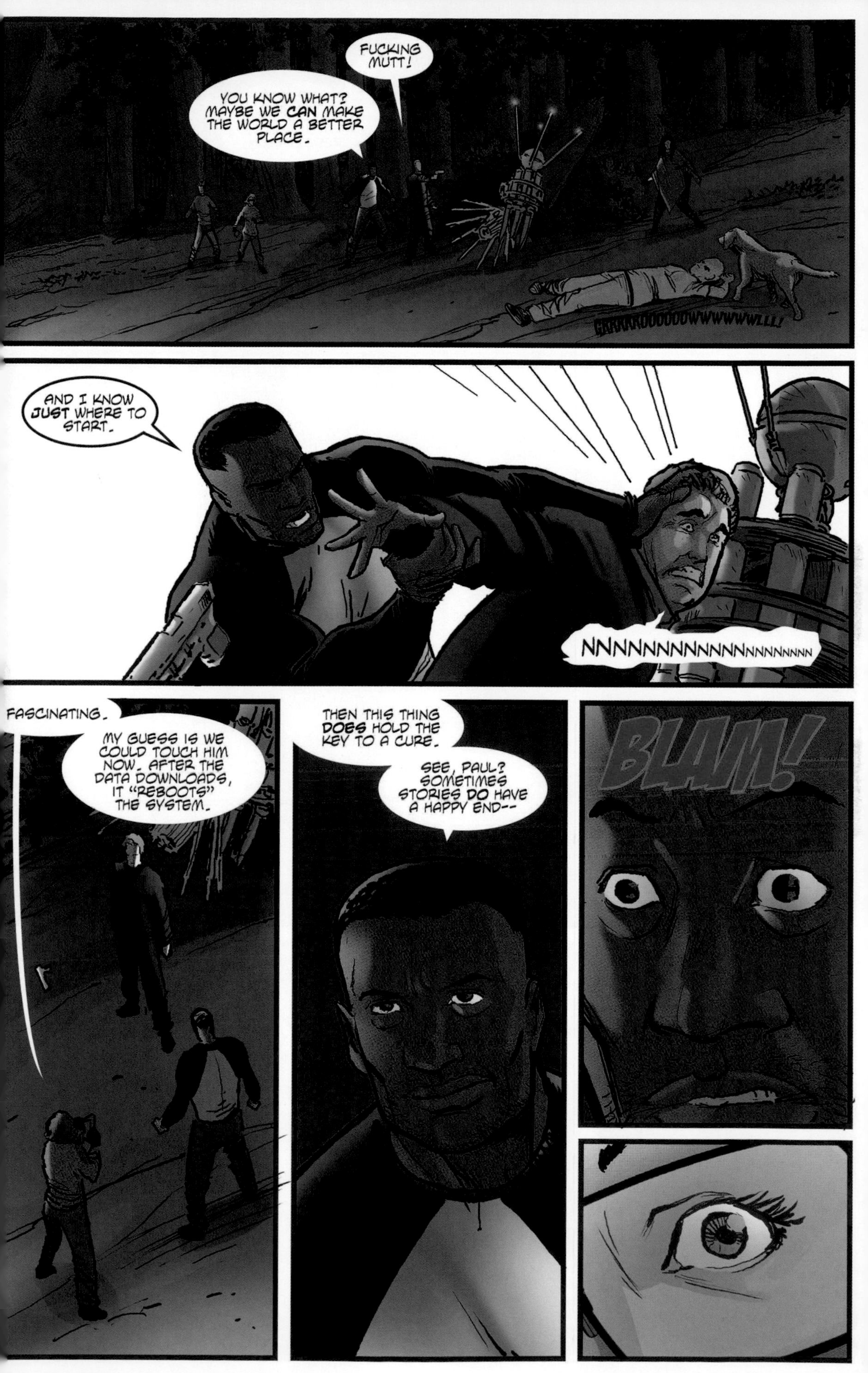
FUCKING MUTT!
YOU KNOW WHAT? MAYBE WE CAN MAKE THE WORLD A BETTER PLACE.
GRRRRROOOOOOOWWWWWWLLL!
AND I KNOW JUST WHERE TO START.
NNNNNNNNNNNNNNNNNNNN
FASCINATING.
MY GUESS IS WE COULD TOUCH HIM NOW. AFTER THE DATA DOWNLOADS, IT "REBOOTS" THE SYSTEM.
THEN THIS THING DOES HOLD THE KEY TO A CURE.
SEE, PAUL? SOMETIMES STORIES DO HAVE A HAPPY END--
BLAM!

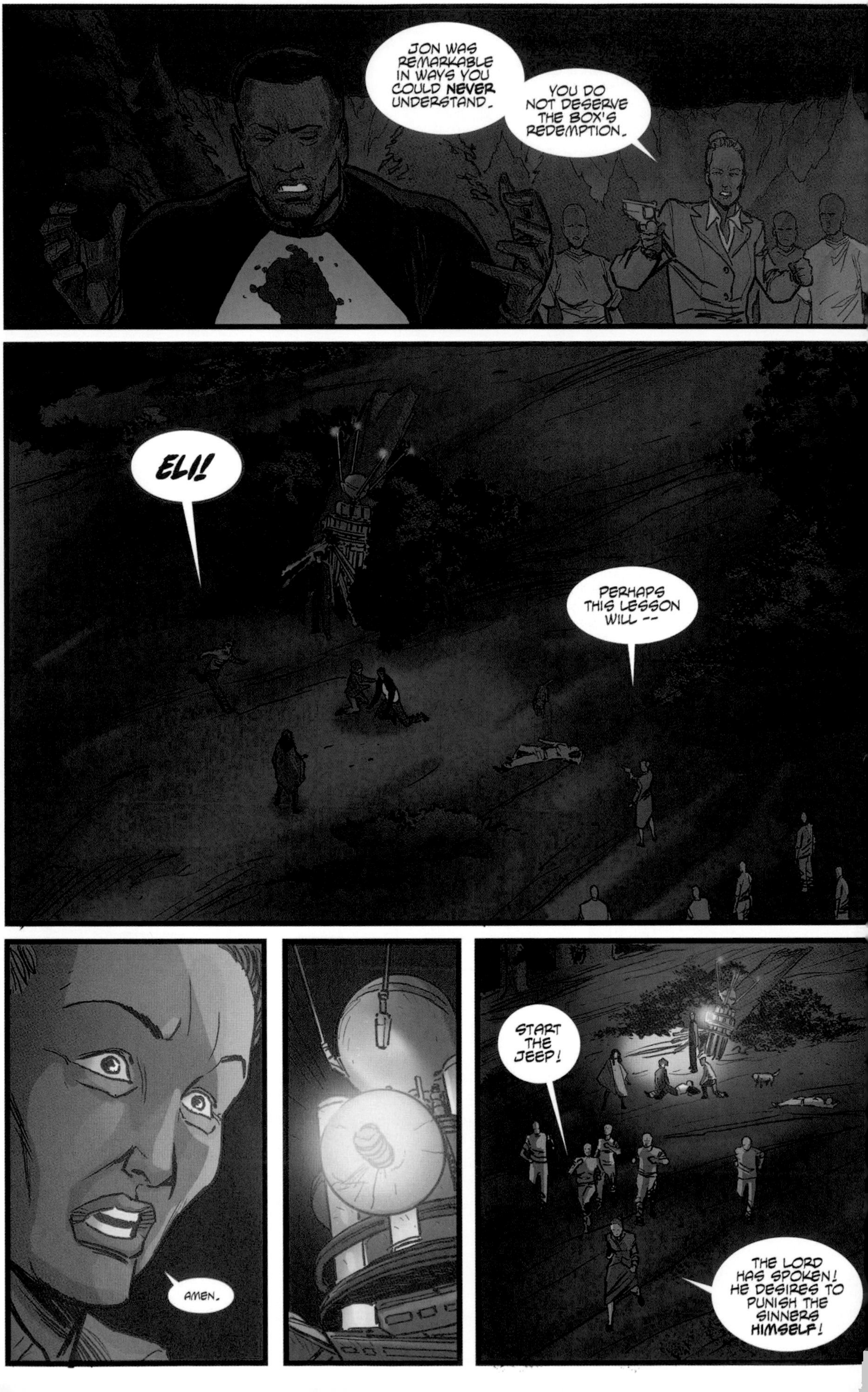
JON WAS REMARKABLE IN WAYS YOU COULD NEVER UNDERSTAND.
YOU DO NOT DESERVE THE BOX'S REDEMPTION.
ELI!
PERHAPS THIS LESSON WILL --
AMEN.
START THE JEEP!
THE LORD HAS SPOKEN! HE DESIRES TO PUNISH THE SINNERS HIMSELF!

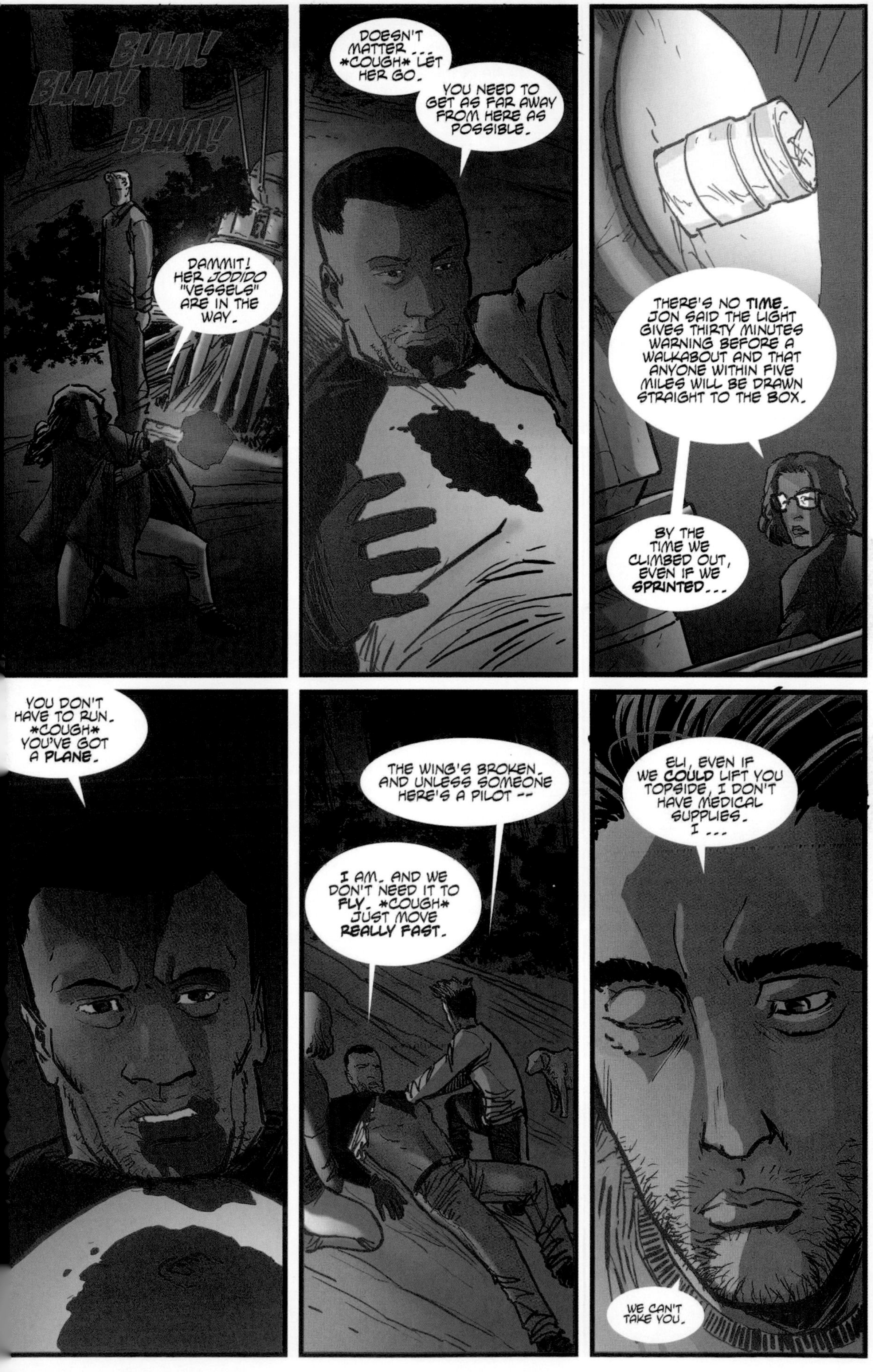
BLAM!
BLAM!
BLAM!
DAMMIT! HER JODIDO "VESSELS" ARE IN THE WAY.
DOESN'T MATTER... *COUGH* LET HER GO.
YOU NEED TO GET AS FAR AWAY FROM HERE AS POSSIBLE.
THERE'S NO TIME. JON SAID THE LIGHT GIVES THIRTY MINUTES WARNING BEFORE A WALKABOUT AND THAT ANYONE WITHIN FIVE MILES WILL BE DRAWN STRAIGHT TO THE BOX.
BY THE TIME WE CLIMBED OUT, EVEN IF WE SPRINTED...
YOU DON'T HAVE TO RUN. *COUGH* YOU'VE GOT A PLANE.
THE WING'S BROKEN. AND UNLESS SOMEONE HERE'S A PILOT --
I AM. AND WE DON'T NEED IT TO FLY. *COUGH* JUST MOVE REALLY FAST.
ELI, EVEN IF WE COULD LIFT YOU TOPSIDE, I DON'T HAVE MEDICAL SUPPLIES. I...
WE CAN'T TAKE YOU.

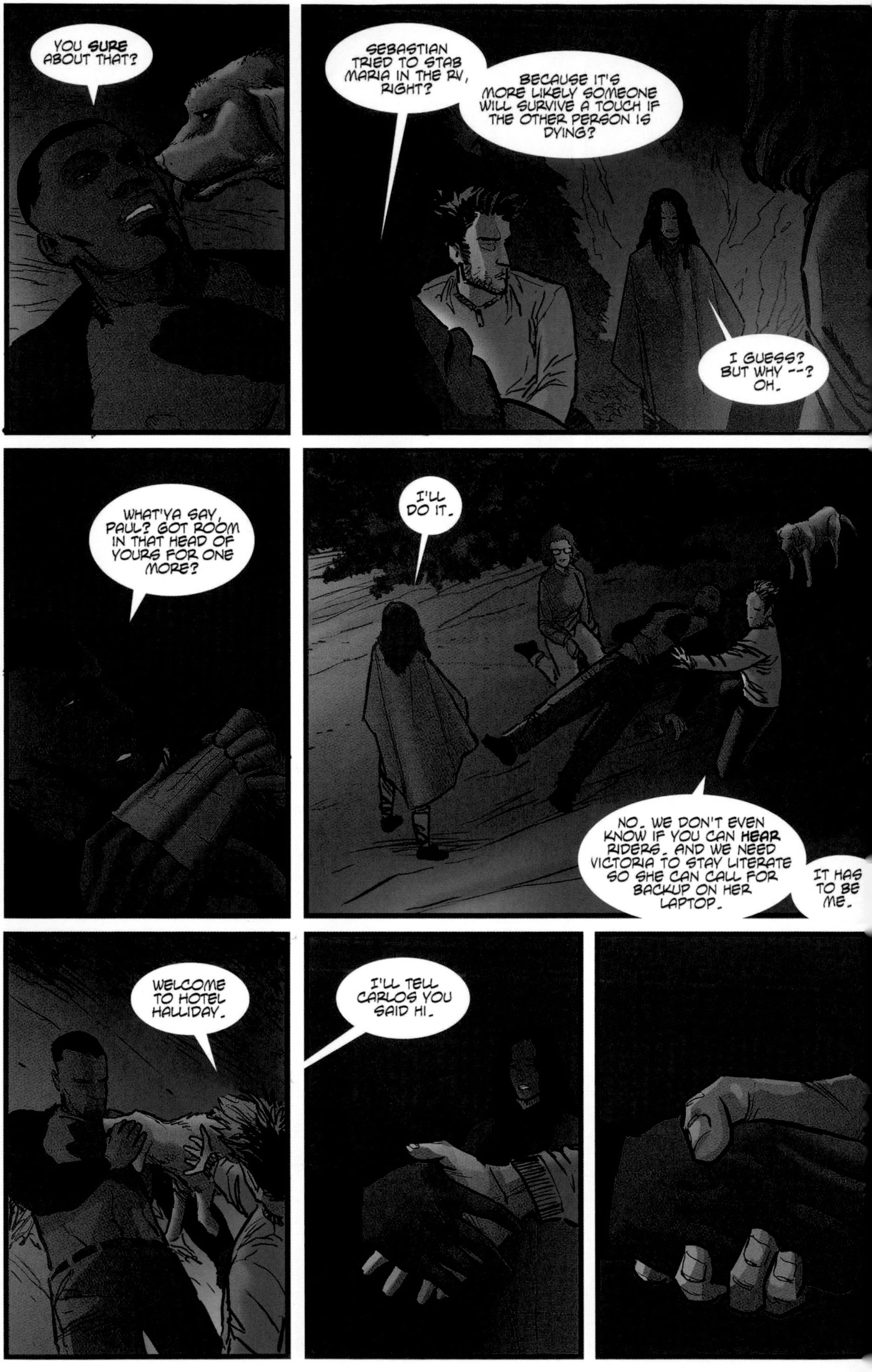

YOU SURE ABOUT THAT?
SEBASTIAN TRIED TO STAB MARIA IN THE RV, RIGHT?
BECAUSE IT'S MORE LIKELY SOMEONE WILL SURVIVE A TOUCH IF THE OTHER PERSON IS DYING?
I GUESS? BUT WHY --? OH.
WHAT'YA SAY, PAUL? GOT ROOM IN THAT HEAD OF YOURS FOR ONE MORE?
I'LL DO IT.
NO. WE DON'T EVEN KNOW IF YOU CAN HEAR RIDERS. AND WE NEED VICTORIA TO STAY LITERATE SO SHE CAN CALL FOR BACKUP ON HER LAPTOP.
IT HAS TO BE ME.
WELCOME TO HOTEL HALLIDAY.
I'LL TELL CARLOS YOU SAID HI.

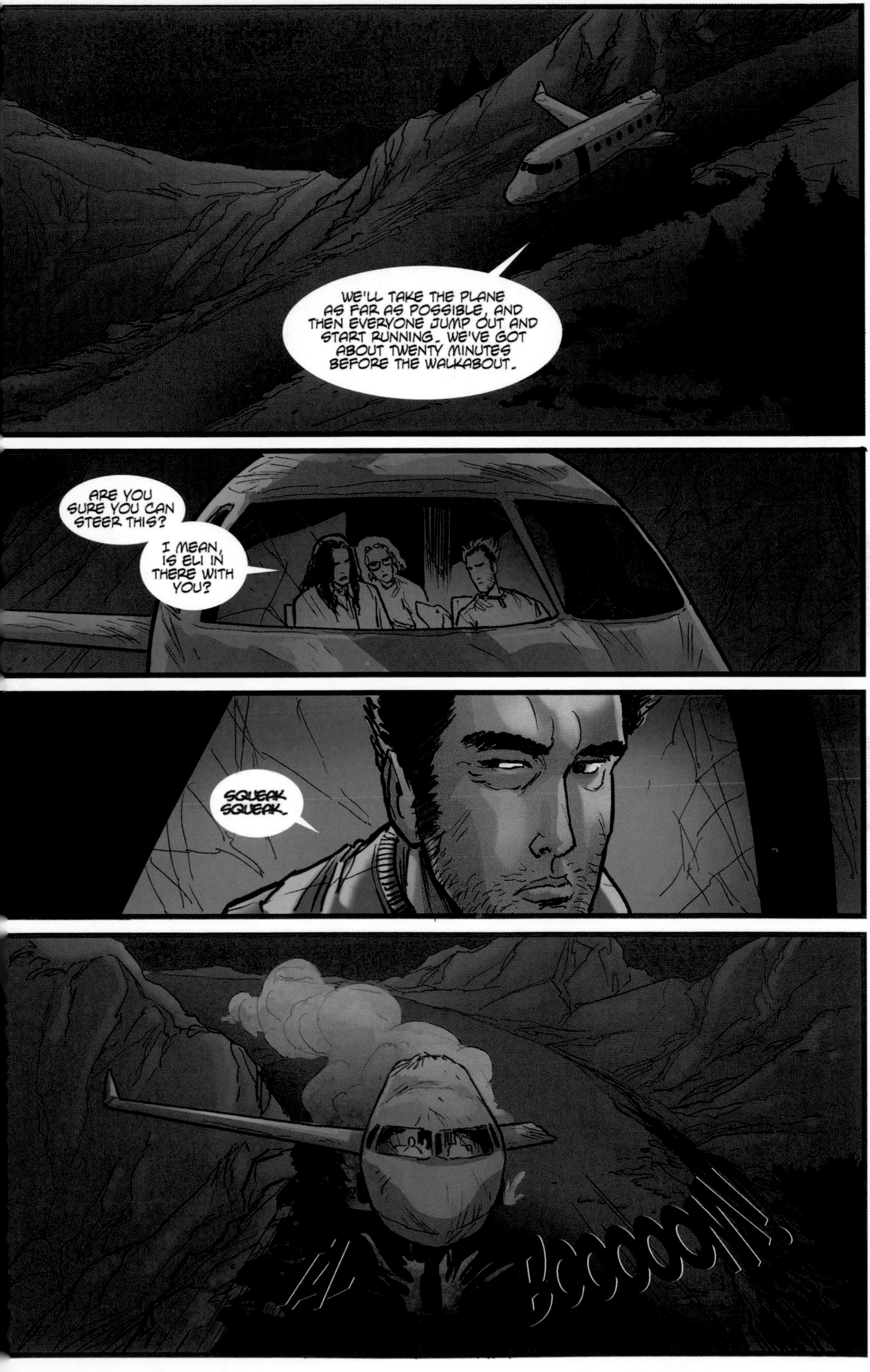
WE'LL TAKE THE PLANE AS FAR AS POSSIBLE, AND THEN EVERYONE JUMP OUT AND START RUNNING. WE'VE GOT ABOUT TWENTY MINUTES BEFORE THE WALKABOUT.
ARE YOU SURE YOU CAN STEER THIS?
I MEAN, IS ELI IN THERE WITH YOU?
SQUEAK SQUEAK.

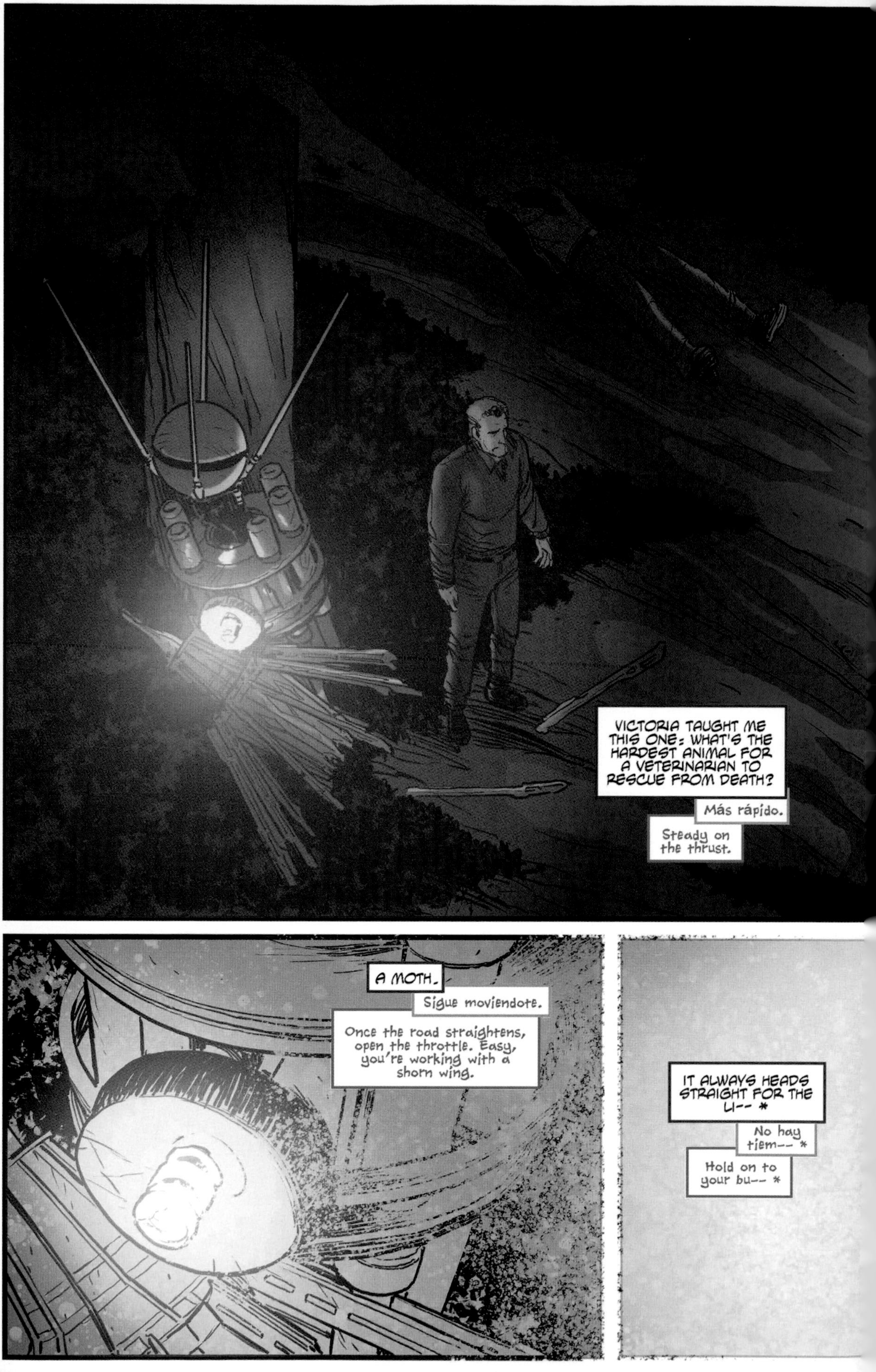
VICTORIA TAUGHT ME THIS ONE: WHAT'S THE HARDEST ANIMAL FOR A VETERINARIAN TO RESCUE FROM DEATH?
Más rápido.
Steady on the thrust.
A MOTH.
Sigue moviendote.
Once the road straightens, open the throttle. Easy, you're working with a shorn wing.
IT ALWAYS HEADS STRAIGHT FOR THE LI-- *
No hay tiem-- *
Hold on to your bu-- *

CLASSIFIED

SECURITY LEVEL:
DOUBLE BLACK

TelChan v0.78, Cpu Cycles: 3000, Frameskip 0, IRC restricted_research.gov

22:01:17* VLS has joined the group. Security clearance confirmed.
!ERROR! GPS not found !ERROR!

22:01:23 <ULS> This may be my last time online for a bit.

22:01:34 <JCK> Run into trouble?

22:01:51 <ULS> Honestly, I have no idea what the hell we've run into, but answers are here. I'm sure of it.

22:02:01 <JCK> Which answers? There are a LOT of questions.

22:02:09 <ULS> The only one that really matters -- what started the Divide?

22:02:15 <JCK> Where are you?

22:02:40 <ULS> I can't tell you that. We both know who's listening.

22:02:46 <ULS> Where is Amy, by the way?

22:03:13 <JCK> An assistant logged in with her account a few days ago. Apparently, there was an accidental contact in the lab. Amy survived, thank God, but the dyslexia prevents her from using a keyboard

22:03:22 <ULS> Oh damn. Hate to hear that.

22:03:24 <ULS> Wait.

22:03:28 <ULS> Amy has INTERNS??

22:03:41 <JCK> Says the one with the chauffers.

22:03:59 <ULS> Ha. Well, in any case, you're the one I need. What do you know about mass hypnotism?

22:04:19 <JCK> Not much. Before the walkabouts started, there was no evidenve that it ever worked. At least not in any reputable psychiatric journal. And considering the ethical implications, it wasn't allowed much room in academic circles.

22:04:26<ULS> Time to update those journals then. Because if there's one thing I can now say for certain --

22:04:29 <ULS> It's definitely allowed.

For the desk of
Gen. Canter

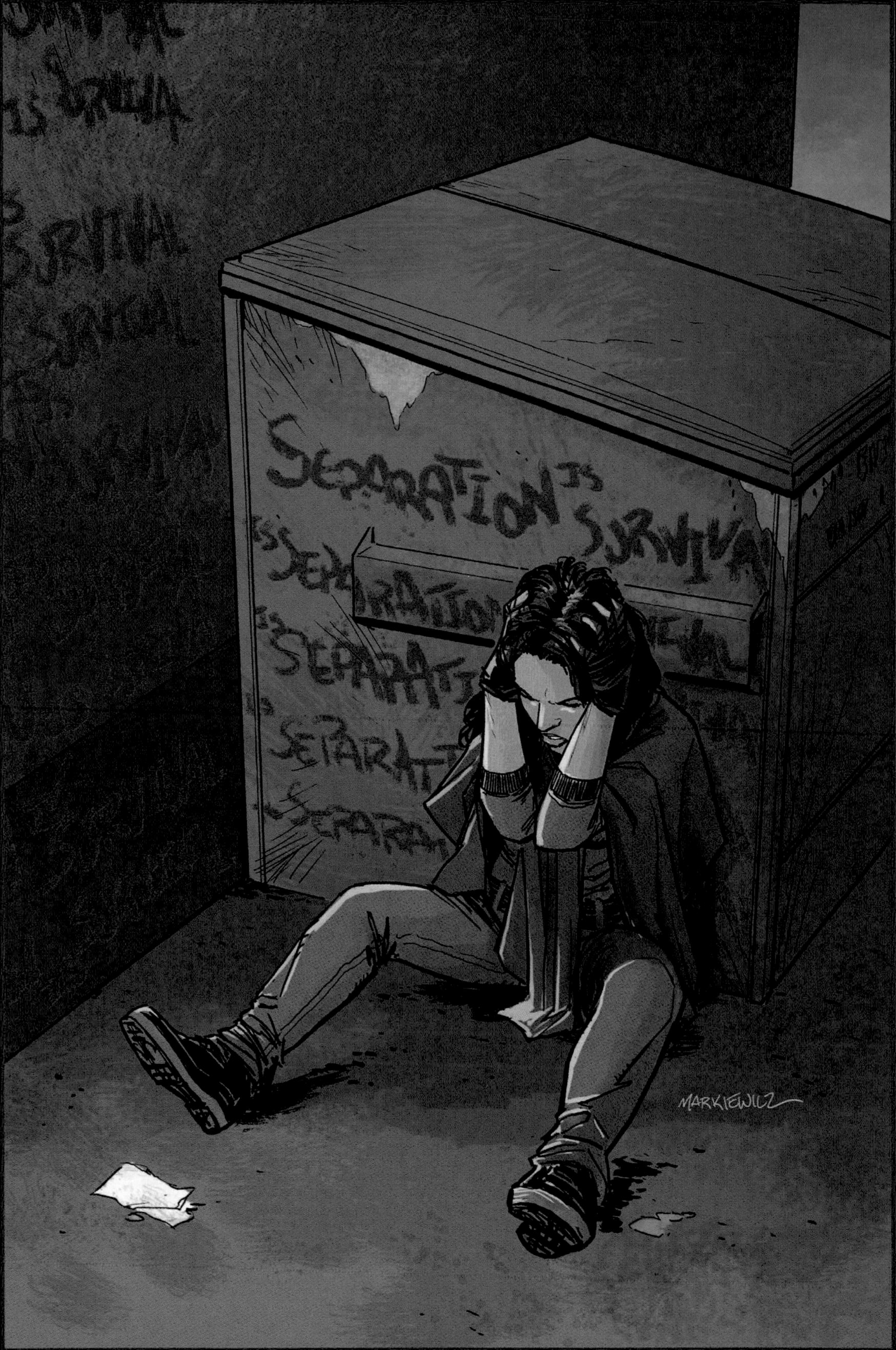
SEPARATION IS SURVIVAL
MARKIEWICZ

ISSUE SIX
COVER ART BY ADAM MARKIEWICZ
COLORS BY MELANIE DARLING

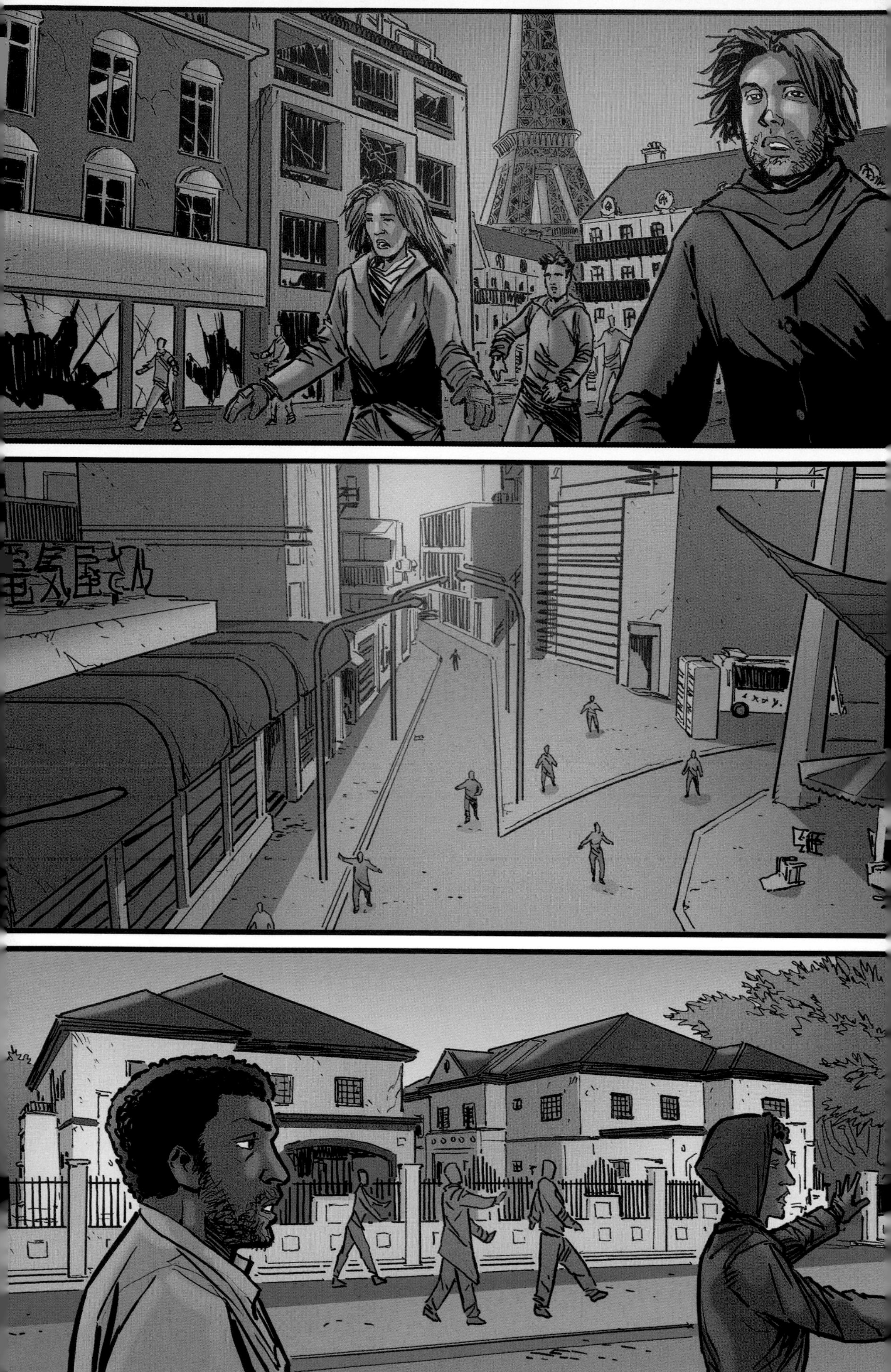

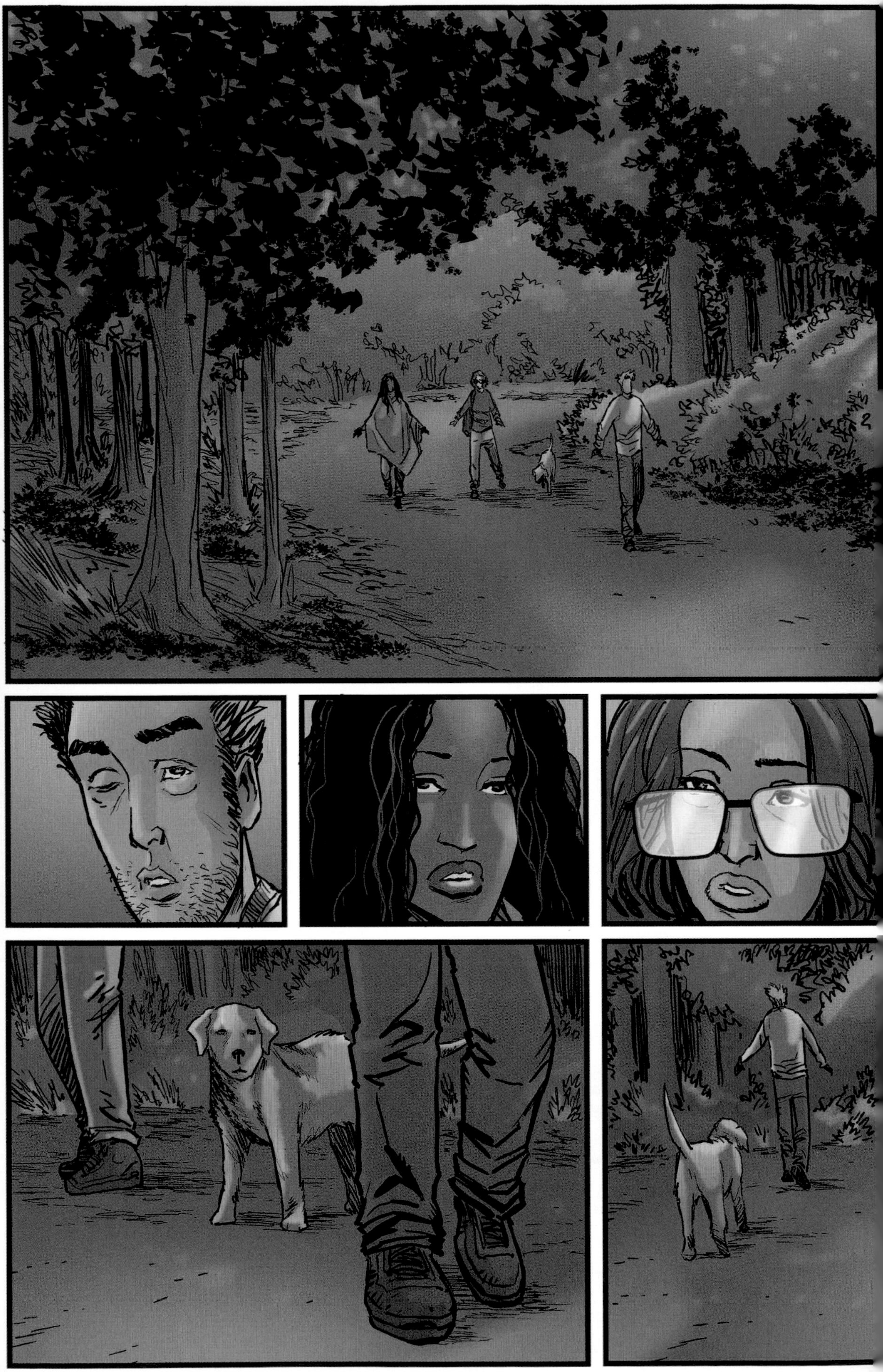

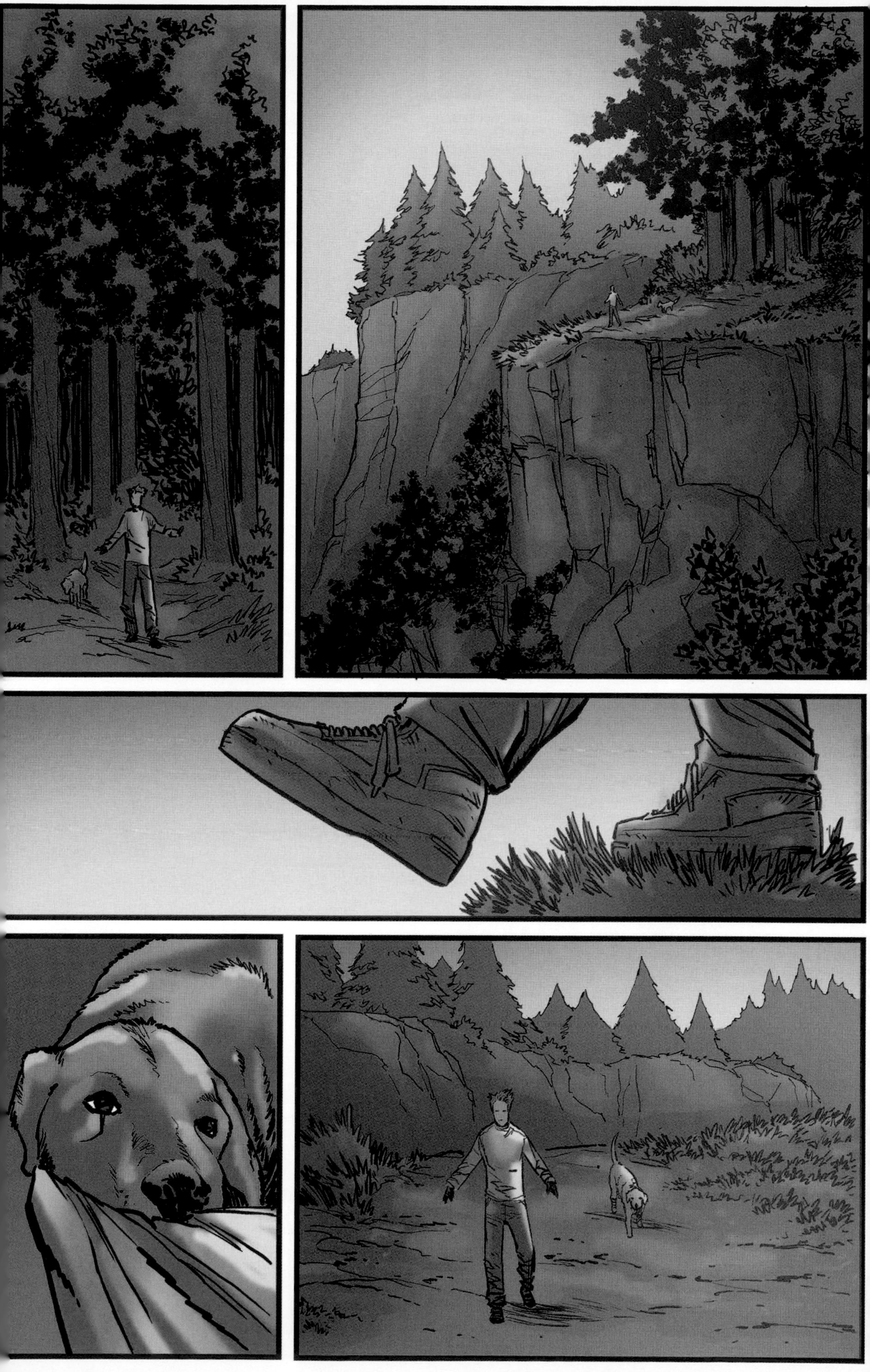

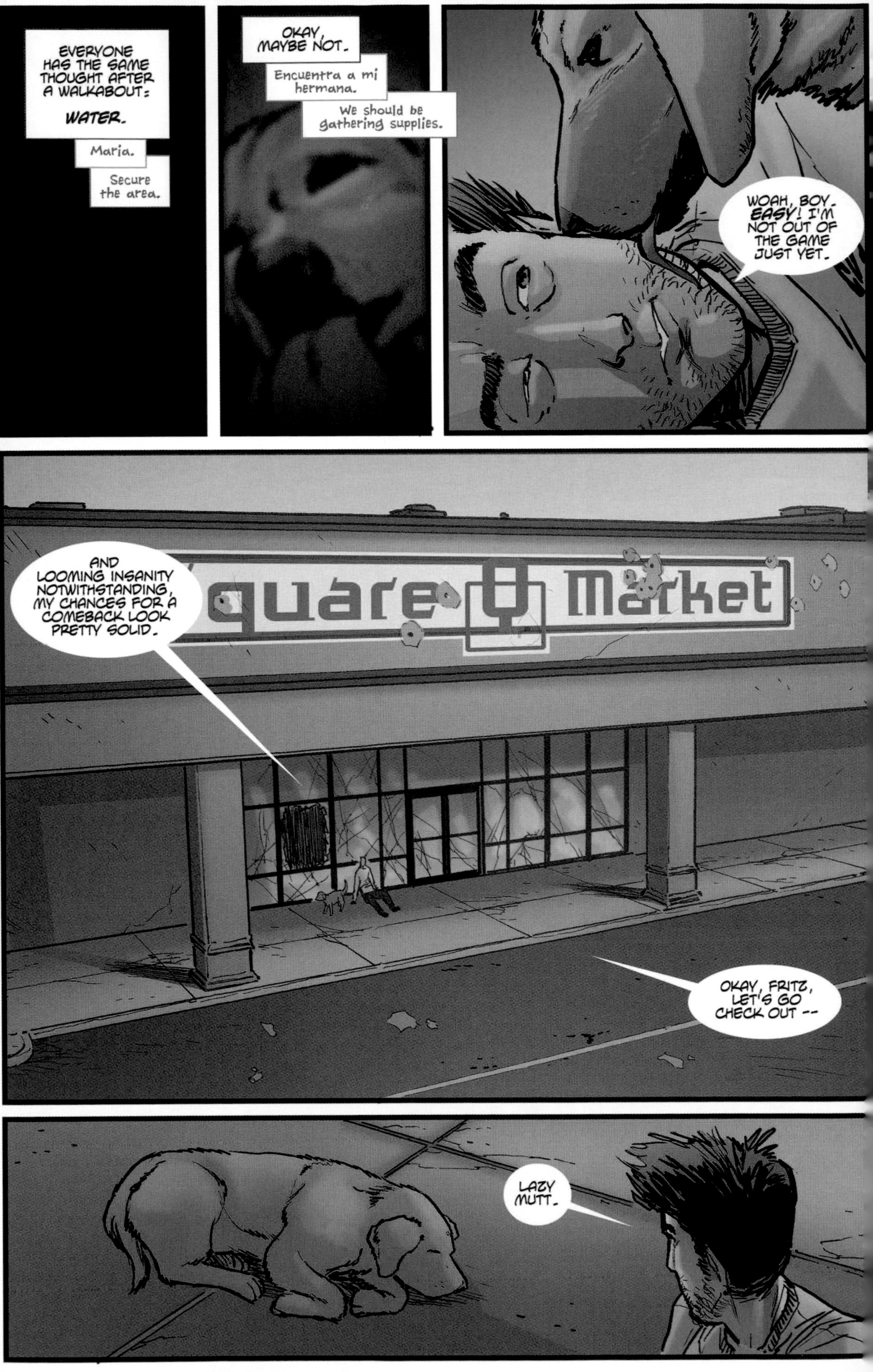
EVERYONE HAS THE SAME THOUGHT AFTER A WALKABOUT:
WATER.
Maria.
Secure the area.
OKAY, MAYBE NOT.
Encuentra a mi hermana.
We should be gathering supplies.
WOAH, BOY. EASY! I'M NOT OUT OF THE GAME JUST YET.
AND LOOMING INSANITY NOTWITHSTANDING, MY CHANCES FOR A COMEBACK LOOK PRETTY SOLID.
quare Q Market
OKAY, FRITZ, LET'S GO CHECK OUT --
LAZY MUTT.

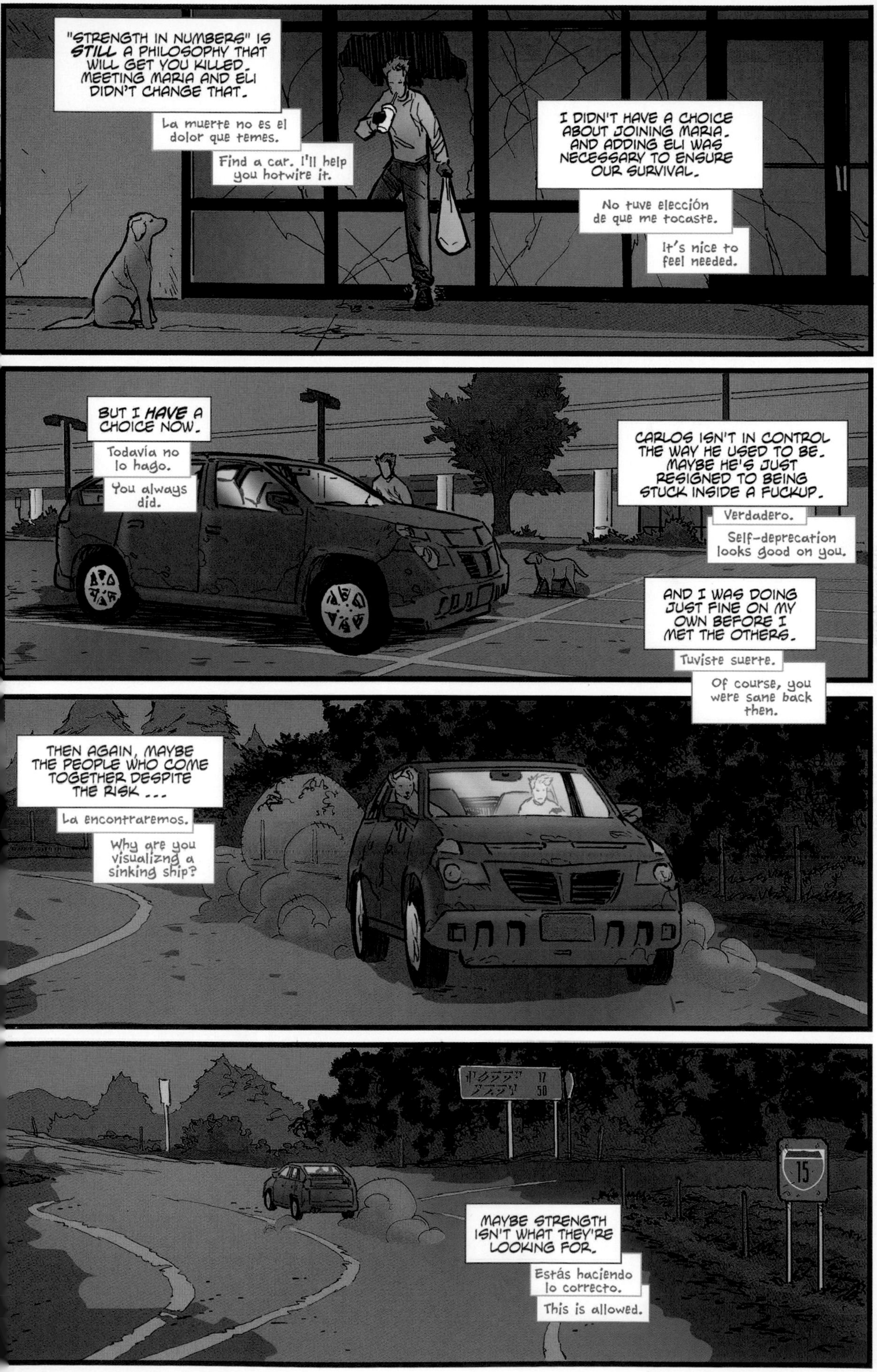
"STRENGTH IN NUMBERS" IS STILL A PHILOSOPHY THAT WILL GET YOU KILLED. MEETING MARIA AND ELI DIDN'T CHANGE THAT.
La muerte no es el dolor que temes.
Find a car. I'll help you hotwire it.
I DIDN'T HAVE A CHOICE ABOUT JOINING MARIA. AND ADDING ELI WAS NECESSARY TO ENSURE OUR SURVIVAL.
No tuve elección de que me tocaste.
It's nice to feel needed.
BUT I HAVE A CHOICE NOW.
Todavía no lo hago.
You always did.
CARLOS ISN'T IN CONTROL THE WAY HE USED TO BE. MAYBE HE'S JUST RESIGNED TO BEING STUCK INSIDE A FUCKUP.
Verdadero.
Self-deprecation looks good on you.
AND I WAS DOING JUST FINE ON MY OWN BEFORE I MET THE OTHERS.
Tuviste suerte.
Of course, you were sane back then.
THEN AGAIN, MAYBE THE PEOPLE WHO COME TOGETHER DESPITE THE RISK...
La encontraremos.
Why are you visualizng a sinking ship?
15
MAYBE STRENGTH ISN'T WHAT THEY'RE LOOKING FOR.
Estás haciendo lo correcto.
This is allowed.

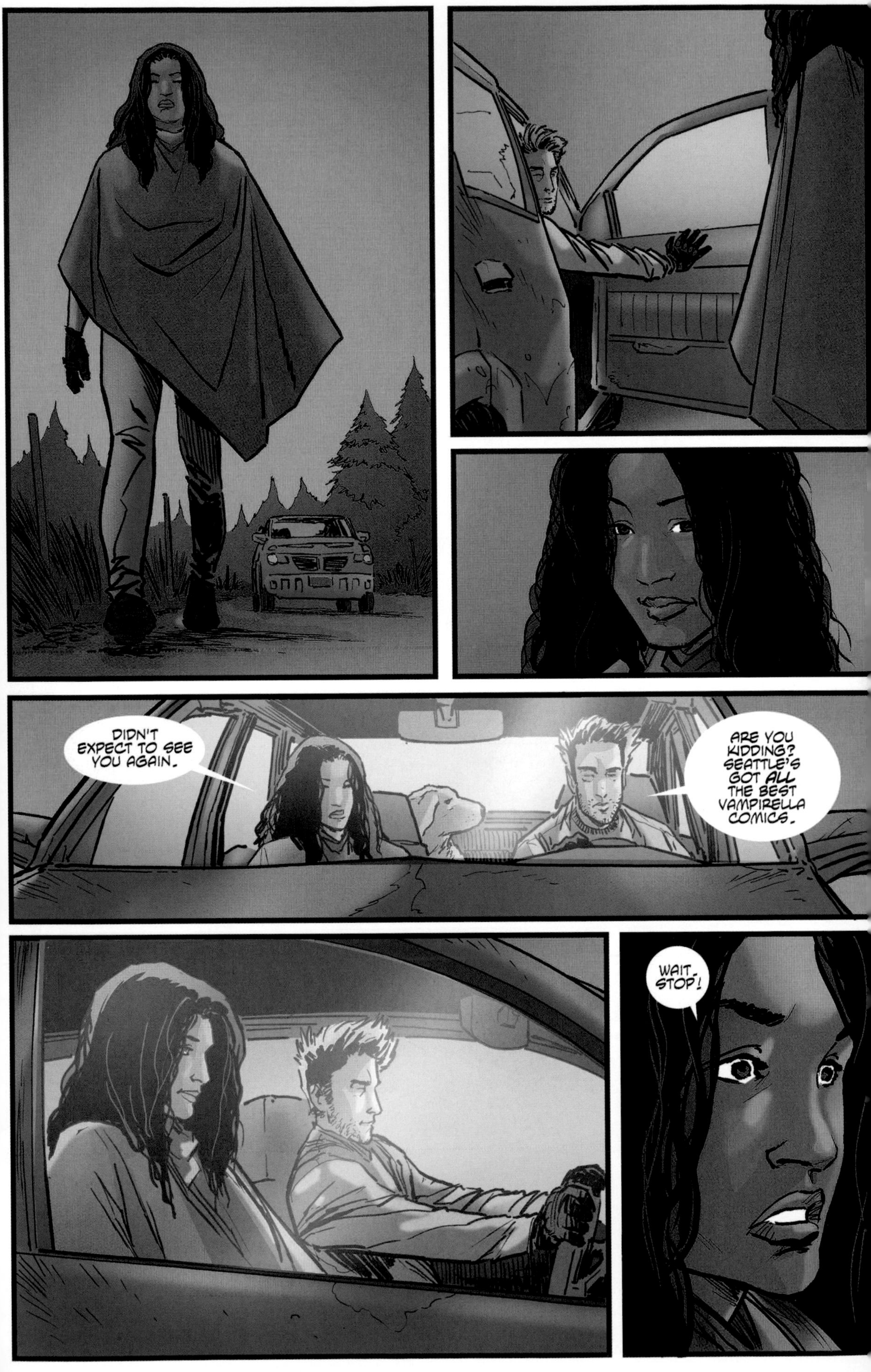
DIDN'T EXPECT TO SEE YOU AGAIN.
ARE YOU KIDDING? SEATTLE'S GOT ALL THE BEST VAMPIRELLA COMICS.
WAIT. STOP!

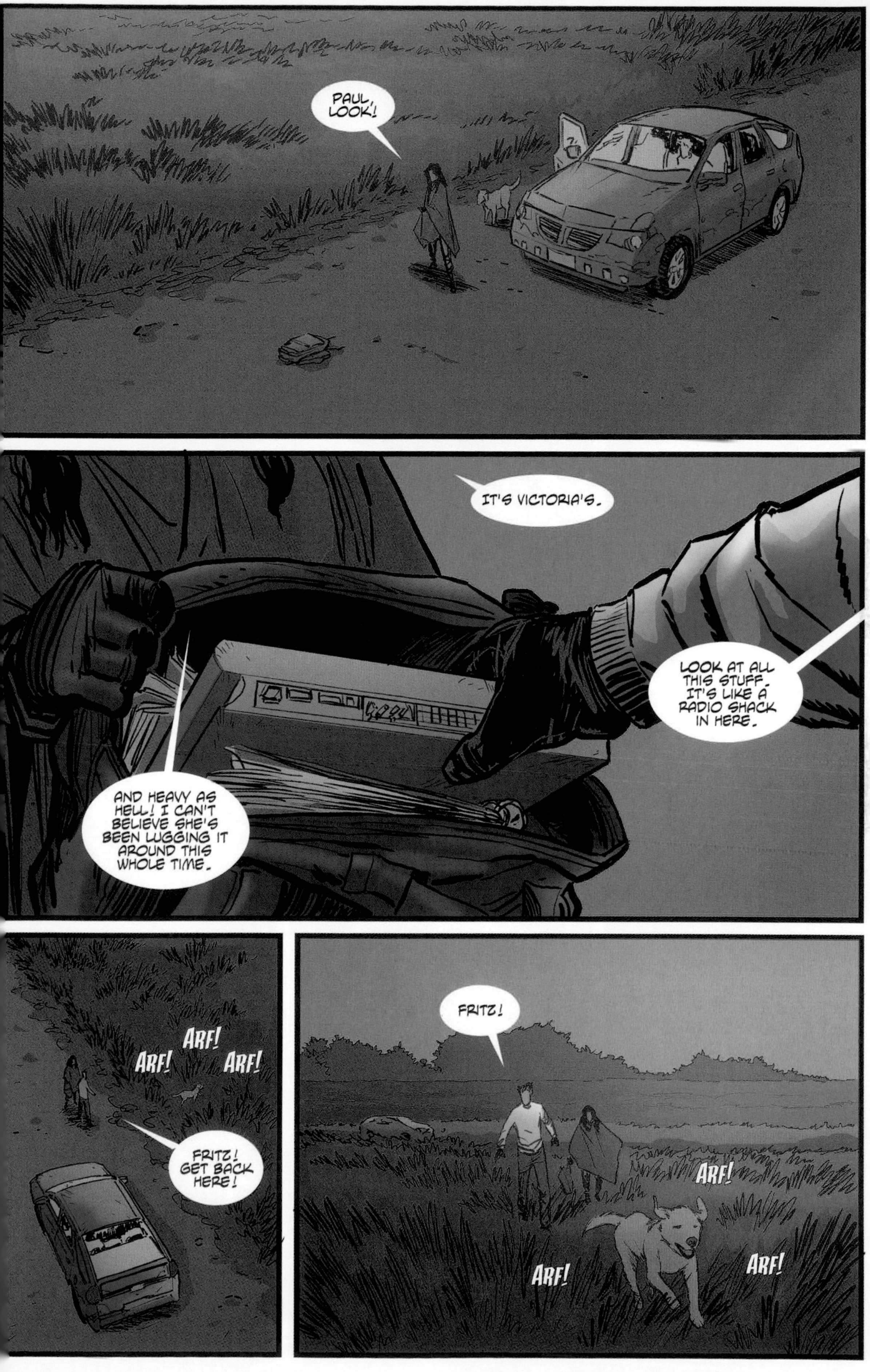
PAUL, LOOK!
IT'S VICTORIA'S.
LOOK AT ALL THIS STUFF. IT'S LIKE A RADIO SHACK IN HERE.
AND HEAVY AS HELL! I CAN'T BELIEVE SHE'S BEEN LUGGING IT AROUND THIS WHOLE TIME.
ARF!
ARF!
ARF!
FRITZ! GET BACK HERE!
FRITZ!
ARF!
ARF!
ARF!

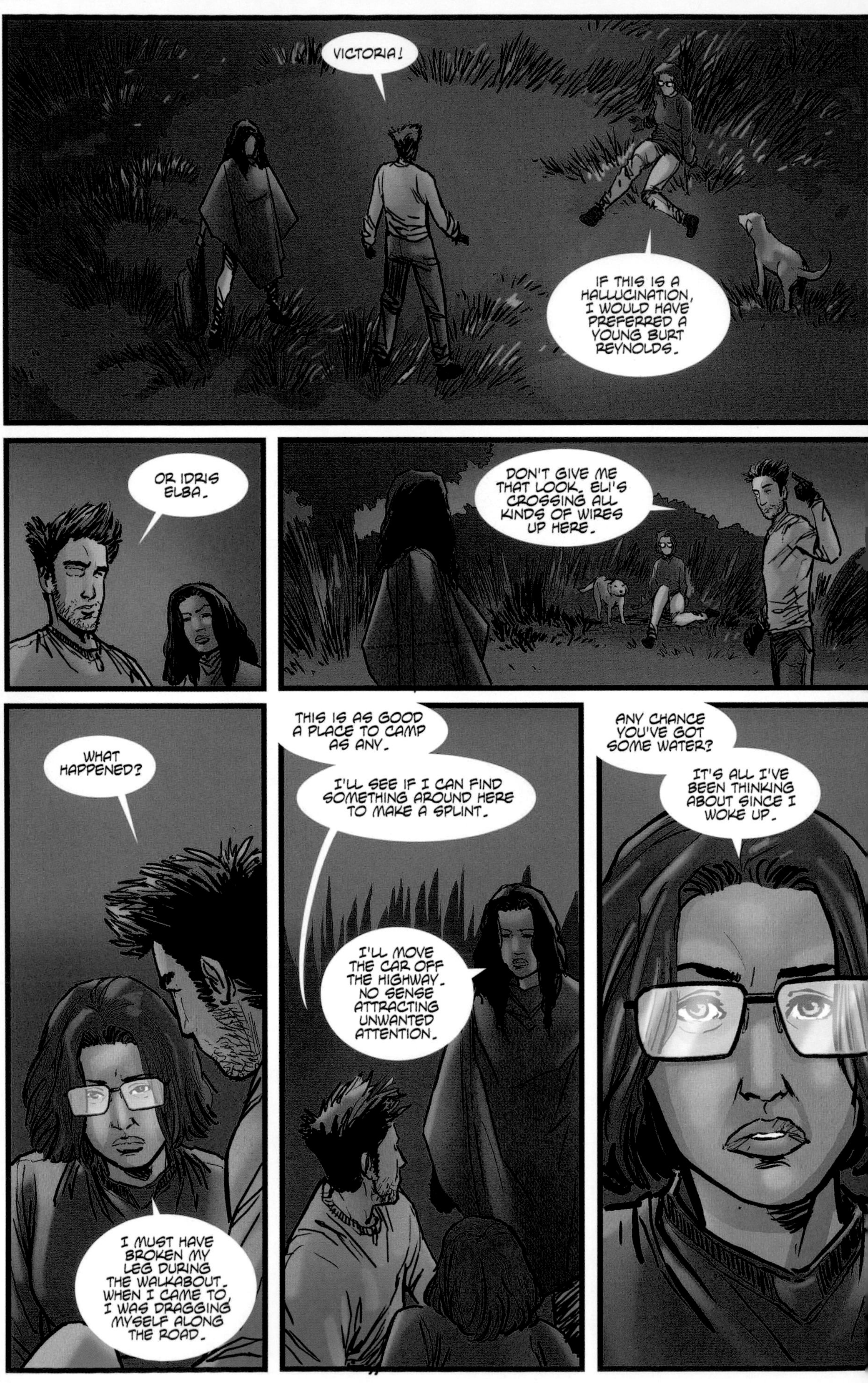
VICTORIA!
IF THIS IS A HALLUCINATION, I WOULD HAVE PREFERRED A YOUNG BURT REYNOLDS.
OR IDRIS ELBA.
DON'T GIVE ME THAT LOOK. ELI'S CROSSING ALL KINDS OF WIRES UP HERE.
WHAT HAPPENED?
I MUST HAVE BROKEN MY LEG DURING THE WALKABOUT. WHEN I CAME TO, I WAS DRAGGING MYSELF ALONG THE ROAD.
THIS IS AS GOOD A PLACE TO CAMP AS ANY.
I'LL SEE IF I CAN FIND SOMETHING AROUND HERE TO MAKE A SPLINT.
I'LL MOVE THE CAR OFF THE HIGHWAY. NO SENSE ATTRACTING UNWANTED ATTENTION.
ANY CHANCE YOU'VE GOT SOME WATER?
IT'S ALL I'VE BEEN THINKING ABOUT SINCE I WOKE UP.

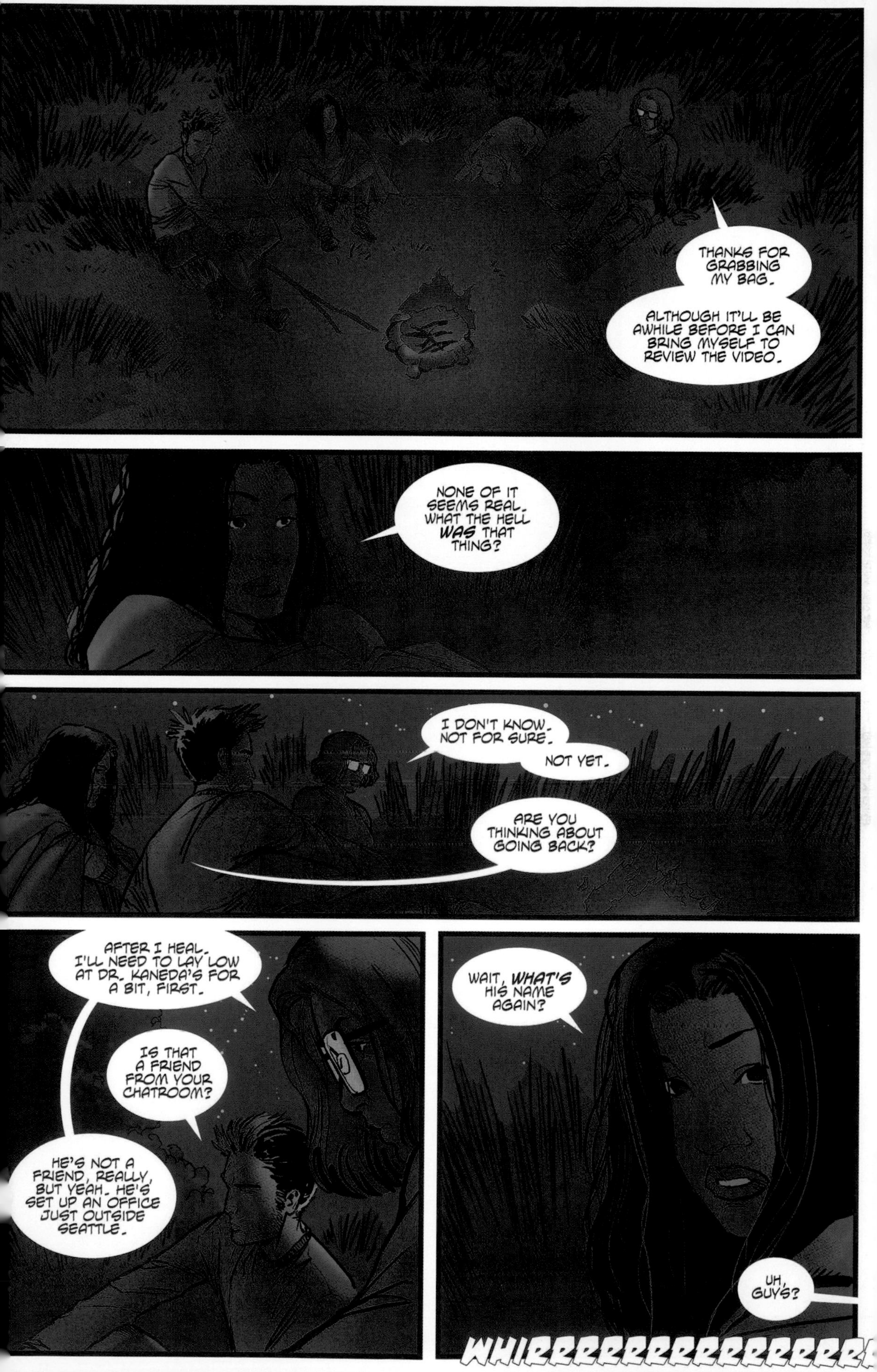
THANKS FOR GRABBING MY BAG.
ALTHOUGH IT'LL BE AWHILE BEFORE I CAN BRING MYSELF TO REVIEW THE VIDEO.
NONE OF IT SEEMS REAL. WHAT THE HELL WAS THAT THING?
I DON'T KNOW. NOT FOR SURE.
NOT YET.
ARE YOU THINKING ABOUT GOING BACK?
AFTER I HEAL. I'LL NEED TO LAY LOW AT DR. KANEDA'S FOR A BIT, FIRST.
IS THAT A FRIEND FROM YOUR CHATROOM?
HE'S NOT A FRIEND, REALLY, BUT YEAH. HE'S SET UP AN OFFICE JUST OUTSIDE SEATTLE.
WAIT, WHAT'S HIS NAME AGAIN?
UH, GUYS?
WHIRRRRRRRRRRRRRRRR

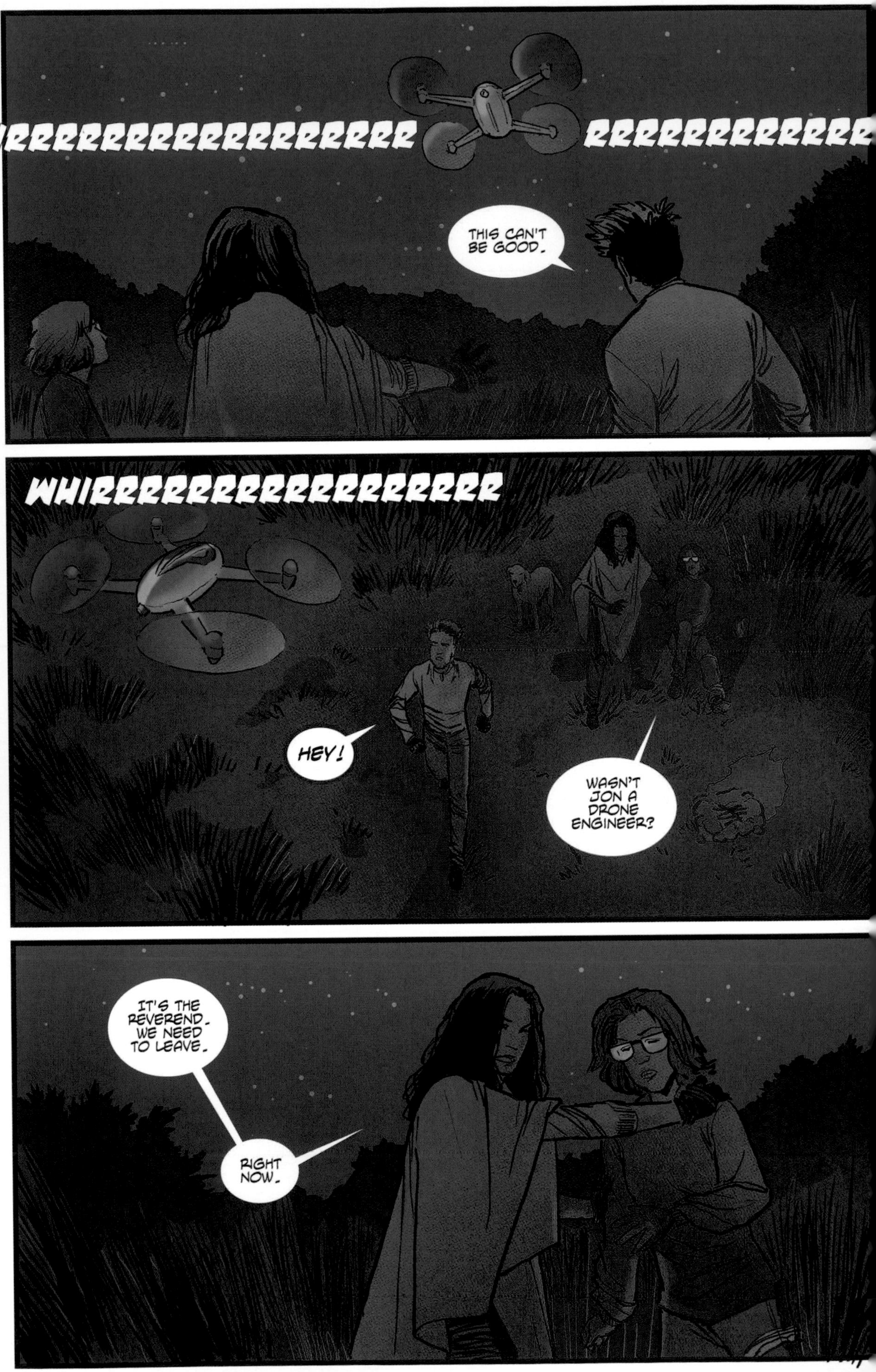
WHIRRRRRRRRRRRRRRRRRRRR
RRRRRRRRRRRRR
THIS CAN'T BE GOOD.
WHIRRRRRRRRRRRRRRRRRRRR
HEY!
WASN'T JON A DRONE ENGINEER?
IT'S THE REVEREND. WE NEED TO LEAVE.
RIGHT NOW.

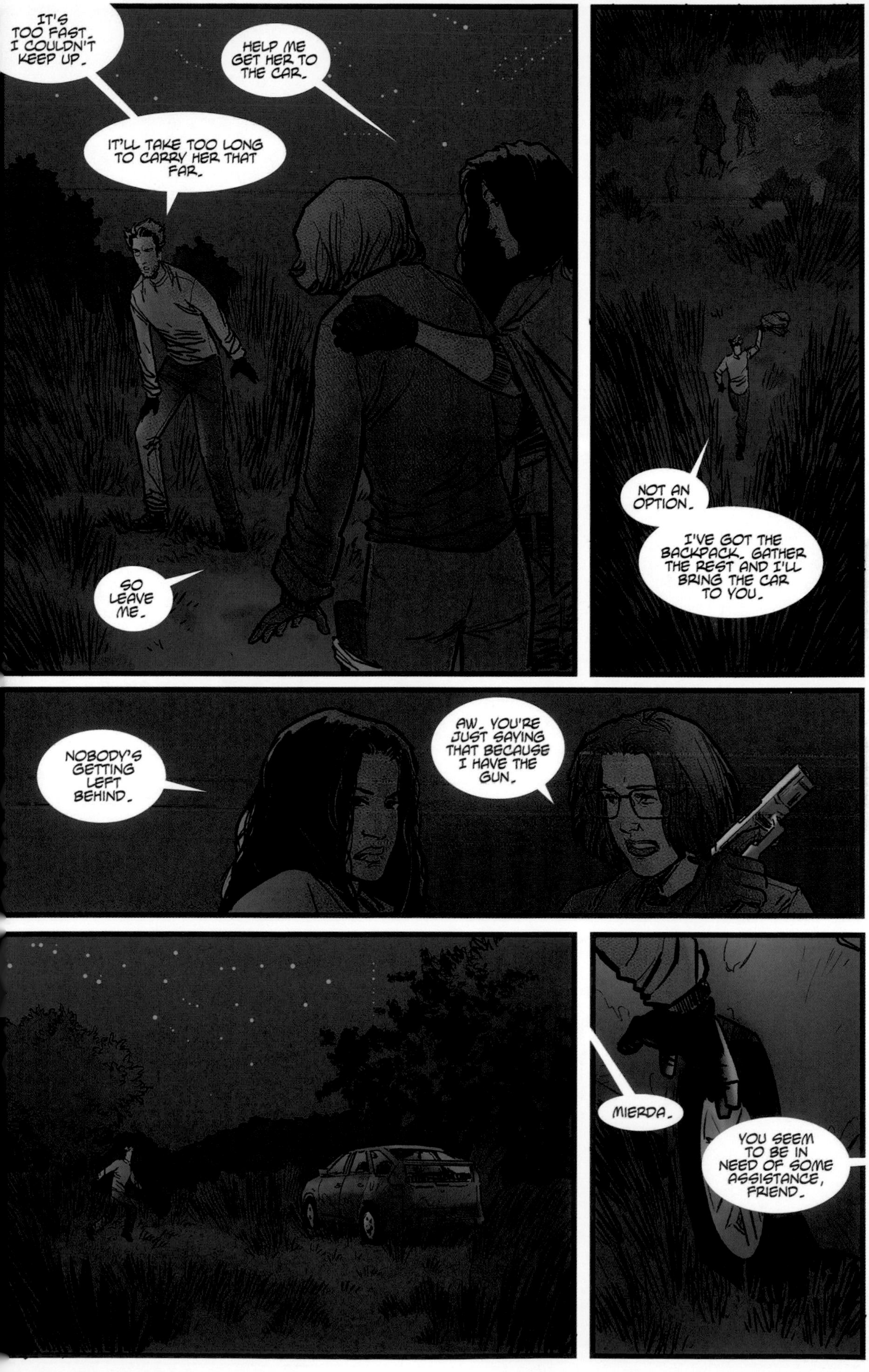
IT'S TOO FAST. I COULDN'T KEEP UP.
HELP ME GET HER TO THE CAR.
IT'LL TAKE TOO LONG TO CARRY HER THAT FAR.
SO LEAVE ME.
NOT AN OPTION.
I'VE GOT THE BACKPACK. GATHER THE REST AND I'LL BRING THE CAR TO YOU.
NOBODY'S GETTING LEFT BEHIND.
AW. YOU'RE JUST SAYING THAT BECAUSE I HAVE THE GUN.
MIERDA.
YOU SEEM TO BE IN NEED OF SOME ASSISTANCE, FRIEND.

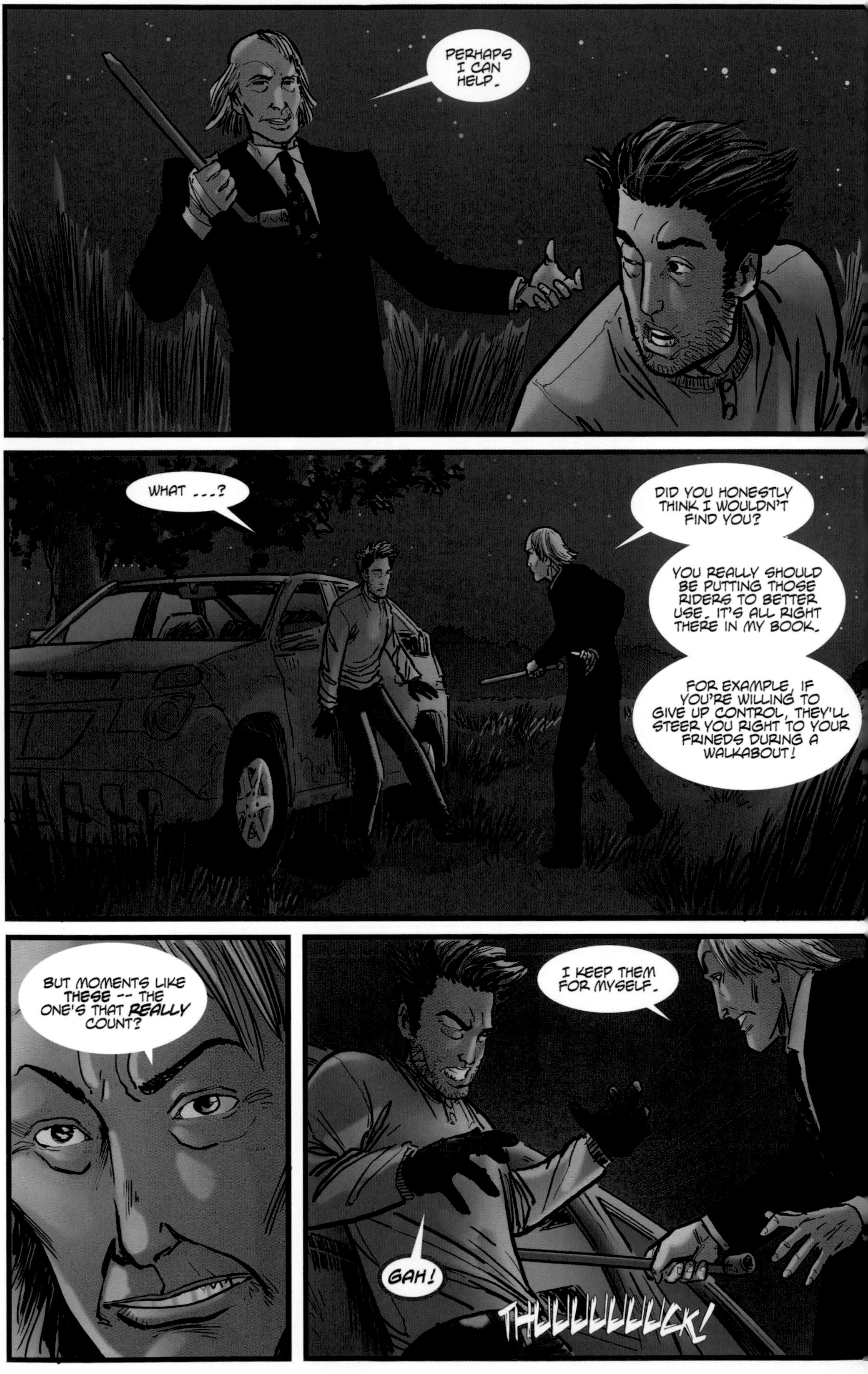
PERHAPS I CAN HELP.
WHAT ...?
DID YOU HONESTLY THINK I WOULDN'T FIND YOU?
YOU REALLY SHOULD BE PUTTING THOSE RIDERS TO BETTER USE. IT'S ALL RIGHT THERE IN MY BOOK.
FOR EXAMPLE, IF YOU'RE WILLING TO GIVE UP CONTROL, THEY'LL STEER YOU RIGHT TO YOUR FRINEDS DURING A WALKABOUT!
BUT MOMENTS LIKE THESE -- THE ONE'S THAT REALLY COUNT?
I KEEP THEM FOR MYSELF.
GAH!
THUUUUUUUCK!

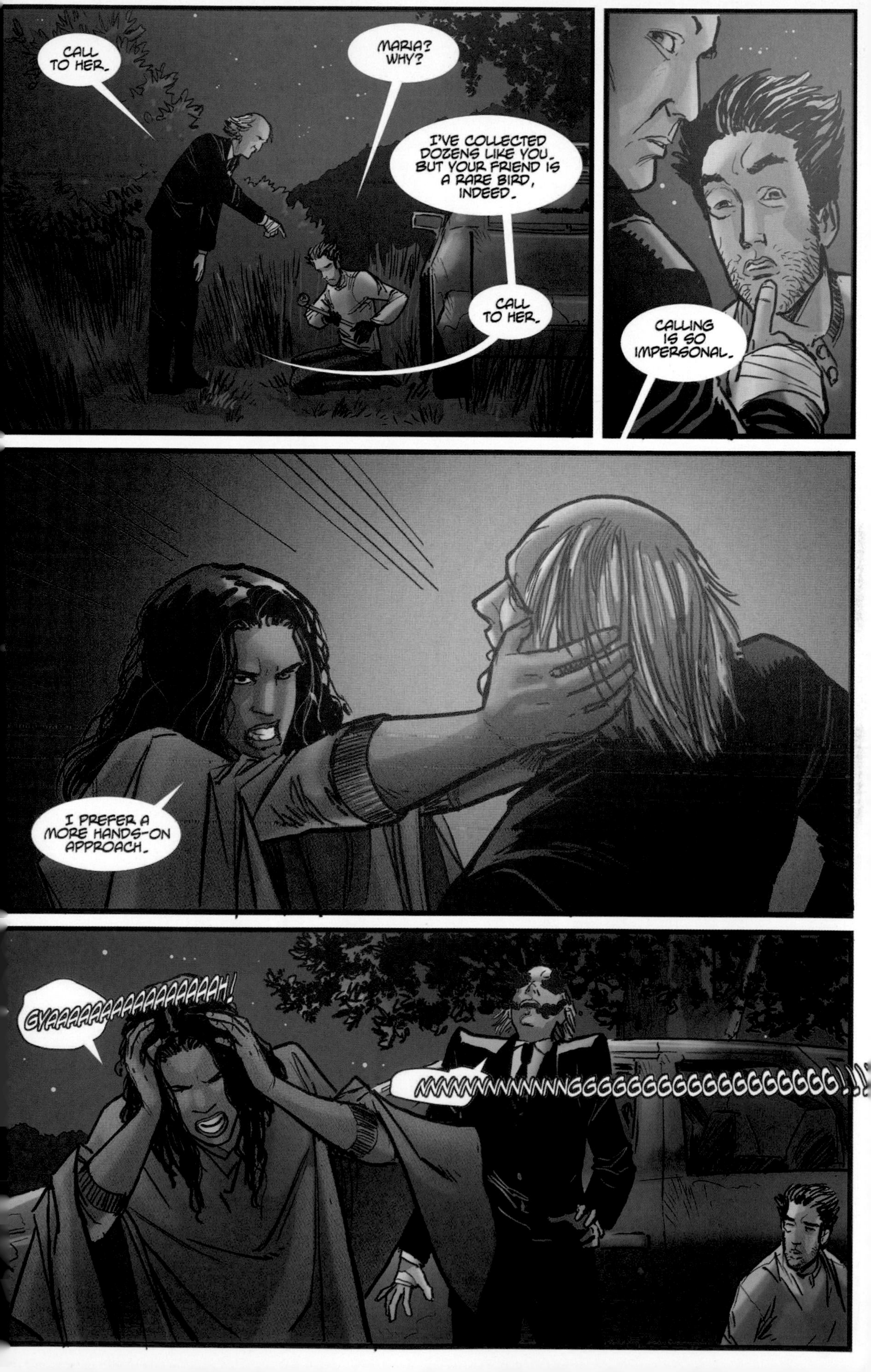
CALL TO HER.
MARIA? WHY?
I'VE COLLECTED DOZENS LIKE YOU. BUT YOUR FRIEND IS A RARE BIRD, INDEED.
CALL TO HER.
CALLING IS SO IMPERSONAL.
I PREFER A MORE HANDS-ON APPROACH.
GYAAAAAAAAAAAAAAAAH!
NNNNNNNNNNNNNGGGGGGGGGGGGGGGGG!!!

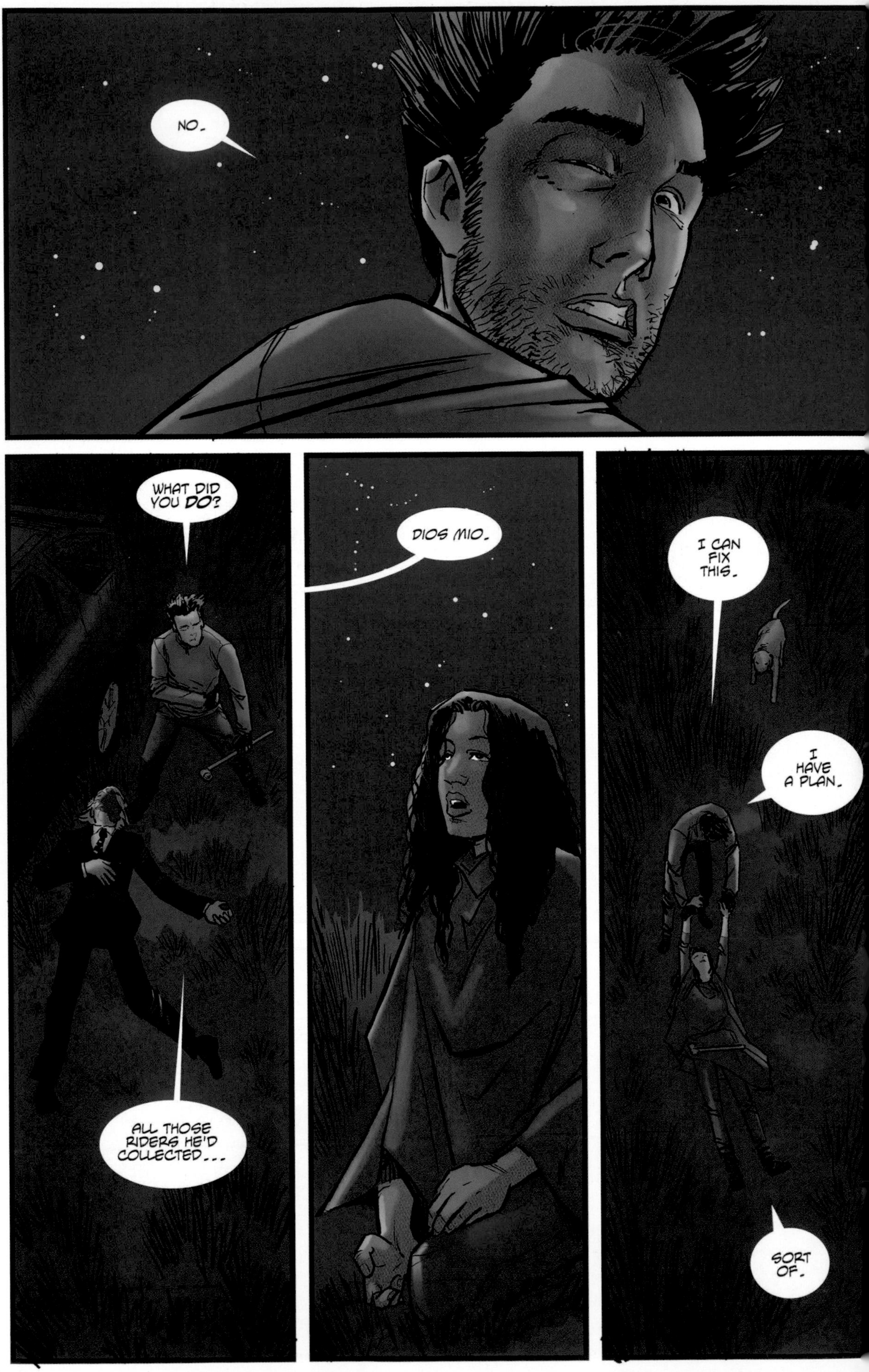
NO.
WHAT DID YOU DO?
ALL THOSE RIDERS HE'D COLLECTED...
DIOS MIO.
I CAN FIX THIS.
I HAVE A PLAN.
SORT OF.

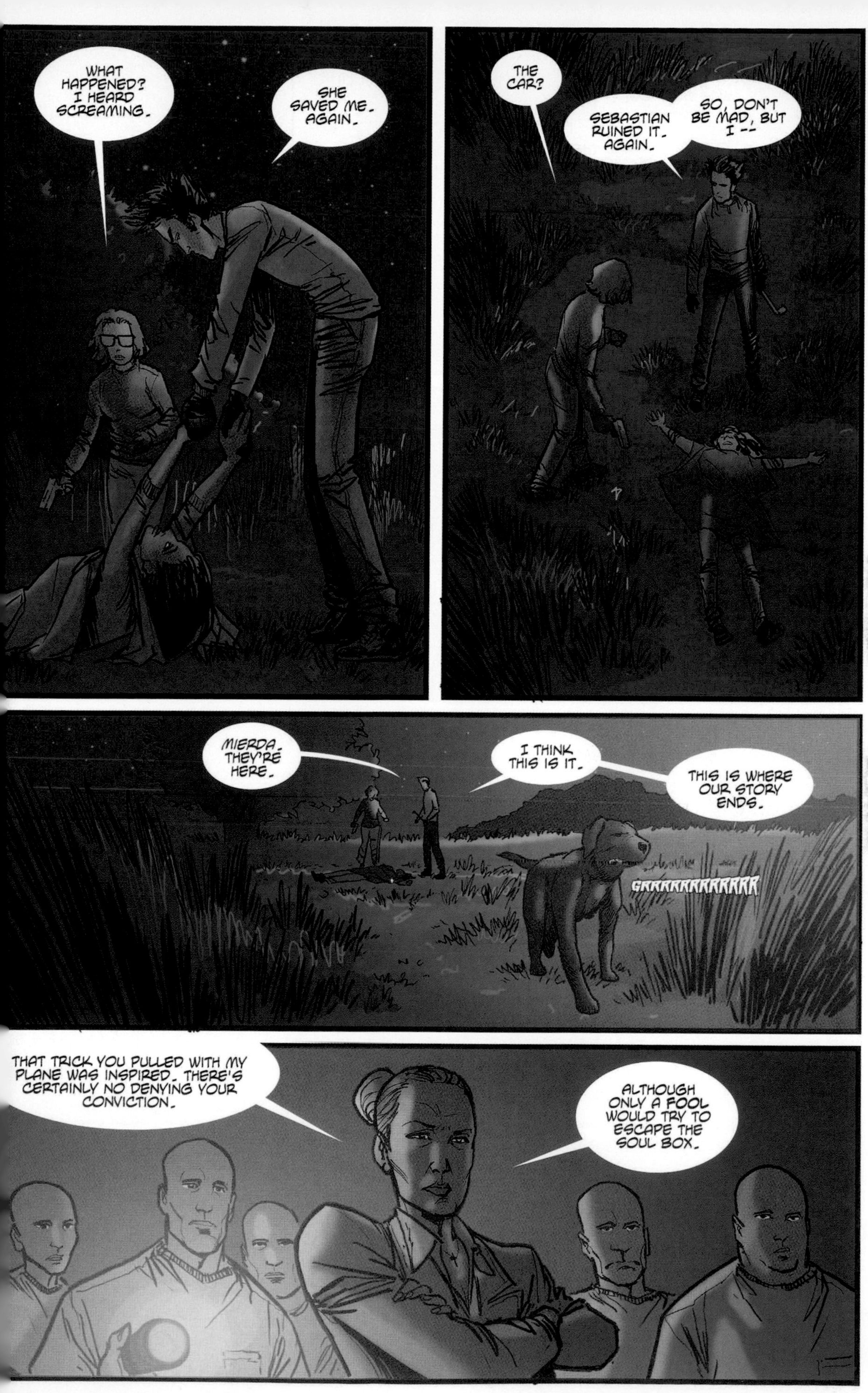
WHAT HAPPENED? I HEARD SCREAMING.
SHE SAVED ME. AGAIN.
THE CAR?
SO, DON'T BE MAD, BUT I --
SEBASTIAN RUINED IT. AGAIN.
MIERDA. THEY'RE HERE.
I THINK THIS IS IT.
THIS IS WHERE OUR STORY ENDS.
GRRRRRRRRRRRR
THAT TRICK YOU PULLED WITH MY PLANE WAS INSPIRED. THERE'S CERTAINLY NO DENYING YOUR CONVICTION.
ALTHOUGH ONLY A FOOL WOULD TRY TO ESCAPE THE SOUL BOX.

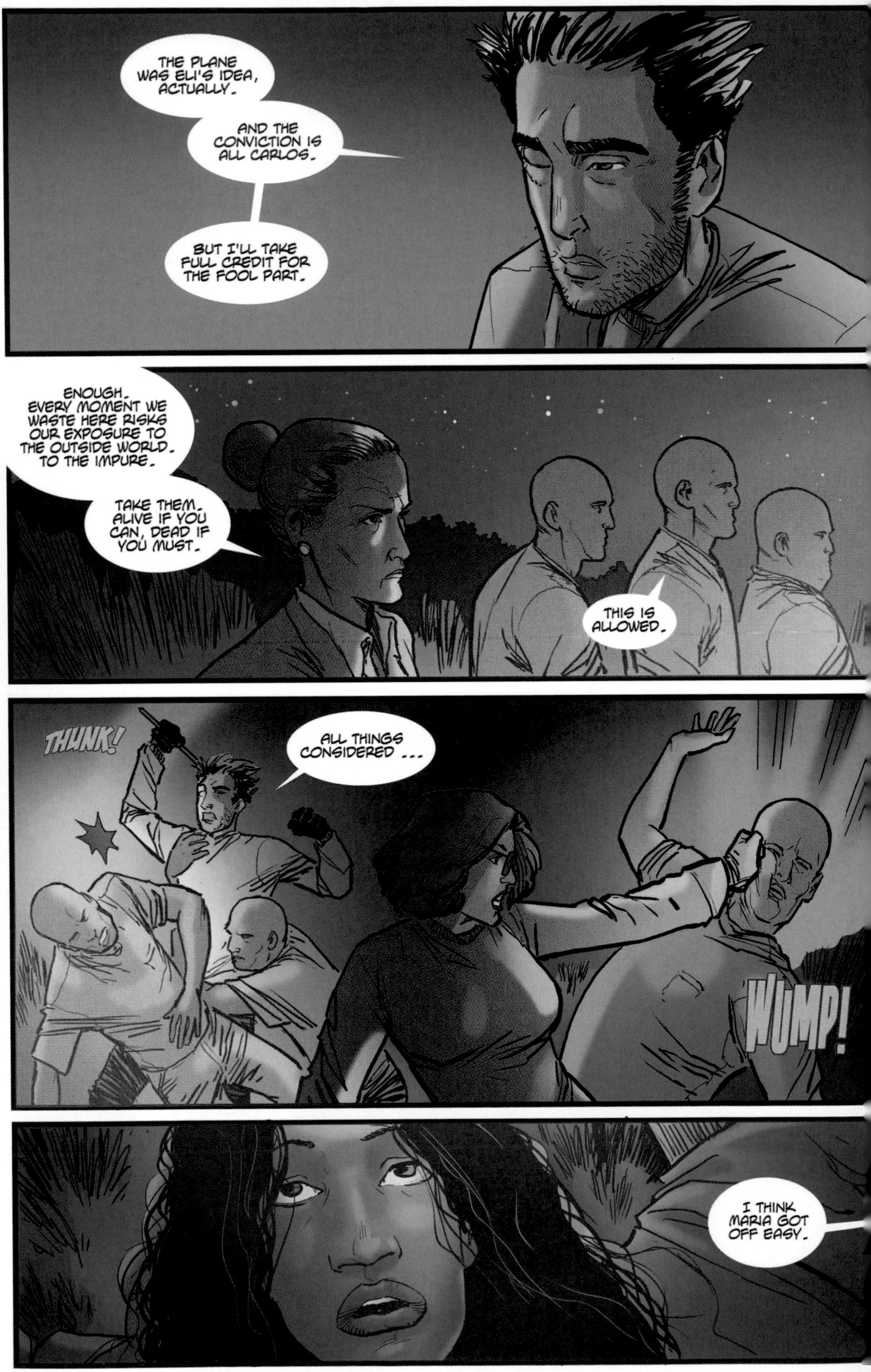
THE PLANE WAS ELI'S IDEA, ACTUALLY.
AND THE CONVICTION IS ALL CARLOS.
BUT I'LL TAKE FULL CREDIT FOR THE FOOL PART.
ENOUGH. EVERY MOMENT WE WASTE HERE RISKS OUR EXPOSURE TO THE OUTSIDE WORLD. TO THE IMPURE.
TAKE THEM. ALIVE IF YOU CAN, DEAD IF YOU MUST.
THIS IS ALLOWED.
THUNK!
ALL THINGS CONSIDERED ...
WUMP!
I THINK MARIA GOT OFF EASY.

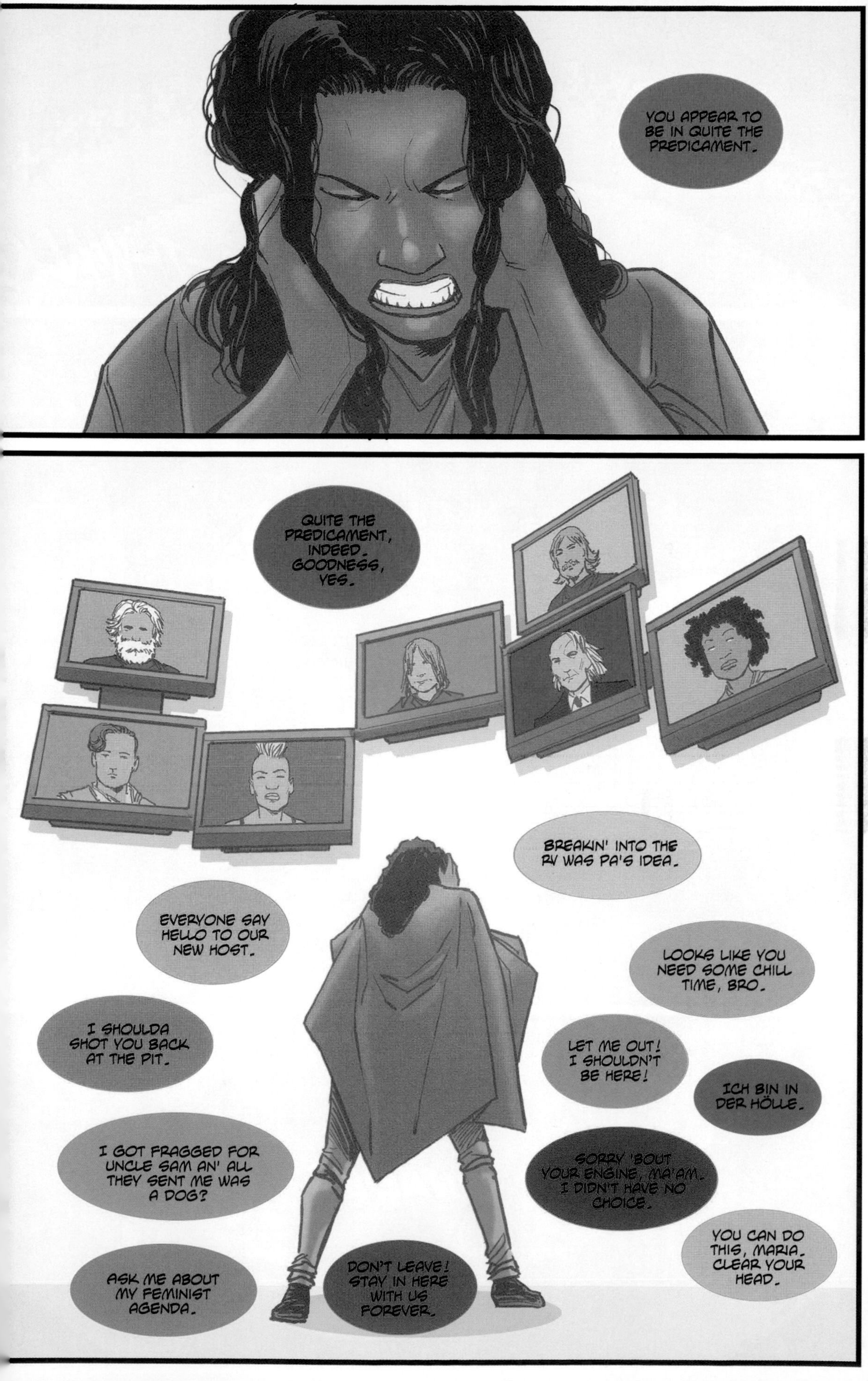
YOU APPEAR TO BE IN QUITE THE PREDICAMENT.
QUITE THE PREDICAMENT, INDEED. GOODNESS, YES.
BREAKIN' INTO THE RV WAS PA'S IDEA.
EVERYONE SAY HELLO TO OUR NEW HOST.
LOOKS LIKE YOU NEED SOME CHILL TIME, BRO.
I SHOULDA SHOT YOU BACK AT THE PIT.
LET ME OUT! I SHOULDN'T BE HERE!
ICH BIN IN DER HÖLLE.
I GOT FRAGGED FOR UNCLE SAM AN' ALL THEY SENT ME WAS A DOG?
SORRY 'BOUT YOUR ENGINE, MA'AM. I DIDN'T HAVE NO CHOICE.
YOU CAN DO THIS, MARIA. CLEAR YOUR HEAD.
ASK ME ABOUT MY FEMINIST AGENDA.
DON'T LEAVE! STAY IN HERE WITH US FOREVER.

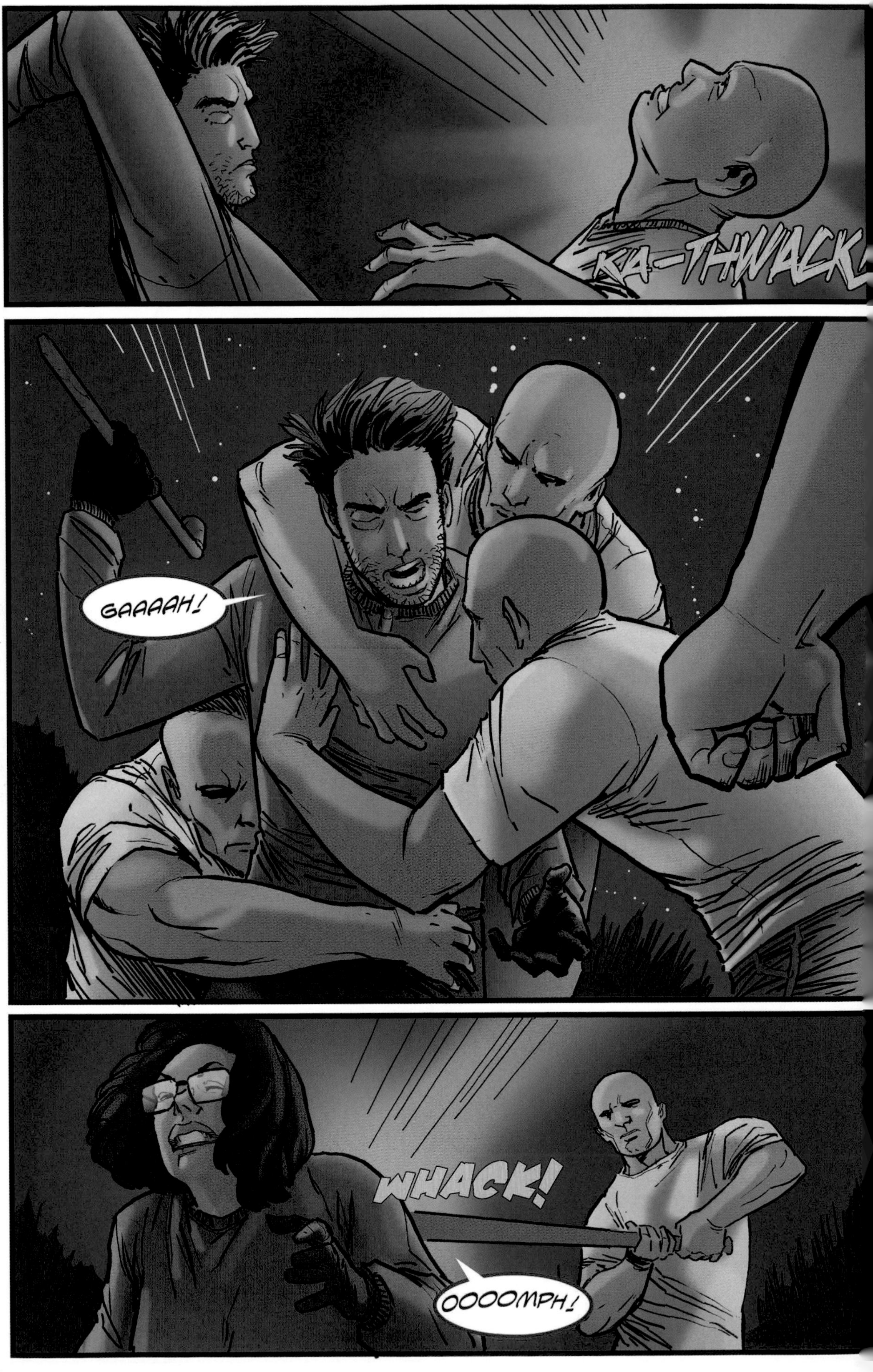
KA-THWACK!
GAAAAH!
WHACK!
OOOOMPH!

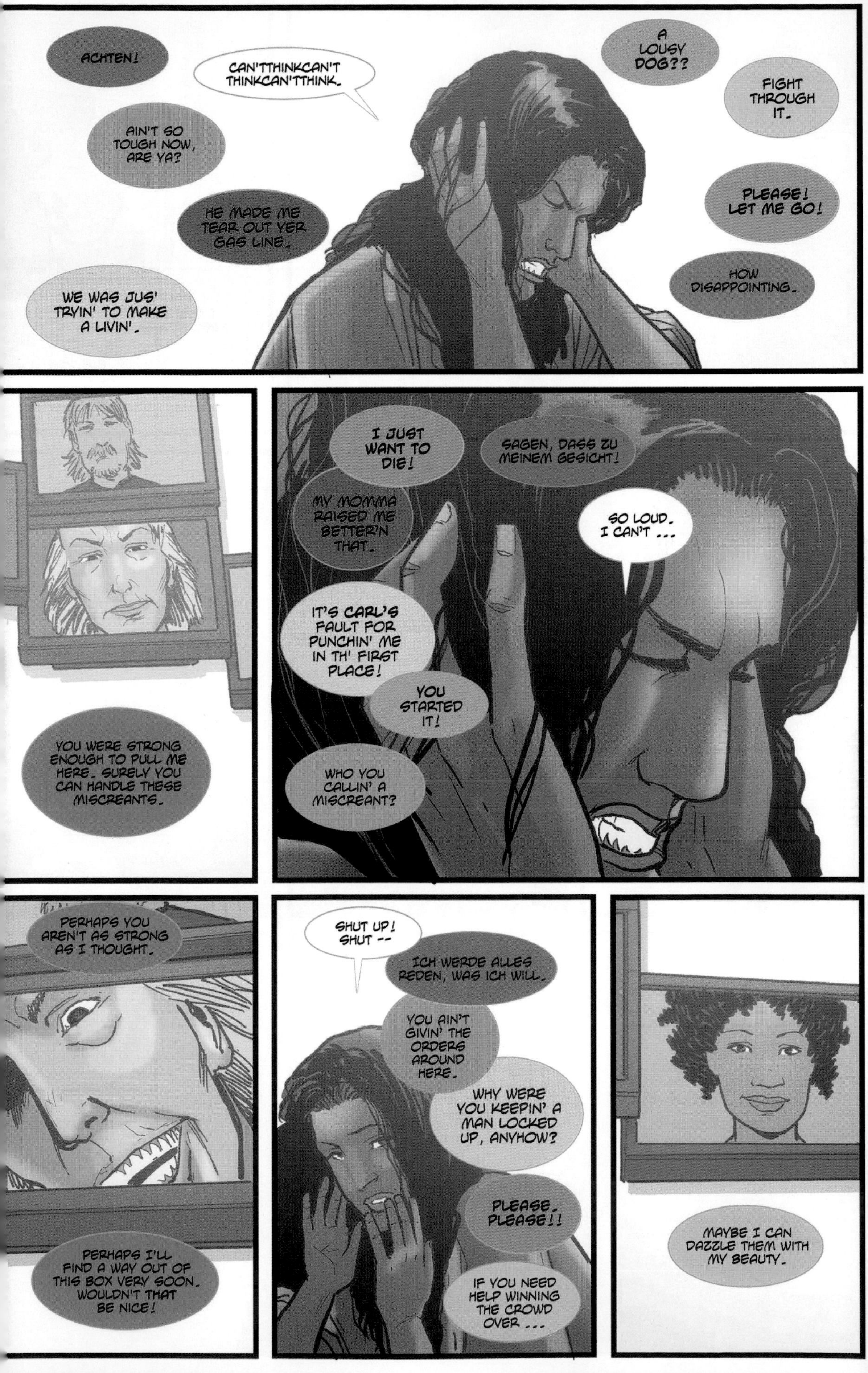
ACHTEN!
CAN'TTHINKCAN'T THINKCAN'TTHINK.
AIN'T SO TOUGH NOW, ARE YA?
HE MADE ME TEAR OUT YER GAS LINE.
WE WAS JUS' TRYIN' TO MAKE A LIVIN'.
A LOUSY DOG??
FIGHT THROUGH IT.
PLEASE! LET ME GO!
HOW DISAPPOINTING.
YOU WERE STRONG ENOUGH TO PULL ME HERE. SURELY YOU CAN HANDLE THESE MISCREANTS.
I JUST WANT TO DIE!
SAGEN, DASS ZU MEINEM GESICHT!
MY MOMMA RAISED ME BETTER'N THAT.
SO LOUD. I CAN'T ...
IT'S CARL'S FAULT FOR PUNCHIN' ME IN TH' FIRST PLACE!
YOU STARTED IT!
WHO YOU CALLIN' A MISCREANT?
PERHAPS YOU AREN'T AS STRONG AS I THOUGHT.
PERHAPS I'LL FIND A WAY OUT OF THIS BOX VERY SOON. WOULDN'T THAT BE NICE!
SHUT UP! SHUT --
ICH WERDE ALLES REDEN, WAS ICH WILL.
YOU AIN'T GIVIN' THE ORDERS AROUND HERE.
WHY WERE YOU KEEPIN' A MAN LOCKED UP, ANYHOW?
PLEASE. PLEASE!!
IF YOU NEED HELP WINNING THE CROWD OVER ...
MAYBE I CAN DAZZLE THEM WITH MY BEAUTY.

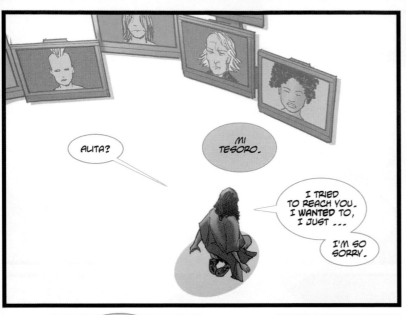

ALITA?

MI TESORO.

I TRIED TO REACH YOU. I WANTED TO, I JUST ...

I'M SO SORRY.

I KNOW. I COULD HEAR YOU.

I COULD FEEL YOU.

BUT THIS ROOM WAS SO EMPTY.

I MISSED YOU.

I'VE MISSED YOU, TOO. AND THERE'S SO MUCH MORE I WANT TO SAY.

BUT IT'S TIME FOR YOU TO GO. YOUR LIFE ISN'T IN HERE WITH ME.

I DON'T KNOW HOW.

YES, YOU DO.

THEN I DON'T WANT TO.

YOU CAN'T STAY. YOU'LL RUIN YOUR EYES.

YOU'RE NOT FUNNY.

GO, MARIA.

I LOVE YOU, ALITA.

FOREVER AND ALWAYS.

IS THIS THE END?

WHAT'RE YOU DOIN', LADY?

EINDEUTIG EIN AMERIKANISCHES DESIGN.

THERE'S NO NEED FOR SUCH DRASTIC MEASURES, FRIEN--

CLICK!

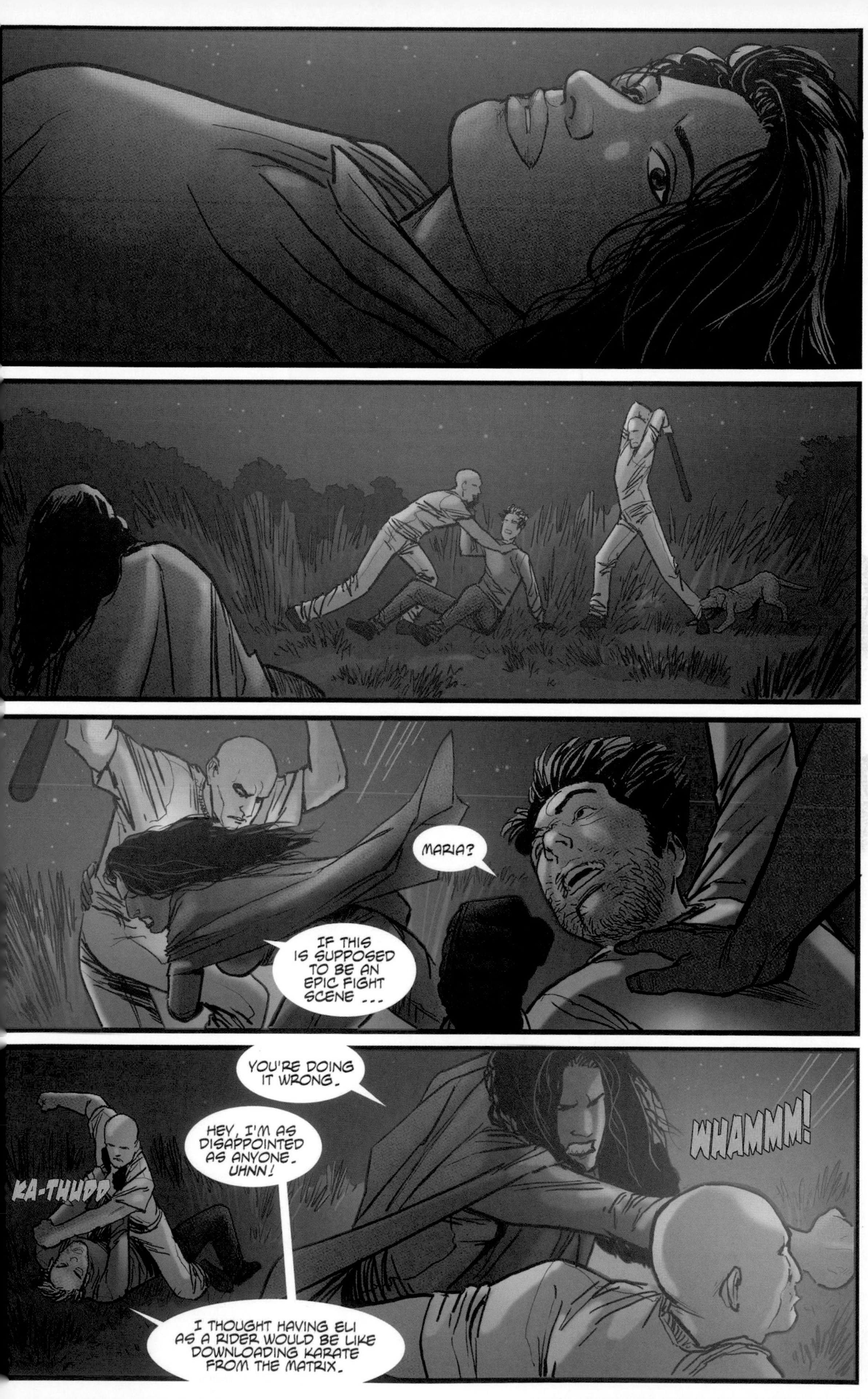
MARIA?
IF THIS IS SUPPOSED TO BE AN EPIC FIGHT SCENE ...
YOU'RE DOING IT WRONG.
HEY, I'M AS DISAPPOINTED AS ANYONE. UHNN!
KA-THUDD
WHAMMM!
I THOUGHT HAVING ELI AS A RIDER WOULD BE LIKE DOWNLOADING KARATE FROM THE MATRIX.

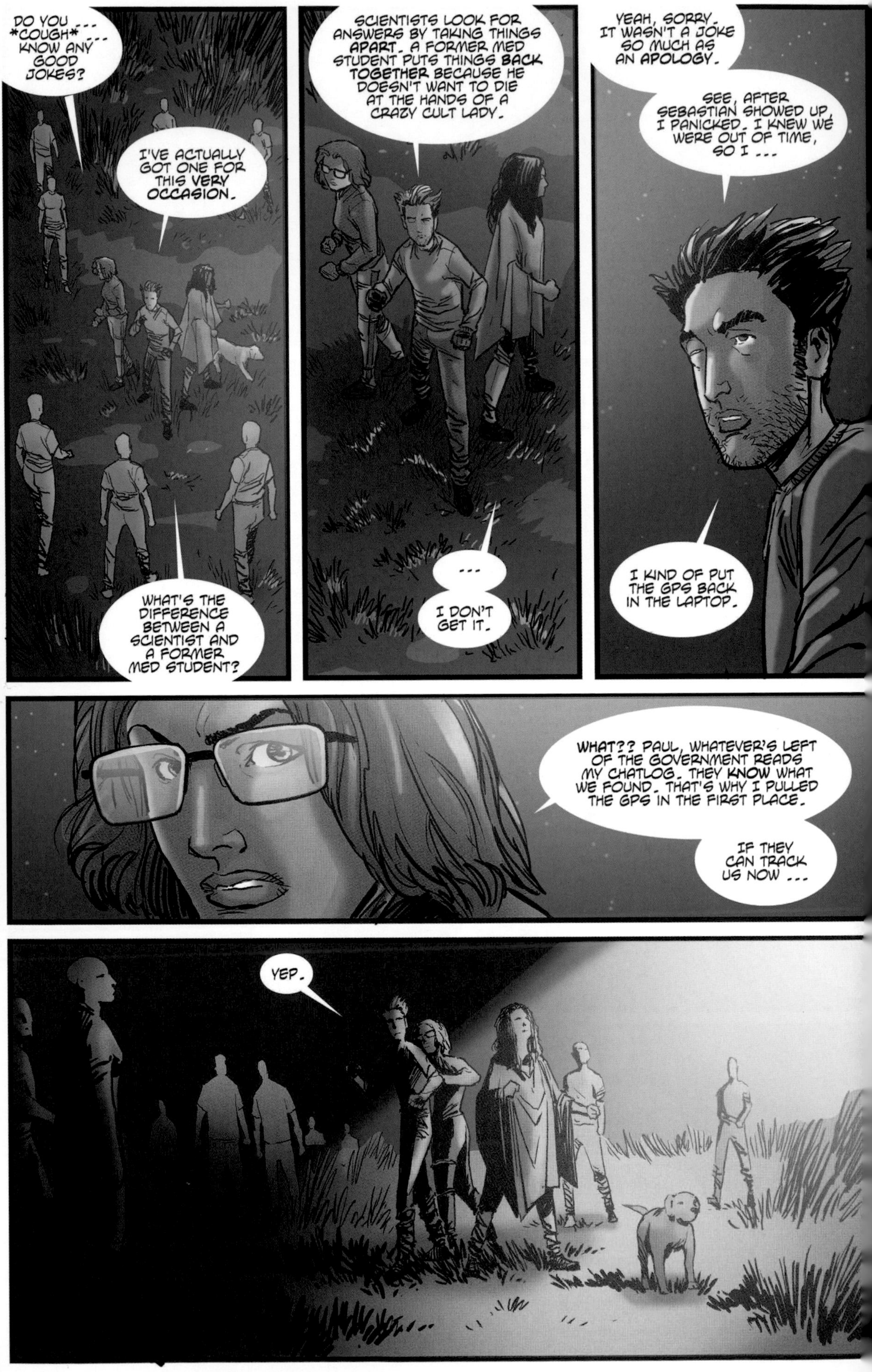
DO YOU ... *COUGH* ... KNOW ANY GOOD JOKES?
I'VE ACTUALLY GOT ONE FOR THIS VERY OCCASION.
WHAT'S THE DIFFERENCE BETWEEN A SCIENTIST AND A FORMER MED STUDENT?
SCIENTISTS LOOK FOR ANSWERS BY TAKING THINGS APART. A FORMER MED STUDENT PUTS THINGS BACK TOGETHER BECAUSE HE DOESN'T WANT TO DIE AT THE HANDS OF A CRAZY CULT LADY.
...
I DON'T GET IT.
YEAH, SORRY. IT WASN'T A JOKE SO MUCH AS AN APOLOGY.
SEE, AFTER SEBASTIAN SHOWED UP, I PANICKED. I KNEW WE WERE OUT OF TIME, SO I ...
I KIND OF PUT THE GPS BACK IN THE LAPTOP.
WHAT?? PAUL, WHATEVER'S LEFT OF THE GOVERNMENT READS MY CHATLOG. THEY KNOW WHAT WE FOUND. THAT'S WHY I PULLED THE GPS IN THE FIRST PLACE.
IF THEY CAN TRACK US NOW ...
YEP.

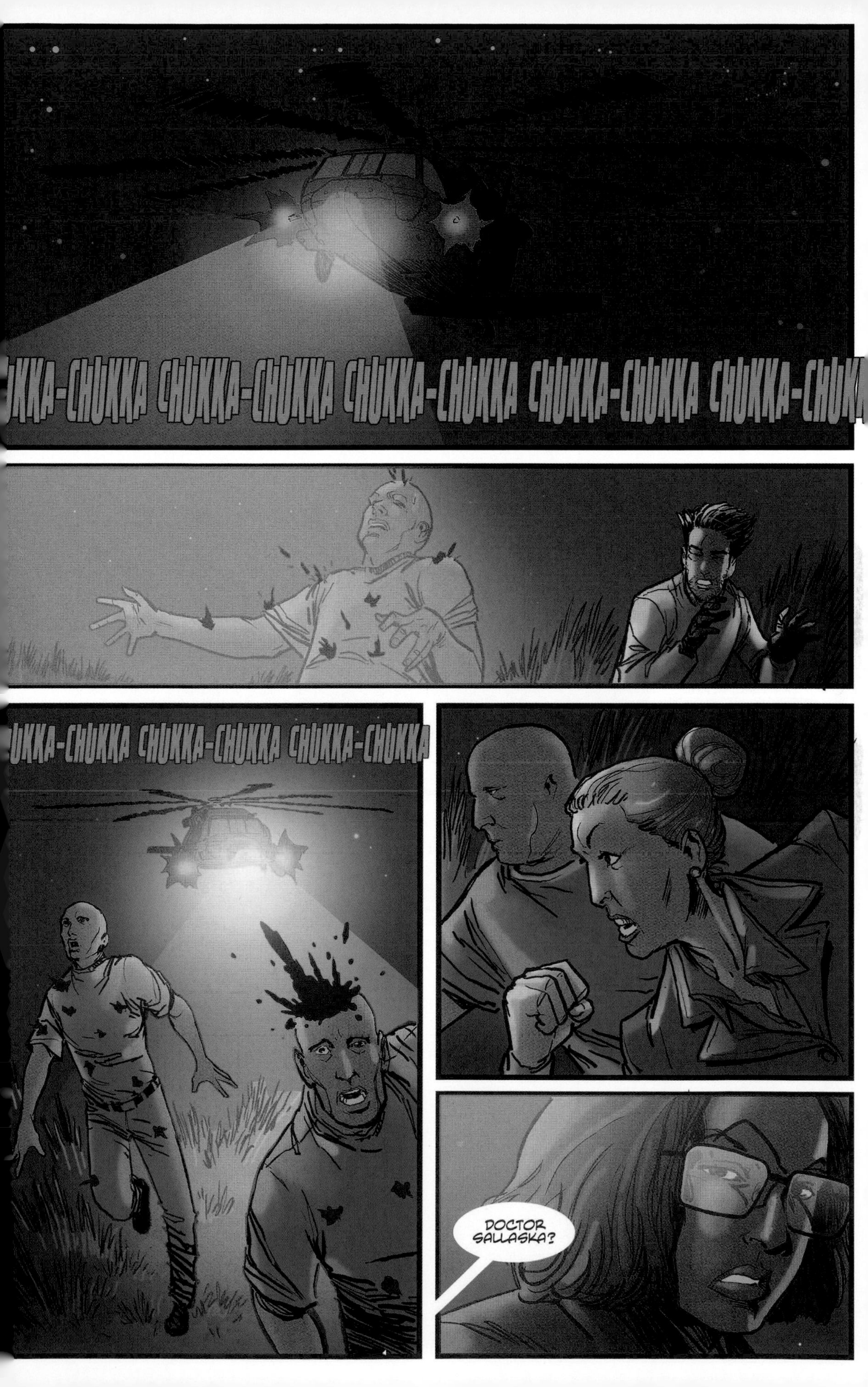

CHUKKA-CHUKKA CHUKKA-CHUKKA CHUKKA-CHUKKA CHUKKA-CHUKKA CHUKKA-CHUKKA
CHUKKA-CHUKKA CHUKKA-CHUKKA CHUKKA-CHUKKA
DOCTOR SALLASKA?

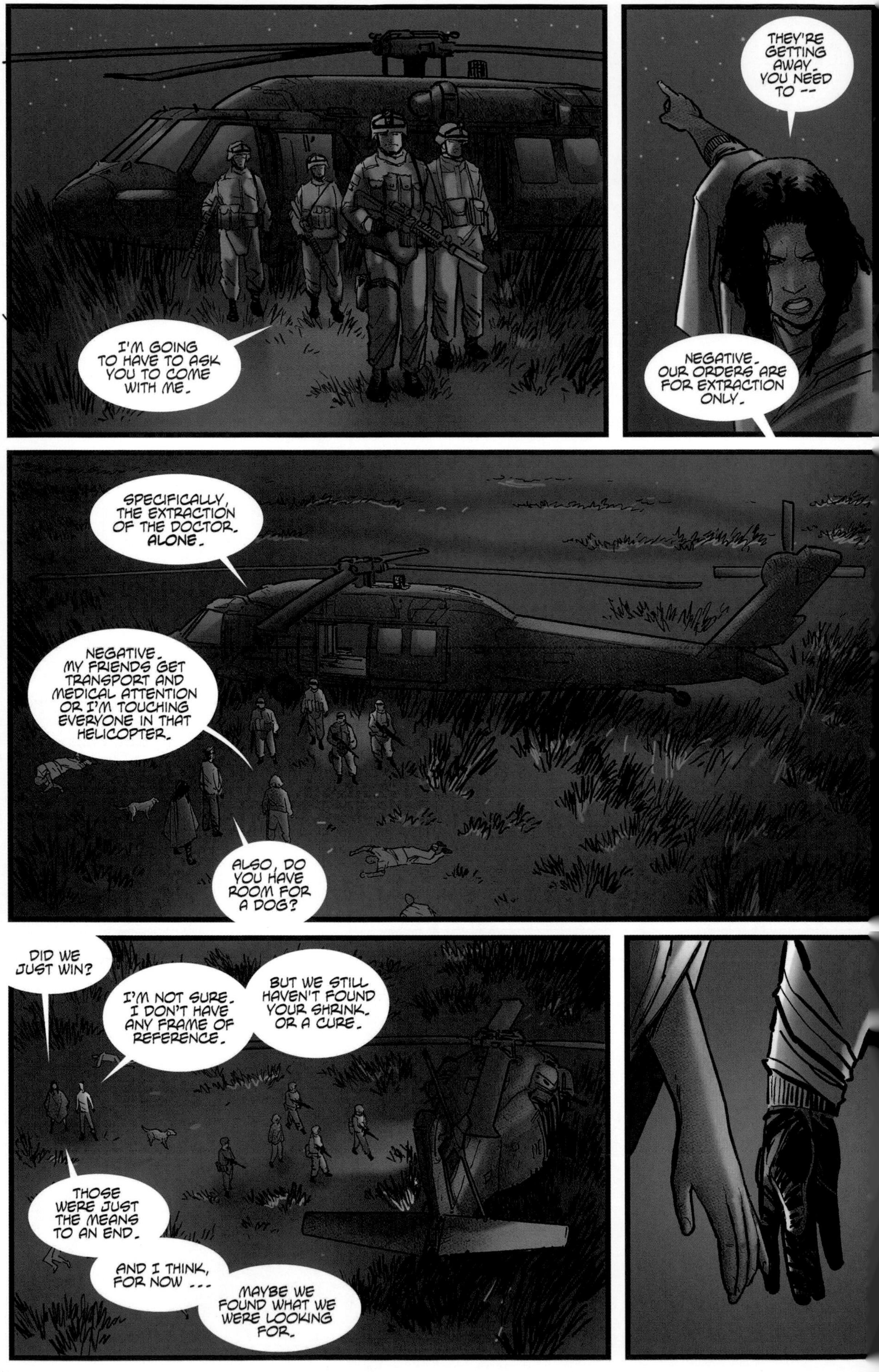
I'M GOING TO HAVE TO ASK YOU TO COME WITH ME.
THEY'RE GETTING AWAY. YOU NEED TO --
NEGATIVE. OUR ORDERS ARE FOR EXTRACTION ONLY.
SPECIFICALLY, THE EXTRACTION OF THE DOCTOR. ALONE.
NEGATIVE. MY FRIENDS GET TRANSPORT AND MEDICAL ATTENTION OR I'M TOUCHING EVERYONE IN THAT HELICOPTER.
ALSO, DO YOU HAVE ROOM FOR A DOG?
DID WE JUST WIN?
I'M NOT SURE. I DON'T HAVE ANY FRAME OF REFERENCE.
BUT WE STILL HAVEN'T FOUND YOUR SHRINK. OR A CURE.
THOSE WERE JUST THE MEANS TO AN END.
AND I THINK, FOR NOW ...
MAYBE WE FOUND WHAT WE WERE LOOKING FOR.

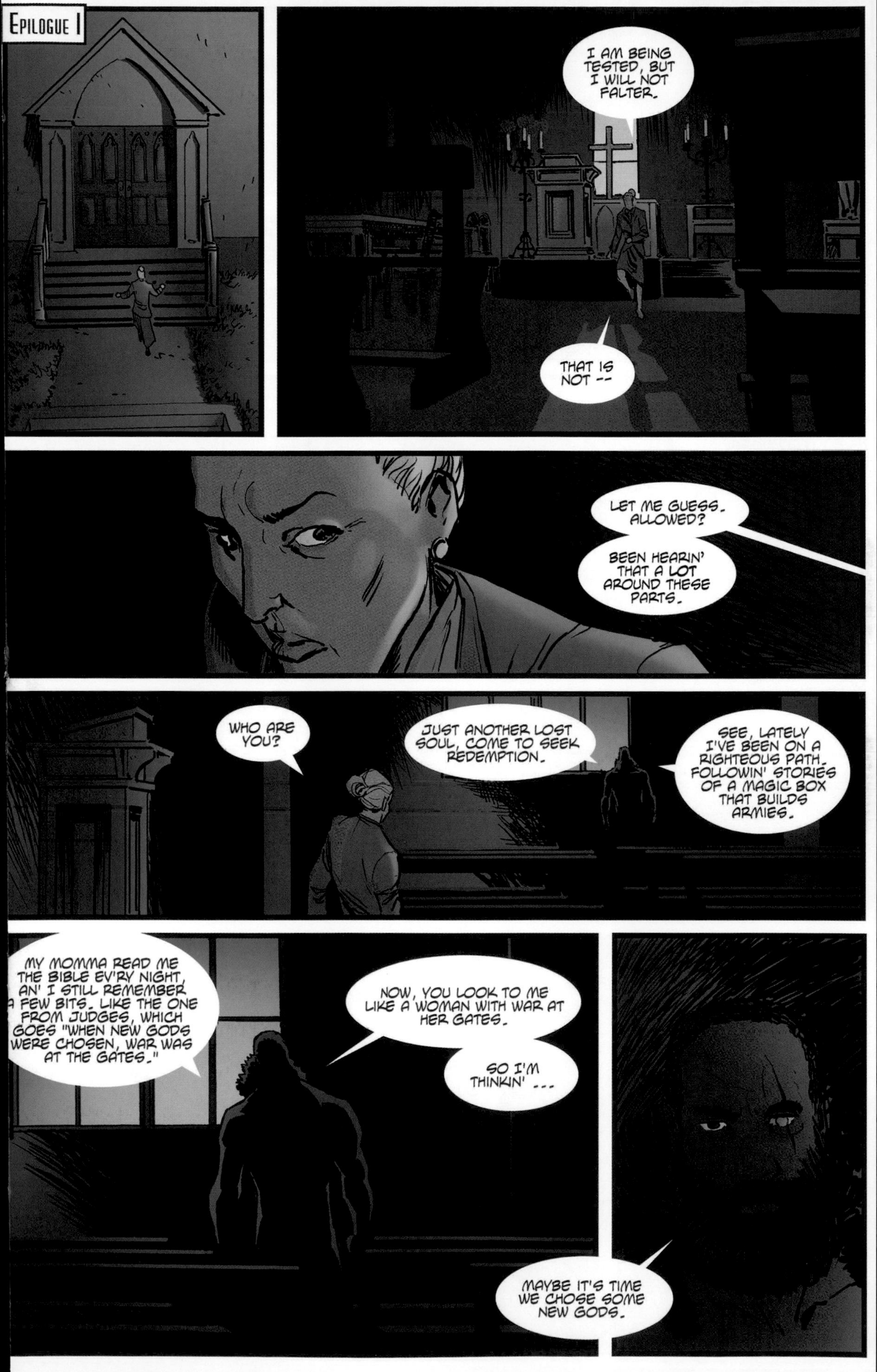
EPILOGUE I
I AM BEING TESTED, BUT I WILL NOT FALTER.
THAT IS NOT --
LET ME GUESS. ALLOWED?
BEEN HEARIN' THAT A LOT AROUND THESE PARTS.
WHO ARE YOU?
JUST ANOTHER LOST SOUL, COME TO SEEK REDEMPTION.
SEE, LATELY I'VE BEEN ON A RIGHTEOUS PATH. FOLLOWIN' STORIES OF A MAGIC BOX THAT BUILDS ARMIES.
MY MOMMA READ ME THE BIBLE EV'RY NIGHT, AN' I STILL REMEMBER A FEW BITS. LIKE THE ONE FROM JUDGES, WHICH GOES "WHEN NEW GODS WERE CHOSEN, WAR WAS AT THE GATES."
NOW, YOU LOOK TO ME LIKE A WOMAN WITH WAR AT HER GATES.
SO I'M THINKIN' ...
MAYBE IT'S TIME WE CHOSE SOME NEW GODS.

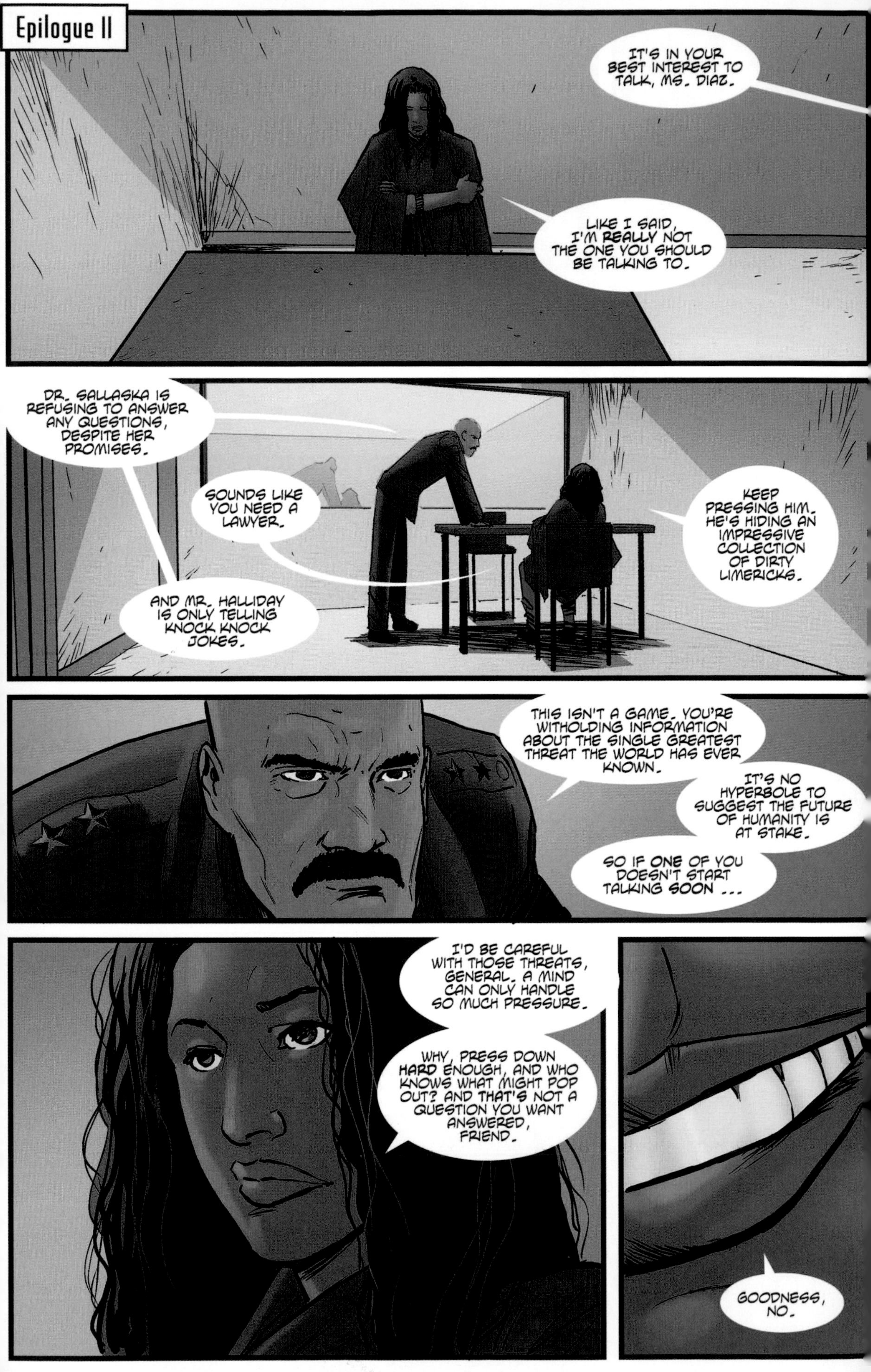
Epilogue II
IT'S IN YOUR BEST INTEREST TO TALK, MS. DIAZ.
LIKE I SAID, I'M REALLY NOT THE ONE YOU SHOULD BE TALKING TO.
DR. SALLASKA IS REFUSING TO ANSWER ANY QUESTIONS, DESPITE HER PROMISES.
AND MR. HALLIDAY IS ONLY TELLING KNOCK KNOCK JOKES.
SOUNDS LIKE YOU NEED A LAWYER.
KEEP PRESSING HIM. HE'S HIDING AN IMPRESSIVE COLLECTION OF DIRTY LIMERICKS.
THIS ISN'T A GAME. YOU'RE WITHOLDING INFORMATION ABOUT THE SINGLE GREATEST THREAT THE WORLD HAS EVER KNOWN.
IT'S NO HYPERBOLE TO SUGGEST THE FUTURE OF HUMANITY IS AT STAKE.
SO IF ONE OF YOU DOESN'T START TALKING SOON ...
I'D BE CAREFUL WITH THOSE THREATS, GENERAL. A MIND CAN ONLY HANDLE SO MUCH PRESSURE.
WHY, PRESS DOWN HARD ENOUGH, AND WHO KNOWS WHAT MIGHT POP OUT? AND THAT'S NOT A QUESTION YOU WANT ANSWERED, FRIEND.
GOODNESS, NO.

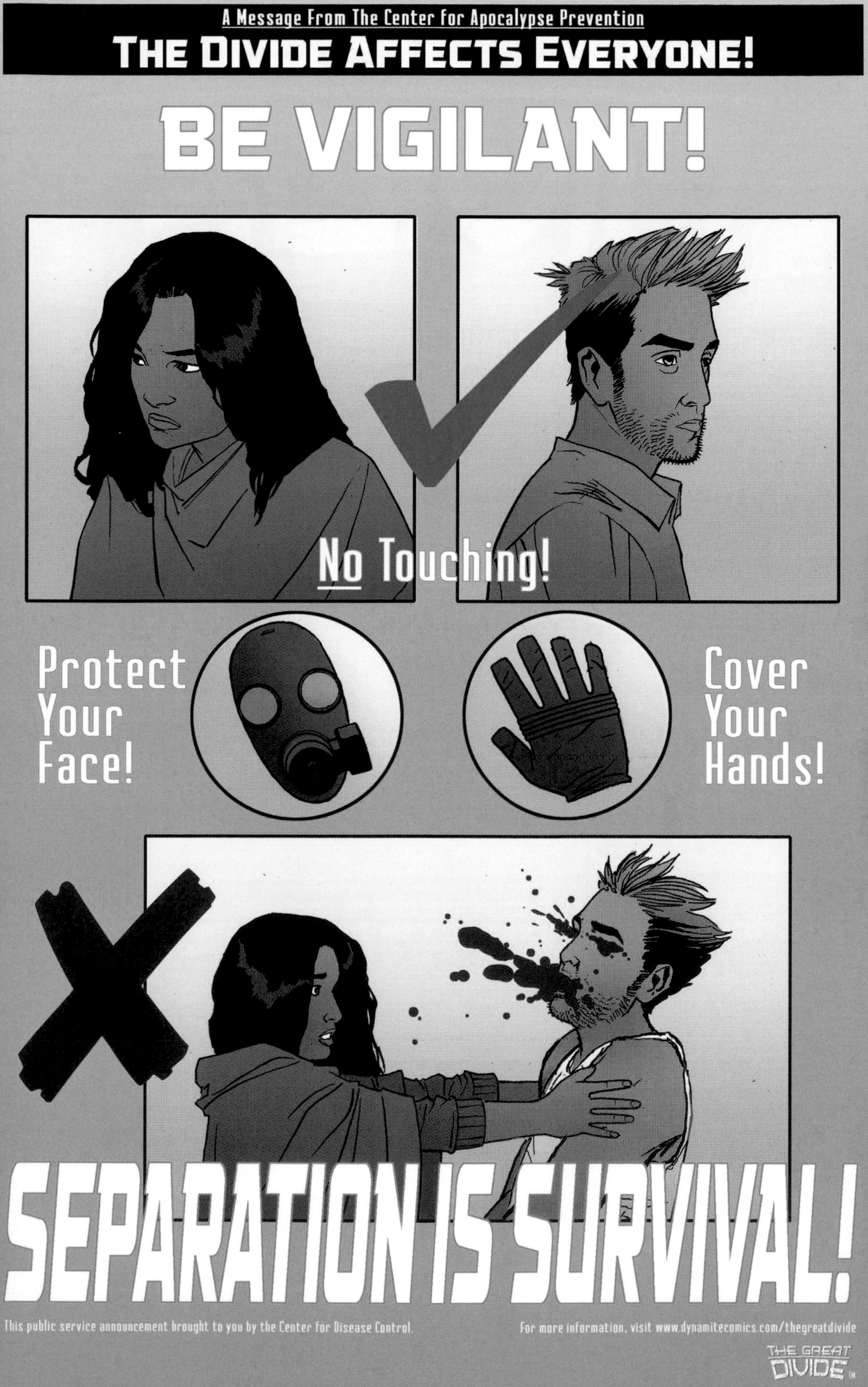
A Message From The Center for Apocalypse Prevention
THE DIVIDE AFFECTS EVERYONE!
BE VIGILANT!
No Touching!
Protect Your Face!
Cover Your Hands!
SEPARATION IS SURVIVAL!
This public service announcement brought to you by the Center for Disease Control.
For more information, visit www.dynamitecomics.com/thegreatdivide
THE GREAT DIVIDE TM

THE GREAT DIVIDE

ENJOY FREE DIGITAL BONUS CONTENT WITH EVERY ISSUE!

ISSUE 1

DOWNLOAD THE SONG "TEOTWAWKI" AT HTTP://TINYURL.COM/TGD001 AND LISTEN TO A DOOMSDAY PREPPER COME FACE TO FACE WITH HIS WORST DISASTER: A FIRST DATE! [MP3 AND WAV FORMATS AVAILABLE].

ISSUE 2

DOWNLOAD PAGES FROM THE GREAT DIVIDE COLORING BOOK: HTTP://TINYURL.COM/TGD002
ENJOY THE ZEN-LIKE TRANCE OF COLORING BETWEEN THE LINES AND TRY NOT TO THINK ABOUT YOUR HORRIFYING DYSTOPIAN REALITY!

ISSUE 3

ARE YOU ENJOYING "THE GREAT DIVIDE", BUT STILL LOOKING FOR
THAT ELUSIVE INNER HAPPINESS? LET SEBASTIAN GIBBS HELP! DOWNLOAD AN EXCERPT FROM HIS
SELF-HELP BOOK "HOW TO HEAR YOURSELF" HERE: HTTP://TINYURL.COM/TGD003 AND LEARN HOW TO MAKE THOSE PESKY VOICES IN YOUR HEAD WORK FOR YOU!

ISSUE 4

DO YOU ENJOY ROLE-PLAYING GAMES WHEN YOU AREN'T READING THE GREAT DIVIDE, BUT FIND YOURSELF ENRAGED THAT YOU CAN'T DO BOTH SIMULTANEOUSLY? WE CAN HELP! DOWNLOAD A FREE CONVERSION GUIDE TO TRANSFORM ALL YOUR EXCITING, VIBRANT GAMES INTO A HORRIFYING NIGHTMARE WHERE EVERY ENCOUNTER COULD MEAN YOUR DEATH: HTTP://TINYURL.COM/TGD004 HAVE FUN!

ISSUE 5

WE ARE PROUD AND HONORED TO PRESENT A POWERFUL COLLECTION OF SHORT STORIES
WRITTEN BY A GROUP OF INCREDIBLY TALENTED WOMEN AUTHORS WHO HAVE CRAFTED HORRIFYING AND THOUGHT-PROVOKING TALES SET IN THE GREAT DIVIDE UNIVERSE FROM A FEMALE PERSPECTIVE! DOWNLOAD YOUR FREE COPY OF THIS AMAZING COLLECTION HERE: HTTP://TINYURL.COM/TGD005

ISSUE 6

THANK YOU SO MUCH FOR JOINING PAUL AND MARIA ON THEIR JOURNEY THROUGH THE GREAT DIVIDE,
AND WHAT BETTER WAY TO END THIS CHAPTER THAN A BITTERSWEET SONG OF LOSS AND INEVITABILITY BY THE AMAZING CITY BELOW? DOWNLOAD YOUR FREE COPY OF "SLEEPING BEAST"
HERE: HTTP://TINYURL.COM/TGD006

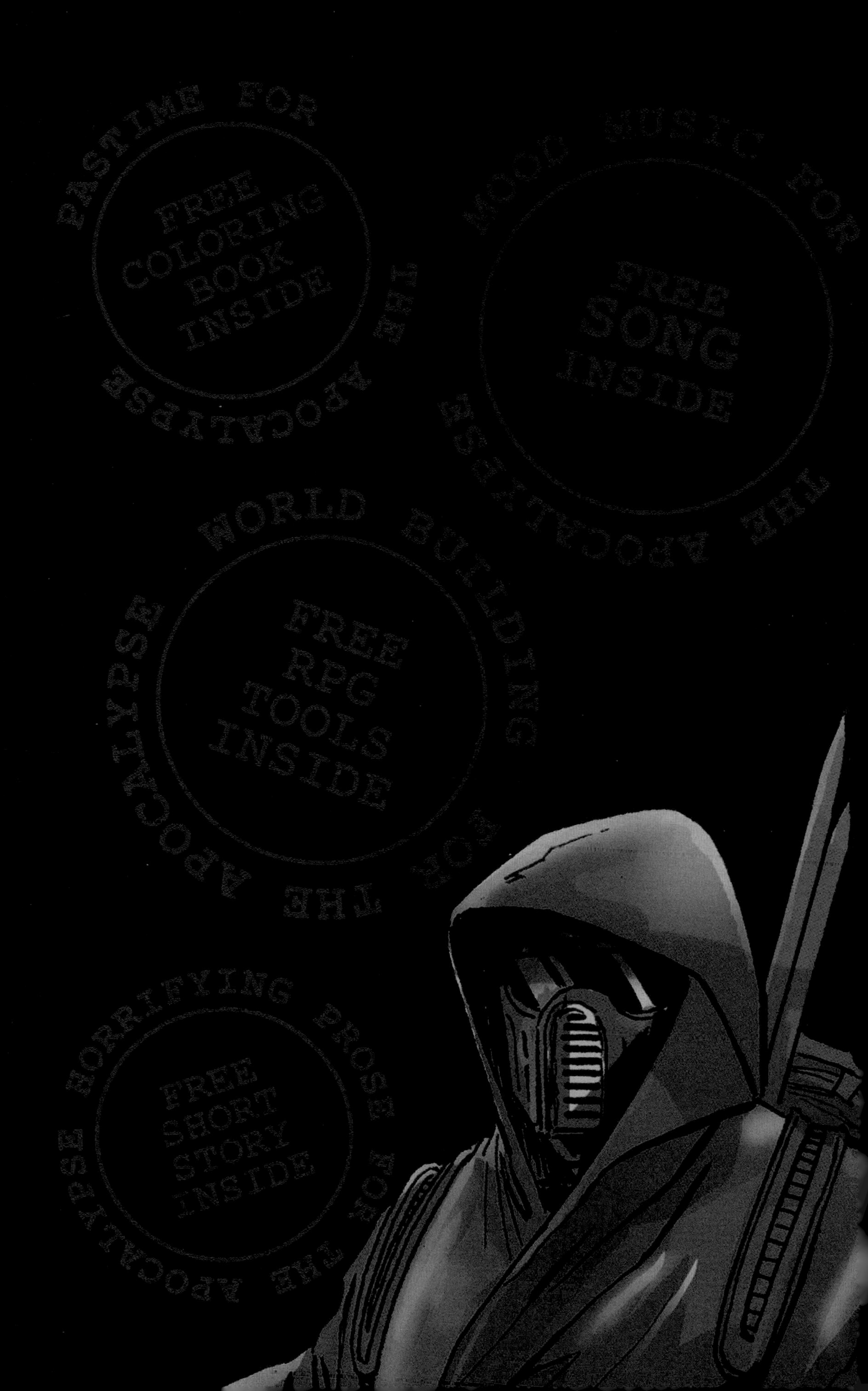
PASTIME FOR THE APOCALYPSE
FREE COLORING BOOK INSIDE
MOOD MUSIC FOR THE APOCALYPSE
FREE SONG INSIDE
WORLD BUILDING FOR THE APOCALYPSE
FREE RPG TOOLS INSIDE
HORRIFYING PROSE FOR THE APOCALYPSE
FREE SHORT STORY INSIDE

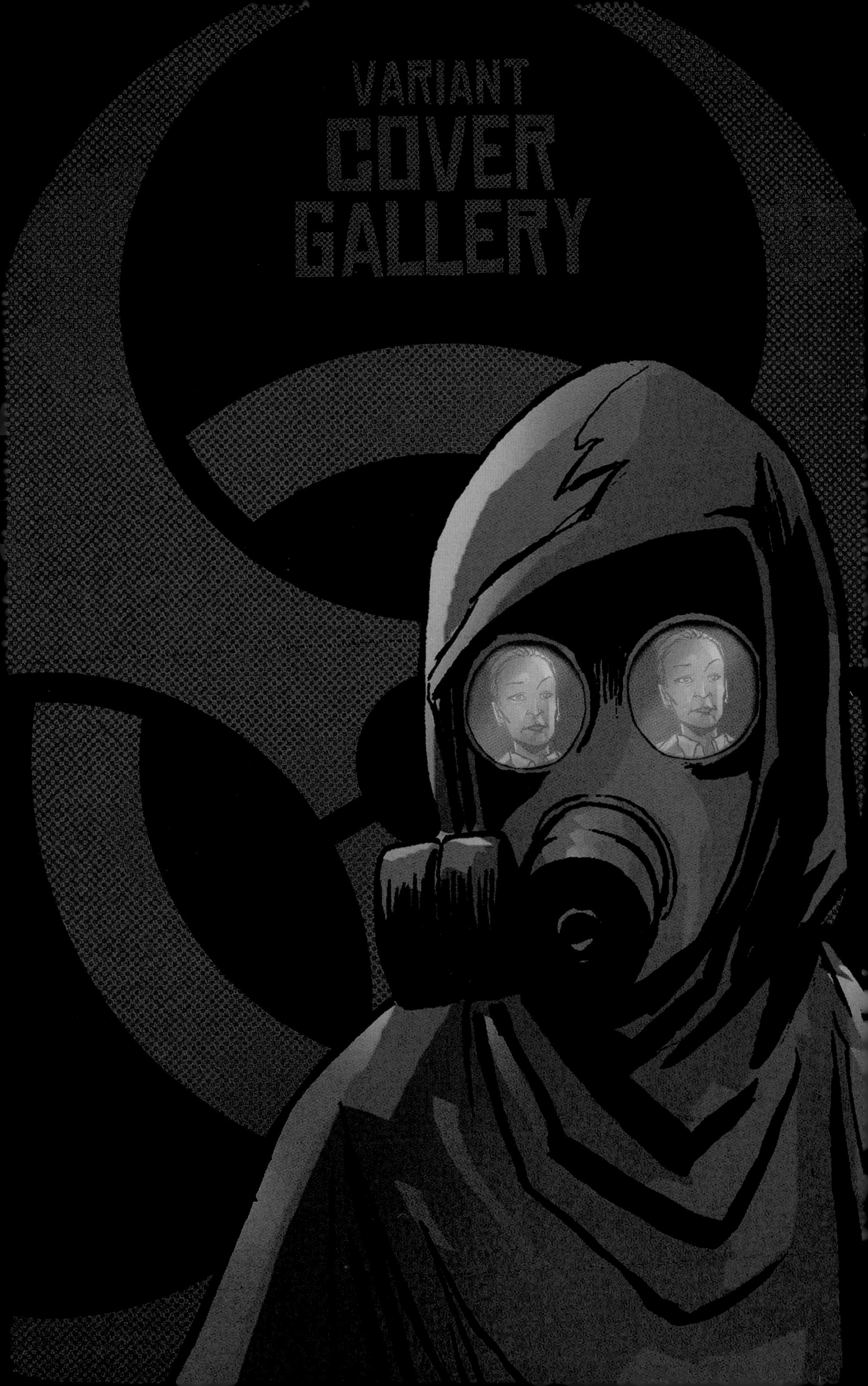
VARIANT
COVER
GALLERY

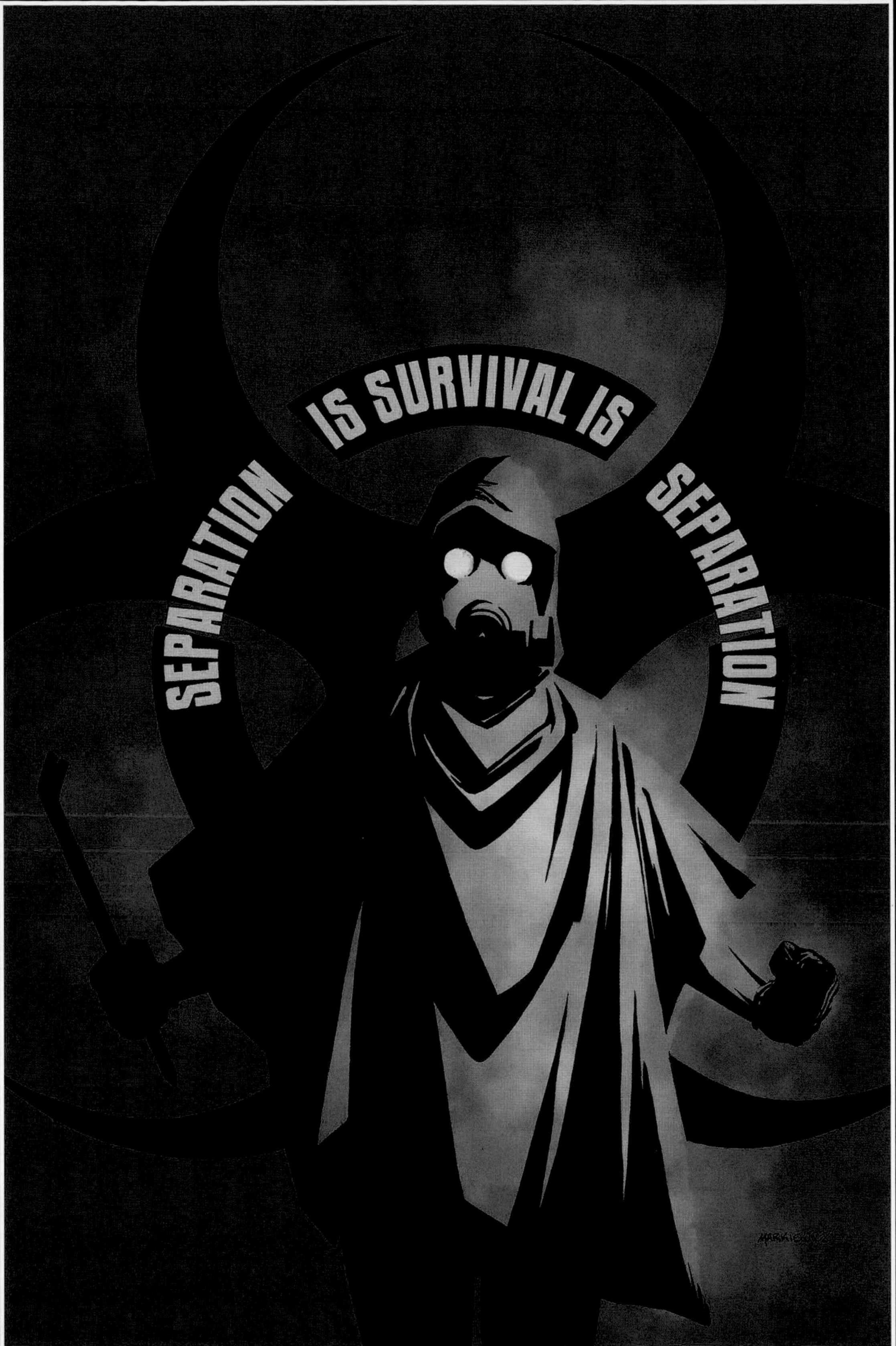
SEPARATION IS SURVIVAL IS SEPARATION

ISSUE ONE
VARIANT COVER ART BY ADAM MARKIEWICZ
COLORS BY MELANIE DARLING

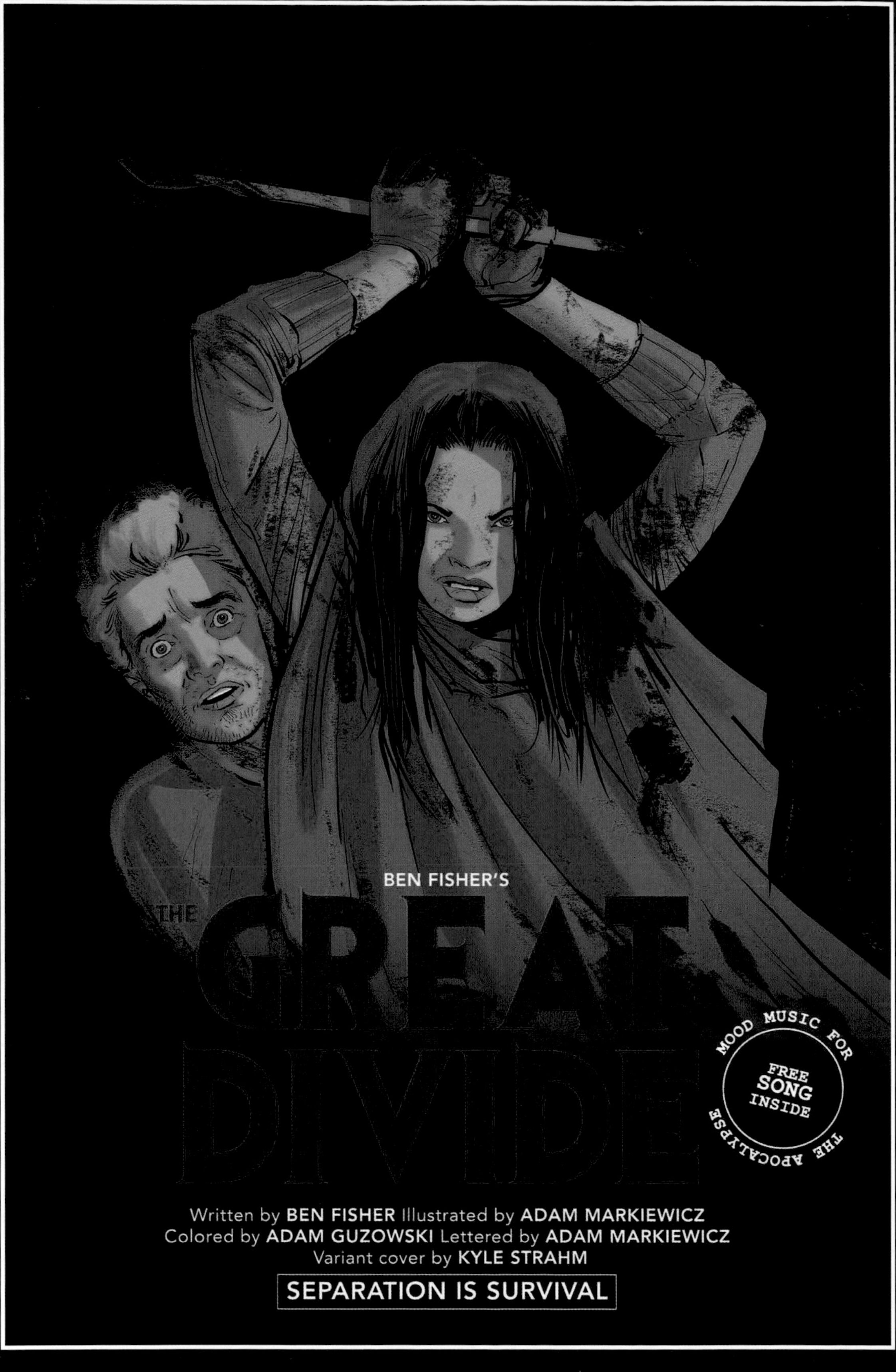
BEN FISHER'S
THE
GREAT
DIVIDE
MOOD MUSIC FOR THE APOCALYPSE
FREE SONG INSIDE
Written by BEN FISHER Illustrated by ADAM MARKIEWICZ
Colored by ADAM GUZOWSKI Lettered by ADAM MARKIEWICZ
Variant cover by KYLE STRAHM
SEPARATION IS SURVIVAL

ISSUE ONE
HOMAGE COVER ART BY KYLE STRAHM
COLORS BY GREG SMALLWOOD

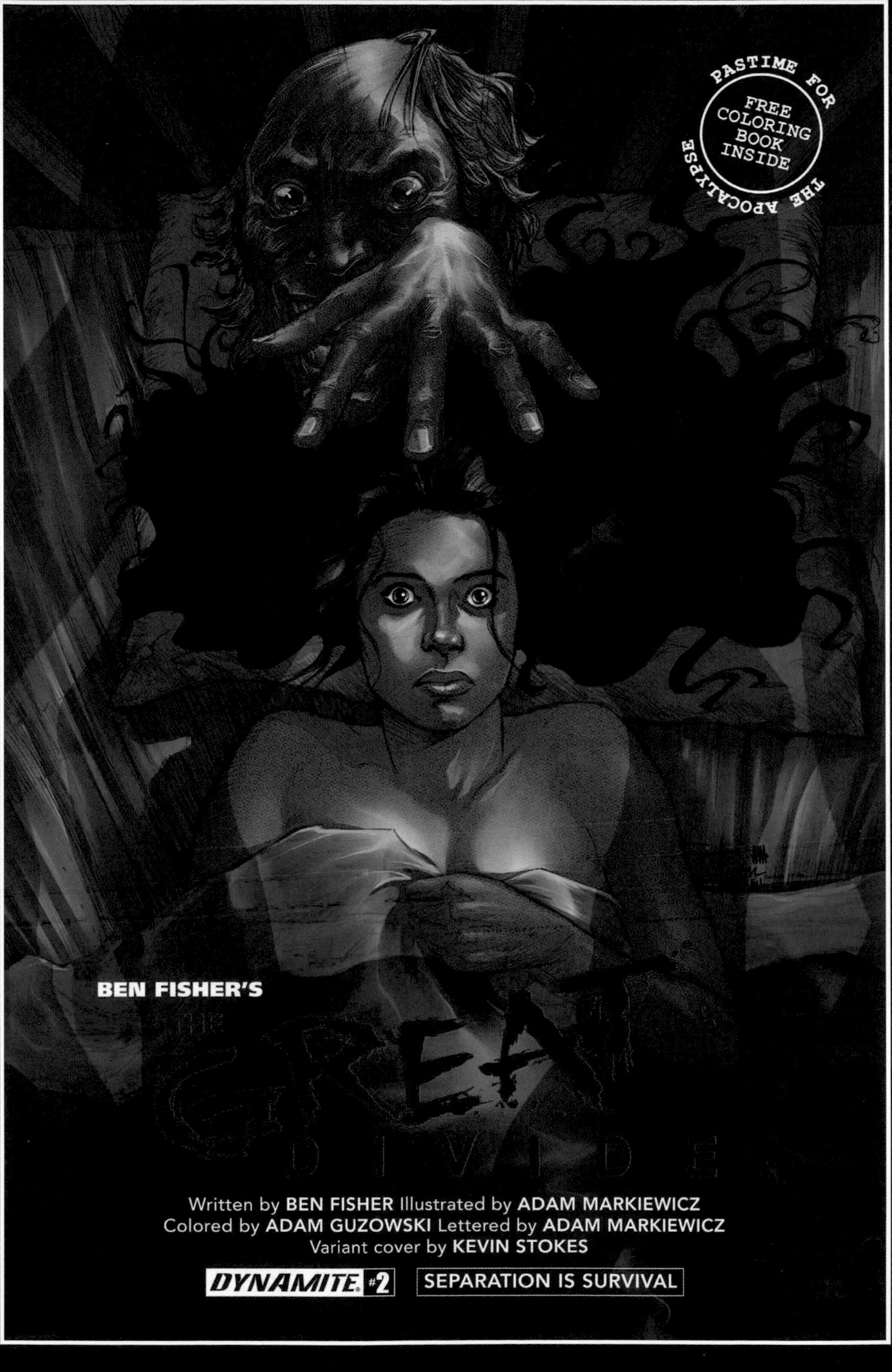

PASTIME FOR THE APOCALYPSE
FREE COLORING BOOK INSIDE
BEN FISHER'S
THE GREAT DIVIDE
Written by BEN FISHER Illustrated by ADAM MARKIEWICZ
Colored by ADAM GUZOWSKI Lettered by ADAM MARKIEWICZ
Variant cover by KEVIN STOKES
DYNAMITE #2
SEPARATION IS SURVIVAL

ISSUE TWO
HOMAGE COVER ART BY KEVIN STOKES
COLORS BY NATHAN MASSINGILL

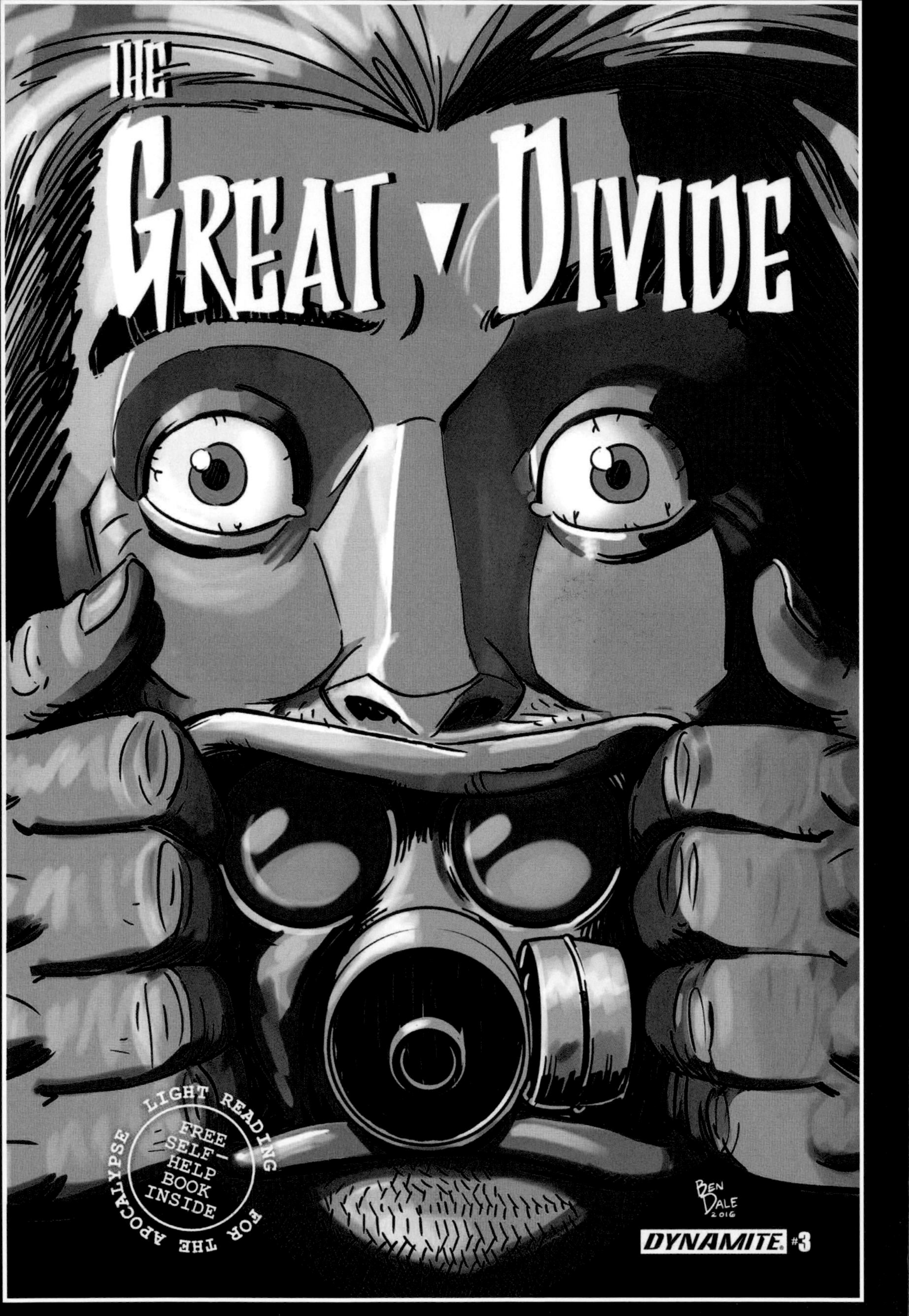
THE GREAT DIVIDE
LIGHT READING FOR THE APOCALYPSE
FREE SELF-HELP BOOK INSIDE
BEN DALE 2016
DYNAMITE #3

ISSUE THREE
HOMAGE COVER ART AND COLORS
BY BEN DALE

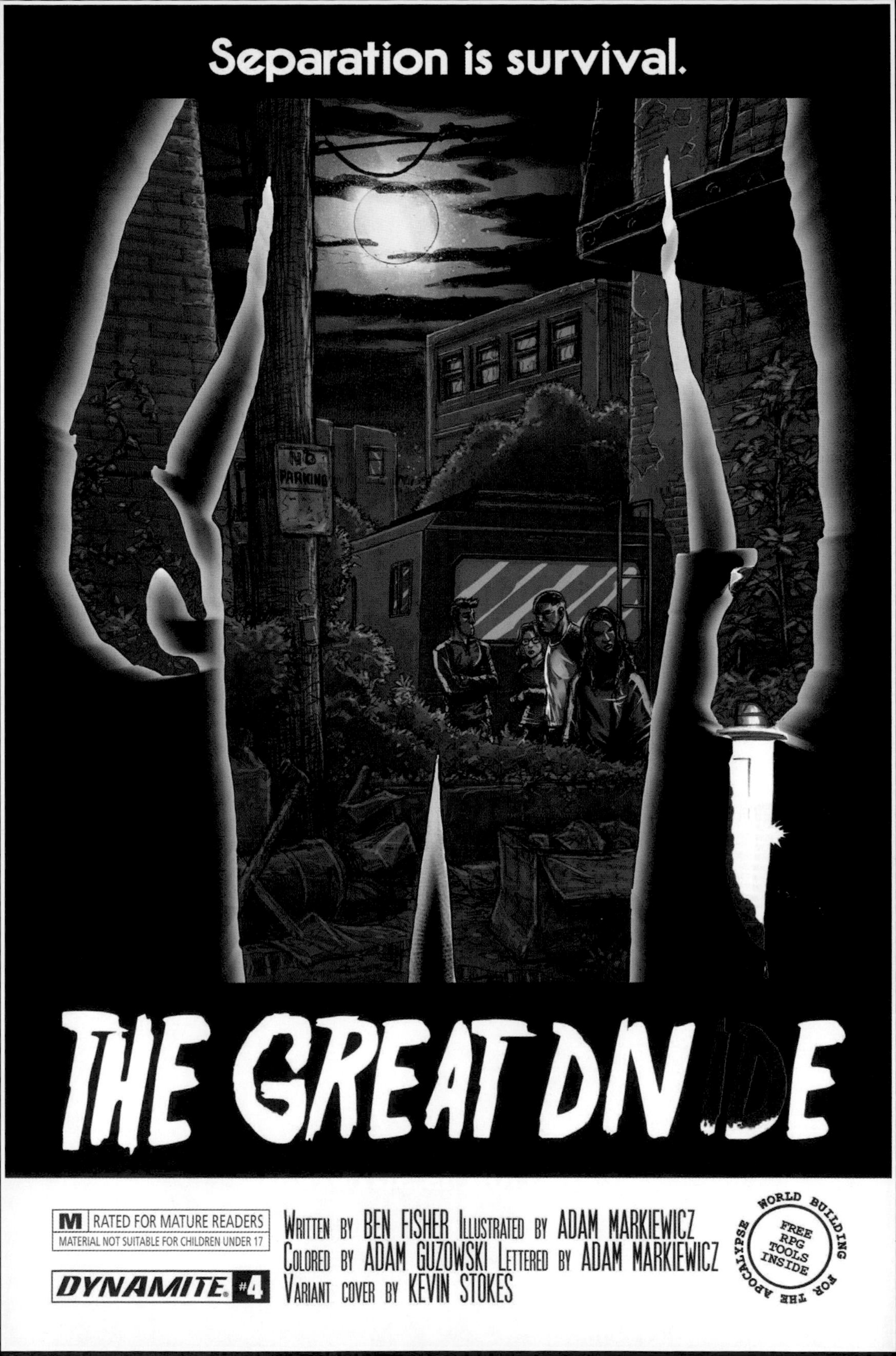

Separation is survival.
NO PARKING
THE GREAT DIVIDE
M RATED FOR MATURE READERS
MATERIAL NOT SUITABLE FOR CHILDREN UNDER 17
DYNAMITE #4
WRITTEN BY BEN FISHER ILLUSTRATED BY ADAM MARKIEWICZ
COLORED BY ADAM GUZOWSKI LETTERED BY ADAM MARKIEWICZ
VARIANT COVER BY KEVIN STOKES
WORLD BUILDING FOR THE APOCALYPSE
FREE RPG TOOLS INSIDE

ISSUE FOUR
HOMAGE COVER ART AND COLORS
BY KEVIN STOKES

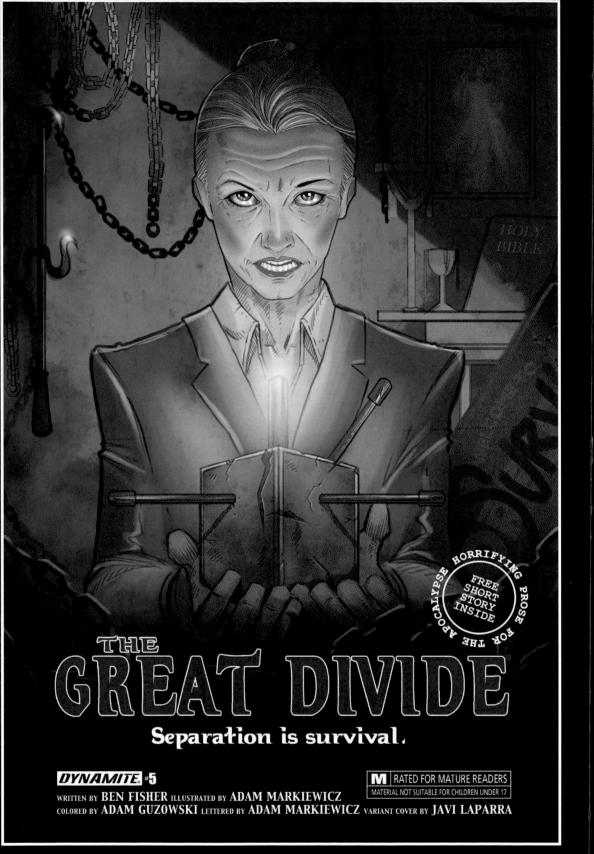

THE
GREAT DIVIDE

Separation is survival.

DYNAMITE. #5

M | RATED FOR MATURE READERS
MATERIAL NOT SUITABLE FOR CHILDREN UNDER 17

WRITTEN BY BEN FISHER ILLUSTRATED BY ADAM MARKIEWICZ
COLORED BY ADAM GUZOWSKI LETTERED BY ADAM MARKIEWICZ VARIANT COVER BY JAVI LAPARRA

FREE SHORT STORY INSIDE
HORRIFYING PROSE FOR THE APOCALYPSE

ISSUE FIVE
HOMAGE COVER ART AND COLORS
BY JAVI LAPARRA

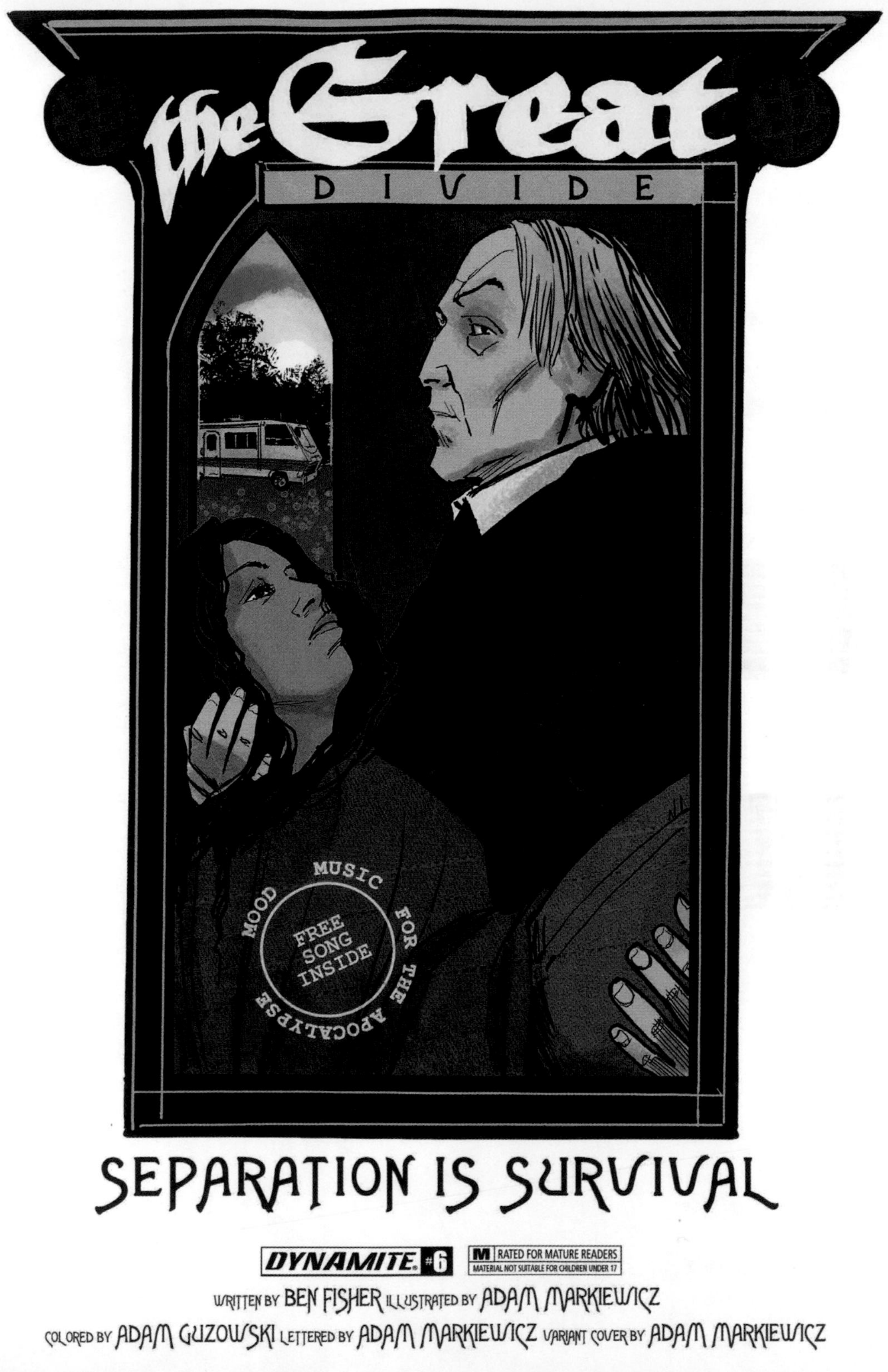
the Great
DIVIDE
MOOD MUSIC FOR THE APOCALYPSE
FREE SONG INSIDE
SEPARATION IS SURVIVAL
DYNAMITE #6
M RATED FOR MATURE READERS
MATERIAL NOT SUITABLE FOR CHILDREN UNDER 17
WRITTEN BY BEN FISHER ILLUSTRATED BY ADAM MARKIEWICZ
COLORED BY ADAM GUZOWSKI LETTERED BY ADAM MARKIEWICZ VARIANT COVER BY ADAM MARKIEWICZ

ISSUE SIX
HOMAGE COVER ART AND COLORS BY ADAM MARKIEWICZ

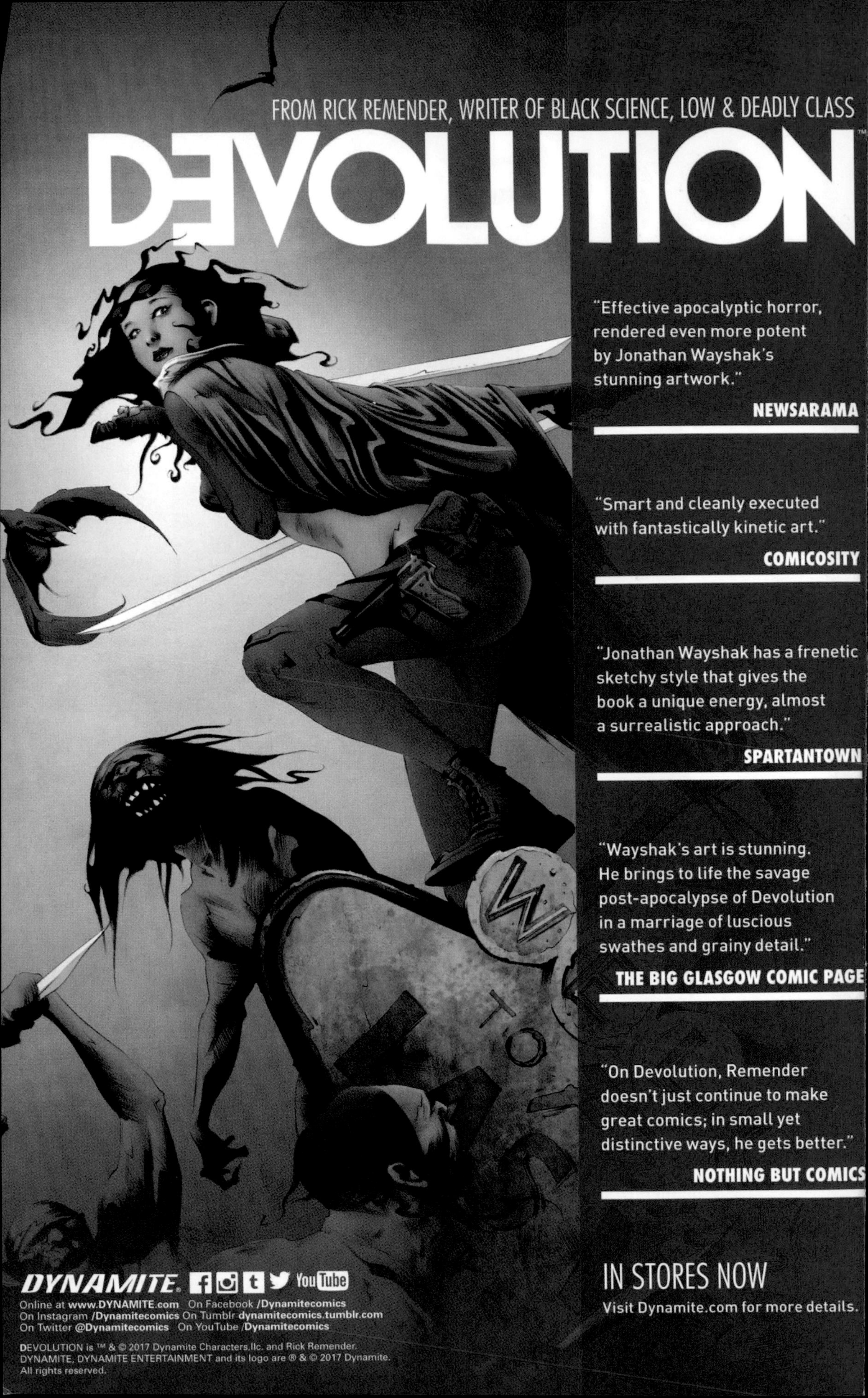
FROM RICK REMENDER, WRITER OF BLACK SCIENCE, LOW & DEADLY CLASS
DEVOLUTION™
"Effective apocalyptic horror, rendered even more potent by Jonathan Wayshak's stunning artwork."
NEWSARAMA
"Smart and cleanly executed with fantastically kinetic art."
COMICOSITY
"Jonathan Wayshak has a frenetic sketchy style that gives the book a unique energy, almost a surrealistic approach."
SPARTANTOWN
"Wayshak's art is stunning. He brings to life the savage post-apocalypse of Devolution in a marriage of luscious swathes and grainy detail."
THE BIG GLASGOW COMIC PAGE
"On Devolution, Remender doesn't just continue to make great comics; in small yet distinctive ways, he gets better."
NOTHING BUT COMICS
IN STORES NOW
Visit Dynamite.com for more details.
DYNAMITE. YouTube
Online at www.DYNAMITE.com On Facebook /Dynamitecomics
On Instagram /Dynamitecomics On Tumblr dynamitecomics.tumblr.com
On Twitter @Dynamitecomics On YouTube /Dynamitecomics
DEVOLUTION is ™ & © 2017 Dynamite Characters,llc. and Rick Remender.
DYNAMITE, DYNAMITE ENTERTAINMENT and its logo are ® & © 2017 Dynamite.
All rights reserved.

CHAOS!
REIGNS AT DYNAMITE®

JESSE SNIDER • JASON CRAIG
EVIL ERNIE
ORIGIN OF EVIL
ISBN: 978-1-60690-414-5

PURGATORI
ISBN: 978-1-60690-741-2

ISBN: 978-1-60690-589-0

Lady Demon
HELL TO PAY
ISBN: 978-1-60690-787-0

TIM SEELEY • MIRK ANDOLFO
CHAOS
ISBN: 978-1-60690-586-9

JUSTIN JORDAN
COLTON WORLEY
EVIL ERNIE
GODEATER
ISBN: 978-1-5241-0290-6

CHECK OUT THESE COLLECTIONS AND MORE AT DYNAMITE.COM